# JOY DIVISION
## PIECE BY PIECE

# JOY DIVISION
## PIECE BY PIECE
### WRITING ABOUT JOY DIVISION 1977–2007
## PAUL MORLEY

Plexus, London

British Library Cataloguing in Publication Data

Morley, Paul
Joy Division : piece by piece : writing about Joy Division
1977-2007
1. Joy Division (Musical group)
I. Title
782.4'2166'0922

ISBN-10: 0-85965-404-4
ISBN-13: 978-0-85965-404-3

Cover photograph by Anton Corbijn
Frontispiece photograph by Kevin Cummins
Book and cover design by Coco Wake Porter
Printed in Great Britain by Cromwell Press

esp 003

# PART ONE:

## Before/Life

### I

Once or twice in the pages that follow I step back for a moment and think about the implications of what I am doing.

## II

**Notes for a narration by the author/for a BBC 6Music radio retrospective of Joy Division broadcast in May 2005 – the 25th anniversary of Ian Curtis' death.**

It has taken 25 years for the story of Joy Division to travel from the dark underground into the commercial light. 25 years for Joy Division to go from rumour, from obscurity, from the ordinary streets where they lived, to being officially named as one of the greatest rock groups of all time – they were influenced by the very best things to be influenced by – the Stooges, the Velvets, Roxy – and they have influenced all the very best things since – Depeche, U2, Nirvana, Radiohead – and no serious modern group can escape their shadow.

No group that wants to do something original and special using guitars, bass, drums, voice and studio can avoid the sound and vision, the sound and fury, the sound and beauty, the sound and space, the sound and time, the sound and delay, the sound and Manchester of Joy Division.

It was 25 years ago that the frantic story of Joy Division came crashing to a shocking stop, and 25 years since the story slowly began. A group, two years old, that was on the go, full of go, forward, always moving into the future, broke up into pieces. Going, going, gone. Eventually, compilations and repackagings and anniversaries and films and memories and books and the enduring strength of their songs would put these pieces back together again. Joy Division have been put back together by time, and something that at the time seemed wasted and wrecked is now remembered with words like these . . .

25 years ago the Joy Division singer Ian Curtis committed suicide two months shy of his 24th birthday.

29 years ago he had four years to live.

Around the time of Ian's twentieth birthday, in July 1976, Curtis saw the Sex Pistols play the Lesser Free Trade Hall in Manchester, not then aware of the presence of his future colleagues Bernard Sumner and Peter Hook. The two shows the Pistols played in Manchester that summer are the beginning of the Manchester music life that includes the Fall, Buzzcocks, Magazine, A Certain

Ratio, the Smiths, Stone Roses, Oasis, Doves, and the Pistols shows were the beginning of Joy Division. The Pistols inspired Manchester music fans to realise that they could make music as well as listen to it. They could be musicians.

In a broken down, bleak and spacious Manchester taunted by the ghosts of the Industrial Revolution and hemmed in by hills, moors and dull grey clouds, Sumner and Hook formed a group with Curtis and drummer Steve Brotherdale that for a brief moment were the Stiff Kittens, and were then Warsaw, named after a Bowie track from *Low*, 'Warszawa'. Their first gig was in May 1977, supporting the Manchester Buzzcocks and the Newcastle Penetration. They sounded more like a slow northern Damned than cosmic rearrangers of rock dynamics, more like a group that couldn't really play than a group who might one day match or even reach further than Bowie's *Low*.

Brotherdale left in August, to be replaced by Stephen Morris, who, like Curtis, was from Macclesfield. Warsaw produced an undernourished home-made EP, *An Ideal for Living*, less the Damned than before but not yet in any way damned. They changed their name because of a London punk group called Warsaw Pakt. They became Joy Division, a name they found in an obscure book about the German concentration camps, *The House of Dolls*, written by an inmate, Ka–Tzetnik, prisoner number 135633. The 'joy division' was a term used to describe units where female inmates were forced to prostitute themselves for Nazi guards.

A group with a name like that had to make music of sensitive, complex power and rare insight to avoid being condemned for indulgent frivolity, for messing around with things beyond their understanding.

By the time they first appeared as Joy Division, at the Pips club on January 25th 1978, around the time Rotten left the Sex Pistols, strangely, they were becoming stranger, and darker, and wilder, and beginning to sound like a group called Joy Division. Space and doubt were creeping into their music – blocky riff music was transforming into something sly, nebulous and alien.

They were ambitious. They took part in a Battle of the Bands record company competition in April at the Rafters club – a sort of *Punk Idol* display by fifteen local bands desperate to get the attention of the London label Stiff. It was their third show with their new name. Joy Division went on last, way after midnight, worked up into a frenzy by the possibility that they might not get a slot, and a fierce desire to impress that shot straight into the heart of their music. Local television celebrity Tony Wilson instantly saw something – in their eyes, limbs and rhythms – and was further intrigued, even delighted, when Curtis insulted him for not putting Joy Division on his Granada TV show. Also around at the time – local promoter turned record producer Martin Hannett and the Rafters resident disc jockey Rob Gretton, who had managed crude Wythenshawe punk popsters Slaughter and the Dogs.

Their anger was not that of banal punks lobbing scowls at the everyday targets of frustration, but more mysterious, less domestic – rage aimed at time, history and the gods, aimed at the self, and fate. Hook, Morris and Sumner all played as if they were the lead instrument, and Curtis' voice sometimes drifted behind the sound. But he was discreetly dominant, truly the voice, the mind, the body of the band. Slowly, he started to move onstage, slowly, he started to move faster, slowly, he turned into a performer possessed, flailing across the turbulent rhythms as if he was physically representing the wired state of his imagination.

They worked with self-sustaining determination during 1978, and gained strength and self-belief. With anti-South philanthropic purpose, Tony Wilson and friend actor Alan Erasmus had launched a local club dedicated to supporting and promoting local talent, and the first night of their Factory Club on June 9th 1978 featured Joy Division, beginning to sound like they'd slipped through the doors of perception, into a wonderland where Manchester could be the charged centre of the universe, yet completely adrift from it.

Local design student Peter Saville produced an eye-catching poster for the show even though he delivered it after the concert was over. The poster for the Factory show was FAC 1 – the very start of Factory Records, the first thought, which would lead to another thought, and so on, until there were so many thoughts they needed to be numbered.

Mr Television Tony Wilson issued his invitation, and Joy Division appeared on *Granada Reports*, the Northwest six o'clock news show, performing 'Shadowplay' – a bare set, the intense group paraded on podiums like a downbeat sixties pop group, moody shots of the city centre as a backdrop, as if Manchester was located on the dark side of the moon.

Wilson and Erasmus turned the Factory club into the Factory record label. They would be joined by Gretton, who backed into managing the group, and who then protected them with his life, Hannett, who as Martin Zero had produced Buzzcocks' punk ground zero single *Spiral Scratch*, and enigmatic imagineer Saville. The name Factory was as much out of the Lancashire mills, the local industrial past, as it was a knowing nod to Warhol's Manhattan community of freaks and dreamers. Also, when most factories in the area had closed down, here was one that was opening. Eventually, as the result of various fun and games, and associated heartache and decision making, the label would have a catalogue of over 400 items, some of which were musical, some of which were ideas, some of which were mere fancies and failed experiments, and some of which were to do with the teeth, hair and travel arrangements of the directors. There was also a nightclub, because Factory understood that the quality of a city's nightlife can have a strange effect on mundane daily existence. Eventually, largely because of this nightclub, which began a little sadly and then ended up a little madly, the stylings, humour and pretensions of the label would influence the city itself, somehow infecting its very atmosphere and appearance.

The first Factory signing was the chamber-punk Durutti Column, remembering music they'd heard in their dreams, or heard whispering in from the moors. Factory decided to release a sampler of northern talents, Joy Division amongst them. The group went into the studio with Martin Hannett to record 'Digital' and 'Glass' – group had found their producer, producer his group, and Joy Division's primitive outlines of ideas about how to make music that incarnated their sense of isolation, intensity and insolence were transformed into grand sonic sculptures by someone who made sense of existence through the shaping, scraping and taping of sound. The *Factory Sampler*, a double seven-inch single, featuring 'Glass' and 'Digital', was smartly packaged as an art object, as if it was a piece of glass, a shiny object of desire that set the template for the anonymous, glamorous and mischievous Factory artwork. The catalogue number – FAC 2.

On December 27th 1978, just about a year old, Joy Division played their first show in London, at the Hope and Anchor. 30 people paid to get in.

The first *NME* of 1979, a look forward to acts likely to break through that year, and Ian Curtis was on the cover, photographed on a Saturday when Manchester was covered in snow. He looked like he belonged there, like there would be many more occasions when he would grace the cover of music magazines. He looked like there was something on his mind. He looked like he figured if you look long enough at anything it will become extremely interesting. He didn't particularly look like he'd booked a trip to the unfathomable abyss. Perhaps he was just wondering about the strangeness of snow.

Meanwhile, in Ian's real life, which was accelerating as crazily as his singing dancing alternative life, he had been diagnosed with epilepsy. He was prescribed strong medication. Strobe lights could trigger a fit. The diagnosis and his sense of always being on the edge of control, of breaking down, seizing up, hitting the ceiling and falling through the floor, would feed directly into the dynamically disjointed 'She's Lost Control', one of the classic songs that were now bursting, seeping, leaping, thrusting up from inside his mind, and inside the group, which were becoming one and the same thing. The fact that there was a positive response to what they were doing intensified Division's self-motivating urgency.

Early 1979 sees their first session for John Peel, a major sign that they were moving outside Manchester, into an outside world which had influenced them, and which they were to influence so much in return, even as they never in the end really left Manchester.

In April 1979, after a false start with an RCA album, angry at corny overdubs that softened and sweetened their music, they started recording tracks with Martin Hannett for their debut album. *Unknown Pleasures* was released in June 1979 – the sound and clatter of a young group from a bruised and battered Manchester escaping their disconnected surroundings and their fractured lives through sound and energy, the sound and fiction of a punk group who wanted to experiment with sound and feeling, the sound and resolution of four idealists produced by a north-western Phil Spector, a post-punk George Martin, a Pennine Eno. He took the zipped, razored riffs of Barney, the plunging, plangent trebled bass of Hooky, the lost, lonely voice and defiant words of Ian Curtis, and gave each contributor all the room they needed – they were in their own zone, miles away from each other, and yet on top of each other. Most of all, he embellished the popping, capricious drums of Stephen, pulled the idea of rock rhythm apart, and then nailed it back together using stoned time and dream space. As he said, he made the drums go bang, but not in an obvious way. This was a subtle, extreme rerouting of the sonic possibilities of rock. Hannett added and removed space, dropped in random rumours of sound, amplified emptiness, created a hollowed out impression of volume and violence. He put the bass and drums way into the future, and the guitar somewhere odd, solemn and disturbing.

Peter Saville designed an audacious, opulently minimal sleeve that said little about who, what, where, when, why, but which said, in an unsaid, unfussy, unconventional sort of way, everything about the music and the makers, who were clearly something of a mystery, sending traumatised signals back from a spaced-out place where nothing was as it seems and Manchester was disappearing into the darkness.

'Transmission' was recorded during the April *Unknown Pleasures* session, but Joy Division were the kind of group and Factory the kind of label not to spoil the flow and integrity of an album by putting on a track that didn't quite belong – it was released as a single in July, and although it sounded like a hit, and would now be heard everywhere instantly, back then it was the kind of visceral exploration of blissful possibilities that stayed a certain secret for the *NME*/John Peel community.

Major labels started calling, but the group loved the madcap Factory, and Factory loved them, and together they made up things as they went along, not looking towards commercial success, but their own version of succeeding, through the power of their music, and the way it changed in response to their artistic needs, not industry demands imposed from the outside. Another exploratory Peel session in November 1979 further established how Joy Division along with Factory were inventing many of the ways independent music would make itself known.

In July 1979, they made another appearance on Tony Wilson's Granada channel, performing 'She's Lost Control'. This was the northern equivalent of the Pistols appearing on Grundy – no swearing, no mock controversy, just a focussed, intense presentation. They didn't appear many times on television, but when they did, they always commanded attention. Later that year, on September 1st, they recorded 'She's Lost Control' and Transmission' for BBC2's self-consciously worthy youth programme *Something Else*. It was broadcast two weeks later. The Jam are on the same show, but it's Joy Division who capture the imagination and make history with an incandescent performance that would be studied for years. A dazzling, driven Curtis, in glamorous glistening greys, with everyday combed hair, looks severely wiped out, in a kind of agony, and yet ready to storm the barricades of eternity. When the music picks up pace, and Curtis starts to move, staring right through time, flinging his body against the space around him, it's as though he's challenging the whole world to pay attention, to dare consider that what he's doing, what he's singing about, is in any way ordinary.

After each live show during 1979, their cult status increased. Ian Curtis had mutated into an explosive performer who was dragging his life, his woes, his responsibilities, his fears and anxieties into the songs and then right onto a stage. The young man who dreamt of being a rock star was now launching himself into stardom by scrupulously revealing his nightmares. The seriousness of what he was doing, using music to escape a life that he was using music to describe, overflowed into live shows that were becoming more and more manic. That his dancing now often teetered into seizures that seemed like mere extensions to the demented choreography added to the danger and excitement of a Joy Division show. A Joy Division song, a live performance, an Ian Curtis display of concentrated desperation was now creating expectations in their followers, it was creating more and more momentum which the group seemed compelled to maintain, at whatever cost. There was no release of tension – Curtis explored all the horror again and again, reliving his torment for those who just thought it was spectacular, demonic show business. There was no stopping Joy Division, and Ian Curtis. It seemed that nothing could stop them.

A combination of a conscientious, grafting work ethic, a basic rock and roll need to enjoy and exploit the attention that was coming their way, and perhaps the bullying of Factory, kept them writing and touring. In late '79, they supported a now chart-topping Buzzcocks on a major UK tour. They recorded 'Atmosphere'. In January, they were touring Europe. In March they started recording their second album, plus 'Love Will Tear Us Apart'.

At home Ian had a wife and a young baby. At work, in the heat of the Factory, the heat Factory was stoking up led by the greedy, myth-making Baron Manchester Tony Wilson, Curtis was becoming an avant-garde rock god with, he felt, a reputation to uphold as someone who could drive himself to the limits, and then beyond, and be composed enough to report back on the dilemmas and demons he was facing. At work, the work of an apprentice pop star, he had a girlfriend, artier, it seemed, and more provocative than what he could find in a Manchester he was leaving behind, or dismissing using his imagination. He was being torn apart, by

18

love, work, stress, songs, and the first distorted signs of a fame that would in the end only come after he had died.

He sang 'Atmosphere' as if he felt that, despite the pain, he was going to live forever.

He sang 'Love Will Tear Us Apart' as if he knew the exact moment when he was going to die.

He sang the songs on *Closer* as if he knew that he was going to die sooner, one way or another, rather than later – even if it was just the death of Ian Curtis the family man, or Ian Curtis the rock singer, one cancelling the other out, not actually Ian Curtis the death of the man.

In March 1980, a French label, Sordide Sentimental, released 1,578 numbered copies of 'Atmosphere', backed with 'Dead Souls' – 'Atmosphere' was Hannett's finest, most deranged yet smoothest moment, as if primetime Spector had produced a Martian Doors, as if Kafka had written a song for Sinatra. It typically came as an extravagant gesture of opposition to the rock-star cult of personality, an opaque, epic representation of intimacy packaged in a gothic gatefold sleeve complete with an essay that quite naturally locked Joy Division into a history of the fantastic along with the Marquis De Sade. Ian had copy number two.

'Love Will Tear Us Apart' was a song about the death of love, ghosted by a shadowy love of death, delivered as if it was a near-cheerful pop tune.

*Closer* was not written or titled to be the majestic close of everything, it just looked and sounded like it was. At the time of recording, all the anguish that Ian was articulating, that the band was supplying the volatile soundtrack to, that Hannett was technologically anchoring, just seemed what was happening at that moment. It was a passing phase: it was a storm they were passing through. When they got to the third album, they presumed, they thought, that the pressure, the emotional and social climate, would all be somewhere else. But no one was really thinking. Everything and everyone was moving too fast. Nothing and no one was moving as fast as Curtis towards a destination he had encoded into his songs.

'Love Will Tear Us Apart' does not appear on *Closer*, just as

'Transmission' did not appear on *Unknown Pleasures*.

In hindsight *Closer* was a series of blatant suicide notes to a number of people in Ian's immediate vicinity, who at the time simply looked upon the songs as immensely powerful representations of emotional collapse that had appalling, yet liberating clarity – not actually an emotional collapse.

The guitars, never as responsible for the melody as the voice, the bass, the drums, or even Hannett's disquieting way with ambient space and incidental noise, were slipping even further into the background, anticipating a Joy Division that never happened, one that might be more Can and Kraftwerk than Iggy and Reed. The drums that previously seemed to follow or provoke the whirling limbs of Ian's dancing now seemed to slip into the spaces between order and chaos.

On April 2nd, 3rd and 4th 1980, Joy Division played four concerts in three days, including a support for the Stranglers during which Curtis smashed into the drum kit. April 1980 was torrid for Ian – more illness, more stress, more fits, a fumbling suicide attempt that forced Tony Wilson to consider guest replacements for Ian in the group while he recovered.

April the 8th, a concert in Bury turns into a riot, as if symbolise to Curtis a world that was disintegrating, a life that was over.

On May 2nd 1980 Joy Division played their last ever show, in Birmingham, in High Hall at the University. The last song they played was 'Digital'. Joy Division shows often had the speed and fury, and drama and tension, of a conclusion to something, the last time anything so intense could be summoned up for the sake of a night's entertainment. This one was no different, except not only did it seem like their last concert, it really was their last concert. Joy Division had taken just over two years, less than a thousand days, to leap to this conclusion.

The tour that would have followed the summer hit that 'Love Will Tear Us Apart' became never happened – jingling, but mostly jangling, in the charts, the song sounded weirdly bright, if a little numb and preoccupied. The commercial success that the melodies, atmosphere and scale of *Closer* suggested was just around the corner never happened.

On May 19th Joy Division were due to start their first American tour. Ian was fretting, tossed and tormented by anxiety, struggling to get himself organised, split by his duties to wife, daughter, girlfriend, himself, group, label, album, America, fans, art . . . struggling to feel well when all around him, life and reality and Manchester and music seemed to be dissolving . . .

Late on the night of the eighteenth of May, Ian watched a film by Werner Herzog and listened to Iggy Pop's *The Idiot*.

'On Sunday I am turning up my trousers, getting ready for the tour,' said Stephen Morris. 'On Monday morning I'm screaming.'

The shock of Ian Curtis' suicide, as much as the brilliance of his words, would account for a fame that was now heading his dead lost way.

On 29th July 1980 Bernard, Peter and Stephen gave their first appearance without Ian at Manchester's Beach Club. They were no longer Joy Division. They were not yet New Order.

**III**

## Introduction to *Piece by Piece*/a collection of writings by Paul Morley about Joy Division from 1977 to 2007.

When I first started writing about Joy Division halfway through 1977 they weren't called Joy Division. This is one of the many reasons why, when I first started writing about Joy Division, there wasn't much to say. For almost a year, as the group struggled vainly to make an impact in a suddenly lively city that suddenly had two or three noted local punk groups, and quite a few not so noted locals, I had nothing much to say about the group. My Joy Division vocabulary was particularly limited. So was theirs.

Initially this was because they weren't even called Joy Division, and then eventually, even when they were called Joy Division, this was because they still sounded like the group they were before they were called Joy Division. Reading my first brief, tentative reports of the group that was yet to be Joy Division, often brief words buried in reviews of other bands that they were supporting, I was nowhere near completely dismissive, but never particularly sure. There was something about them I quite liked, an idea trying to connect with itself, an impressively misshapen bass guitar turn of phrase, a sudden drop in guitar noise, a stray word of wonder and darkness coming up for fresh air, a look in the eye that was somewhere between scared and momentous, a sudden fitful movement from their lead singer that fell about somewhere between sweet, nervous twitch and sweeping leap into the unknown, but I always seemed to be writing about their potential, what they could become, rather than what they were. For a while I was willing something to happen, sometimes more optimistically than other times. The group themselves, experts at keeping themselves to themselves from quite an early stage, were also willing something to happen, to calculate perhaps how to fit together the bass with the guitar, to come to some conclusion about how the voice would find a place, and what the drums should be doing so that they opened everything up, specifically those earthly factors connected to space and time, rather than pinning everything down to the floor, with punk flatness, where nothing could move.

Enjoying my first few months as a gig reviewer for the *New Musical Express*, I was already relishing, without really understanding, the power and influence I had to celebrate or condemn, and was happy to slam and knock groups who didn't live up to my specific but unfocussed standards. I didn't know it, but in a way I was learning how to write, even as I was writing and being published in a famous, and notorious, national music paper. I was learning how to write while covering the work of local bands whose members I knew and went to gigs with, and who were in their own way learning to do what they were doing as they were doing it.

The young men who were first Warsaw, and then something else entirely, were learning as they went along just what it was to be a rock band, just as I was learning as I went along how and what it was to be a music writer. We knew only too well what we wanted to be, the high, heavy and mind-stirring standards to aim for. We were sure what our dream of achievement was, and we set off with a mixture of naivety, optimism, stupidity, excitement and crude, instinctive talent to try and make it all come true, not really sure if that ultimately meant ever being known beyond a few people in a small local community. But we had to try, because the alternative was staying who and where and what we were, sticking around the time and place we found ourselves, buried in a dusty, desolate post-industrial North that was heading nowhere but back and beyond into its own fixed and to us at the time irrelevant history. The past was all around us, dominating, crushing the present, and what we wanted was the future, a future that would take us with it, to a place wonderfully unspecified. Somehow we knew that the best way to find this future was to help imagine it, to think it up, to force it into place. Without ever really explaining it to ourselves in this way, we were on a mission.

As Joy Division slowly put themselves together, survived their unsteady early months, found their name, searched for a sound, discovered their allies and colleagues and supporters, taking almost a year after their first show to begin to become the group we now think of, I was never entirely convinced, but always stayed positive. I vaguely knew the members of the group. I went to gigs with them, drank in pubs with them. I can't remember the details of what we might have talked about, but then I can't remember any conversations I had with anybody during 1976 and 1977. I can only make guesses about where I was and what I was doing and who I was with based on the fact that I started writing about music during this time, and this became a kind of diary offering clues as to who I was and what I was up to.

This slight friendship may account for the fact that, whenever I reviewed the group who were to become Joy Division, I was never as hostile as some. Some reviewers were so hostile it seemed they were instantly dedicated to wiping the group out of history, as if they were metaphysical warrior-spies travelling back in time to ensure that Joy Division would never, in their own time, exist, and be what we now think, or know, or are finding out, that they

23

were, and are. These spies had information that Joy Division would produce important material that would become a major factor in some unimaginable 21st century ideological war.

It was vital that they were stopped, when they were merely Warsaw, of no use to anyone, a group that just vanished overnight after a few earnest performances, stomped on with seemingly inappropriate force by agents anxious that the provocative, imaginative stimulation of Joy Division never took place. How else to account for the need of some early reviewers to so quickly decide that this group, after a little rehearsal and a couple of shows, were so definitively hopeless? Warsaw, though, perversely took strength from the aggressive negativity of some early reviewers, and the indifference of many of their audiences, and used this initial antagonism to fire their energy. It took some time, though, for this energy to build.

I didn't sneer at the group's early efforts, but I didn't wholeheartedly cheer. I never claimed after their first few shows that here, shockingly, gloriously, out of nowhere, wearing grey trousers, Cheshire frowns, Lancashire shoes, serious ties and neatly ironed shirts, was the greatest rock group of all time. However friendly I was with the group, and however much I would like to have said it, it just wasn't true, and it would have looked like stupid and transparent local favouritism. I took my role seriously enough to make sure I never made absurd claims about the local Manchester musicians. I knew enough to make sure that when I announced in the pages of *NME* that, say, Howard Devoto was the most important man alive, there was some kind of justification for it.

Oddly enough, I could justify the statement about Howard Devoto then, and actually now more so, now that the history of the time has begun to settle into hard, irreversible shape. (In a few short months, Devoto promoted the Sex Pistols performances at the Lesser Free Trade Hall, played a dozen or so scalding, compressed shows with Buzzcocks, as if Ornette Coleman had fused with Iggy Pop, recorded the austere, incendiary potted punk history of *Spiral Scratch* and bossily formed Magazine to send the language of punk spiralling off into a multitude of potential directions. His mighty, particular brain was leaking all over the city, and as a consequence, as he said in one of his songs, the future ain't what it was.)

With Warsaw, quiet, inarticulate lads whose brains weren't really bubbling like Devoto's, I could tell, perhaps, that even though the kind of group they talked about being hadn't yet materialised, it was always worth giving them the benefit of the doubt. They were working hard, even as they had day jobs, to achieve their dream, the first stage of which was to give up those day jobs, and become full-time musicians. I think we talked about Brian Eno, Patti Smith, John Cale, Kraftwerk, Can, Iggy and David Bowie, which would have been about as intimate as we were going to get, and perhaps I was subconsciously intrigued enough to be patient enough to see how they could turn their influences into their own sound.

Possibly, we didn't talk about music at all, and I am merely guessing in hindsight that this is what we must have talked about. I presume we must have talked about new records, and upcoming gigs, and what Howard Devoto's new group Magazine were going to sound like. I suppose we agreed on the kind of new punk music that we liked, and the kind of punk music we were disappointed by that just seemed to be copying the early pioneers, the Clash, the Pistols, Buzzcocks. I think we were taking very seriously the idea that it was important to invest our time and energy into music that was intelligent and innovative rather than superficial and obvious. But I might just be assuming that's what we were talking about, considering everything that has happened since.

Perhaps we lent each other albums that we had saved up for and bought at the tiny new Virgin Records store just off Piccadilly. Perhaps we made plans to travel to the nearby cities of Liverpool or Sheffield to see X-Ray Spex and the Rezillos. Perhaps we stood next to each other and nodded knowingly, or jumped about like thrilled white kids struck dumb and lucid by something so new it just seemed entirely right, when Talking Heads and the Ramones played at the Electric Circus. Morrissey was just a few yards to our left, his head in his own particular clouds. Perhaps we just gossiped about girls and football. Did we mention Jean-Luc Godard, T. S. Eliot and Neu? I don't think we ever did.

I think, after guitarist Barney showed me some artwork he had designed for the debut Warsaw EP, that we might have talked about swastikas and sundry nazi imagery, just so that we all knew where we stood in terms of our relationship to the particular kettle of fishiness, but, again, I am just assuming that's what we must have done, because what has happened since indicates that this is how it must have been. History takes shape based on the events occurring after the fact as much as at the time, as facts, guesses and memories are pummelled into a shape that resembles something we might call truth, until we decide we might as well call it truth.

At the time I never factored in the reality that, as the Warsaw boys and I talked in tiny back-street Manchester pubs, about Manchester City and/or the relationship between Sun Ra, Ezra Pound and the MC5, I was already something of a professional. I had become the local Manchester critic for the *New Musical Express*, able to give exposure to local groups in an influential magazine where every week we would read about mythical giants like Bowie, Eno, Ferry, Jagger, and the mysterious seeming new New York where the future was forming by the drugged, driven second around the mouths, hair and t-shirts of punk pop poets like Richard Hell, Patti Smith and Tom Verlaine.

When three members of the group that became Joy Division, plus a drummer who was to drop out of history the way some drummers do, played their first show, the advance literature advertising the show – I imagine a few posters and leaflets, but mostly just word of mouth – announced that they were to be called Stiff Kittens. This was a name offered to them by the manager of Buzzcocks, Richard Boon. A keen, active part of the local music community rapidly forming during early 1977, he was pleased to help out these eager, slightly distracted young lads. For a while, rumour suggested that the name was in fact recommended by Pete Shelley, the Buzzcocks guitarist and new lead singer following Devoto's smashing, melodramatic exit. He thought of the name possibly because his pet cat gave birth to some kittens that quickly died. At the time, the idea of using a name given to you by someone who was to some extent a local pop star seemed to give your group a kind of boost. You were flattered by association. Buzzcocks, after all, had already released a real, if defiantly surreal, seven-inch EP record on their own New Hormones label, *Spiral Scratch*, which had received great reviews in the national music press and was selling thousands of copies around the country. They were negotiating with major labels in London. They surely knew what they were doing.

The group had been leading up to this show for a few months, and somehow their indecision about a name symbolised that they were not really sure about what they were and who they were. You need a great name to help create a truly great group, a name that uses language to almost invent new words, representing a new approach not just to pop music, but to life, art and the very next day. A great name for a group can make every day seem like it's going to lead to a great very next day, not least because of the songs this group produces on the back of their great name.

They, the group who were to become Warsaw, and then something else, just wanted to be in a group, because in Manchester, in 1977, a few months after the Sex Pistols had visited the city on four occasions with noisy, hysterically precise messages of support and inspiration, new groups were forming by the week. Hidden away in derelict rehearsal rooms and cramped houses across an area that stretched from the mazy centre of the city out into the unassuming suburbs nestled on the edges of hostile moors, scores of concerned young men were forming themselves into the shape of some kind of new rock group that mixed glamorous rock history with rock-solid local accents. Some of these groups imagined that being in a group like the Sex Pistols, causing trouble and potentially even threatening the stability of the government, the music industry and the nation itself, would be some kind of laugh. Some of these groups were quite happy to sound like the Sex Pistols, as if that was easy, just a case of cutting your hair, rubbing together a couple of chords, smashing drums, and shouting loudly about snot and royalty. Some of these groups knew that to sound like the Sex Pistols or the Clash was utterly missing the point, that to capture the spirit of those groups you must not sound like them, but sound like the next step on, even the next step after that, if not the one after that.

When the group that would be Joy Division played this first show, on Sunday May 29th, in 1977, at the Electric Circus, supporting Buzzcocks and Newcastle's Penetration, they were known as Warsaw. The name was an improvement on Stiff Kittens, but only just. Its source was a David Bowie song from the *Low* album – which contained music that seemed to drift up from someplace that was exactly between Manchester and Mars – but you couldn't really tell. It seemed a little dull, a little dented, and even a bit thick compared to the names of the Manchester groups that belonged to the intelligentsia. The Fall – with its blunt, cloudy hints of the mind of Albert Camus – and Buzzcocks and Magazine, these were the groups Warsaw had their immediate eye on, groups that had been inspired by the Sex Pistols – and Bowie, Eno and Can – not to sound like they were merely copying others, but to sound worthy of existing alongside the greats. It was early days, already Buzzcocks and the Fall sounded like they might actually have created cracking uniqueness . . . and forming in the shadows, somewhere between the Manchester Ship Canal and the view from Franz Kafka's office window, you could just tell from the name Magazine, and rumours that they were covering Captain Beefheart and setting Beckett to song, that Devoto's new outfit were not going to be routine. Warsaw sounded like they'd just opened up an atlas, as if their imagination didn't travel further than just nicking the name of a city, or turning an exotic Bowie title into something flat and featureless. (Oddly enough, *Low* would have been the better name, but at the time that was a bit like calling yourself *Hunky Dory*.)

This first Warsaw show was reviewed in the *New Musical Express*, because I was the local reviewer for the paper, and I was at the show, excited as always to be reviewing Buzzcocks, the first group I ever wrote about for the *New*

*Musical Express*. At the time, I didn't think about it, because what was happening was just happening, and I took it for granted that I was reviewing for the *New Musical Express*, the best music paper in the world, even though it had been my ambition since I was fourteen to write for it. Now that I was writing for *NME*, it seemed absurdly natural, or it was a dream that I didn't want to ruin by thinking about it too much. I didn't think about how odd it was that Warsaw were playing their first ever gig as a group that was roughly based on the idea of a group, and their first nervy, tentative moments were going to be reviewed in a national music paper. I hadn't yet fully realised that when my reviews were published in the *NME*, the local groups who were reviewed didn't see pale, skinny me from Stockport, just turned twenty, with crude new Richard Hell haircut and cheap straight trousers, proud and stunned that I was getting space in the *NME*, actually having my name in print, but the *NME* itself, which was kind of a big thing. They were, in a way, however new and fresh and unformed, being seen by the nation. It might be important for their careers, even their lives, that they got positive attention in music papers like the *NME*.

The first thing I wrote about Warsaw was this review of their first ever concert. I didn't write it thinking I must be careful about what I say because it might become something read in years to come, saved not just by books but by a vast new electronic saving system which will hang onto just about everything ever written and become a version of the consciousness of the entire planet. I wrote it, I think, thinking, I want to be a great writer, better than I was last week, and I want to get across the feeling of what it is like to be in this very special place at this very special time, and for whatever reason I happen to be the one getting a chance to write about it. I might just have thought, I hope the *NME* accept this review, and print it without changing it much, and don't give it too silly a headline. I may well have written it wondering whether I should send it by first class post, or second class.

At this stage, I was posting my reviews, which created, for me at least, an intoxicating kind of magic – I would post the reviews at my local postbox around the corner from our Heaton Moor house, addressed to the slightly intimidating and quite cryptic live editor Phil McNeill, and then, a few days later, this review would appear in the copy of the *NME* that I would buy at the newsagents a few yards from the postbox where I had posted it. Sometimes the review I had written might be on the same page as something written by the established *NME* writers such as Nick Kent, Charles Shaar Murray and Ian MacDonald, writers I had read and loved since the early 1970s. It was almost too much to bear, seeing a piece of my writing actually printed in the *NME* underneath a review by Kent or Murray, who were so famous they would actually have their own pictures in the paper at the top of their interviews. I would buy the *NME* at the newsagents, check my review, and walk in a kind of daze back to my house, daydreaming about how astonishing it would be if one day my photograph would be printed in the paper above something I had written.

The second thing I wrote about Warsaw was in a piece for the *NME* about the Manchester music scene as it was forming in the months after the Sex Pistols concerts during 1976. I barely mentioned them, mainly because they barely existed, had hardly played, had only a handful of songs, and it was not possible to detect the shape, and depth, of a future Joy Division in the way they played. There was no way anyone could have predicted that such a thing, such a noise, such a story lay ahead. Warsaw seemed destined to fade away, perhaps becoming a kind of footnote to the Manchester post-punk history, like the blazing, magnificently primitive Worst from unsunny, unlikely Preston. I said as much about Warsaw the second time I wrote about them, an opinion based, more or less, on a couple of quite rocky shows, and possibly the fact that as friends of mine, people I actually knew, like school friends or something, they seemed to be just an example of the kind of workmanlike local group that never went beyond their own area. The only thing, perhaps, on their side, which I seemed to be detecting, as if through a swirling mist, was their absolute self-belief, and their commitment to the making of themselves into something special.

They hadn't begun to master how to turn their ideas and ambition, their references, taste and style, into their own music. This same inability to turn dream into reality was also true with my writing, which, like Warsaw, was full of hopeful energy, and ambition, and primitive technical ability, and a desire to avoid dispiriting cliché. I wanted to invent new ways of writing about music, because the writers I liked best tended to write about music in a way that almost verged on a kind of fiction, underpinned with what seemed to me to be fervent intellectual bite. My ambition to be a new Richard Meltzer, Nick Tosches, Lenny Kaye, Nick Kent was not yet achieved, beyond the occasional worked-up hint that I could be more than a keen, curious fanzine writer lifted above my station by a music paper looking for new writers to report on the new post-punk music that was emerging fast and furious around the nation. During 1977, I was proving quite useful for the *NME*, writing not only reviews of established bands visiting Manchester – my first live reviews for the paper after my life-changing Buzzcocks review were of Mott, David Essex and Cockney Rebel – but energetically and conscientiously covering the Manchester music inspired by punk. The editors at the *NME* might not have believed that what was happening up north was as vital and fascinating as I was making out, but they were content that a thriving new area of musical activity was at least being covered.

I didn't mention it at the time, and I've since learnt that it sometimes does help to reveal personal background to what you are writing, to explain certain passions, even the occasional inconsistency, but my Manchester piece was written a few days after my father committed suicide at the age of 40. It might be a surprise to you – it is to me – that I write in the piece that 'Manchester is a great place to be' just days after my father had in a deliberately suffocating way issued his ultimate verdict on the quality of the area. I think I was trying to convince myself that all was well, give or take the obvious, which I was obviously going to keep to myself, or at least I was keen not to let my father's rude interruption spoil the party that I was having as new Manchester venues opened up, and new people, who I could call my friends, were forming a community that I had a part to play in.

The review of Buzzcocks, Penetration and Warsaw was published the week before my father drove from Stockport down to Gloucester and dramatically cut off his supply of oxygen, until he was in no need anymore of oxygen. It was published a couple of weeks after I posted it to Phil McNeill, who sometimes took his time working out whether what I had written had any grounds in reality. Sometimes he just waited until he had a hole to fill, was lacking review copy, and would slip in one of mine. Sometimes the post was slow, and a review of mine would trundle into the live reviews section a couple of weeks late.

I only realise that this was the last review published in the *NME* before my father died as I write this, that this review is perhaps the last thing he ever read that I wrote – if indeed he was interested in reading what I was writing, or was in any kind of state to be bothered, although in his briefcase, found next to his body, there were a number of copies of my fanzine *Out There*, which contained the first thing I ever wrote about Buzzcocks.

I think new things about my father's death just about every day, especially now I am ten years older than he was when he died and the amount of history and experience that accumulates in my imagination ready to be sorted through reaches sensational proportions. This growing memory often features an appearance by my father, who died just as I was becoming the someone I am today, the writer, and indeed the writer of large amounts of material about the year 1977, when my father died, as well as Bolan, Presley and Groucho, and I saw the first concerts by Warsaw, the

Fall, Pete Shelley's Buzzcocks and Magazine.

I think of him heading toward certain death, a position he had practically established for himself, reading this review of Buzzcocks, Penetration and Warsaw, wondering what on earth I was going on about, but perhaps relieved that I might be able to survive, somehow, without him, because I had found some kind of odd calling, and, at least, had a job. I had found work, which I often think he worried about – that I would never really find a job, a career, in the way that he never did. That I would drift from one failed occupation to another, until finally I drifted into a kind of cul-de-sac of hopelessness, where the only occupation that seemed likely was a final cancelling out of ambition, a dive into a vacuum where you do not, as far as we know, need a job.

Apart from his funeral, and the inquest, writing the Manchester article is the one vivid memory I have of the dense, done-in days following his death. Our sprawling, depleted semi-detached house in Heaton Moor was still and somehow always dark, and I sat cross-legged in the front room at a large, pale green, metal office typewriter my father had salvaged from somewhere he was working and gave me for my eighteenth birthday. I was sat on a brand new carpet, which I believe was the colour of death, that he had himself cut and nailed into position the weekend before he matter-of-factly set off for the abyss.

Using all the inside knowledge I had picked up going out just about every night in the few months leading up to my dad's fairly inconvenient self-destruction, I made what was happening in Manchester at the time seem, almost, to be a matter of life and death. I might have written it in such a way even if my father had not died, but the feeling that I am on some kind of adventure, determined to put Manchester on the map, and therefore put me on the map, is infused with a sense that, offstage, off the page, just beyond my immediate thoughts, something else is going on, or emphatically not going on. Something has apparently just happened that forces me to cling onto reality by exaggerating, or just honestly relating, but with a sense that I have just been issued with some kind of challenge, the nature of things at the time.

There is no doubt that, after the suicide in our family, my writings, about music, Manchester and myself, all of which fused for a while into one mysterious element, were written with a sense of urgency and importance, as if somehow I could escape this ferocious blow to my universe, or make sense of it, by concentrating on my imagination and its immediate surroundings. Eventually, the band that became Joy Division became the focus for this intense concentration, but at the time of writing, the Manchester piece in the *NME* was the first sign of how I was trying to deal with the shock of what had just happened. Howard Devoto, my first real local music love, was attracting all my striving, excited attention, and the thought of him, how I could write about his volatile alertness, was influencing my desire to write about music in a way that matched, and then surpassed, my favourite writers. The Fall, roughly magnificent after just a handful of their own shows, their very first at the end of May, six days before Warsaw's, seemed to be another way I might target my urgent need to find – as anxious, learning writer and grotesquely disappointed, shook-up and aimless Stockport lad – hope, salvation and certainty.

In the end, the Fall, as anchored to the bastard backstreet eloquence and snappy, stubborn extremism of their singer Mark E. Smith, were just too committed, wonderfully but savagely, to writing songs that appeared to me to be always locked in a place that reminded me too much of the place I found myself in the seconds, minutes, hours and then, to an extent, months and years after I learned of my father's suicide. Mark E. Smith didn't provide me with the idea of change, of rebirth, that I was looking for. He was exactly what he was always going to be as soon as the first Fall played their first show, as if he had already picked out in his buggered, brilliant head the songs and albums and jackets and rhythms and melodies and gigs and drinks and arguments and shoes and musicians and marriages and blackouts and birthdays he would live through in the decades to come. He couldn't possibly pack all that livid, lived-in life into one first night, but he could begin as he meant to go on, knowing that it was going to take about 50 years to spew and splatter his existential pop spleen right into the jerky heart of a cold, unforgiving universe. When Warsaw began, there was no such plan, no such sense of destiny. There was just a vague idea based on a vague urge connected to a vague feeling that ahead there was a sort of vagueness that it would be quite pleasing to somehow sort out. I identified significantly with this kind of vagueness. Mark E. Smith's coruscating confidence in his own terrible, fully formed genius verged on the indecent, and, although extravagantly entertaining, did not point me towards intellectual and emotional salvation.

There was absolutely no way at the time that I would have imagined that I would one day transfer my antic, nervous, post-death-of-father allegiances to my raw, profoundly unsure mates, Warsaw, or what – would you believe it? – they were to become. After all, by the time I wrote the Manchester piece, they were so young, they were so new to being, that they didn't yet know how to walk, or talk, or come up with a combination of riff and rhythm that could, depending on the circumstances, call into question the very foundation of consciousness. They were still crawling, and any consciousness, and questioning of, was only appearing in the most basic, blatant ways.

In the Manchester piece, making my second quick, friendly mention of the group that were to become Joy Division, I almost relegate them from history before they have a chance to properly apply for a place. Oddly – possibly because of where my head was as I wrote the piece, somewhere inside the typewriter I was banging on as grief gathered around me in my house, settling on my shoulders like a kind of breathing, seething dust – I express near-affection for Slaughter and the Dogs. This group had almost caused me to be thrown out of the second Sex Pistols performance at the Lesser Free Trade Hall, for heckling their lead singer, and, I am ashamed and/or pleased to say, throwing peanuts at him. I am not too sure why I had peanuts with me at the time, but they seemed to be the correct missile for hurling at a group who I considered to be, let's say, not quite as sensational as the other group who supported the Pistols that night, Buzzcocks.

However it happened, writing in my Heaton Moor front room under a darkened sky, strapped in by a determination to finish the piece – because you never know, having just been through what I'd been through, I might never write again – I seem almost jauntily confident about Slaughter and the Dogs' future. I had made my mind up after what must have been maybe three performances by Warsaw that their future was not so assured. My predicting skills seem a little shaky in this piece, possibly because I was a little disconcerted by the abrupt removal of my dad, who had been clearly amazed that I had done what I said that I'd do, get a job on the *NME*, which I think to him was about as likely as me reading the news on the BBC from the heart of the sun. He was so amazed he decided he might as well finish his life early, not bothering to hang around and wait for the moment I would interview, say, Mick Jagger. I might also have been a bit erratic in anticipating the ultimate direction of pop history, because everything in Manchester was happening so fast that the few days I had taken off, due to unforeseen circumstances, from my main task of going out and maintaining contact with the very scene I was here commenting on meant that I was momentarily out of touch. I wasn't around to witness what was happening, and I momentarily lost my grip on the history that was forming around me.

Luckily, in my very first mention of Warsaw, who would end up as Joy Division, who would end up ending up, I finish on a fine note of optimism. This is how it should be. It is a necessary part of the history that the writer who ends up writing for 30 years about Joy Division first mentioned the group, or the group that were to become the group, in a favourable light. He spotted something, just, at the very beginning of a story that eventually would be told in a number of different ways, in a number of different forms, including the way he chose to tell it, which included as much speculation, if not more, than fact.

And so I found myself at the beginning of the story of Joy Division, which was removed, slightly, from my own story, which was connected, immensely, to the story of my father's suicide, which, as you can imagine, was the end of his story. There might, indeed, be something in the idea that as my father's story ended, the story of Joy Division more or less began, which gave me something to write about, and which also ended in suicide. Even with my experience of suicide, and the way suicide takes you by surprise even when you knew it would happen all along, that second suicide was still a hell of a surprise. Along the way it might be that as I wrote about one suicide story I was writing about another suicide, even if I didn't know it, even if at the time one suicide hadn't yet happened, even if I didn't admit that just as much as there was a suicide in the story of Joy Division, there was also a suicide in my story.

I watched Warsaw play their first shaky, innocent show, in close proximity to Manchester's finest and most fundamentally, but deliciously, eccentric. Suicide, anyone's suicide, was a long way from my mind. First of all, I had to think of something to say about this new group who I liked as people, and who I wanted to be good, even great. Once that was out of the way, once I'd found some words that to some extent accurately set up the situation, words that in the long run would reasonably fit into the history that words like this help provide, who knew what was going to happen?

## IV

**Live review – Buzzcocks/Penetration/Warsaw, Manchester, 29 May 1977, *New Musical Express* (published 18 June).**

There is undoubtedly a great deal of refining and cleaning to be done on Buzzcocks' material before the album they can so definitely record comes along, but the essential material exists. Their established repertoire is one of the most packed and highlighted of any new band, only its unfinished quality and Pete Shelley's occasionally faltering voice standing between the band and a welcome, traditional pop album full of catchy, danceable potential hit singles.

The qualities of Buzzcocks' tunes lie not in any aggression or rawness but in their tightness, pace, in their ability to lay a 'memorable melody' over a basic drone riff, to surprise with twists and hooks and often to equate words with music.

Buzzcocks are, dear *Sun* readers, a pop group not a punk-rock group. It needs either Mickie Most or Brian Eno to be brought in to emphasise that point. The band have the material; now it's all down to performance.

Their development as a pop group – closer to Herman's Hermits than the Velvet Underground but with sharpness and sympathy, anger and frustration bleaching the teen romance with realism – dates perhaps directly back to the time the legendary Howard Devoto left the band. Where Devoto would quote Georg Büchner – 'Every man's a chasm, it makes you dizzy when you look down in' – Shelley would quote Gary Glitter – 'D'you wanna be in my gang?'

The songs from the Devoto period, including all four tracks off the multi-levelled EP *Spiral Scratch*, are still played, but less harshly, often with a sense of naïve vulnerability. The new songs are sheer Shelley and more directly commercial than previous tunes. They are mostly love songs, but they have things to say, without forgetting the little things in life. They are very poppy: 'What Do I Get?', 'Love Battery', 'Whatever Happened To', and 'Fast Cars', produced properly, are all hits.

At the Electric Circus at the end of May they played a spirited if hardly inspired set, interrupted by faults and buzzin' and things. Being local heroes they could do no wrong. Their first encore was 'Love Battery', the second a repeat of the standard 'Boredom', during which Shelley's amp packed up. They departed to cheers. Buzzcocks are unique: time will tell.

The Fab Four were ably assisted with supplying all with a high above average quidsworth by two bands and two almost legendary local characters.

Warsaw have been searching for a drummer for many weeks, their stickman for the night uncovered only the night before. There's a quirky cockiness about the lads that made me think for some reason of the Faces. Twinkling evil charm. Perhaps they play a little obviously but there's an elusive spark of dissimilarity from the newer bands that suggests that they've plenty to play around with, time no doubt dictating tightness and eliminating odd bouts of monotony. The bass player had a moustache. I liked them and will like them even more in six months' time.

Manchester's one and only new wave beat poet then ambled up to the mike, the stringy, impossibly wordy John Cooper Clarke. His genuinely individualistic poems are thick, funny, rhythmic and plentiful. An eagerly awaited first volume of word shots is a guaranteed best-seller.

Penetration travelled down from Newcastle, and are the kind of new wave muzak exponents every town should have. They seemed nervous and oddly angular except for the faintly erotic boiler suit clad chick singer, who aimed hard for psychotic stares but seemed put out by the vigour and enthusiasm of the Manchester audience. There was an overeager reaction to Penetration's unimaginative and bulky set, but any band who can conclude with such a compact version of 'Free Money' I'll go see again.

The evening was finished off by the new wave's very own Alf Roberts, Jon the Postman, whose acapella 'Louie Louie' routine, executed with the vigour of a starving puma – snarls, swearing, punching – is a well loved treat on local stages. Buzzcocks may well bring both Jon the Postman and John Cooper Clarke along to future gigs. You have been warned.

# V

**An early summary of the Manchester music scene, post-Sex Pistols – *New Musical Express*, 30 July 1977.**

Manchester as a Rock and Roll town just didn't use to exist. It fed dutifully off London, and there were frequent visits from groups to the big halls; Free Trade, Belle Vue and Hard Rock.

Manchester had its place on the provincial touring lists alongside Birmingham, Newcastle, Liverpool, and Glasgow, but towards the end of 1975 it looked like losing even that position among the groovy out-of-town venues.

There were a few low-lit dives where bodies jerked moronically and automatically to what was at times termed 'progressive' and 'underground' rock; records churned out repeatedly and monotonously until it reached a stage of spoon feeding. A few local bands performed proudly, regurgitating the same spoon-fed sounds. Some of them smiled occasionally.

I tell you, it was a very boring place to be – it had no identity, no common spirit or motive. It was probably a reflection of the country at large.

Just as Manchester was about to fizzle out completely, Howard Devoto formed a group, Buzzcocks, and wrote the words to a song, 'Boredom', 'You know me I'm acting dumb. You know the scene, very humdrum. Boredom, boredom, boredom.'

A year later, people smile, know each other, help each other, are part of each other. It's a recognisable community. There are more venues, smaller and friendlier; the glorious Sunday nights at the Electric Circus, Rafters, the late lamented Oaks and the Ranch Bar. A lot more minor groups visit and 90 per cent of the time are eager to return.

Manchester is a great place to be now. There is grimness, determination, humour and awareness. The scene has unfolded rather than exploded but it's very much there and alive.

Howard Devoto is not acting dumb anymore. The scene isn't humdrum anymore. Certainly not in the Devoto vicinity. He resides comfortably among his favourite homely artefacts in a place called Lower Broughton, and spends his time answering the phone, taming weasels under the cocktail cabinet, and smiling at the quasi-Brechtian get-up-and-go influences in a great deal of what is quaintly termed 'new wave rock'.

Lower Broughton lies messily, with plenty of those red-brick, cracked-window locations popular in mid-sixties pop snaps, just outside

Manchester. And right now Manchester is the centre for a happening, menacing, attitude-rich movement that – to use an easy and no doubt misplaced equation – rivals the mythical creative flush of sixties Liverpool in its fun, potential, and importance.

Things are happening in Manchester. Devoto knows, quietly. Devoto is important, quietly. Unique; a stupid word, but in this case true.

Devoto used to be the singer and lyricist for Buzzcocks, Manchester's first new wave band, but he discovered that he is perhaps more a dramatist than a performer. Typifying his skilful, almost absurdist dialogue technique with lyrics is 'Boredom', surely a genuine classic. The song is a curious assimilation of the central force behind Samuel Beckett's play *Waiting for Godot*, which, equally curiously, relates to the initial idealism of punk/new wave; that the pattern is desperate and yet the movement paradoxically hopeful.

Devoto left Buzzcocks six months back, one of the reasons being a cleverly masked reluctance to perform on stage. He's still searching for a comfortable way to perform his work. His importance, and that of Buzzcocks, cannot be overlooked in terms of Manchester's growth to what it is now; a pretty hot place to be.

For a start, it was Devoto who first brought the Sex Pistols up to Manchester – twice – thus establishing an early reputation that Manchester was a good place for punk bands to play. This was back in June '76. Devoto realised the importance of the Pistols from early on; 'The Pistols certainly helped lead the way for me. Some of our songs had been around not quite formulated for a few months before I saw them play. I'm not very good at envisaging finished musical product. I knew *what* I wanted to say but I couldn't see *how*. The Pistols made me realise how I could express what I was trying to say.'

The Pistols were the final influential ingredient in a strange creative stew. Devoto already knew that the music should be fast: '. . . The Stooges, obviously. It was so simple almost anyone could play it, but it was effective. That was what I wanted.'

Devoto is an individualist, more in love with vitality and vigour of personality than morality. He has more control of language than any of his immediate contemporaries and more complexity. This was another factor in his quitting Buzzcocks: a frustration that fans and critics alike tended to overlook the subtleties of his presentation, ignore the rich and lively language of the songs.

'I formed Buzzcocks' – a pop group whatever else – 'because I wanted to get across what I was saying in the market place, not in a small office in a tower block. People, I wanted people to hear.'

That people largely missed in performance the intense overlay of repetition in 'Boredom'; the vain and humiliating urgency of desire in 'Time's Up'; the sharp fusion of terror and habit in 'Breakdown'; and the odd surrealistic vitality of 'Friends of Mine' (all tracks off their *Spiral Scratch* EP) is, to understate, unfortunate.

For the first few months of what must loosely be termed 'the Movement', Buzzcocks evolved alongside the Clash, the Damned, the Pistols and the rest to much the same universal misunderstanding and were the *only* new Manchester rock band.

They played one of their first gigs at the Ranch in Manchester, the congregation centre for those with pins in their sleeve, frustration (however mild or forced) in their heart, and action in their mind; much the same as the lower level of the Roxy. 'It was from here that we thought that something would happen, that bands would form,' says Devoto. 'A lot of what Buzzcocks tried to do in the early days was inspire.'

In fact, not a lot happened. Slaughter and the Dogs gradually remodelled their ideals, and the Drones cautiously materialised out of some hazy previous incarnation. Little else.

At the end of '76 Manchester had two visits from the 'Anarchy' tour, which undoubtedly intensified the city's reputation as a place to play and inspired many more fans into the fold, so to speak.

During 1976 Buzzcocks had led the way in Manchester, showed what could be done. Early 1977 was when Devoto bade farewell and *Spiral Scratch* was released. Buzzcocks now gained Pete Shelley, whose warmth and sympathetic psychological acuteness is in direct contrast to Devoto's mystery and invulnerability, and who contributes Peter Pan vocals and off-the-wall guitar. Steve Diggle plays furious elbow-tugging rhythm guitar, Garth is on courteous bass and John Maher on almost technoflash drums.

Their abstract avant-garde style has set them way apart from anyone else on the Manchester scene. Shelley's new songs are propelled by genuine social and personal indignation, his interpretation of Devoto's work possibly the correct procedure – a natural performer idiosyncratically delivering the songs of a natural writer. There is something precious, special and different about Buzzcocks that's still waiting to be exploited.

Howard Devoto, meanwhile, has not disappeared. No way. His involvement with Buzzcocks still exists, via both management and New Hormones, the label which released *Spiral Scratch*, and which he co-owns with Richard Boon, Buzzcocks' manager. But it's as an artist that Devoto

39

can and should excel. Devoto is not a minor writer! As far as I can see he is not content to sit back and accept a passive role. Like Samuel Beckett, who has surely influenced Devoto more than anyone or anything, his prominent theme is the absurdity of existence.

Devoto is forming a group to play 'fast and slow music', probably for record only. Wait.

From highbrow to glorious lowbrow pop music and Manchester's two top shots for the huge gap only Eater and the Hot Rods ever looked like filling; Fast Pop. The Drones and Slaughter and the Dogs are the groups in question, and if Buzzcocks are by far and away number one, then these two bands have worked admirably hard for the number two spot in popularity.

It's been a good few months since I viewed the lamentable debut gigs of both these bands, and since then it's been intriguing and gratifying to see them both sharpen their ideals, dragging their previous faiths into new disciplines. Surely this is the initial basis for what has sprouted into an increasingly ugly monster – speed, aggression, beat enthusiasm, a variable amount of ego fulfilment plus frustration and that essential anti-apathy ingredient.

The differences between the two bands date from previous incarnations – the Dogs very much Bowie-Ronson/Reed, the Drones a wishful attempt to supply the missing link between Quo and Iggy. Probably both would still be turning out the same thing if not for the Ramones, Rotten and Strummer.

And that's the point; their songs are now faster, tighter and sharper and more exciting. Both bands are unrecognisable compared to their beginnings, and that's the way it should be. Both have commercial possibilities and neither mind a little manipulation as long as they're stars and get to sign a few autographs. There was some talk a while back of them doing a tour together, which would have been a whammer if not for conflicting personalities (aah . . . healthy rivalry) and difficulties about who would go on first (it would've had to be a sharing arrangement!).

The development of the Dogs has a slightly perverse quality about it. At the beginning their hammy theatrics detracted from whatever quality their flashy glam rock had, but gradually the frills were dropped and they concentrated emphatically on sheer musical impact. Playing with the Damned in London at the end of last year they were a shameless bubble-gum rock band, thrashing out with enthusiastic abandon rough, cute, speeded-up 'Suffragette City/Queen Bitch/Sweet Jane' variations that couldn't but fail to delight.

They played it refreshingly straight visually, which was thought by many to be a hindrance. Playing with the Damned didn't help, and these days the

Dogs are visually just plain silly. Lead singer Wayne Barratt covers himself in talcum powder, which once was a neat idea, and guitarist Mike Rossi, who knows all the right moves, mercilessly crams them down the audience's throat. Visually they impose when they don't need to; their music does it all for them. Simply, the band seem to have become sloppy, appear reluctant to continue the shrewd sharpening of their approach and, since the beginning of the year, have become static.

But who can deny that they've a great future? I want to see them on *Top of the Pops*. It's their natural habitat.

The Drones' natural habitat is the stage. At times they echo the thrill and thrash of Quo at full throttle, but their songs are too short and well constructed for any monotony to set in. They have no great songs but a series of up-front sharp moves that aim purely for the body and the feet.

Their improvement since the early days is marked. The difference between, say, the early version of 'Hard on Me' (a track off their new EP *Temptations of a White Collar Worker*) and the new version is like the difference between Kiss and the Ramones. On stage they refuse to let up, and although it's difficult to see in which direction they're heading, they are fine entertainers and definitely for you if Led Zep flipped you until the Damned swayed you.

If these are the three biggies there are others aiming to challenge. It's since March things have noticeably developed. The nice people at the Electric Circus wisely booked new wave acts for each Sunday, and the late lamented Oaks in Chorlton saturated May '77 with little-known London groups like the Genet-nasty Siouxsie and the Banshees, the Vibrators, the Adverts, and the degraded beauty of the Slits.

The two literary catalysts for Manchester activity – *Ghast Up* and *Shy Talk* – stuttered out their first editions; primitive popzines, potentially important, nervously requesting interviews, urging involvement. Manchester buzzed.

As Buzzcocks' *Spiral Scratch* sales reached the 8,000 mark, as Slaughter and the Dogs' single 'Cranked Up Really High' was released on their Rabid label, as the Drones prepared their *Temptations* EP the next wave of Manchester bands finally surged into view, cementing the city as perhaps the healthiest, most uncluttered new music centre. The Fall, Warsaw, Ed Banger and the Nosebleeds, the Worst; something for everyone.

The Fall have prompted quotes like 'I thought the Clash were political until I saw you.' Their approach is perhaps too serious – maybe they strip rock of its fun? Perhaps they're not even a rock 'n' roll band? They are. The guitarist's slashing chording is the anger of frustration solidified into burning sound, the simplicity of the lady keyboardist's embellishment a self-mocking intrusion. The singer is an angry, concerned narrator, the rhythm clever and neutral.

Their words are voiced, clipped ideologies, entertainment for radicals maybe – but they have something to say and they try to say it to as many people as possible. A Henry Cow approach, the contradictory collision of form and content always apparent in such earnest and undiluted political quests should prove an interesting barrier to overcome.

With the sad demise of the Derelicts, the Fall could stand alone as a genuinely committed, politically agile rock 'n' roll band, without, say, the Clash's superficial fluency.

Warsaw are one of many recent new wave functional bands; easily digestible, doomed maybe to eternal support spots. Whether they will find a style of their own is questionable, but probably not important. Their instinctive energy often compensates for the occasional lameness of their songs, but they seem unaware of the audience when performing.

Ed Banger and the Nosebleeds are interesting but only in a mild, smirky way. They used to be a terrible collection of directionless yobs carving out laughable mish-mash songs for largely uncaring audiences, until a guy called Vini – who used to run the Oaks – grabbed hold of them and shook them into the disciplined, artless new wave functionals they are today. With correct manipulation – and Vini has the consciousness and fingers to work the strings wonderfully – they could fill the gap left by Hello.

There is no gap for the Worst to fill. Only the Slits' early gigs or the odd Prefects passages give some idea as to the Worst's expressionist style. They are a Punk Rock group; new wave is such an effeminate term. They stand for all the freedoms that can be imagined. They voice brutal imaginations of blurred everyday themes – urban alienation, distortion, depersonalisation – and their style is, by liberal intellectual standards, destructive and antisocial.

The band use the most primitive techniques and riffs imaginable, and their singer squalls words about oppression, depression, and most other -essions with a Kevin Coyne-like intensity.

Their act is split into five or six sections, each of which is different each time it's played. They improvise words on the spot, most often distilled shorts; *Daily Mirror* rape stories, dole statistics, *Forum* explanatory articles, all crudely illuminated with terse verses, and demands for action.

Dole queue rock? 'Fuck, I'm glad to get paid for doing nothing,' singer Allan explains. The song 'Gimme the Money' greedily explores his attitude while 'Police' is a furious account of paranoia as awareness. The Worst are agonising and totally enjoyable.

With Buzzcocks, the Fall, and the Worst, Manchester has two genuine *new* wave rock groups (new as in . . . new), and possibly the only genuine punk rock group. They are certainly three of the most provoking, eccentric and entertaining of new (and thus all) British rock bands.

The cause of Manchester buzzing so hard on the new wave front (the beach?), not only in terms of music but with an undeniable sense of communal comradeship and involvement, is difficult to explain completely. It's been a cumulative effect, painfully slow initially, that's sped almost too fast to see lately. It was initiated certainly by the first two Pistols gigs, continued by the second two on the 'Anarchy' tour, and maintained by Buzzcocks' steady willingness to remain in Manchester and be repeatedly, often derogatorily tagged a 'Manchester Band'. Then there was this merry month of May when the Oaks venue brought two London bands up who proved that if you had something to say you could say it with narrow technique (Slits and the Banshees). It all helped.

Definitely apart from the bands that I've numbered, there are more in preparation, and yet more tentatively/rashly/cockily performing debut gigs, a lot of fans inspired more by what they see immediately about them than anything happening elsewhere.

The refusal of (inter)national record labels to venture away from London is unfortunate, but a blessing in disguise. It's forced the big three Manchester bands to release the discs they were long mature enough to record on their own labels; Buzzcocks typically leading the way with New Hormones, and the Dogs and the Drones trotting frustratingly behind with Rabid and the 'S' label.

A side issue: both the Dogs and Buzzcocks were featured prominently on the *Live at the Roxy* compilation. In the same vein, the Bent label aims to release a Manchester compilation LP with a view to resultant singles, and both New Hormones and Rabid have solid plans for the future.

The ideal would be for none of the Manchester bands to have to resort to signing for the big labels, but Richard Boon has hinted that New Hormones could possibly continue and be distributed by whatever label Buzzcocks sign for, which would open the gates for the company to indulge themselves in certain esoteric experiments. Rabid also looks to be more than merely a vehicle for releasing the first Slaughter record, with Bent Records, set up by Dave Bentley, a brave attempt at setting up a liberal local label, maybe a Stiff equivalent.

Away from the, er, new wave buzz, Manchester's Sad Café (now signed to RCA) are doomed for middling stardom with their lush bed-ridden rock. Gags, Bicycle Thieves, Harpoon, and a few period-piece heavy three-piece bands continue to juggle bravely out on a limb. The former three are quite competent and have been known to thrill, but in the light of what's happening elsewhere it all seems a little uninspired.

The legendary Spider Mike King was doing seven years ago what Graham Parker did last year to gain respect. He's still doing it now but that's not the point. The point is his lack of confidence, which I doubt he'll ever overcome now. And I know why; ignorance. No one cares/cared.

Tom Yates has met similar obstinacy from the punters. Yates sticks to his gentle and beautifully crafted originality as contemporaries like Roy Harper, John Martyn, and Richard Thompson claim deserved success, having turned to rock and electricity. Yates can hardly remain a cult for much longer, and his perceptiveness, guts, and timeless music deserve a far larger audience than the local folk club circuit. But . . . Manchester City will win the league.

And then, as sixties Liverpool had its literary scene, its Henris, Pattens, and McGoughs, so Manchester has its John Cooper Clarke, fitting snugly into the scene with a disarming modesty. His words dovetail neatly into Shelley/Devoto's, much as the Liverpudlian poets' did to Lennon/McCartney.

Clarke's a total non-conformist, a grinning rebel, a comic, ironic, and relevant observer of the thing called society. Both New Hormones and Rabid want to sign him. His delivery is just right. He's the next link in the chain after Rimbaud, Chuck Berry, Mike Harding and Pam Ayres. Significantly, when Clarke recited with Buzzcocks in Manchester, people were clapping, cheering, and even dancing to the biting rhythm of his poems. In London the reaction was (cough) lukewarm.

How too would Jon the Postman fare in London? A fan unable to merely spectate, his famous dance is a test for any visiting group; if the band's winning, he'll start twitching until eventually he'll be in full flight, playing imaginary guitar on his beer bottle, sweat pouring pints. He's also prone to climb on stage after a group's performance and deliver a solid accapella version of 'Louie Louie'. Local rumour has it he wrote it.

No, I'm not assuming that London's dead, although it seems to run on automatic drive, self congratulatory; a little like that glossy supplement *Sniffin' Glue*. And I'm not telling you that Manchester's manna. But it *has* got an identity like London's got a lump.

The only thing we ain't got is an all-girl group (c'mon Denise!) and a central 'factory' to organise and help proceedings. Richard Boon is quietly working on that. To distort something Jon Landau said introducing his infamous 'It's Too Late To Stop Now' article, 'There's a stack of excitement in the air.'

## VI

29 years after I wrote the Manchester piece for the *NME*, it was time, so it seemed, to write a large essay being nostalgic about the time I was making up Manchester for myself, and passing on the information in the *New Musical Express* for anyone who might be interested. I always find such exercises useful in helping me to piece together a memory that I discovered, after years of not noticing, or pretending not to notice, had been shattered by my father's death.

After 29 years, a lot of the events and happenings that occurred in Manchester in the years after those two visits by the Sex Pistols had become increasingly well documented, even as they seemed to me to be something that happened in a dream. The early gigs, the bands, the venues, the characters, the cults, the crusades . . . the idea of Manchester as filtered through the warping magnifier of Factory Records, the idea of Manchester that had eventually twisted into a cartoon version of that early, curious, cocksure energy which became known as Madchester, eventually all of this meant that, after all that, some of which was life and death, most of which was song and dance, Manchester had established itself as a historic music city.

By the time I wrote the essay for *The Observer*, to publicise a box set of northern music that I had compiled for the Warners label, the momentum of Manchester, the speed of thought, the rapid motion that was carrying myself and others along out of our teens and twenties and into the 1980s, had drawn to a close. The burst of activity that had happened within the music had spread out into the actual geography and architecture of the city, and Manchester was clearly a changed place, a modern environment, largely because of the impact of pop culture, and the response the city had made to the ideas and thoughts of those early post-punk innovators.

It's not as simple as saying Manchester slipped into the 21st century as a forward-thinking city because the punk generation found a way to connect its desires and determination with the traditional radical energy of the city, its history as the first industrial city, as a location with commitment to progress. It's crazy, although oddly it can be done, to map a journey, some muffled, defiant adventure, from the suicide of Ian Curtis to the opening of a Manchester Harvey Nichols. It's just as crazy, but I've attempted it and sometimes pulled it off, to chart a course from the shorts that A Certain Ratio wore as they danced to their very own barking, grievous dance music to the number of boutique hotels that existed in Manchester by the early years of the 21st century. What came out of the mouths and minds of Tony

Wilson, Rob Gretton, Alan Erasmus, Peter Saville and Martin Hannett might well have meant that a fictional idea of Manchester took its place nestled within and around the reality of the city.

It's too simple to say that the Manchester skyline has been transformed because of Peter Saville's designs for Joy Division and New Order. It's not quite right to suggest that a new Manchester rose out of the commitment of Factory Records to be not just a revolutionary independent label but to be above all a Manchester record label. There's always money involved in such change, and the connection between money and politics, and in a way the new Manchester is more a commercial zone than an idealistic urban zone devoted to the poetic fusion of pleasure and intellectual liberation.

There's no doubt though that Manchester moved into the future when for a time it seemed as though it was sinking back into a past it would never escape. The first people to really believe that Manchester could move into the future, that change was important especially in an area that had initiated some of the most important technological, creative and environmental changes in modern times – in a way, the birthplace of the modern – were those people that used punk music, and then post-punk music, to work out how ideas and ideals would keep alive this progressive spirit.

In this narrative, where Manchester punk music kept the city alive and ready to change when it was under attack from direct and indirect external forces, the story began when the Sex Pistols visited the city in June and July 1976 and played the Lesser Free Trade Hall. At the time it happened, even in the months that followed, we didn't pay too much attention to these visits, as everyone was just getting on with the urgent business of responding in the ways that best suited the individuals' talents to the taunts and provocation of Johnny Rotten. We didn't dwell on them. It took time to start marking the anniversary of these visits, and to consider how much of an impact they'd had on the way the city looked, and how it thought about itself.

I didn't write about those shows for over twenty years. One of the many things those two shows taught me is that there is no time to look back if you want to get things done. Johnny Rotten's immaculate glare, his burning, fanatical stare of fury, pointed just one way – into the future. Whatever you took from the past was attached to you, and came with you without dragging you back.

The time to look back is when it's time to move the events into history, and to make sure that the events make it into history with some of the original integrity and excitement intact. Eventually, for better or worse, I decided it was time for me to remember those times, or at least to work out how much I remembered. This piece for *The Observer* was one example of how I was, after nearly 30 years, starting to write about the times that had made me the kind of person that naturally loathed sentimentally looking back. I was looking back, but determined to make the events of those times seem as relevant now as they did then, because they were about something that was important, how a local community of sharing thinkers can make their ideas have real impact on their physical and metaphysical environment.

What follows is an overlapping sequence of events, a series of beginnings and recollections that are constantly changing as the writing draws up more memories, and more connections. Slowly, remembering something that at first seems to be remembering something that never really happened becomes the remembering of something that is as close to fact as it is possible to get, blending together memory, guesswork and language. I've started writing a piece about how the Sex Pistols' visits to Manchester led to such emphatic change, always searching for some clue as to exactly why these visits ended up being so important. I've found that I have begun this piece on a number of occasions, and what follows are just a few examples of these beginnings, one of which temporarily completes itself as the *Observer* essay.

They demonstrate my search to find, eventually, the perfect way to begin the perfect summary of the impact those visits had on a number of individuals who were present. In the end I suppose I want this perfect summary to be so detailed and accurate that it actually has the quality of fiction. I want the summary to be so totally true it's as unsettling and incredible as a dream. The more dreamlike it is, the more accurate, somehow, it will be. Facts can reduce reality to a state of ordinariness which often contradicts the actual experience. I wanted to remember a sequence of events that ended up having such huge influence without undermining the beauty of this sequence and reducing it to mere assumptions.

The following versions are examples of a work in progress. Eventually more and more different versions of the same thing will appear in various publications, or just places where they can be found, as I keep this particular past alive by never assuming that there is one definitive way of describing what happened and one way of ordering the facts. There are thousands of different ways of describing the same thing, and in the gaps between each version, at the edges of each version of each possible truth, exists something close to the truth.

What happened during those Sex Pistols visits, and what happened in the months after, led to, among other things, the drastic, seething songs of

Joy Division, the unbelievable death of their singer, and their eventual lingering afterlife, which went beyond Manchester and looked likely to head out into a potential eternity. It seemed to me wrong to attempt to create one still version of those events, as that is not in the spirit of what happened. It seems to me that it's more appropriate not to create a settled version of events, but to keep the versions of events always moving, and therefore part of the current world, not part of a disappearing world, a world losing its shine, its permanence, a world where nothing can happen because it has already happened.

What the Sex Pistols shows, and then Joy Division's music, taught me is that anything can happen, as long as you accept that the relationship between the past, the present and the future isn't necessarily as obviously organised as we are often led to believe. I am still where I was, there, always, watching, waiting and working out, in the Lesser Free Trade Hall in 1976, at the Factory Club in Hulme in 1978, as the Sex Pistols make their moves based on the drive and drone of Iggy and the Stooges, as Joy Division count out their ways of reconfiguring the dynamic density of the Stooges. Everything is always building up to various kinds of climax. The past doesn't necessarily have to stay in the past. The past doesn't have to dim. It can stay where it once was, completely in the present, and perpetually turn into the future.

## VII

**Essay about Manchester and Liverpool circa 1977, for the *Observer Music Monthly*, May 2006**

In 1976, if you were a teenager in and around Manchester, a city falling apart, moaning and groaning under Victorian clouds the colour of limbo, still covered in war dust, streets seemingly weakly lit by gas, an economy financed by pounds, shilling and pence, and you a/ read the *NME*, b/ wanted to write for the *NME*, or just sent them letters every week, signed Steven, or Morrissey, c/ were intimate with the Stooges, the Velvets, Patti Smith and Richard Hell, d/ were poor but had a few pence in your pocket, or e/ were so bored with *The Dark Side of the Moon*, which didn't seem as much fun as the dark side of the moon, you'd go and watch the Sex Pistols twice at the Lesser Free Trade Hall on June 4th and July 20th 1976.

Those two history making shows – as has been reported again and again, as I'll report on again and again, maybe later in this piece, so that somehow eventually the full real details start to emerge, and the astonishing true history of it is definitively established – started the process which led to the actions which inspired the creative energy and community pride that pieced the city back together again which led to it being filled, splendidly and somehow sadly, because what is modern is also sort of mundane, with light, lofts, steel, glass and sophistication.

Over a hundred years after the nineteenth century Industrial Revolution, which seemed destined to crush the area into dust and isolation as the world it inspired moved Manchester out of the way, an Emotional Revolution happened that would push Manchester into the 21st century. This happened because Johnny Rotten showed Howard Devoto a way to positively exploit his interest in music, theatre, poetry and philosophy. Devoto, let's just say it, for the hell of it, because the story has to start somewhere, with a bang, or a legendary punk gig, was the man who changed Manchester because he had a few thoughts about what needed to happen at just the right time in just the right place, because he arranged for the Sex Pistols to play in Manchester before the rest of the country had caught up with the idea that there was any such thing as a Sex Pistols. In the audience for the Sex Pistols shows were Mark E. Smith, Ian Curtis, Howard Devoto and Morrissey, four of the greatest rock singers of all time, directly challenged to take things on. Johnny Rotten was like some kind of psychotic lecturer explaining to these avant-garde music fans exactly what to do with their love for music, the things they wanted to say, and their unknown need to perform.

Buzzcocks formed in time for the sold-out second Pistols show, where Beckett met Bowie, or so it seemed to me, as I followed them from gig to gig in the new clubs mysteriously opening up underground in cramped drinking dives or overground in grubby pubs and decaying old bingo halls. Buzzcocks, brainy bubblegum sour-pop, with Pete Shelley on cheap guitar, with the viciously smart Howard Devoto s(t)inging songs that had already abstracted the idea of the Pistols' rock punk into something seething with thought, history and jokes, two-minute songs about something and nothing that mixed up the minds of Ken Dodd, Ornette Coleman, Marc Bolan and Franz Kafka. Our very own Buzzcocks, who joined the travelling carnival with the Pistols and the Clash, and who showed everyone in Manchester who a/ read the *NME* or b/ wanted to form a band the route from nowhere to more or less somewhere.

1976 ended with the Sex Pistols' Anarchy Tour playing Manchester twice – most places in the country wouldn't allow the group inside their boundaries even once. They played the Electric Circus, a heavy metal venue a couple of miles up the Rochdale Road in Collyhurst, abruptly co-opted by a new scene that needed venues to cope with this new audience swiftly coming to life. The Pistols sort of felt like a Manchester band, and there was Buzzcocks, local lads, playing – plotting – with them as they invaded and outraged this dull, drab land.

Coach trips would be organised, leaving from Piccadilly Gardens in the centre of town, 75p a ticket, heading for places around the country where the Pistols would be playing under various aliases, to avoid the censoring wrath of local councils. Malcolm McLaren, the Pistols' manager, would put the whole coach load on the guest list. The young people of Manchester, including various Buzzcocks, would arrive to see the Spots – the Sex Pistols on Tour Secretly – in Wolverhampton, and walk straight into the venue, into the very heart of the deliciously forbidden action.

Just after Christmas 1976, using a loan from guitarist Pete Shelley's dad, Buzzcocks recorded four tracks for their *Spiral Scratch* EP, with Martin Hannett, then Zero, local lad from the dark side of Mars, the city's Spector, the region's Eno, the man who produced the sound of Manchester, forcing the spacey, twisted highs and thumping lows of his life into the local, cosmic and carousing music that would soon follow the Buzzcocks. *Spiral Scratch* was released on the band's own New Hormones label at the end of January 1977. Four brief songs, four monumental miniatures, four stabs in the light. It was meant merely as a memento of the adventure they'd been having, a way of recording this lively little local disturbance. They hoped to sell at least half of the 1,000 copies so they could pay Pete's dad back.

The *Spiral Scratch* sleeve was black and white, the music was black and white, the landscape their songs occupied was black and white, it was the last time Hannett's production would be so black and white. The vivacious intelligence and dry, saucy wit was smuggled in behind the coruscating austerity. It was as though the group was clinically scrapping bloated rock history, and locating a very particular position where things could start up again. Perhaps, if you like, *Spiral Scratch* was the first real punk record, the birth of alternative indie culture, the rich, compressed source, ideologically if not sonically, of all the music that has come and gone since that could be labelled punk, post-punk, new wave, grunge and so on.

At least, at the time, I was claiming its importance, boasting on its behalf, the person who had shoved Morrissey out of the way to become the local *NME* reviewer and whose first review was of the sixth or seventh gig played by Buzzcocks. (Billy Idol's Chelsea were supporting. Devoto looked like he was an emaciated glam rocker from a sci-fi Poland.) I was making out that this record, by people I now knew, and saw every time they played, had a kind of power that would last forever. I believed it in one way, knew and felt and could explain why it was so special. I also sort of believed none of this would ever go anywhere beyond the city limits, would never mean anything in, say, the next year, or in 1980, even as I started to follow Buzzcocks out of town, to Liverpool, Leeds, London.

I never imagined 30 years later I would be writing up my memories in *The Observer*, talking about this local EP that I sold in the Stockport bookshop where I worked at the time as if it actually had become the historically important artefact I sort of fantasised it was at the time. I argued passionately with sceptics, usually from down south, that *Spiral Scratch*, which they heard as a collection of lively but spindly songs, all attack and no knickers, was going to one of the most important rock records in what one day might perhaps be history.

We never thought we were ever going to be nostalgic about what was happening. We would die first, or retreat into a Rimbaudian silence. The me I appear to have been back then – bursting into 1977 as an *NME* writer covering the music scene in a city where it was opening up just as I needed something to write about, like a bridge folding out in front of me, taking me over a choppy ocean to wherever I was heading – would tell the me I appear to have become to fuck off for being so nostalgic. This now me would not tell that then me to fuck off in return, mentioning the financial difficulties of a Rimbaudian silence lasting more than a few months, and the off-putting end results of an early death. I wouldn't tell him to fuck off, because I am aware of the 1977 he/I was about to have, which made Manchester the best place in the world to be and the very worst place all at the same time. It became a place to escape into, and a place to escape from. During 1977, lost to myself as I was following the creation of this endlessly exciting new music scene, my father killed himself. The year split into two. One 1977 where everything collapsed and closed down. One 1977 where the world was opening up.

If you a/ read the *NME* and b/ had started a fanzine that was a Manchester reply to Mark Perry's *Sniffin' Glue* – I had, and Perry wrote, snarled, me a note, saying that my effort, *Out There*, printed on glossy paper, looked posh like *Vogue* – one week you'd be seeing the femcrazed Slits in a pub called the Oaks a moneyless two-mile walk from my house in Heaton Moor. The next week back at the Oaks you'd be hearing a freshly formed Siouxsie and the Banshees still working out their sound. You'd be writing poems about Gaye Advert for fanzines called *Girl Trouble*.

As John Cooper Clarke matter-of-factly said about what happened following the release of *Spiral Scratch* – one thing would start another. 1977 was the year everything sped forward fast and faster over itself as things led to other things, as local action spurred more local action, and by the middle of the year it seemed as if there was a gig to go to every night at a new venue, a new band to see every week with a new take on things, and hordes of local eccentrics, enthusiasts, loners and hustlers suddenly having places to go and ambition to fulfil. Suddenly, there was a community.

Oddly, odd bod Cooper Clarke popped out of his own life as, naturally, a living, rhyming punk poet, just what was needed at the time. We sort of took it for granted that the scene would include a demented poet who made you laugh before some group or another got angry about something or other. A skinny vision in specs and bone-hugging black falling from the front of *Blonde on Blonde* into the streets of Salford, speaking hardcore nasal Manc years before everyone else, fitting just fine on bills with Buzzcocks and the bands that were about to take part in the one thing leading to another, bands who hadn't yet sorted out their names.

By mid-1977, the instantly intimidating and incendiary Fall were up and slouching, savagely, playing thin tinny ultra-noise blasted into cryptic song, fronted by that creepily normal looking maniac first spotted violently heckling Paul Weller – 'fucking Tory scum' – when the Jam played, a little too camp and suited for local taste, the Circus. The Fall's first show seemed to be played in front of an audience that consisted entirely of the Buzzcocks. Mark E. Smith's earliest performances, where he was often playing in tiny clubs or rooms that sometimes seemed to be where you were actually living, where there was no stage, so he'd be just inches away from your face and on the same level, were possibly the angriest thing you would ever see in your life. It seemed he was being so angry on your behalf. You sometimes didn't think he'd make it to the next song, let alone 30 years and 30 albums, all of which sound like they sounded as soon as they made sound. Some of them sound like they were made before they even existed. The Fall channelled into their songs through a harsh northern filter a night's John Peel show from the mid-seventies, one of the darker, stranger ones that had played as if it was all one track some rockabilly, some dub, some psychedelic pop, some garage punk, some New York punk, some English punk, Canned Heat, the Groundhogs, Peter Hammill, Henry Cow and Faust. They might in the end be Manchester's greatest, if only because there have been at least twenty Falls, one Fall leading to another, all of them with the same lead singer, who's always the same and never the same twice.

In 1977, I somehow managed a band, the Drones, whilst simultaneously giving them bad reviews in the *NME*, because I couldn't bring myself to tell them to their face that they were a little bit too corny for me. I played and sang alongside photographer Kevin Cummins and Buzzcocks manager Richard Boon in the Negatives, the local po-faced joke group who deleted their debut EP, *Bringing Fiction Back to Music*, the day before it came out, mainly because we never bothered to record it. We played a lot with the Worst, a punk group that made the Clash seem like Rush. Alas, their 60-second rants about police brutality and the National Front were never recorded. In my mind, and it might well have happened, a key Manchester event in 1977 was an anti-Jubilee night that featured the Fall, the Worst, the Drones, the Negatives, John Cooper Clarke, Warsaw and Jon the Postman. Buzzcocks would be in the audience.

Warsaw never made it, possibly because they weren't that good. They played on the closing night of the Electric Circus, the venue the locals had taken over and which had only lasted ten frantic months before being shut down. We had plans to save it by occupying the premises after a two-night farewell show on October the second brought things to an end, but it never came to anything. There was no time to be sentimental. Something else was always happening, because one thing was always starting another. By then, bands were playing at the Ranch, the Squat, Rafters and the Band on the Wall. If you go in search of these places now, none of them have been turned into supersmooth loft apartments like the Haçienda has. They've just disappeared into thin air, as if they were never really there, or they're broken-down buildings not yet touched by the modernisation that's spreading through the city, or they're rusted doors that seem permanently sealed and give no clue of the chaos and noise there once was on the other side. Chaos and noise that ended up helping to build the Haçienda club, where people now live as if they're dead in tune with the modern world.

Warsaw became Joy Division, who would, in way or another, make it. They played their first gig in January 1978, about a year after the release of *Spiral Scratch*. It was the month when Rotten quit the Pistols and formed, as if he'd had them in his pocket all along, Public Image Ltd. The events started in 1977 couldn't stop just because 1978 was in the way. Howard Devoto had left Buzzcocks after a dozen or so gigs and the *Spiral Scratch* EP, deciding that what had become known as punk was all over now that it was known as punk. He'd met Iggy Pop and handed him a copy of *Spiral Scratch* with the immortal words, 'I've got all your records. Now you've got all mine.'

His new group Magazine accelerated into the brand new hard and cerebral post-punk zone with their furiously articulate debut single 'Shot by Both Sides', released in January 1978 along with 'What Do I Get?' by Pete Shelley's Buzzcocks, which dreamt up punk pop. Joy Division's music was changed beyond belief from that of Warsaw's by the involvement of Martin Hannett, whose influence helped bend their music into, and out of, shape. The musical difference between Warsaw and Joy Division was the difference between the Sex Pistols and PiL, the difference between sleepwalking and exploring outer space. By 1978 Manchester had Magazine, Buzzcocks, the Fall and Joy Division, music, rhythm and thinking which you now hear streaked across more and more new bands.

Watching from the inside but on the outside of everything, the doomed Steven Morrissey still dragged himself around town, and tried to get involved. He was slowly planning his revenge on all of those who doubted he'd be anything other than the strange, slightly retarded boy waiting for something that would never happen, who wrote letters to the music papers. In May '78, the Factory Club had opened in decaying Hulme, which led to Factory Records, which led to the intensification of the one thing starting another, which has led to Manchester today, with a brand new history as one of the world's greatest music cities, with a brand new future as the hip, renovated place to live. The Factory designer Peter Saville, who generated images, accessories and styles that made and remade Factory's shifty, shifting mystique, is the city's creative director. The young man whose vague project was to invent a record label like no other by raiding the design history of the twentieth century is now in charge of inventing the idea of Manchester being a city like no other. A city that has become what it has become for better and worse because the Sex Pistols visited in June 1976 and something started to happen.

I've been putting together a compilation of music from the cities of Manchester and Liverpool between 1976 and 1984, called *North by North West*. The compilation follows the music that was being made in the two cities because a group of people, an adventurous underground collective looking to establish their own identity, were suddenly shown by the Pistols, and the Clash, that they weren't the only ones having these thoughts, listening to that music, fancying themselves as the boisterous bastard children of Warhol, or Nico, or the New York Dolls, or Eno, or Fassbinder, or Marcel Duchamp.

Manchester and Liverpool were only 30-odd miles apart, and Eric's was one of the best music clubs of the period, so a few of us in Manchester would often make the journey in less than an hour, but the way the two cities' music developed during the few years after punk was vastly different. You can tell the difference by the names of the groups from the two cities – Liverpool names were eccentric, told stories and showed off, Echo and the Bunnymen, Teardrop Explodes, Big In Japan, Wah! Heat, Lori and the Chameleons, Orchestral Manoeuvres in the Dark, Dalek I Love You, Frankie Goes To Hollywood – while the Manchester names were more discreet, and oblique, looking for meaning in the shadows and shadows in the meaning: Magazine, the Fall, Joy Division, Ludus, Durutti Column, the Passage, New Order and, ultimately, the Smiths. The music, while it shared the same influences, and was inspired by the same English punk personalities, sheered off in different directions. Only the Bunnymen and Joy Division retained any kind of remote atmospheric contact, feeding right into U2.

The Liverpool scene started a little later. Historically it was tough to know how to avoid the trap of appearing to be creating another Merseybeat scene. Throughout the early seventies, only Deaf School, a self-conscious sort of panto Roxy Music, gave any clues as to how to form a new Liverpool band without being the Beatles. The Yachts were quick off the mark, but their exuberant power pop was never going to be any kind of catalyst.

The Spitfire Boys formed after Eric's opened in October 1976 as a members club, allowing it to stay open until 2am, and started to put on the Ramones, the Damned, Talking Heads and Johnny Thunders'

Heartbreakers. The Spitfires were playing Ramones covers on a Warrington bill with the Buzzcocks and the Heartbreakers, by May '77, had a name given to them by New York's Wayne County, and as the only Liverpool punk group at the time, would support all the visiting punk bands. They were the first Liverpool punk band to have a record out, but in a way their take on punk was a false start, and was soon overtaken by the Liverpool scenesters, jokesters, gossipers and posers who acted like superstars when their only audience was each other. The Spitfire Boys, too trad in their taste and sound, just didn't have the flamboyant, competitive sense of glory that was the essence of the new young Liverpool. There'd been an underground since '75, glam followers looking to create a New York-type scene around their love for Bowie and Roxy, but for a while it was more clothes, and hair, than music, and the vitriolic immaculate poser Pete Burns was the city's ultimate face, with makeup better than any music he ever made.

Perhaps Liverpool was in some ways slow to get going because they didn't have the Sex Pistols visit twice. The closest the Pistols got was Chester sometime in the autumn of '76. The big change in Liverpool happened when the Clash played Eric's on May 5th 1977, and Joe Strummer spent hours talking with half of Liverpool, or at least the half of Liverpool that was a/ reading the *NME*, b/ wanting to form a group, c/ living more or less with each other, d/ working out what particular pose would save their lives, or e/ hating/bitching about members of other Liverpool cliques and clans and cults that just weren't cool enough, pretty enough, arty enough or good enough.

Three local pals were there for the Clash show. They were always there. There were at least a hundred regulars who turned up every week. The awkward, shortsighted Ian McCulloch, the gloriously garrulous Pete Wylie and the freakishly self-assured Julian Cope. They became a group that talked a lot about being a group. Wylie called them Arthur Hostile and the Crucial Three. McCulloch hated the Arthur Hostile name, and so they became simply the Crucial Three, a group who just talked about being a group, and how legendary they would be. Eventually, each member of the Crucial Three would form their own band, and Wylie's Wah! Heat, Cope's Teardrop Explodes and McCulloch's Echo and the Bunnymen would all play their first gig at Eric's – Teardrop and Echo on the same night in late 1978, a few days after the first performance by Orchestral Manouevres in the Dark, electro-pop pioneers slipping between scenes and crossing over into Manchester, releasing their debut single 'Electricity' on Factory Records, with the full Factory treatment – a glorious Martin Hannett production, a gorgeous Peter Saville sleeve and occasional contact with Factory's inspired, infuriating television personality spokesman Tony Wilson.

If the Liverpool scene was a kind of surreal sitcom, then living next door to the Crucial Three, underneath OMD with their synths, and across the road from Pete Burns and his wife Lin with her kettle handbag, were Big In Japan. The Crucial Three loathed the camp, play-acting performance tarts Big In Japan, who were a kind of reverse super-group, a training ground for extrovert Liverpool characters destined for fame and notoriety. They contained Holly Johnson (later of Frankie Goes To Hollywood), Bill Drummond (producer, impresario, founder of Zoo Records, KLF), Ian Broudie (Care, Lightning Seeds), Budgie (Slits, Siouxsie and the Banshees) and scene queen Jayne Casey (Pink Military, avant-garde impresario, and later spokeswoman for the Cream nightclub). Jayne shaved her head, screamed, wore lampshades for hats, Drummond wore kilts, Holly would also be bald with two plaits strung over his face. One song, 'Reading the Charts', was Jayne reading that week's top 40 over a load of feedback. Big In Japan became so hated a petition was organised that raised 2,000 names demanding that the group stopped. They did. Nothing could stop Echo, Teardrop and the various Wah! incarnations from taking over the pop world, except their own vanity and vulnerability.

As well as the compilation, I've also been working on an essay for a book of photographs by Kevin Cummins that follows the Manchester music scene from the time the Sex Pistols played their two shows in June and July 1976 – stop me if you've heard this before – all the way past New Order via Happy Mondays and the Stone Roses through to Oasis, Doves and beyond. There's also a book I'm writing about the North itself – exploring the psycho-geographic idea of the North as a real place, and a dream place, and the differences and similarities between Liverpool and Manchester, Lancashire and Yorkshire. The book examines what it is that makes you northern, and what it means to be northern, and northern for life even if you move away. The sleeve notes for the compilation, the essay for Kevin's book, the book about the North that searches for the moments that sealed the northernness inside me, and this very piece I'm writing for the *Observer Music Monthly* could all begin with the same words, because in the end it's not about passively looking back, but acknowledging that history happens, and that's what makes the future:

*Eight days after the Sex Pistols played their first public date supporting Eddie and the Hot Rods at the London Marquee on the twelfth of February 1976, two college friends from the North, Howard Trafford and Pete McNeish, borrowed a car and drove down to High Wycombe. The Sex Pistols were playing a show at the College of Further Education, supporting Screaming Lord Sutch. Howard and Pete wanted to see and hear for themselves this new thing that promised 'chaos' and not 'music'. This implied that whatever music there was, it was worth driving hundreds of miles to experience. After all, these two friends from the Bolton Institute of Technology had been drawn together because of their love for Captain Beefheart, Can and Iggy Pop, and the understanding that if you formed a band you should know your way around the Velvets' 'Sister Ray' inside and out.*

*They liked what they discovered in High Wycombe, so much that, not only did it focus their ideas for the band they were putting together, but they were inspired to change their own names. In the new world the Sex Pistols were roughly creating, a change of identity seemed necessary. Trafford would become Devoto – Latin for 'bewitching' – and McNeish would become, romantically, Shelley – the name he would have had if he'd been born a girl. They would become Buzzcocks. They had the unusual desire to actually bring the Sex Pistols up to Manchester, and closely studied a tape they'd made of the gig so that they could work out what the Pistols were doing.*

*If you lived in a city like Manchester, in the mid-seventies, you didn't really think of forming a band, unless that band sounded like it was from London, or even Los Angeles, or the middle of nowhere. There was nothing around to show you how to do it. Bands came to Manchester but they didn't really come from Manchester. It was the same with Liverpool. Then, inside a couple of years, all that was to change.*

## VIII

A variation and extension of the previous piece, and/or a possible introduction to a book of photographs of northern musicians, or an essay about northern music between 1975 and 1980/to be further changed/extended as an introduction to a book of photographs of Manchester musicians by Kevin Cummins/published autumn 2008.

Eight days after the Sex Pistols played their first public date supporting Eddie and the Hot Rods at the London Marquee on the twelfth of February 1976, two college friends from the North, Howard Trafford and Pete McNeish, borrowed a car and drove down to High Wycombe. The Sex Pistols were playing a show at the College of Further Education, supporting Screaming Lord Sutch. Howard and Pete wanted to see and hear for themselves this new thing that promised 'chaos' and not 'music'. This implied that whatever music there was, it was worth driving hundreds of miles to experience. After all, these two friends from the Bolton Institute of Technology had been drawn together because of their love for Captain Beefheart and Iggy Pop, and the understanding that if you formed a band you should know your way around the Velvets' 'Sister Ray' inside and out.

They liked what they discovered in High Wycombe so much that, not only did it focus their ideas for the band they were putting together, but they were inspired to change their own names. In the new world the Sex Pistols were roughly creating, a change of identity seemed necessary. Trafford would become Devoto – Latin for 'bewitching' – and McNeish would become, romantically, Shelley – the name he would have had if he'd been born a girl. They would become Buzzcocks. They had the unusual desire to actually bring the Sex Pistols up to Manchester. Howard Devoto, already noticing that the Pistols' singer was more poet than hooligan, actually put that dream, part nerdy, part philanthropic, into practice.

And so a little over ten years after Bob Dylan played the Manchester Free Trade Hall, when his new electric approach to folk provoked a certain John Caldwell to brand him a 'Judas', the Sex Pistols played the smaller annex theatre, the Lesser Free Trade Hall, tucked into the wings of the building. Dylan's historical appearance at the Free Trade Hall was on May 16th 1966 – for a time the Judas incident appeared on a famous bootleg album mistakenly entitled *Live at the Albert Hall*, its Manchester roots shrouded for years.

You can read all about that concert in a book written by local historian C. P. Lee, who, by the time the Pistols travelled north for their date with destiny at the Lesser Free Trade Hall on June 4th 1976, was a member of a local psychedelic comedy revue troupe, Alberto Y Los Trios Paranoias, sort of the Bonzos dipped in Zappa with a side order of the Firesign Theatre. For a while, just before the Sex Pistols turned up in the early summer, it seemed as if the Albertos were the only Manchester band around. If you lived in a city like Manchester, in the mid-seventies, you didn't really think of forming a band, unless that band sounded like it was from London, or even Los Angeles. There was nothing around to show you how to do it. Bands came to Manchester but they didn't really come from Manchester. The sound and content of early seventies bands that came from Manchester, like the Bee Gees, 10cc and Sad Café, didn't seem to have much to do with Manchester, or the North of England.

Over in Liverpool, just over 30 miles away, the new generation had a different problem. The Beatles had produced a Liverpool scene that had taken over the world, and it took some self-belief to try and come up with something that wouldn't be soaked into the all-pervading idea of nostalgia for Merseybeat. The impact of the Beatles froze Liverpool in time. In Manchester, there was always the chance, even though it was never originally in the Mancunian mentality, that you could become the best Manchester band ever – after Buzzcocks, Joy Division, the Fall, Magazine and the Smiths fought over that for a few years, the next wave, involving the likes of Happy Mondays, the Stones Roses and Oasis, were closer in their arrogance to the Liverpudlians that arrived in the late seventies. It started later in Liverpool, mainly because they didn't get the equivalent of the Sex Pistols' two shows at the Lesser Free Trade Hall.

The Free Trade Hall was the best local venue for any music fan living in Manchester throughout the sixties and seventies. Whatever you liked, eventually it, or something very like it, would arrive. The Free Trade Hall was something special, somewhere between intimidating, and grown up, and intimate, especially if you had managed to get a seat for a show in the prized front-row area of the stalls that ran from AA to JJ.

I saw my first ever pop concert at the Free Trade Hall in 1971. The folk-tongued wizards of weird, Tyrannosaurus Rex, had just shape-shifted into the spectacularly glamorous T.Rex and were having hits where eerie white swans throbbed with erotic promise and hot love rained from the sky, and an audience of bewildered hobbity hairy hippies were being rudely shoved out of the way by screaming teenage girls with glitter under their eyes, waving satin scarves. I was on my own in row HH. I imagine a skinny twelve-year-old Morrissey in National Health specs also on his own sat breathless and moist nearby.

Bowie visited for an early first blistering showing of his brand new space-age Ziggy, in front of one of the smallest audiences I'd ever seen at the theatre. By the time he came back as Aladdin Sane a year later, the hall was packed. Roxy Music beamed in, out of a world where Dr Who would be played by Duchamp, with both Eno and Ferry as potential future doctors, supported by a ludicrous Leo Sayer. Mott the Hoople's equipment failed to arrive and an embarrassed Ian Hunter played an acoustic set. (The next time Mott came they were up the road at the Palace, supported by a quite entertaining heavy mock group called Queen.) Tangerine Dream sent the theatre into space. Black Sabbath dragged it back down to earth and buried it. A hooded John Cale and a sleazy Lou Reed passed through, but not together, bringing tantalising hints and threats of a New York that made Manchester seem a little . . . provincial.

The decision to have the Sex Pistols play a rather posh little theatre instead of a squalid, cramped dump was inspired, although largely economics-driven as it only cost £25 to hire it. It added secretive, somehow artistic power to the event, seeing this exotic anarchic cult rumour sneaking into a nation's imagination via the pages of *NME*, *Sounds* and *Melody Maker* in a venue that was attached to the place where you usually saw your music, but which was strangely separate. The only other events that tended to be held at the Lesser Free Trade Hall were avant-garde theatre productions and experimental classical music. The Pistols fitted just fine, even if in the end they were a depraved pop group who played songs by the Monkees as well as their own antsy, pushy anti-anthems.

The Sex Pistols show at the miniature Lesser version of the main Free Trade Hall on June 4th 1976 has now entered history as much as the Dylan 'Judas' concert. Documentaries have been made about it, it has its own book, and it featured in Michael Winterbottom's film about Factory Records, *24 Hour Party People*, a true story based on lies, or a made-up story based on truth. The book about the show is called *I Swear I Was There*, because only between about 41 and 103 actually attended, but in hindsight hundreds of people felt that they should have spotted the signs, and been there. By early June, this group, with a singer called Johnny Rotten, had been openly hating hippies and pub bands and playing at least a dozen chaotic gigs, all of them closely covered in the music magazines who were quickly sensing a vivid new scene. If you were interested even slightly in new music, and had already tuned into the diseased New York night dreams of Patti Smith and Richard Hell, and the born-again New York ultra-pop of the Ramones, you didn't have to read between the lines. Here was a group whose singer was actually sending the vague young people of wherever they happened to be in the dead, decaying nation a direct internal message – 'I want people to see us and start something, or I'm just wasting my time.'

I swear I was there, 4th June, 1976, and my memory of it, challenged over the years now that the gig has been enshrined as one of the greatest gigs of all time, was that there were closer to 40 people there than 100, and most of them were male music fans far too young to have seen the '66 Dylan. Howard Devoto, the surreal promoter, likes to push it up to about a hundred, but even if you count the startling entourage of freshly painted and punctured proto-punks that accompanied the Pistols as if they'd tumbled out of Jean Cocteau's *Alice in Wonderland*, making it seem as if us locals were actually wearing clogs and flat caps, there weren't enough people in the small theatre to make it seem more full than empty. I was on my own, making my usual anxious, excited leap from bedroom to venue, from daydreaming to approximate real-life experience. We now know enough about the others there to almost be able to name everyone else present, because in an abrupt instant a Manchester scene was created. The members of the groups that were to become Joy Division, the Fall, the Smiths and of course Buzzcocks and then Magazine were there – the singers-to-be Mark E. Smith, Devoto, Morrissey and Ian Curtis. (Buzzcocks guitarist Steve Diggle was mistakenly directed towards Devoto and Shelley by Pistols manager Malcom McLaren, who was outside the hall hawking the gig to passers by, dragging people inside hoping to fill the empty seats. Diggle was looking for someone else, but McLaren thought his face fitted with Shelley's and Devoto's.)

The man who would go on to produce some of the greatest new Manchester music, Martin Hannett, was there, along with other curious people, including Tony Wilson, who would form the label that ended up for better and worse defining and dictating the atmosphere of the new Manchester – Factory Records. Mick Hucknall was there. An intense young musical fan we would know as Jon the Postman was there – eventually no

Manchester gig was complete without it finishing with a mass stage invasion begun by the 21-year-old real-life postman, grabbing the mike and snorting out an extended acapella improvisation based around a version of 'Louie Louie' that made it sound like some kind of demonic Lancastrian voodoo.

At the first Pistols show the support band was Solstice, a longhaired group in flared jeans and cheesecloth shirts looking twice their age. Devoto and Shelley's group were not yet fully formed, certainly not ready to make any kind of history, and Devoto asked a group from his college in Bolton to fill in. They played cover versions of jam-songs by the Welsh Grateful Dead, Man. The difference between their take on rock music and the Pistols was like the difference between the theatre of Agatha Christie and the theatre of Antonin Artaud. It made the moment of shock even more pronounced, to watch the frankly amateur example of the typical local group for whom music was a kind of trainspotting hobby, and then to witness the future as a group who clearly knew their way around 'Search and Destroy' and, it seemed, even *Trout Mask Replica* snarled at us that there was no future. More than anything political, more than anything that was to do with fashion, this was a private gathering of the most avant-garde Manchester fans of music, who suddenly found a focus for how to exploit their knowledge of strange cult music. It was the equivalent of a lecture by Charles Darwin. Suddenly the rules of the world, the laws of your entire existence, were rewritten. Local limits were shattered. Minds were blasted open. We all sat in our seats, as if it really was a lecture, marvelling at the mobile, mocking face of Rotten as he marvelled at us pale, shy northerners who hadn't yet worked out how to open their mouths and use their eyes and ears just like him.

A few weeks later, the Pistols returned to the same venue, and this time it was sold out, and the Buzzcocks were ready. The music was still not really called punk. I was to make my own stab at naming this nameless music that was now being followed by tribes of fans quickly connecting with its attack and language that seemed to surge out of their very own environment – in *Out There*, the fanzine that was my reaction to what was happening, I called the music 's rock' . . . 's' for surge, for sensation, for stun, for speed, for the 's' in Patti Smith, the Ramones, Television, the Clash, the Stooges, and at the beginning and end of the Sex Pistols, and also for the music's sensational seriousness, the sense that this was music to believe in because it clearly believed in something. Once I heard Buzzcocks' curt, turbulent and emotional songs, it wasn't too far fetched to suggest the 's' was also for self-conscious, for self-confident, and for the 's' in existential.

Devoto and Shelley had taped the Pistols' High Wycombe show, and they'd studied it extremely closely, as if it were a scripture, a series of codes to decipher and turn into their own series of cryptic signals. The Pistols played giddy sixties songs by the Who and the Small Faces. Buzzcocks played the Troggs' 'I Can't Control Myself'. Rotten's edgy Englishness was sucked into an American sneer following years of exposure to Iggy Pop. Howard's Leeds/Bolton northernness was bent around Rotten's north London Iggyism, and he sneered too, so that if you didn't listen clearly you would not notice that his lyrics were teeming with literate wit, dazzling wordplay and knowing symbolic urgency.

At the second Pistols' Lesser Free Trade Hall show, Buzzcocks were bottom of the bill and went on first. Wythenshawe's mouthy Slaughter and the Dogs, three months old, had chatted up McLaren, boasting that their apparent following would help sell out the show. They played the kind of shouty, snotty punk that revealed they hadn't studied the Pistols' ways and means as ruthlessly as Devoto and Shelley. They knew their way around 'C'mon Feel the Noize'. A bandwagon had already started, and Slaughter and the Dogs had hungrily bounded onto it.

It took a little time for things to settle after the visits by the Pistols. The various witnesses who'd been inspired by this wildly liberating challenge spent the remainder of 1976 working out what their response would be. Buzzcocks would be drawn into the heart of the new punk movement, supporting the Pistols, becoming a major name in the initial punk list alongside the Sex Pistols, the Clash, the Damned, the Slits and Siouxsie and the Banshees. They were the first sign that whatever this new music was, wherever it was heading, it was not going to just be from and about London.

By the end of 1976, the controversial Anarchy package tour led by the Pistols and the Clash visited Manchester twice, when most of the councils of most towns and cities were refusing to allow the tour to play. Buzzcocks became part of it, replacing the Damned. The tour visited a crumbling old bingo hall at the centre of some wasteland in Collyhurst called the Electric Circus. The Circus, previously just an ordinary venue for ordinary bands to play, was first and best known of the venues that were about to host the new local bands that were beginning to work out what they should be called.

Just after Christmas 1976, Buzzcocks borrowed some money from Pete Shelley's dad and swiftly recorded four tracks with Martin Hannett, aka Zero. These tracks, 'Boredom', 'Breakdown', 'Time's Up' and 'No Reply', would become the *Spiral Scratch* EP, released on their own New Hormones label at the end of January 1977 in an edition of 1,000 copies. To some extent, this was meant merely as a Manchester memento of a movement that might not necessarily go anywhere, a personal souvenir of the journey in their own minds from High Wycombe to Anarchy. The EP, in many ways the first genuine British punk record, the very beginning of alternative indie culture, is a stark sounding map of how a group fired their influences – Can, Eno, Iggy, Velvets, Dylan – into guitar punk songs that were of pop length and which told detailed stories about action and inaction. It was pop music with philosophy peering in, or out.

Certainly, it was the first post-Sex Pistols Manchester punk record, and it was as northern as rain, flat, grainy and commonplace yet shot through with the glamour, the gift, of consciousness, a hybrid of wild eloquence and a subdued, dry orderliness. Devoto was somewhere between twenty and 24, somewhere never fully established at the time, and while the songs were definitely fraught with the longings of youth, they were also somehow shaken by the lamentations of age. He seemed to be describing how he was gambling for control of his slippery life. He was contemplating, more or less, the transcendent through the gritty resistances of human vulnerability.

The record could only have been made in the months after the Sex Pistols set off their explosions, but the four songs were as packed and feverish as four extremely literate and profoundly timeless short stories. The succinct sub-savage sound was pure 1976 but the sentiments were not so particularly set in time. What was certain was that the abrasive, even resplendent intelligence of the record, the energetic precision of the record and its undeniable belief in piercing smartness even as it was speeding along on the surfaces of compressed riff and rhythm, created the template for the Manchester music that was to follow. The bands immediately following the example of the alert, quivering and cutting Devoto Buzzcocks and their punk rock-inspired devotion to the life of the mind – and in time we can see that they were in particular the Fall, Joy Division and Devoto's own Magazine, all in their own ways trenchant and otherworldly – were never likely to settle for the crude, the simplistic and the mundane. Because of *Spiral Scratch*, the greatest Manchester music that followed was mad keen on getting stuck into the imagination.

## IX

Those of us who fell for punk in Manchester, in the months after the Pistols pointed out that in modern Britain there was much afoot, started to go to exciting new venues which opened up, some of them in the same places where previously we had witnessed old, stale bands. We would meet at the Squat, the Ranch, the Oaks, and regularly at the Electric Circus, places where we could plot and plan and exalt in the feeling that what we were doing had revolutionary motives. We were part of a new, developing department of dissent, a conspiracy of freethinking radicals darting through the margins of the city, operating in a seductive underground, crusaders collaborating in the construction of a new city, even a new universe, made up out of feeling, music and pleasure. We felt that we were at the very beginning of something, the best place for young people to be, rinsing our environment of oldness and forcing a fresh future into place. We were part of a secret community meeting in unknown parts of the city where you only gained access because you knew where the entrance was and what time it opened.

As the Manchester writer for the *New Musical Express*, I reported on the sudden (it seemed suspicious) closure of the Electric Circus, an established rock venue that had only been booking punk/new wave bands for a few months.

At the time, it seemed as though a little bit of our power, our freedom, even our ability to function as thinking human beings was being snatched away along with the Circus. It was like we were letting down the Sex Pistols – who had been demonised with tabloid ferocity by most of the world, but who we thought of as zealous Dada political pioneers, demonstrating how to positively rearrange the world in three fantastic moves.

It is amazing that we all fell in love so much with this grotty hall in the middle of nowhere, a near ruin rising up from ruins, a place – half hole, half utopian camp site – that only lasted for a few months. But, as I hinted in the sleeve notes to a cheap and gimmicky ten-inch LP souvenir Virgin Records released a few months after the event, we were young enough and sure enough, and magnificently self-obsessed enough, to believe that, in the very act of going out and discovering ourselves at the same time as we were discovering new music, we were changing the world. Eventually the spirit that was generated amongst aficionados, fanatics and latecomers finding a common purpose in the raving night-time chaos and order would curl around a couple of other fracturing cultural disturbances and alight in a new form, in a new building in the centre of town that was christened the Haçienda.

Those who thought of the Haçienda name remembered the passions excited by a few nights out at the Electric Circus, and the raging disappointment when it was all shut down. You can therefore draw a multicoloured, crooked line between the life and soul of the Electric Circus and the smoke and dreams of the Haçienda. The Haçienda would eventually become a modern block of apartments where you could live in a kind of loft-like urban echo of Madchester itself, as if your daily existence had its own Factory catalogue number. (Got up and made some toast: Fac 5,789.) The Electric Circus just seemed to implode, leaving nothing behind but a small patch of wasteland in the shape of a sauce bottle.

In the middle of my urgent notices about the Electric Circus, the band that eventually paid for the Haçienda – whether it was with Joy Division or New Order money – are barely visible amongst all the noise, community spirit and outrage. Warsaw are just about clinging on, joining in, definitely in the right place, but not yet the right time, and with the wrong name. The longer they held onto the name, the paler and frailer they seemed to become.

In the sleeve notes for *Short Circuit: Live at the Electric Circus*, written just a few weeks after the concerts took place, I got the month wrong, saying that the final nights were held in November, not October. Within months my grip on memory, the past as represented by hard facts and a certain strict correctness, was slipping, and I was losing track of exactly when things happened, and in what order. Events were melting away in my mind. For various reasons, I was heading into the future and not looking back if I could help it, not least because right behind me was the death of my father. Right ahead of me, I decided, were more times like the times I had at the Electric Circus, and I couldn't wait to get there.

As I sped into this future I tended to forget many of the traces I'd left behind. Eventually I would make it far enough into what seemed like the future to feel secure enough to look back, and try to make up what I'd forgotten.

**X**

**Live review of the last days of the Electric Circus –** *New Musical Express*, **22 October 1977.**

It starts with Panik and finishes with chaos: fun, confusion, and a little sadness. The final two days for Manchester's best venue, closed by directives from Above: The Last Weekend At The Electric Circus – twelve groups, a poet and Jon the Postman.

Saturday wasn't too tremendous; a little pseudo-serious, no real rock 'n' roll atmosphere. Manicured Noise (demonic experimental types), the Swords (beefy-fun punk types) and Big In Japan (abstract pop-punk types) all failed for varying, unfortunate reasons to materialise.

It was really a night to get drunk, not strive for cheap publicity. A night to strut and sweat and laugh. Only Steel Pulse gave what it takes.

There's nothing like an oasis of cheery reggae amidst lifeless fast-chording. People moved, fell over, some collapsed.

The Drones, surprisingly Manchester's first punk/etc group to break into the land of the full-page music paper ads, finished off the evening in their usual immaculately rehearsed style. They're one of the country's best at what they do: standardised, chiselled, sterile fast pop.

And that was Saturday.

Now Sunday *was* special. Just like the Circus's short history, not stunning, but I wouldn't have missed it for the world. Virgin's Manor Mobile – rock 'n' roll's Tardis – recorded The Weekend, and if Virgin make most of their pickings from the Sunday night they'll produce a RELEVANT, genuinely interesting compilation.

Warsaw had disappeared from the surface for a few months, and weren't honestly missed. But their re-emergence is a pleasant surprise. They've been thinking; the set was well-paced, there was some style and some force.

The Prefects' music is artless fast rock meets studied avant-garde, with a shaking of bone dry humour and gentle immature wisdom. Abstract and serious – which is not to deny them their constant wry sense of humour. They're good fun, intriguing and at times a little scary. Not a fashion band – a lasting band.

Like the Prefects, the Worst are not out of any packet. They're a punk rock group. There's not many of them. Most of their songs are called we're gonna make this one up.

Nevertheless, amongst their repeated numbers are some real classics. 'Vim',

'LSD', 'Pass Me the Vaseline' and 'Gimme the Money' are not poor songs. This night they were plagued with all sorts of major technical irritations, but they still came over strong enough to almost dominate the audience.

If you're totally destroyed by the mess punk/etc has degenerated into, verging on despair at the lack of imagination etc, go see the Worst and the Prefects. And the Fall, for that matter. A potentially great group, they relay their messages amidst semi-complex, if surprisingly catchy, structures. They are angry, committed and genuine. They play long sets; they have so many strong songs they're almost too much to take in one sitting – punk/etc's Henry Cow.

And still more to come. Fittingly for the last night, Howard Devoto's new band Magazine made its stage debut with a tantalising glimpse of brilliance.

Just three songs: 'The Light Pours Out of Me' and 'Shot by Both Sides', based around simple motifs and stretched and elaborated menacingly, and 'I Love You You Big Dummy', based loosely around the Beefheart roll – done months back by Buzzcocks but now harsher, staggered and direct. During 'Dummy' Devoto draped an absurd punkette dummy/doll around his person, making tentative grips with performance and projection.

Buzzcocks topped the weekend. Structured pop, paced, solid, catchy and solid. They're unafraid to experiment with song lengths, subject matter and rhythms – the group for '78.

After Buzzcocks' set the band suddenly burst into the 'Louie Louie' riff, and five minutes later 50 people were on stage, Buzzcocks members lost amidst the headbangers. The mess was cleared up quickly, but the peak it seemed the evening was heading for never arrived. An anti-climatic finish to a wonderful evening.

## XI

**Sleeve notes to** *Short Circuit: Live at the Electric Circus*, **April 1978**

Every Sunday – save when I charmed my way into a vehicle driven much steadier to its destination than away from it – it was a twelve pence ride on a number 112 bus from Piccadilly, outside Littlewoods. Out past the Sabbath-quiet, ghostly centre shops, easing into the next ring out of the city centre bullseye towards the first hints of the suburbs, those early conceived square blocks and high-rises now festering, and spiritless, past second-home corner pubs, then off the buses at Collyhurst Street. Damning, blitzed, stumbling, crumbling half-occupied blocks of flats, once perfect, text-book architectural dream homes – many bearing the requisite legend in the window, 'This is occupied.'

The overlarge shed of red brick with dirt, cobwebs, moss, more dirt, so small really but large inside-Tardis effect – and on one end of the building the tatty canvas banner that hung forlornly proclaiming: The Electric Circus.

Sunday Night At The Electric Circus. Can we ever forget it – or describe it? The Circus opened around October 1976 (chronology is approximate, especially during 1977 when time seemed compressed and inverted), a place, usually to drag yourself to in the line of duty, where 'club' groups bashed out sorrowful, uninspired sets for slow, tiresome clumps of student/hippy/heads. In the early months of the Circus' existence attendance was not exactly rigorously necessary. The place seemed what it was: a filthy, converted working man's club/cinema 'The Palladium'. As a rock club it was a dusty, apathetic, pitiful anachronism.

But there were early exceptions that proved how dowdy and dead-end the regular, routine dates were. Out of four or five dates throughout the country, the Anarchy Tour visited the Circus twice, a foretaste of the strange, euphoric atmosphere in the months ahead. The Buzzcocks played there a couple of times at the end of 1976, once supporting Slaughter and the Dogs and the other with Chelsea. The place was atrociously attended, which probably explains the club's owners' (Allan and Graham) initial reluctance to book these peculiar new guerrilla rock bands whose popularity, if it existed, was probably transitory anyway. The Buzzcocks of late 1976 was a different Buzzcocks to the bittersweet quartet we love so much today. Howard Devoto on pained, uncomfortable vocals, Peter Shelley on mangled, screeching sawn-off guitar, and only now that these two receive relative rewards and fame for their artistry can we achieve perspective in a traditional, sensible manner on just how good that band was. When they played the Circus – desperate, crucial sets – I remember perhaps 40 featureless faces. Yet fifteen months later, with separate groups, they both dent the top 50, when they are less desperate, less crucial, less ecstatic. Explain this, an eternal paradox of rock 'n' roll.

Explain the surreal phenomena when the Electric Circus finally opened its doors to energy. May 4th 1977 I think it was. The Clash, their White Riot Tour, was the true landmark of change. The Electric Circus seemed to come alive. There was a thick glorious atmosphere of ecstasy, energy, euphoria that was recaptured and intensified more or less every Sunday throughout the next six months.

Such a short time, but a vibrant community was established, based on love (audiences at the Electric Circus were *very* intimate), energy, idealism, escapism. Everyone seemed to know each other, posing became all but redundant, it was a different world that was cloaked in a spirit I've never felt anywhere else.

And if you didn't get drunk for the first time or make an utter fool of yourself or dance without inhibitions or make your first acquaintance with illegal substances or spew up at regular intervals during an evening or French kiss with someone of your own sex or fall asleep for hours on end or eat glass or . . . then you weren't really a part of the Electric Circus club. Even a few of the older kids who'd hung about dirty and bored outside the Circus on gig nights, a little curious as to what happened within those walls, were soon regular visitors in new straightlegs and tank-tops.

Only those cruel *Sunday People* infiltrators and those bemused BBC2 *Brass Tacks* personnel were non-members.

Really, I suppose, the Circus had to close. Such intense activity couldn't continue indefinitely. It was burning itself out with so much energy. And the closure, if nothing else, established immediate martyred legendary status.

The cause of the closure is controversial and best left alone, something about fire regulations and maximum dancing room, though the anger at the time almost materialised as a heartbroken occupation of the building. The closure did give us an excuse for a weekend of orgasmic indulgence and it was a hell of a way to go. November the first and second. A hundred bands wanted to play. Fourteen or fifteen did.

A weekend where all the energy and friendly corruption and intimacy and tears and noise and dancing and drinking of six months were crushed to be savoured, as if into a jar. This album has made tangible a little bit of the contents of that jar, and because that final weekend party seemed to specify, in terms of music (the artless, the artful, the terrible, the funny, the different), the spirit that the Circus was ultimately about. The album gives a small glimpse of those times. It's not comprehensive, it doesn't claim perspective, nor greatness, nor permanence, nor accuracy, it just helps strengthen messy memories and offers a taste to those millions of outsiders who could never get to the Electric Circus.

Those who played included:

| | | |
|---|---|---|
| The Fall | – | Science Fiction. Music of structure and insight. Tantalising. Accusing. Compelling. |
| John Cooper Clarke | – | Loony. Been going for years. The Electric Circus helped in putting him where he is. The willingness of the audience to give chances . . . They clapped and danced to Cooper Clarke every time he performed, realising immediately you must not take this man seriously. |
| The Drones | – | Pulp. Representing those groups who for a year experienced brief minor fame cos for a little while we just wanted to dance. |
| Steel Pulse | – | From Birmingham. To keep dancing. |
| Buzzcocks | – | Where do you begin . . . To tell the story of how . . . When the album was made superstars only in Manchester's minds. Now . . . the Circus' favourite act. |
| Joy Division | – | Warsaw on the night. Representing those groups who had something to say but faltered in articulating. Half formulated. |

Find another audience prepared to eagerly assimilate such diversification. That was the key, the open-mindedness of the Circus audience.

Peter Shelley sat in the dressing room after it was all over. There were a few of us hanging about, not saying much, a little tired. Peter picked out on an acoustic guitar the rough chords to 'Breakdown'. 'Well,' he said, head hanging down, guitar playing getting slower, 'that's the last time I play the Electric Circus.' He meant it.

And, of course, there was Magazine. The Worst (who must have played the Electric Circus more than anyone else), the Slugs, V2, Panik, the Negatives, the Prefects, Jon the Postman, Gorton Jerry, Big In Japan who didn't quite make it, Penetration who would've loved to, and some names to reveal the guilty: Denise, Joan, Tony, Lindsay, Linder, Tony II, Maggie, Martin, John, Daphne, Jodie Deep, Steph, Gavin, Malcome, Pete, Mauve, Graham, Joey, Lindsay II, Syd Sylver, Carol, Toni Lee, Carole, Big Dave, Steve for the sounds, Alan Dial, Martin, John, Woody, Candy and Karen, and hundreds more whose names elude but whose faces will never.

# XII

Warsaw were forced to change their name. They did so, with secretive, serious, unexpectedly self-possessed style – a little sprig of genius among the wild weeds – and their choice, with its bleak Holocaust connotations, veered close to a little controversy, if you bear in mind the way Barney introduced a song on the final night of the Electric Circus with an unstable, wound-up mention of Rudolf Hess, and the little drummer boy cover of the Warsaw EP *An Ideal for Living* – which seemed a little unironically 'Tomorrow Belongs to Me' – and the fact that Barney liked to read war writer Sven Hassel, and Ian was not averse to immersing himself in the dark, evil side of history. Were they naïvely messing around with sinister business way beyond their understanding, or just inching closer to working out how to conceptually organise their fascination with strangeness and otherness in ways that were deadpan, provocative and wildly exciting? By choosing the name, which had such a weight it ended up feeling somehow weightless, had they made an internal decision, consciously or not, to produce rock music dedicated to explaining the inexplicable?

Whereas the name Warsaw was flat and unexceptional, somehow bogus, the name Joy Division seemed to flow into and out of history, it seemed to have fierce, moving qualities always just hovering out of reach. It had a serene outerness that hinted at tumultuous inner life. Everything changed once they had such a name, a name that rescued four young men from the obscurity Warsaw was enclosing them in, a name that demanded extravagantly extreme music. For a while they still sounded more Warsaw than Joy Division, but even just the change of name meant they were so much better than Warsaw.

At the time, when you heard that a group called Joy Division were playing a gig, even though you knew they were really Warsaw perhaps having just one last shot at making it, you were intrigued by the idea. Joy Division just simply sounded like the kind of group that should be great. With such a name, the boys that were Warsaw now had a lot to live up to. They had a lot of work to do. The thing about the Warsaw boys, mutating into Joy Division as 1977 swept, or stuttered, into 1978 – they were never afraid of hard work.

# XIII

**Extract from A-to-Z sleeve notes written for a compilation of Northwest post-punk music for Warner Music, *North by North West*.**

j.  Joy Division played their first gig at Pip's in Manchester in January 1978, crawling out of the spotty, tired skin of Warsaw who ended up playing Iggy's 'The Passenger' in a desperate attempt to impress a largely uninterested audience. Were they giving up the ghost already? Perhaps their problem was that they were trying so hard to play together, to sound tight and coherent, that they just sounded rigid and pedestrian. What they needed to do was play together by not really playing together, by following their own instincts and just letting the bass, guitar and drums exist in the same time but not necessarily the same space. (Or the same space but not necessarily the same time.) But they were too tired by now. A new name might be the seed out of which their new life would sprout. Their very last show as Warsaw was on the last night of 1977.
Also in January 1978, the Rotten Sex Pistols split up, and Magazine released 'Shot by Both Sides', two events which seemed to signal the dead end of what had become known as punk as a musical phenomenon. Joy Division would become leading players in the next stage of development, as passionate music fans who turned to punk not because of the fashion but because of the idea that music could be radical and avoid deadening cliché. Post-punk enabled new groups to find a way to work out their edgy, difficult influences and start to experiment with form and content. The Sex Pistols turned into Public Image Ltd, the Buzzcocks Devoto turned into the Magazine Devoto, and Warsaw were now Joy Division. At the time the third of those changes didn't seem as thrilling as the others. On April 14th 1978, Joy Division played their third show, taking part in the Stiff/Chiswick Battle of the Bands Challenge at Rafters on Oxford Street, where the winner of a night's auditions would get a deal with Stiff or Chiswick Records. I can only remember what I can remember, which was that a deadpan joke pop group I was in called the Negatives, who were novelty enough to have quite suited Stiff Records, were also playing that night, and Joy Division were livid with us because, they claimed, we were making things run late and it looked as if they wouldn't get to play. They kicked in our

dressing room door, so the story has developed, although I don't ever remember it being the kind of night where there were dressing rooms, and acted like they might actually hit one of us. When Ian Curtis was in one of his moods, you didn't want to get in his way – he might have been able to distil those moods into gloriously anguished and exhilarating song, to transfer his frustration and anger into rapturous rhyme and reason, but in their raw state, they were abrupt and unpredictable, and he looked quite capable of taking you on, and taking you somewhere you didn't really want to go. You didn't want to get on Ian's nerves. His nerves had a life of their own. At the time, Joy Division felt they were outside of the elite Manchester system, unloved and unwanted, and would have been quite happy to have signed to a London label and escape an indifferent Manchester. No one seemed to care about them. Even the name change hadn't changed much. The idea that getting in their way was a novelty punk group made up of exactly the people who they considered were not exactly helping them achieve their ambitions was too much.

Tempers were rising. It was chaos, as well over a dozen bands milled about fighting to claim their short slot. I think we played, I like to think as the missing link between William Burroughs and Pere Ubu, more likely as the Manchester version of Big In Japan whom I had seen in Liverpool muck around on stage with a kind of demented cool. Maybe we didn't play, and just allowed Joy Division, at that time largely an unknown quantity with not many followers, having not yet shaken off their basic, blundering Warsawness, to play their show. By the time they got on stage long after midnight, with most of the audience gone, they were in a furious mood, and played a set of such desperate intensity it scared off Stiff and Chiswick. It won them their spiky, good humoured and subtly militant manager, Rob Gretton, who up to then had been in the Slaughter and the Dogs camp. The funny thing was, he was born to be the manager of a group like Joy Division who were in exactly the circumstances they were in as marginal underdogs with boundless determination. Their fiery performance also attracted the interest of notorious local television presenter Tony Wilson. Wilson, possibly influenced by Malcolm McLaren, possibly because he fancied himself as an avant-garde philanthropist, possibly because he just liked the attention you got being at the centre of things, had a strong desire to support the fast changing Manchester musical community. The Shelley and Devoto New Hormones end of things were well spoken for. He needed new blood. At Rafters, Joy Division sang their songs as if it was bloody imperative that they did so, as if they were prepared to bleed over the ignorant and unconvinced, and although it wasn't too clear what on earth they were singing that required such passionate intensity, it was possibly along the lines of make life beautiful! make life beautiful! Or, get out of our fucking way. They all but broke out of the chains of Warsaw.

When the driven, voluble and perversely poetic light entertainer Tony Wilson opened his Factory Club at the PSV/Russell Club in Hulme on June 9th, 1978, Joy Division played alongside Durutti Column and Cabaret Voltaire. Peter Saville's poster for the show, famously delivered late, was FAC 1 in the Factory catalogue. ('And he was late every time after that,' said Wilson. 'Someone later told me he had been two months late with his first piece of commercial work, just before he did the poster. That should have told me.') In my memory, this is when and where Joy Division became the Joy Division you would recognise as Joy Division. Joy Division assaulted our senses that night.

There were a few more people in the club than on the stage, but not many, and Ian Curtis quite easily spiralled off the stage into our midst. The music seemed to lift him up and fling him about, as if he was possessed by its power. There was a look in his eyes that wasn't at all like the look in his eyes when he was offstage, off duty, although I had seen hints of that look when he confronted me that night at Rafters and suggested he might turn to violence if I didn't let his band go on before my band.

He was being carried somewhere. He was seeing things that we couldn't possibly see. He was deep and pained in the glorious fury of a performance. He skidded through the scattered members of the audience unafraid that he might crash into us. We were all sort of dressed the same, in dark fairly shapeless clothes that weren't ironed too well and which made us look like we were crawling into, or out of, a short story by Gogol. We stood still not daring to look him in the eye, even though we knew exactly who he was. At least, we knew the young man who had arrived at the club, and probably we would know the young man who would leave the club. As the singer of Joy Division, we didn't know him at all, he was racing away from us as he stunned the air around him with explosive movement never before seen in Manchester, or anywhere else for that matter.

Luckily, material they'd recorded for a department of RCA as Joy Division between the Rafters revelation and the Factory debut never officially appeared – the group hated the synthesisers that one of the producers put on, reedy, day-glo disco synths that made the music we think of as having a deadly humanity and a grim brilliance sound quite ordinary if not a little camp. Funnily enough, Martin Hannett was to put electronics on the album that eventually became the Joy Division debut, *Unknown Pleasures*, but they were more newfangled, and he made the whole thing sound like the music was whistling off the moors via the industrial history of Manchester into the technological future – as if the moors were on Philip K. Dick's Mars. The band put up with that, give or take the concerns one or two had about the fizzing, phasing drum sound Hannett conceived, which to some at the time seemed the rhythmical raving of a stoned mad professor.

On 15th July 1978, Joy Division played Eric's in Liverpool. The Crucial Three (Julian Cope, Ian McCulloch, Pete Wylie) would have been in the audience. By then, Joy Division were already beginning to sound like they could actually be what I thought they were by the time they recorded the howling, mesmerising 'Transmission' – the most spectacularly electric rock group on earth who played their stunned, uneasy music with a kind of religious conviction. It was not clear how or where they had bought the golden ticket that was taking them further and further away from Warsaw, but however it had happened, they were beginning a unique journey, now accompanied by the kind of important Manchester insiders – Wilson, Gretton and Hannett – that had previously spurned them.

# XIV

Meanwhile, I was still not entirely convinced, and where I was obediently standing in place at the moment it was happening, not throwing back glances with the clarifying benefit of hindsight, having no idea what was going to happen, still remembering Warsaw, I continued to view Joy Division as an experiment that hadn't yet been completed. There was no way that we knew at the time that Joy Division were actually going to become Joy Division.

They were obviously moving forward, getting better all the time. I was liking them more and more every six months, and I dutifully explained in the *NME* the steps the group were making as they turned from the group who had thought up the name Joy Division to becoming the group that would be worthy of the name. They were on their way to becoming the group that you didn't keep comparing to other groups, but which you would compare other groups to. In the background, busy and a bit belligerent, the endlessly amused and sardonic Rob Gretton was now helping them, and wherever the group would go, so would he, protecting them, guiding them, arming them with an arm around their shoulders, getting them work, as sure as anyone that they were his dream group and could conquer the world.

At this point, they were still likely to sign to a London label. Factory Records was not yet anything other than a late-night conversation Tony Wilson would be having, after reading the news for Granada Television, or sailing through the city on a cloud of ego and restlessness with his best mate Alan Erasmus. Peter Saville was stuck in a room somewhere solemnly loading himself with information about twentieth-century graphic design, not yet knowing he might be able to turn his studies and his fascination with enigma and the elaborations of imagery into commercial, and artistic, surfaces and signals. Martin Hannett was, in a manner of speaking, working out just how to make drums sound like a burst of hail against a windowpane.

I was still working out if I could become the kind of writer who could explain the magic power of music without reducing everything to a cluster of mere descriptive facts, hoping that, in my world, I was making the same sort of move Warsaw had in going from nowhere to – what the hell – Joy Division.

## XV

**Live review – Joy Division, Manchester, 20 May 1978,** *New Musical Express* **(published 3 June).**

Joy Division were once Warsaw, a punk group with literary pretensions. Warsaw Pakt forced them to change names.

They disappeared for a while at the end of last year, and have re-emerged with their new name, an EP and their pretensions even more to the fore.

Their record attempts to communicate in an almost tangible way all the abstraction of Buzzcocks' *Spiral Scratch*. It is called *An Ideal for Living*, and is on the Enigma label. It proclaims on the sleeve that 'this is not a concept EP, it is an enigma.'

Despite all this, the record is structurally good, though soundwise poor, a reason it may not be widely released.

They're a dry, doomy group who depend promisingly on the possibilities of repetition, sudden stripping away, with deceptive dynamics, whilst they use sound in a more orthodox hard rock manner than, say, either the Fall or Magazine.

They have an ambiguous appeal, and with patience they could develop strongly and make some testing, worthwhile metallic music.

# XVI

**Live review – Joy Division, Manchester, 4 September 1978,** *New Musical Express* **(published 9 September).**

Those familiar with this young quartet mainly through their excitable appearance on the *Short Circuit* pretty package, and to a lesser extent with their self produced *An Ideal for Living* EP, unimpressed by their ordinariness but detecting deep in their industry and pretensions a potential for making a more effective, ambitious music, should look to Joy Division now.

In months, they have matured considerably. They have learnt to sculpt, not merely to emit. They are now not instinctively fast and frenzied, but animated and volatile. The crucial substances in Joy Division's original expression, the dynamics and vigour, have been lifted out of a surrounding morass of clumsiness and unsureness, and elaborated on, sharpened up. A new-found sensitivity. From a punk group with minimal awareness and ability, to a music group with eloquence and direction.

Previously crude and inarticulate, painfully overworking an idea to nothing, using minimal deviations or patterns in a song, they now twist, punch, turn within a manoeuvre, never resting, never spilling.

Joy Division use basic guitar, bass, drums, voice, it's still riff, rhythms and coherence. But its form and execution drag it away from rock tradition – different introductions, different shapes, different conclusions.

Their music is mercilessly attacking, it rotates, persists, repeats, always well balanced.

Ian Curtis on voice, reacting to the music as if on a hot plate, discovers the scope within tonal limitations – uses his vocals for force; blankly impressed emotions, bitter and angry. Not tuneless, not tuneful. Flat and intent, a fourth instrument.

Lyrically, philosophically, their ideas and intentions are lost, the peril of fast communicative music performed with poor equipment in dire venues. This could be an advantage – they may be advocating a police state and restrictions of freedom for all the listener can discern.

Joy Division's old songs (written as Warsaw), once blunt and hollow, are now fuller, keen and more pointed, with a new-found sense of time, tension and suspension.

That Joy Division can be dropped, without qualms, into the same sweet packet as Magazine and the Fall is significant of their growth. Growth that introduces new difficulties – greater responsibility, deeper commitment. An audience will drift towards them (towards fashionable metal-industrial exploits), but Joy Division will need to fight the tendency to dilute brand new standards to seduce a larger audience.

This could be Joy Division's peak. On the verge of a compromise – or on the verge of something greater? Right now they make provocative and invigorating music, somewhere on a line between the conventional and unconventional practises of Penetration and the Banshees. That 'good'.

# XVII

I am not sure why, in the following extract, I describe Alan Erasmus, a founding member of the Factory collective, as a 'tramp', but, even three decades after he helped form the Factory label with Tony Wilson, I would still find it difficult to describe his role, and indeed his activities before Factory. I treasure a solitary memory I have of Erasmus the actor appearing in an episode of the Carla Lane sitcom *The Liver Birds*, as a doctor with one line. It gives the story, as framed around Factory Records, a constant sense that it was always in a way an extravagant sitcom; it had the classic line-up of five men, and the occasional whimsical female, sitting around a bar, or a workplace, grumbling about a disappointing world, whilst having a series of madcap adventures as they set about trying to make it better. Their adventures were located on the frontier of two worlds, that of death, and that of play. Erasmus to some extent played the role of straight man with mysterious past, and mysterious future.

There is no doubt though that Factory would not have been Factory without Erasmus. Although it was Wilson who had the nerve, skin and gusto to talk the whole thing up, and sell the enterprise from the very beginning as if he knew all along that its importance would only start to be fully acknowledged years later, and it was Saville who fantasised the shape and appearance of the record label, it was Erasmus who made sure that it all connected to what we might under the circumstances call reality.

Perhaps amongst a gang of transgressive northern surrealists – and Gretton and Hannett had definite surrealist tendencies, even as they attended to the practical matters of organisation and sound – Erasmus was the one true realist. On the other hand, he was just as likely at a moment's notice to slip out of reality's way, and as the years have gone by he's drifted out of the picture, to the point where he's becoming a kind of lost legend, a mere rumour, never known to engage in any kind of recollection about the early days, glorious heyday and chaotic decline of the label. He seems less and less real.

Above the mobile, imperial mythmaker Wilson, the traumatised, mystic technician Hannett, the rambling, dramatically pragmatic and stoical Gretton, the hedonistic, high-falutin' visionary Saville, it was Erasmus who supplied the pure mystery. However present, or absent, he was during the conception, running and collapse of Factory, Joy Division's romantic, sceptical label, his contribution alone ensured that Factory was itself a work of art, and often a glorious conceptual joke.

It was never Erasmus that contacted me, asking if I could find a way to mention the new activities of Factory. It was Wilson. It wasn't Erasmus who kept calling to see if I could somehow get a review of Factory's first record, a double seven-inch, into the *NME*. It was Wilson. (I was having trouble, because the LP reviews editor wouldn't take it as it was, as such, a single, not an album, and I was not yet senior enough to be given more than a couple of singles columns a year, and when I did the editor didn't consider the sampler a single. Factory's first release existed in a kind of limbo – it was neither one thing nor another, an exotic, impractical single/album hybrid.)

It wasn't Erasmus who pleaded with me that the entire future of the label depended on me getting a review of the sampler into the paper. It was Wilson – I found out later he did the same thing with other music writers. But possibly, in the room as Wilson made the calls you imagined Erasmus was there with him, quiet, watchful, wondering not how much money they might make out of this unique, modestly local, precarious new venture, but how consistently surprising, provocative and playful they could be.

# XVIII

Preview of *A Factory Sampler* – *New Musical Express* ('Thrills' section), 2 December 1978.

Manchester noise nightclub the Factory, a welcome rock venue, soon takes the inevitable next step from staging to recording.

Incorporating the diversity of Rough Trade Records with the sharply eclectic marketing processes of New Hormones, Factory Records is run by co-directors actor/tramp Alan Erasmus and graphic designer Peter Saville. With the ever-enthusiastic Tony *So It Goes* Wilson inevitably involved, it will release an attractive double EP sampler of acts and artistes who have appeared at the club over the last few months. The EP (FAC 2) includes three tracks from abandoned comic John Dowie, produced by C. P. Lee; two pieces from Cabaret Voltaire's cult cassette, produced by themselves; two songs from Joy Division, produced by Martin Zero; and a couple of fascinating dub-psychedelia exercises from Durutti Column, produced by Zero with Laurie Latham.

A devious sampler out to both seduce and introduce, its packaging is thoughtful and unusual, its implications exciting. It is provisionally set for mid-December release, priced an irresistible £1.50.

Future Factory Records projects remain endearingly vague; FAC 3 (FAC 1 was the original Factory venue poster, designed by Saville) looked set to be a twelve-inch disco single from the Tiller Boys, but internal confusion has temporarily shelved that. Factory express interest in the Distractions, the Negatives and current musicians' favourites Manicured Noise (ask Vic Godard, the Banshees, Wire what they think of M. Noise – politely, of course).

Send Factory Records your cassette: The Factory, Hulme, Manchester. Let's all take risks this Christmas!

85

# XIX

Tony Wilson, who north-westerners knew as a jaunty TV presenter who had a future as a quiz show host or, if that failed, a weatherman – which probably accounted for the long-term suspicion of him as a genuine pop-culture radical – used his grandmother's inheritance to pay for the pressing and packaging of the *Factory Sampler*. It wasn't quite clear when he made his plugging calls whether he was just concerned about getting his money back, or that he fully intended to turn Factory Records into a going concern, an absurdist record label, a business always on the verge of glory and collapse, a catalogue of records, distractions and occasions that somehow linked Karl Marx with Andy Warhol.

I eventually persuaded a reluctant Monty Smith, the *NME* albums review editor, a ZZ Top fan, to give some review space to the *Factory Sampler*. The review appeared some months after its release, which fell in with Factory timing. Factory's first record sold out of its initial limited edition run, and Wilson and company ended up making a small profit on the release – some said about £80. A few months later, after releases by groups with names such as Orchestral Manoeuvres in the Dark and A Certain Ratio, Factory would release the Joy Divison album *Unknown Pleasures* as Fac 10.

## XX

**Record review – *New Musical Express*, 31 March 1979.**

*A Factory Sampler* -
**Joy Division, the Durutti Column, John Dowie, Cabaret Voltaire (Factory Records)**
Conceived and executed by a handful of acute Mancunian idealists (Tony Wilson, Peter Saville and Alan Erasmus), *A Factory Sampler* attempts to represent the nature of performers who appear at the Russell Club, Manchester on Friday nights – the Factory.

The Factory eagerly and consistently concerns itself with staging rigorously and obstinately uncompromising modern entertainers whose music and attitude doesn't desire or pretend to be comfortable, comforting or complacent. Some pretty strange, terrible and wonderful people have been known to play there. 'It's nonsense really' is the Factory motto and 'some of it's not' is its aside.

Factory Records' first release is a nine-track double EP sampler of acts and entertainers who have been associated with the club, smartly packaged in shimmering silver, the design a tender, indulgent situationist parody. Factory Records joke as much as they poke. They are not pretentious, they are affectionate.

None of the acts on *Factory Sampler* complement each other – the listener doesn't feel they should – and angles and ideas jut out all over the place. Four compartments. Four noises. For anyone.

Compartment one – aside – Joy Division: Two patient, intent pieces, 'Digital' and 'Glass', their structure subtly suppressed, dryly and dully produced by Martin Zero. Two blurred depictions of desperation and desolation, the missing link between Elvis Presley and the Banshees. The drive and decisiveness, the separation and interaction of each instrument, their unusually supple positions (high bass, drums to the front, meandering guitar) and the deep, round vocals will surprise those whose knowledge of Joy Division is limited to their sluggish EP and their dire *Electric Circus* contribution. More proof of Division's intelligent development. How much longer before an aware label will commit themselves to this individual group?

Compartment two – beside – the Durutti Column: Two rough, restless examples of an ambitious music the group spent many months attempting to perfect before splintering and all but disintegrating in the latter few months of last year. An uneasy, fluctuating blend of the extreme atmospheres and differing shapes and patterns of dub and psychedelia. Produced with restraint by Martin Zero and Laurie Latham.

Compartment three – seaside – John Dowie: Three irrational, indignant little snaps, 'Acne', 'Idiot' and 'Hitler's Liver', deftly accompanied by members of the Albertos and artlessly produced by C. P. Lee, Dowie's arresting and vigorous delivery is, as always, on the edge of mania, and the seaside humour provides the sampler with a certain balance considering the oppressive, ponderous aura of the other three sides. As you smirk, you're nudged.

Compartment four – decide – Cabaret Voltaire: Neil the *NME* editor opines this Sheffield trio are a bunch of pretentious berks. Me, I think the theoretical input is more attractive than the musical output. So there!

It's not a particularly constructive parallel, but when the Human League 'drop sounds' onto the floor, they do so into a box so that the sounds collect and form; CV 'drop sounds' and let them spread, and the mix and flow is never definite or distinct enough – or shockingly random enough. A collection of ordinary electronic sounds and tricks without design or discipline and rarely worthwhile – as in atmospheric or alienating, edgy or evocative. Splodges and splatters. Ebbs and echoes.

What next for CV? Research.

The sampler's sound is often untidy, and in a way the selections seem like leftovers – but leftovers that invite search. In five years' time rock and pop will be utterly different in form and content to what is foolishly accepted as being pop and rock now. And it'll still be changing.

Factory helps it along its way. A game of love. The only way.

## XXI

By the beginning of 1979 it was time to write a follow-up to my 1977 Manchester piece. New groups were emerging in Manchester all the time, inspired by being in Manchester at the exact time they were, in the lively, moving months after the Pistols changed everything, when suddenly there were possibilities, and you could make your own records, and be written about, and even played on the radio – if only by the wise and ever observant John Peel in the murky, magical late night shadows at Radio One. In this piece, I had more confidence in expressing a formative post-punk manifesto now that I had been writing for the *NME* for over two years. I was unashamedly and confidently using the paper to project an ideological zeal and a belief that the best new rock needed to be serious and uncompromising and always moving forward. This attitude was undoubtedly because of the detached, philosophical Manchester thing that meant that the first lines you heard on *Real Life*, the debut Magazine album, were, 'I've got this bird's eye view/and it's in my brain/clarity has reared/its ugly head again.' The song was called 'Definitive Gaze'. 'So this is real life,' it went, 'you're telling me.'

This *NME* article concentrated on three bands who I felt would become as known during 1979 as Magazine, the Fall and Buzzcocks had during 1978. I guess I was right about one in three, although at the time, if I'd gone on the quality of the conversation, and based future success on how the musicians articulated their views and presented their mission, I would have suggested Joy Division would not break through. They seemed a bit baffled by their status and trajectory.

Of the three groups I selected, they were the ones who couldn't really talk about themselves and their ideas. An interview with Joy Division consisted more than anything of pauses, sighs and a jumpy sense that they couldn't wait for the whole interrogation to end. Rob Gretton, their wily, stubborn manager, tended to sit in on interviews, not going out of his way to hide the satisfaction he was getting from the difficulty journalists found themselves in, as they attempted to extract information, even revelation, that might match the tremendous power of the group's music. Sometimes it seemed as if you were still interviewing Warsaw, even though they were now, to a large extent, Joy Division, and Rob Gretton was watching over them with a twinkle in his eye that wasn't necessarily completely benevolent.

We met on a Saturday morning in the grim and grimy Brunswick pub at the bottom of Piccadilly station. This was in the years before self-consciously hip boutique hotels started to spring up near the station, before there were European-style trams streaming through the city, and when the centre of Piccadilly looked like it might be headed for ruin, not renovation.

Not much was said about not much. My questions seemed to nudge the group into deeper and deeper silence. Perhaps we were all silently working out how tall each of us was. We could point the finger at Ian as being the tallest, even if he did stoop a little as if worried he was standing higher than everyone else.

Mostly the group talked matter-of-factly about how hard it was for them to make an impact, and explained the details of how they got their gigs, and the small likelihood of them ever being able to make some kind of living out of being Joy Division. Stephen the drummer was so quiet it was almost noisy. Perhaps all that was in his head were the riveting beats and rhythms that kept his life steady.

Ian dragged deep on a cigarette and sipped his thoughtful way through a pint of bitter. Perhaps, a few hours later, he thought of something to say that wasn't so prosaic. Perhaps he didn't want to say too much because he didn't want to be judged by what he said as a diffident 22-year-old in a future that might end up a little twisted by fate, a little smashed by circumstance. He was instinctively ensuring a kind of secrecy that would eventually help nourish his posthumous reputation.

Despite how withdrawn he could be in interviews, maybe hiding most of what he was thinking for whatever personal reason, and how opaque his band mates could be, not wanting to give the game away just in case in the end there was nothing to give away, I was slowly finding more and more to say about them. There was more of a story, even though the story mostly consisted of them looking, or waiting, or hoping, or praying, for a break.

After their first *NME* interview was over, they obediently trooped off into the snow that seemed specially laid on for the occasion in a blanketed city that appeared evacuated of fellow citizens. They had their photographs taken in a city that had visited from a dream. They didn't say much while that happened either, certainly nothing to suggest they were aware in the slightest that those photographs would be looked at for years, and eventually make it into art galleries and books.

On the other hand, Steve Solomar of the gracious, almost gothic Spherical Objects, and Dick Witts of the desolate, lacerating Passage, talked with considerable fluency about their plans, with expertise that wasn't just musical and artistic but also financial. They were working out all sorts of business strategies in terms of their independence, and determining how the early punk spirit was going to survive and evolve in a world that was threatened by the uncompromising ideological fervour of the participants.

For a moment, in a conversation I had with *New Musical Express* editor Neil

Spencer about whether he was going to make a mistake in putting Ian Curtis on the cover of the first issue of the year, I hesitated a little. Spencer was only prepared to give a part of the cover to Curtis, handing out other shares to other NME-supported newcomers, but at the time, giving cover space to an unknown and at that point unsigned rock band was something of a risk. He wanted to know if perhaps he was putting Curtis on the cover too quickly, building up a level of expectation that the group would have problems dealing with.

I hesitated, because, remembering the conversations I had with the respective lead singers of the bands, Ian was the quietest, the least articulate, and didn't seem as prepared for the future as the other two. I paused, because Solomar and Witts talked with penetrating persuasiveness and an intellectual rigour that seemed positively Eno-esque.

Witts' understanding of why the Sex Pistols were not just conceptually but musically important was compelling. His analysis of the way 'Anarchy in the UK' was recorded, picking up on how Steve Jones played the bass by simply copying the melody line to create a distinctive tonal effect, was extremely astute. (Jones played the bass during the recording session in the temporary absence of Glen Matlock. Not being a bassist, he took the simple option of copying the vocal melody, but this helped produce the disconcerting rock power of the track, which seemed traditional but was somehow experimental.) I also liked hearing the way Solomar talked about music, and had a kind of sentimental sympathy for the fact that, being older than most post-punk musicians at the time, this was his last chance.

Solomar, though, looked like a gentle primary school teacher. Witts looked like the probing academic he actually was, even though his vigilant, jagged, guitarless group were somehow the missing link, the actual passage, between the Fall and Wire, and could be as dark and persistent as Joy Division. In photographs, Solomar and Witts were the quiet, shy ones. In his photograph, Ian looked like he might have been ill at ease in an ambiguous world, but he wasn't going to show it. His photograph said everything that he never said in the interview. Curtis looked like the star. Curtis made it seem like we'd been expecting him.

Spencer fanned out the photographs of the three in front of us. No contest. The pure, indelible stare of Ian Curtis slipped onto the cover of the NME at the beginning of 1979. By the end of the year, Solomar's group had hopelessly disappeared into the kind of void that once seemed to be beckoning Warsaw. The Passage left behind some enlightened cult classics, and took their places more or less as a footnote in the Fall story. Joy Division had proved, not so much by talking but by playing almost non-stop, and releasing fantastically tender, uncannily turbulent and romantically excessive records, that they were worthy cover stars.

## XXII

**A piece on various Manchester bands including Joy Division –**
*New Musical Express*, **13 January 1979 – Ian Curtis' first music-press
front cover.**

Over the last few months there have been definite dislocations in the way
the British rock business is structured that are both depressing and satisfying.

The major labels have managed quite easily to steady themselves after the
cutting commotion of '75/'76, and have carefully invested in and subdued
the activity. They did their jobs, only the most careless making mistakes.

Economically the dozen or so new bands captured and marketed
represent a fair future. The consumers are responsive and, most importantly,
young – and the bands themselves have generously been given more
control over their careers than is usual within the system.

So the labels have done well. They've diverted and diffused a dangerous
movement and are making money. And it seems that 90 per cent of all
consumers are satisfied.

These new investments are tiny next to the current gargantuan financial
and statistical realities of the brainwashing disco/compilation/TV packages,
but supply an illusion that the labels are offering choices, and were
necessary so the labels could control and dilute the movement.

Now the good news.

Totally separate from the Business's assiduous activity here's a whole
mass of diverse and distinct new rock musicians whose activity is implicitly
concerned with preventing this suffocation of choice.

Imagination and individualism currently dominates rock – if not
commercial rock – like never before. Take a look around you . . . but not
where the Business tells you.

This genuine underground music reaches a small, enthusiastic audience,
and despite the reserved and/or reactionary decisions of many fans who, for
example, continue to demand the vague ideals of '75/'76, dourly dismissing
the eclectic and exciting new force of synthesiser units with depressing
abruptness, this audience is going to flourish as it becomes obvious that the
major labels have manufactured a new pop muzak, however irresistible, out
of an important revolution.

We should be writing books about the birth of rock 'n' roll, not
obituaries. We should be fighting the control of the radio and labels, not
derisively ignoring this underground.

Because ultimately it's not that anyone is denying anybody else the right to purchase Showaddywaddy or Travolta or Yes or Gen X or whoever in droves, as amusing or saddening as it is. Simply that there must be choice. We need choice.

For examples of the wide choices that exist in rock, obscurely but certainly, let's look to Manchester. The new music exists anywhere and everywhere. No one is ashamed or nervous of making music. Manchester I know best.

The amount of music in Manchester would be substantial even if it was spread right across the nation and not just housed in a limited locality. But you may not be aware of this – because once the industry struck with Magazine and Buzzcocks, failed with the Drones and the Dogs, and was puzzled by the Fall, it scurried away.

Manchester, however, created its own network. Rabid Records you'll already know. But apart from Rabid there are three record labels that aren't purely group vehicles.

New Hormones, which operates from 50 Newton Street, Manchester, will soon release records by the Tiller Boys and Ludus, and re-release *Spiral Scratch*.

Factory Records (86 Palatine Road, Didsbury, Manchester) release at the end of this month a strong sampler containing music from John Dowie, Cabaret Voltaire, Durutti Column and Joy Division.

Object Music have released records by Spherical Objects and the Passage, with a handful more planned.

The three groups who interested me most are Spherical Objects, Joy Division and the Passage. All are totally committed, totally assured, totally independent.

Spherical Objects are a quintet who were conceived in June 1976, initiated in May 1978, and formed around the delicate, driving songs of Steve Solomar.

Solomar stumbled accidentally upon Frederick Burrows (bass), John Bisset-Smith (guitar), Duncan Prestbury (keyboards) and Roger Hilton (drums) . . . after auditioning 100 musicians. He himself is 28, passionately involved with music 'ever since I was twelve,' sensitive, shrewd and ambitious.

'I'd been in bands long enough to know now what I want, and I've got reasonably strong ideas on how I want to present it.

'I found that musicians of my own age were very cliché-ridden so I looked for younger musicians where the chances of them being less spoilt were greater. Everyone in the band has freshness, they're all twenty or under, and they play effectively without in any way being virtuosos.'

Solomar's unswerving confidence in his own ability and style was quickly established with Spherical Objects, the first group he'd felt completely happy with. They first performed on May 28 last year after five months' careful, systematic rehearsals, and by July 10 were in Manchester's Arrow/Indigo Studios recording an album, *Past and Parcel*.

Solomar has such faith in his own highly esoteric, archly flamboyant music.

'At the time we recorded the album,' he calmly recalls, 'we'd done three gigs. But I knew that the material I had for the album didn't have to be embellished too much – there's great variety in our music. And I knew the band was ready.

'The actual content of the album I'd had ready for over a year. It just seemed a logical step to produce one, on our own Object label.'

Their first single, 'The Kill', was released at the end of last year.

'I could see, from other material we had, that there was going to be a logical progression. The first album, then two singles, then the next album. That would have been logical. The flow wouldn't have been as logical if the single had been the first release.'

Although the album was done quickly, it isn't sloppy. *Past and Parcel* is simply and sensibly packaged, and despite being recorded and mixed in ten hours ('all one takes and live') the sound is clear and clever – a necessity for what is a naturally fussy music.

Recommended price was £2.50p.

'To finance the record meant borrowing about 800 quid. I took months preparing the processes. At £2.50p we still make a profit, something you normally wouldn't do with a *single*. This week we have sold the last of the original 1,000 pressing, so it's taken five months. We're re-releasing it in April.'

Solomar is convinced record companies could drop their prices incredibly. Due to increased costs the next pressing of *Past and Parcel* will be £3.75. 'But there will still be a difference of about a pound between ours and EMI's. It is very feasible to do it so cheaply.'

The tightly structured music is hardly imitative or naïve. By regulating distinctive influences – Love, Buckley, Reed are heavily discernible – alongside their own fully charged elegance the group achieves a music that is distinctly eclectic yet undeniably original and special.

It is very personal, uncommon music, irregularly based with versatile, individual embellishments from Bisset-Smith's delicate, introverted lead and Prestbury's subtle, illuminative keyboards.

At the time of recording Solomar's voice was a little weak but is now beginning to leave behind its Buckley taints and become eerie and capable in its own way.

The very curious Objects sound is totally unlike anything else anybody else is doing. Two rag dolls on the cover with a six-inch nail driven between their hands to crudely seal them together supplies a gentle symbolic clue to the nine songs' subject matter.

Concerning his music, Solomar is objective; baffled about its obscurity without boasting.

'I think the album is really underestimated,' he reasonably concludes. 'I feel the potential audience for Spherical Objects is quite huge. One thing this band has that most groups haven't is that there are definite sixties roots. There's no way we sound like a sixties group, but there are all sorts of things that are subtly in there. A lot of other new bands that I really like have their roots in '76 and nothing in the sixties.'

It's not hard to bracket Spherical Objects within the scope of Pere Ubu and Talking Heads once awkward prejudices have been discarded.

'Those groups rooted in '76 are conscious of working within a certain scene. Our songs reflect something far greater than that. Life in our times, whatever. Because even though a part of what I write is personal experience, a far great part is observer experience.

'It's very difficult to control what you write in a number of ways. The most important thing is selecting what you've written. There's a certain area that philosophically or conceptually the group is working within – the album was centring on relationships between two people, the traditional relationships, the upward swing, the downward swing.

'Other material that we have – enough for two more albums – shows us not necessarily concerned with relationships between two people, but with human relations and human behaviour. That's a central area our records will continue thematically.'

Up to now Spherical Objects have remained stoically independent, but Solomar has no illusions about the ultimate need to join a record label for purely financial reasons, and paradoxically, because of the freedom such a coupling would offer; the records labels have the money, thus the power to promote, and that power will be directed out of basic greed as long as the companies organise and dilute the artists and not the other way round.

The musicians must have more say.

Solomar sees this latter object as possible if the record companies became saturated with confident, capable musicians who could alter the narrow-mindedness.

What is needed is more and more groups cultivating a fresh commercial music that the labels cannot ignore, backed up with strength, honesty and intelligence.

'There's two sides to signing a deal. The main problem is finance. I don't see any reason why, if we had a deal retaining artistic control, we couldn't put out music exactly as we want, advertising it how we want. Buzzcocks are a shining example. I don't see any reason why we couldn't do exactly as we would by keeping our independence, but with the finance helping to promote us, to get us heard.

'Also on the next album it would be nicer to spend five days recording it, and with a deal we might be able to double that. The more time you have the more hold you have over your music.

'It's wholly financial really. There's no chance of us going professional if we ignore the major labels and stick with Object. For instance, I've got a nine to five job in an industry (Solomar is a computer analyst) I've been with for twelve years and, to put it mildly, I'm very fucked off with it.

'I know the record business sucks, but I'm not disillusioned because I knew from the very beginning what it was like . . . but if we had control there would be no problem.

'I fully realise that if a company signed us they would attempt to push us in certain directions, but I think the sound that we make is commercial as it is without us having to compromise in any way.'

The rest of the group fall in with Solomar's idealism.

Prestbury: 'If you want to do anything constructive in music you've always got to stand closely by what you want as a band, and I'd rather have the whole thing explode and come to nothing than have to compromise. I am prepared to carry on until people become interested . . .'

Hilton: 'Take a case like Steel Pulse: when they started they were really exciting but since joining Island they've been like a Radio Two job . . . cassette in the car thing . . . nothing like the old band. And that's an example of what seems to happen to bands who sign to large labels.'

Solomar: 'It would be difficult for us to supply any freedom of choice in our current position, because record companies can obviously give a lot more promotion to their choice than we can to ours. But if we don't get a contract this year we will still release an album on Object in the autumn. We will carry on regardless.'

A disciplined romantic, Solomar saw the possibilities of Object Music as an actual label, and not purely a temporary group vehicle, once all the hassles involved in recording the album had been overcome.

'I wouldn't have formed the label without having my band on it, because that initially gave the drive and the groundwork. But once that was done it just seemed logical.

'What I plan is for there to be quite a lot of releases on Object this year. We're planning releases by three Manchester bands – who'll get 50 per cent of profits after costs have been deducted. What will probably happen is that after a lot of activity on Object Music this year it will be either wound down to a large degree next year, or we'll stop production to concentrate on wherever Spherical Objects have reached at that time. It may be possibly kept over to release things I find interesting.'

The first non-Spherical Object release on Object Music is edgy, frantic four-song EP *New Love Songs* from passionate experimental rock trio the Passage, who incorporate the economic, emotional aspects of rock, the harshly academic determination of experimental music plus the spontaneity and detail of jazz.

The trio consists of classically trained percussionist Dick Witts, who spent three years with the Hallé orchestra and who has played much experimental music, keyboardist Lol Hilton, and bassist Tony Friel – who contributed much to the early Fall sound.

'The same line-up as ELP,' chuckles the effervescent, irrepressible Witts. 'It's extraordinary the number of people who come up to us and say that we really need a guitar . . . who can't adjust to our sound.'

Following the relentlessly intelligent and smilingly opinionated Witts' trail to forming the Passage is curious and, in its way, complimentary to rock as a proper, positive twentieth century music of action and vigour.

Witts is totally classically orientated, from the orthodox to the avant-garde, progressively and experimentally inclined because 'that's a defence you set up as a percussionist.'

He'd been playing experimental music and becoming increasingly dissatisfied with its conventions and limitations.

'All the balls has gone out of it. It's not developing in any direction at all. Experimental music stagnated after the Second World War . . . and what I wanted to do was something that was very direct. In experimental music you can play a piece that lasts 40 minutes and you ask people what they thought . . . y'know, you've been playing for 40 minutes, thinking all the time, creating, and they say, "Oh yeah I really like that bit about two thirds in, that was really nice."

'Y'know there was no criteria . . . you wanted to know something had happened. And you didn't. Whereas in rock, you know when you've played badly or well, or when it's working. So that's part of why rock appealed. The other part of it was why deny tonality? . . . why deny keys? What's happening in rock – even with Cabaret Voltaire or This Heat – is there's a kind of tonal basis to what they're doing, a key . . . whilst experimental music had become obsessed with getting things down on paper . . . it became very atomised.

'So why deny tonality? Let's use it in other ways; a progressive state of music. It's not that I'm particularly interested in music developing per se, just 'cos it needs to progress, because it seems that the role of the contemporary composer is as a researcher to discover the marketable commodities of the future. That's something I'm against. What we've got to find is something that exists as a critique of existing society. Music is one way of doing that. Music is about time and energy. You don't play a piece of music and suddenly there is a revolution, but music is necessarily concerned with attitudes of mind and other possibilities of using time and energy.

'On that level we shouldn't be concerned with progress for its own sake. It should be geared to some social end. So that's why I became interested in rock. Like the Fall were doing some really interesting things.'

But surely if there were some interesting things happening in rock, and its superficial purpose was attractive, there were equally fascinating things happening in experimental music. Both have their elements of stagnation and their positive elements.

'No no. There are possibilities in rock that haven't been tapped, avenues that I'd wanted to explore. Tony, coming from the other end, would probably say something else.

'Sure, Steve Beresford in experimental music is superb. He spreads across the whole range of music. One minute he'll be playing slinky ballads, the next minute something violent, then something else. What he's about – and this is very important – is change, continual change. I don't mean for the sake of it but for a particular social end.

'I like the idea of continual change because I don't want to see a society that is so formulated, so static, bureaucratic in that sense, but one that is continually revising its forms and actions. There's a lot of change in a Passage set. There's a lot of different things happening – music that goes from one extreme to another. My songs are experimentally based, and Tony's are rock based, but there's still a fluidity.

'Y'see, I first came into rock through David Bedford, who was an avant-garde composer who first got into rock by arranging things for Mike Oldfield. But if you've heard the stuff he did . . . he took what seemed to me to be the most stupidly stagnant aspects of rock and he milked all the rest, and all you were left with was the most awful tepidity.

'It did nothing. I thought that was all wrong. There must be other possibilities. I thought this before forming the Passage, which is why I became interested in the Fall; the most important change was – chichi cliché – the

Sex Pistols at the Lesser Free Trade Hall. I went because I'd read something John Peel said, that they were doing something completely new. And they were! There's a difference with what the Pistols did between *repetition* and *insistence*; in "Anarchy" the bass line and the melody are the same; they're parallel and the chords are parallel to the bass and thus the melody, and that's similar to eleventh century Organum. What happened there was that there was a very firm Christian ideology being promoted by a bunch of hoodlum monks and the way they did it was through parallel insistence in music.'

From all this – his own refined enthusiasm for the potential sounds of experimental music, Bedford's mistakes, the Pistols' impact, the Fall's strengths, rock's actual social justification and purpose – Witts arrived at the Passage.

It's interesting that he should wish to play rock considering his background, and that he felt that there were definite aesthetic avenues to follow. As much proof than anything else of the actual purpose and success of the '75/'76 turmoil, and how valid rock can be as a communicative social force.

To those who say this new underground lacks the fun, spirit, beat, and soda pop dressiness of what's accepted as rock 'n' roll (still), or that the exponents are producing music that is at best a slightly idiosyncratic intrusion on rock's mainstream intrusion, I'd answer that the Passage, a trio making technically precise, theoretically sound classical rock music, are anything but difficult and dour.

Witts is aware that above all else rock should be dance music. The Passage are fast, furious, monochrome, simplistic, satirical as well as being decisive and suggestive.

The four tracks on the EP took three hours to record, and the group are slightly puzzled as to why it took so long.

There is nothing elaborate about them. They are a rock 'n' roll group. But adventurous. And the opening line to the heavily ironic anti-sexist 'Love Song', 'I love you because you've got a cunt,' is one of the most naturally funny things I've ever heard in rock.

But if the new rock underground is exhaustively diverse and imaginative, not only does the industry ignore it, but also a large part of the rock audience, thanks to a number of preconceived and probably perfectly rational prejudices.

Something Spherical Objects' Steve Solomar said is apt here; 'Ideas are sold to people, and ideas were sold to people very well in 1976, so that there was a very recognisable scene in 1977. Whereas now there's a very diverse and more interesting scene. And because it's more diverse it's much more difficult to sell to the mass audience. And there's also those people now who in ten years time will still identify themselves with being Sex Pistols fans, with being punks, in the same way that there are people who will forever be Grateful Dead fans, forever Beatles fans, forever Elvis fans. People who identify with that and who will never move from it.'

Rock today is a valuable combination of pop, avant-garde, theatre, discovery, classic sixties rock, punk – wildly eclectic and probing, but very little of it is overground.

Intuitive conservatism rules OK. Yet rock itself is innovating more than at any stage before – in its use of electronics, the scope of its lyrics, the extent of its ambition, the nature of its motivation, the strength of its overall content.

Rebel music still. Youth music still. Does anyone care?

Maybe it's not only conservatism but laziness too. We all complained a lot two years ago, got very excited, but now it's very easy to accept things served up for us when they are as attractive as Buzzcocks, Public Image, Clash. It's easy to avoid going out to look for music anymore. So whilst rock is vibrant and challenging, it appears dead, stale, because commercially it is.

Joy Division have been together two years. And after talking about the streamlined effectiveness of Spherical Objects and the cheerfully straightforward Passage, the Joy Division tale is pitiful and sorry.

None of the group has the articulation or assertion of a Witts or a Solomar; they've had to struggle spitefully to survive.

Their two-year development is a scruffy patchwork of naviety, mistakes, gullibility and indecision, yet – gloriously and significantly – their actual music has developed from clumsy three-chord exuberance into an open spatial rock sound that discreetly alters rock instruments' accepted roles in a subtly different, equally appetising way to that used by the Banshees or Public Image.

Their music is rhythmic and integrated, their songs sullen and angry. They're not sure why or how, they're very vague about musical development, it's just something that instinctively happened. And it's happened totally isolated – 'We never felt part of anything, except in the very early days.'

Called Stiff Kittens during early rehearsals, they changed their name to Warsaw for their first performance – supporting Buzzcocks and Penetration at the Electric Circus on May 29, 1977. In August the line-up settled on Bernard Albrecht (guitar), Stephen Morris (drums), Peter Hook (bass) and Ian Curtis (voice).

The painfully nervous Curtis (in total contrast to his absolutely demonic stage antics) falteringly recalls the naviety and numbness of those early days:

'We were just learning how to play, really. At the time it was just, aw, we're doing it, we couldn't believe it, really we didn't think about it. It was just great to be doing it. None of us had ever been in a group before.'

Romance that was quickly to be crushed.

By the end of '77 the quartet changed their name, thanks to the temporary Warsaw Pakt, and considered their material good enough to record. About this time they contributed to the Electric Circus shutdown festivities, an example of their early muddy riff routines, 'At a Later Date', turning up on the commemorative *Short Circuit* biscuit after some typical confusion and unsureness.

'We didn't even know we'd been recorded, and in the end we chose the wrong track to put on the record. Royalty wise, I think we owe Virgin.'

Managerless and clueless, they blindly set about making their own record. A certain studio seductively offered to record, press, engineer and label it for them, and greedily they accepted.

Dismay when they heard the queasy quality of the sound . . . and they decided not to release.

A handful of cold gigs broke them into 1978 . . . 'Material-wise, everything seemed to be clicking into place. But at that time we felt very detached from things. No one was helping us. It was very disillusioning, but in fact it urged us to carry on . . . sort of "we'll show them."'

Their early blunders were totally their fault. They were inordinately stupid. Even at the beginning of '78, when their material had strengthened, their navïety had not been dispelled. Just prior to employing the sensible organisational ability of ex-Rafters DJ Rob Gretton, who gently smoothed over the group's blunders and gave them an actual direction, they signed a particularly dubious contract with an eccentric major record company subsidiary to record an album, an adventure that has only just concluded.

The collection of songs they prepared for that project is structurally sound if direly produced, but may yet surface remixed by Martin Zero.

Zero, Rabid's house producer, has taken an avid interest in the group's progress, and persuaded Rabid boss Tosh Ryan to distribute their discarded *Ideal for Living* EP (later issued on the Anonymous label as a twelve-inch with a far superior sleeve than the Enigma seven-inch.)

Zero also produced the group's insinuating, atmospheric contributions to the Factory double EP sampler, 'Digital' and 'Glass'. Thanks to Gretton, Zero and Factory, Joy Division enter '79 in an unpredictably strong position. They're surviving. They're growing up.

'Sometimes we felt like finishing, but it was because everyone ignored us or interfered that we kept thinking we'll show them. Now we've reached a point where we all work (at day jobs) and we need to give up work to continue . . . but it's not worth signing to a record company unless they can supply you with a living.

'We'd like to stay on the outside. We'd love it if Tony Wilson said he'd pay us to do an album on Factory. That would be great. We can't afford to do it ourselves, which we'd want. But you either stay outside the system or go in totally and try and change it.'

As Dick Witts implies, the new wave is experimental music, possessing all the advantages of rock and potentially containing all the pitfalls of a concealed, incestuous music. It is alert and active. When Witts helped set up the Manchester Music Collective eighteen months ago (collectives are usually the homes of obscure experimental musicians), the Fall and other rock musicians attended the first meeting, conscious of the need to work without relying on the industry.

This is rock concerned with alternatives, rock scorning rigid routines.

The Collective developed well during 1978 although Witts feels perhaps it's already stagnated a little, setting up a circuit for a number of interesting new rock groups who could play, borrow equipment, experiment. Manchester Mekon, Spherical Objects, the Passage, A Certain Ratio, Grow Up, the Elite etc. Joy Division etc.

Curtis: 'The Collective was a really good thing for Joy Division. It gave us somewhere to play, we met other musicians, talked, swapped ideas. Also it gave us a chance to experiment in front of people. We were allowed to take risks – the Collective isn't about music that needs to draw an audience.'

'Groups in the Collective were basically exposing the fact that society has been constructed in a certain stinking way and can be reconstructed. Groups performing for a reason . . .' Witts develops.

'In rock you have to use practical images, what goes on in rock music is fantastic, far more complex than anything that goes on in experimental music. Because it's an absolutely natural social thing.'

This new underground of musicians, and we're talking about a whole list of names (Scritti Politti, Prag VEC, ATV, Passage, Cabaret Voltaire, Gang of Four, Fall, Subway Sect, etc etc etc) have many motivations; ostensibly to entertain themselves, criticise society, fight the industry, suggest, contrast, defy, deny, retain and elaborate on rock's myths, recognise that rock demands are continually changing, to supply provocative entertainment, to continue offering choice.

The need is for something positive. You can only con yourself for so long. Do you want to pretend that you're comfortable or accept you're confused? Or don't you want to think at all? The Passage, Spherical Objects and Joy Division are there if you want them . . .

## XXIII

When *Unknown Pleasures* was released on the Factory label, I did not review it for the *NME*. This may well have been because, in the *NME* office on Carnaby Street, I kept playing a cheap, tatty cassette of the album that Rob Gretton had sent me and telling everyone I could that this was, at the very least, the album of the year. It was decided – perhaps in a meeting I was not invited to – that I might be a little extravagant in my praise, and that even if the record was worthy of tremendous approval, if I was the one doing the approval some might feel, well, he *would* say that, wouldn't he?

Perhaps I was just relieved that a group I had claimed were growing stronger and stronger, with intensifying moral fibre, had actually proved it with their debut album – just, to be honest, in the nick of time. It had taken two years of fits and starts, movement and vulnerability, on and offs, mistakes and misfires to produce a proper debut album, and it seemed to me it was a dark, specific classic.

I guess I got a little worked up, and even the title got me going. To make matters worse, I have a vague sense that when I showed people the cover – which consisted of a lot of deadly black and a stern shimmer of frosty white spasms, and when it came to name of group and title of album a dramatic, almost extraterrestrial blankness – I sort of swooned, like a young girl in the presence of something so impossibly handsome it could only cause breathlessness and a temporary loss of sight.

At first sight, to some, Peter Saville's album sleeve design could be interpreted as a little unfinished, or at least a bit on the inappropriately delicate side. At first hearing, those who had imagined Joy Division to come storming out of the speakers with a music that was going to lunge for the throat and crush the skull were disconcerted to hear a bright, fickle outbreak of nervy drumming that seemed more deprived than depraved. We have since had the experience of listening to Martin Hannett's production of Joy Division, feverish hallucinations of the live sound of the group, their monstrous, careering ruthlessness transformed into interior clarity, intimate extroversion technologically compressed into fierce introversion. Without that experience, the first thought of many was that Hannett had squashed Joy Division flat, sucked up all of the violent zest, and replaced it with a strangely subdued subtlety.

With experience of listening to Joy Division, and an appreciation of how Martin Hannett was creating another group, one that existed in haunting parallel to the less nuanced but more aggressive live version, we can hear that *Unknown Pleasures* sounds perfectly like it should. It is exactly the record it should be. It makes more sense the more that time goes by, because Hannett wired the music so that, as oddly ancient and spaced-out as it instantly sounded, pre-industrial and post-industrial, it would never seem dated.

I'm not sure exactly what I would have said at the time about the record, had I reviewed it for the *NME*, other than revealing total enthusiasm for the way the group, with whatever assistance, had fashioned a seething masterpiece that confirmed Joy Division's brand new grown-up status, and also demonstrated how far rock music had come in the three years that took it from fast punk anguish to fast-slow post-punk anxiety. I would have tried to show off a little, wanting to prove that, just as Joy Division had come a long way since they were little more than a group once called Warsaw, I had kept up with them with my writing.

I might have made a case for suggesting that it was no use pretending that you could hear this album and know all that it had to say in a single charged moment. There would always be more to hear in the songs, I was sure. You would be able to go back to the music repeatedly, and it would never lose its powerful allure, its cryptic combination of discretion and a bizarre kind of showmanship. Something hyper-serious at its core would always be heating up.

I might not necessarily have mentioned the titles of the songs or described too explicitly the sound, as in my writing about music I was increasingly determined not to spoil mystery by being too literal. I preferred to let things unravel, to find ways of writing about music that exposed how I felt about the music in the way I used language, and put words together. Sometimes I was disposed to put words and sentences together in ways that verged on the random, even the incoherent, as a way of defining the initial excitement I felt on hearing the music, and not possibly undermine that excitement, the sense of discovery, by using language to control the emotion. On the other hand, just finding the one sentence, the one combination of words and punctuation, that might actually get to the heart of what was happening in the music – it might in the end be just one word, perfectly placed amongst others for ultimate effect – was worth the apparently haphazard combination of lines and paragraphs that led me to the breakthrough. One great, succinct, quite shocking sentence amongst others less, shall we say, fortunate was the reward – certain meaning had to be discovered by hacking through the terrible uncertainty of language. Attempting to fix things in place by pretending there was only one truth in the way we hear music seemed to me to be despicably insincere and totally cynical.

Consequently I was beginning to experiment with the way I was writing about music, finding ways to summarise the experience of listening to the music, to represent the way music affected my mood, resisting the pressure to produce an apparently objective response. I think I would have used the release of *Unknown Pleasures* as a chance to experiment further with my music writing, preparing a review that was an impression of a review, a series of sketches, a list of provisional responses, an admission of the guesswork involved in music criticism. Such a review might possibly have lacked certain amounts of information, mirroring the way the album sleeve itself kept the traditional pieces of rock artwork information hidden, in order to make the experience of the record seem more like an unfathomable, tantalising mystery than just another easily assimilated slice of commercial reality.

I had decided by now that the majority of critics writing about music more or less repeated the same rudimentary bits of information, so if you needed to know the basic facts about an album they would be easy to find elsewhere. My job, I concluded, was to try and find phrases and sentences that judged the quality of the music in a more abstract but ultimately more powerful and invigorating way.

The more I liked a record the more I felt the need to explain my passion in as fresh a way as possible, holding onto the first feelings and compulsions I had when I heard something without polishing away the initial bloom, even if this freshness sometimes descended – or ascended – into prose verging on, in a mainstream music paper context, the obscure. I felt that to be too specific about a piece of music undermined its intangible, churning power. I thought that there was a place for the conventional, detailed type of rock writing, but because there was so much of that kind, felt that there should also be an alternative, a way of writing about rock music that represented how you might feel listening to the music rather than who played what and what track was at the end of side two. Sometimes, I got it wrong, sometimes, I got it right. I was still finding my range.

This is possibly why the *NME* didn't let me review the album. There was slight concern that in response to the record I might write a poem, or draw an eye with the word 'singe' scrawled in the centre, or superficially reveal more about myself than the record, because my attitude was that the more you revealed about yourself when writing about music the more sophisticated your description of the music actually was. My editors weren't so sure. They wanted balance, they wanted facts. They wanted track listing and credits. The facts I was interested in were a little too farfetched, to the point where I though that a piece of fiction was the best way to write about music. Sometimes they let me get carried away, but not this time. Someone else reviewed the record.

I had a lot to say about Joy Division now that they had released such a severe, molten album in such an explosively reserved sleeve with such corrosive songs with their serene, vibrating titles, but for the moment I had to keep it all to myself. During 1979 Joy Division turned into the kind of group they had always wanted to be, one that was being taken seriously by more than just a few local enthusiasts. During the year of their transformation from hardworking minor cult to Peel favourites with a well-received debut album released on a hip new label, I didn't get the chance to say much about them directly, but I mentioned them as often as I could while writing about other bands. This was also, perhaps, why the *NME* didn't let me write as much about them as I wanted to – I seemed a little obsessed, as obsessed as only a music fan who had become a music journalist and whose favourite band was from his part of the world could be. The *NME* editors might have decided I was expressing the kind of temperamental enthusiasm for something that weeks later would be transferred to some other obsession.

I wrote a review of a Secret Affair concert at the Rainbow in 1979, after which I had been attacked by skinheads and slashed across the mouth with a Stanley knife. The review I wrote of the Secret Affair show was written in the hours following the attack in the kind of shock that was like a compressed version of the shock I was still trapped inside following the news of my father's death. The review turned into an abstract rant about the fact that Joy Division's 'Transmission' was not being played on the radio and was not the hit it so obviously should have been. This seemed more important than writing about Secret Affair, a mod group whose music seemed as conservative and stiff as their suits.

I could find a connection between Joy Division not being played on the radio and the fact that I could be attacked in an ordinary London street making my way to the tube station. Actually, although I never went close to mentioning it, I could find a connection between the lack of Joy Division on daytime Radio One and the fact my father considered the world so hopeless he decided to pursue an extremely dangerous course, just in case hope lay where you would least expect it, somewhere beyond this life.

I couldn't understand a world where such an obviously fantastic pop song was not where it deserved to be, high in the charts. It didn't occur to me that if I waited 25 years songs a little like this, at least round the edges, with less of a sense of urgency, would regularly make the charts. I didn't want to wait.

In 1980, now established as one of the *NME*'s more senior feature writers, at least when I didn't so much experiment with my writing as just tell stories about pop personalities, I interviewed Sting in Bombay. Sting's group, the Police, were then the biggest British pop group in the world. While I was waiting for a world where groups like Joy Division were the biggest pop groups in the world, I was happy to explore the world that actually was, even if it wasn't quite what we thought it would be after punk. Within minutes of meeting Sting in a Bombay Hotel, he started talking to me about Joy Division, knowing that a way to impress me, and win me over, was revealing he was aware of my favourite group – indeed aware that they were my favourite group. He was probably convinced that I had reviewed *Unknown Pleasures*.

I wasn't destined to review Joy Division's second album, *Closer*, either. In the end, once all this turned into a kind of story that would be filmed, retold time and time again, and marked with anniversaries, and I had a minor part, there was just an assumption I had reviewed the two albums, and some people could even quote the reviews they thought I'd written. In the way that these things happen, it seemed as if everything written in the *NME* about the group was written by me, that I must have written about Joy Division every week, because people remember it that way. My off-page, or concealed, excitement during 1979 that Joy Division had completed their transformation from caterpillar to butterfly, along with the fact that I wrote the early reviews and then wrote about them for 30 more years, created the illusion that I had written about everything they ever did. People imagined what it was I had said about *Unknown Pleasures* or *Closer*, based around a memory of the time that was itself based on what happened years after the event. Their version of what I wrote but didn't write was close to what I probably would have written. I didn't have to write the reviews for people to know what I would have said in those reviews.

Once Joy Division became rock legends – as much because of what was not written about them but seemed to be as what was, as much because they themselves didn't say much before, immediately after, and especially during their experience, and kept all mystery alive – I would be asked for comments about the group. Often this would be because of something I hadn't actually written at the time, although by then writing something this surely confirmed that I had indeed written it at the time.

When *Uncut* magazine asked me for a contribution to their 2005 list of the greatest pop-culture artefacts of the past 50 years, I of course chose Joy Division's *Unknown Pleasures*. It was an obvious choice for me to make, as of course I had reviewed it when it came out, and pointed out with utter certainty that it was a masterpiece. Except I hadn't, except in my own head.

I was interviewed by Paul Lester, who compressed my hour's ramblings into the appropriate *Uncut* length – nearly 30 years later, the unambiguous, autobiographical fervour I would have brought to the review, the uproarious, post-adolescent bedroom-fan craziness, the lack of directly specific details, the resolute insider enthusiasm that the *NME* decided was not required, at least from me, is undimmed.

## XXIV

All great groups have a diarist that gives them context and believes in them, that goes out of their way to explain why something is special, and why it will last. I felt like I had a mission. I didn't really think about what it was at the time, but in the end it was something to do with building up a myth, reading things into something that may or may not be there, but which if you say enough times with enough conviction, then they become truth, they become real. It's how history gets made – the louder voices saying the most emphatic things in the most determined way possible. I remember saying to people who looked at me like I was insane: 'This is the best album ever made.' I think it *is* the greatest album ever made. Even the sleeve is so sensual and sophisticated, immediately announcing some kind of intellectual break with the past, speaking instantly to exactly the kind of people who at the time would be looking for such a sleeve and therefore such a record.

*Unknown Pleasures* had a weird clairvoyant quality to it, as if it was anticipating its own place in history, even as it was being made in turbulent, very present-day circumstances. It sounded crazy to say all this at the time about a local band – it sounded like you were a young naïve journalist wanking off, reading too much too quickly into something that may yet just sink down into ordinariness. The florid, almost violent language I was using to describe them led their manager Rob Gretton to call me a cunt, and it was kind of true – although Rob tended to use the word 'cunt' as a compliment, or at least as a way for him to hide behind his true feelings, and I sometimes think on the quiet Rob was happy for me to pile on the fan frenzy because in a way it confirmed some of the things he was thinking, if not so hysterically.

I didn't review it for the *NME* because, I suppose, they wanted a more measured response, something a bit more businesslike, and I was there trembling and weeping and acting in a spirit of manic speculation like the lead singer was going to kill himself or something, like I was demanding sainthood. It was as though, as far as the *NME* editors were concerned, or was this my paranoia, that because they were from Manchester, it couldn't have any great value – there was still that slight parochialism, and that sense that an independent record was one step up from something coming out of the bedroom, a kind of hobby.

Not many months before, Joy Division sounded like a fairly ordinary punk band. Suddenly their concerns were more spiritual, existential, they'd been through a kind of crisis, or just needed time to sort themselves out, or a helping hand in the form of Martin Hannett, their energy seemed more focussed and original. Yet I recognised from songs that were abstract, grandiose and gothic the landscape they were describing – my local area. In a guitar lick or a drum pattern or Ian singing about the blood of Christ, you'd go, 'Oh, it's Stockport!' 'There are the hills outside Macclesfield,' 'That's the sound of Salford drizzle,' 'There's time hanging limp in the still air above Manchester' – that's exactly what my editors were worried I was going to say, as if they knew the first line of my review might be, 'What strange places one wakes up in,' and I'd then go on to describe how Joy Division 'play the present' but none of it would date, and then, for God's sake, I might have ended the review with 'God help us all,' or 'they find a delicate balance between the ideal and the real, between the pragmatic and the impossible,' or 'nothing is likely about masterpieces,' or 'almost everyone in the twentieth century has become somewhat of a detective,' or the one I think I might have selected, if only to see the look on my reviews editor's face, although I would have been very sincere about the thought, 'the songs offer impressive evidence just how much beauty the talented can wrest from fear.'

Because of Martin Hannett, and what I was ready at the time to call 'the sobbing, stabbing bliss of precision', each instrument was in its own individual space. Hannett used space as a kind of fifth instrument. The weird noises hovering there and thereabouts at the edge of the sound, and therefore at the edge of the imagination: a double-snare influenced by disco, but put in a more haunting, chilling context. It was unbelievably exciting, as if whole new feelings were being articulated, and whole new sounds dug up. Somehow, Hannett – the Eno, the George Martin, the Phil Spector of the piece – allowed Joy Division's innocent exploration of rock dynamics to become a new language. He managed to plant the sounds into the psyche of the future.

1979 was filled with great and important post-punk albums, representing the experimental energy of the times, and it was saying a lot at the time to place it as album of the year – there was Gang of Four's *Entertainment!*, Wire's *154*, Public Image's *Metal Box*, Talking Heads' *Fear of Music*, the Raincoats' debut, Throbbing Gristle's *Twenty Jazz Funk Greats*, the Fall's *Dragnet*, This Heat's debut, the Slits' *Cut*, Swell Maps' *A Trip to Marineville*, the Human League's *Reproduction*. I made it album of the year in the *NME* poll, and it ended up as the third best album of the year behind *Fear of Music* and *Metal Box* – some at the *NME* might have thought that was too high, that the overexcited votes from fanatics like me were messing up the canon, but in hindsight it was more or less right, although those above it have subsequently lacked the same mythical momentum and overall influential power as *Unknown Pleasures*.

*Closer* was the soundtrack to all other kinds of emergencies, but it was more the shock of the new with *Unknown Pleasures*. We had Ian's death to contend with once *Closer* came along, and that made everyone extremely biased about how they approached the music. We can't really imagine a world where Joy Division grew into the 1980s, we are stuck with the fact that they stopped dead just as they were about to cross over into a new zone. But what an *uncanny* start. *Nothing*, my book, was named after the final track 'I Remember Nothing', and the idea of calling the sides [of *Unknown Pleasures*] Inside/Outside was the seed from which ZTT ['80s record label for which Morley was agent provocateur] grew. The mythology was exotic yet brutal. Looking back, it was always destined to end the way it did, sudden, after just a year or two of graphic chaos, because then it all became a kind of fiction, with a life of its own. But it can only have had the life it has had because the music was something more than just Manchester post-punk music that in the chronological order of things came just after the Sex Pistols and just before the decade when the world started to go pop.

Would they have been bigger than U2? I'm not sure, because there was something about Ian's experimental nature, a man so uncompromising he killed himself. I think their sound would have been electronic, but it would have been far darker than the band that crawled out of the shadows of Joy Division. With Ian they would have been more disturbing, and disturbed. He was definitely entering dangerous territory. He was slipping from Kraftwerk to Throbbing Gristle, and a third Joy Division album would have been a little more depraved than what had gone before and what in fact came, a bit more burnt-out and jarring.

Did I see him between the two albums? Yeah, strange meetings in clubs and pubs, at bus stops, as we took our position in this time at that place, playing our roles in a narrative we didn't even know we were involved in, but we were very sheepish. It was a little like – what did people say to Dylan when he made *Blonde on Blonde*? There was a sense of northern embarrassment in everyday engagement. There was no kissing of feet. We took it for granted: he was a fucking genius, but not when you bumped into him at the bus stop. He was interested in what I had to say, but it's not like we ever talked about any of the things happening in our lives. One of the things that twists everything I wrote about Joy Division and, again, led to Rob Gretton calling me a cunt, was that this was all happening in the shadow of my father's suicide, so it all meant even more to me. I mean, I was reading things into the group that alarmed even Barney and Hooky. But then in a way so was their designer Saville, so was Wilson – just because the group didn't know what was lurking inside their music didn't mean it wasn't there.

## XXV

By now, when I was given the chance, I was thinking of more and more things to say about Joy Division. After a few months of good behaviour, and a few words from various editors limiting the extent of my experimental writing to just a few hints, the *NME* let me review a Joy Division concert. The group were accelerating toward an ending we now know, intensely writing, regularly recording, adding up the Peel sessions, fitting in their own gigs together with support shows to bands like Buzzcocks and the Stranglers, as though this was all leading to inevitable success, as opposed to a discriminating and vivid stillness.

At the University of London I think I heard 'Love Will Tear Us Apart' for the very first time – I knew instantly more and more people were going to hear the song, so thrilling in its desolate simplicity, its sense of solitude and atomic aloneness – and chatted a few minutes before I heard it with the singer. We didn't talk about anything to do with the intense personal pressure and accumulating metaphysical confusion that he had so elegantly crystallised in the song. To be honest, I don't really remember what we talked about, but I am pretty sure we didn't talk about anything to do with his music, or his love life, or how long he thought he had to live, and whether death in the end would possess more live-ness than life, if only because it, death, was so damned patient. I didn't really have any technical questions for him, and he didn't make any mention of the fact that, as a potential suicide, he was in fact talking to the son of a suicide. Can you imagine how such a conversation would have butted in on reality as Ian and I continued eking out the kind of small talk we tended to have when he wasn't angry with me or I wasn't interviewing him?

This then would become one of those conversations I must have had with my father before he died, a last one, a final one, where you later try and remember the things that you said because, once the next set of circumstances reach their catastrophic conclusion, and you move into the next unlikely set of circumstances, you really want to know what was said. There might have been some kind of clue about what was going to happen very soon, even just because, at the end of the conversation, no particular plans were made about meeting up sometime later.

These kinds of conversations disappear into a place that isn't even the past. They disappear as if they never even happened, or as if they have yet to happen. They make you realise that a large amount of what happens as you live ultimately becomes as hard to remember as a dream you forgot, as if it only happened in an imagination that never quite believed in itself.

I can remember the show because I wrote a review. The review doesn't quite capture what I felt as I watched Joy Division play that night, perhaps because I was on my best behaviour for the *NME* and didn't dare write the kind of review that might have better represented the evening's performance, at least in the way it reached into my present, or my presence, and spared no expense in convincing me that music can, broadly speaking, set you free.

This other review would have been over 5,000 words long, and I would need to rewrite it every now and then again to ensure that it didn't keep the past in the past by implying that what has happened is losing its energy because it has, quite simply, happened. I think in this review I might have mentioned that the truly great thing about Joy Division's music was that it made everything seem as if it was about to happen even if it had already happened. Their music made it seem as if time itself was building up tension, always building, always flowing forward, always about to happen, in order to open up space, and liberate the future. If I did say that – and eventually I would have modified the thought until I crept closer and closer to articulating the essential excitement of watching Joy Division live – it was edited out. The drawing I would have submitted with the review of an ear with the words 'the hardness of light coming over the hill' written across it would have been screwed up by my editor into a ball and set on fire.

Meanwhile, Joy Division had written one of the greatest pop songs of all time – once revised, in a future essay, this sentence will decide that it is the greatest pop song of all time – and were about to record it. Ian Curtis, in grey flannel trousers belted high on his waist, hair freshly washed, strapped on his white teardrop guitar, turned his back on the audience, found where to put his fingers on the fret board, slowly turned around, closed his eyes, and found his position in relationship to Hook's apprehensive, isolating bass, Sumner's frail, illuminating synth and Morris' incandescent, flickering drums. He then started to sing, with specific, peculiar serenity, about what had become, once everything was taken into account, the story of his life, now that it was being put out of joint and, come to think of it, about to end.

## XXVI

**Live review – Joy Division, University of London, 8 February 1980,**
*New Musical Express* **(published 16 February).**

I didn't know which way to turn. In every corner of the second floor of the anonymous university building there seemed to be some group demanding attention.

Blackpool's Section 25 I missed – PiL-Lite, somebody said, whether as insult or not I don't know. And Honey Bane's Fatal Microbes I couldn't stand, though I wanted to. The Smirks I forgot all about. Killing Joke were the worst, heroically adding nothing at all to the latent seventies post punk beats and bashings one or two turned into their art.

I wandered around looking for a time machine. There's one. The sign said the future was none of my business, but I found the present for the first time all evening.

I walked through a door and Joy Division had started their first song. Live entertainment. Start here.

Joy Division at the University of London was a sell out. The guest list was huge. Their impact was substantial.

Seeing Joy Division, if you are properly tuned, is a jarring experience. The music keeps coming, trenchant, serene, steady, hard, almost an orgiastic celebration of the decent fact that Joy Division have arrived at a noise and form that is distinctive, instinctive and immeasurably dynamic. The introversion and singularity of the four musicians is fitfully held under control, and private music is forced out into the open. The tension is startling.

The presentation is as grey and bland as the noise is volatile and deeply black – singer Ian Curtis' comical trapped butterfly flapping the only real stage movement, a visual representation of the struggle inherent in Division's music. As Richard Jobson said, Division's music is genuinely violent, and it's the violence of beauty rooted in beastly desire, the violence of breakdown, inhibition, failure, fatalism . . .

It could be vanity, it could be impatience, even nervousness, but during a Joy Division set, outside of the songs, you'll be lucky to hear more than two or three words. Hello and goodbye. No introductions, no promotion. Good or bad? Inside the songs, careful words – setting, situations, dilemmas, images that are primitive and anxious. Joy Division are a powerful act of make believe, their songs like desperate bits of nightmares, clearly drawn, potent and personal. But Joy Division's dreams are the inescapable places where we live. It's all suggestion rather than direction or dogma.

Joy Division sped through their early songs, with intensity of feeling and concentration, and without totally relenting the shadows and suspense. The group pointedly proved that they still work well away from the re-established mainstream, forging ahead down the same slippy corridor of experimentations. They played more new songs than old (untitled but I guessed two were 'Sound of Music' and 'Colony' – they didn't play 'She's Lost Control' or 'Transmission' or 'Disorder' or . . . name your favourite) and these new songs give no suggestion of Division stagnation.

These new songs show that Division's music is as natural as PiL's, not held down by the grey hand of limitation and expectation. Division aren't conforming to pressure or pattern. The songs revealed a new extension of their language and possibility, and considering that live the songs are true caricatures of recorded versions, how these new ones will end up is a good mystery. But Joy Division are still coming up with new ways to alter the shape, emphasis and texture of their music. The new songs are as organised, hostile and spacious as the last set, but there's all round intensification, further emphasis on the lead bass and the active drums, even an overall simplification.

The songs have extreme, para-melodies, and some have no bass, some no guitars. Synthesisers and bass with the drums, or two guitars. The new single 'Love Will Tear Us Apart' is one hell of a 'classic' – bass, synth, drums, voice, Curtis hugging a white guitar up to his chest but rarely using it. The song's mobility and fluidity shows how much potential there is in the simple contrasting and connecting of instruments that Division use. It's a staggeringly melodic and momentous piece.

For 'Isolation' they have the same instrumentation, but it's more withdrawn and estranged; a song they wrote only days before that reveals Numan and Foxx as true fools.

The full new introduction of synthesiser has not damaged the coherence and balance of the music in any way, it simply increases the amount of mood, atmosphere, ephemeral terror Division are capable of achieving. The encore is a confident, compelling utterly withdrawn ballad, something like a dislocated and depraved improvement upon Bowie's 'Heroes'. So impressive.

Part of Joy Division's 'success' is the breadth and certainty of the reactions they inspire. For this performance there were three obvious ones: love, penetration and stimulation is one all in its own, and if I wasn't tied down by language and responsibility I could attempt to explain. Simple frustration; that the group didn't lay out for selfish delectation their eloquent standards.

How ironical! And old fashioned derision. A dissenter behind me, with a spiteful snort, reckoned Joy Division are the new Pink Floyd.

Joy Division's music is physical and lucid, music about uncontrollable emotions, impulses, prejudices, fears. The group have turned inarticulacy and vagueness into concrete, disturbing impressions of the most degenerate, deepest desires.

It's simple music, but not simple-minded; cryptic but not impenetrable.

As Danny Baker said to me, Joy Division are due some sort of backlash, but he's not the one to do it. If the group had shown the slightest indication of slackening or straightening out I would have attacked. But they are now better than they have ever been.

Joy Division will tear you apart. Still.

## XXVII

**An interview with members of Joy Division conducted in 1991 for a documentary about New Order/Bernard, Stephen and Peter around a table remembering the past/remembering a trip up the motorway and the arrival of new realities/dealing with it in their own way.**

Bernard: Ian Curtis, our ex-lead singer . . .

Stephen: Oh, heady days . . .

Bernard: . . . became epileptic. He had a fit as we were driving at night after a gig.

Stephen: Which put me under a lot of pressure . . . I was driving the car.

Bernard: Hang on, hang on . . .

Peter: I wasn't in the car.

Bernard: Ian had a fit in the car and we had to take him to Luton Hospital, at which time Stephen got really, really upset because this meant we couldn't go to the service station . . .

Stephen: To get some fags. I had to drive the bloody car . . . up and down the motorway . . . where's the hospital . . . is he alright . . . what's going on? And then the hospital turned out to be non-smoking, and so the fact I'd nicked Ian's fags while . . . he didn't need them . . . was a complete waste of time.

Bernard: And the point of this story is that Stephen was more upset about the fact he couldn't have a smoke than about what had happened to Ian.

Stephen: (*sheepish*) I knew he'd be alright.

Peter: You bastard, Steve.

## XXVIII

While I was in India with the Police for the *New Musical Express*, Joy
Division were in Islington, north London, not far from where I now lived,
recording the follow-up to *Unknown Pleasures*. On a personal note – what
else can this story be, considering I am writing it, but personal? – the group
had recorded their first album in Stockport's Strawberry Studios, a few
hundred yards up the cobbled hill from the bookshop I had worked in
before I started writing for the *NME*. They were now recording their
second album in London, metaphorically a few hundred yards up the hill
from the *NME* offices where I now worked.

I had headed for London once the *NME* offered me regular work, and
the chance to write features about leading pop groups like the Police, and
to meet Marc Bolan, Patti Smith and Debbie Harry. Although a furious
Tony Wilson – possibly shouting at me on behalf of the opaque and
reclusive Alan Erasmus – was appalled that I was leaving Manchester, and
what he saw as my indigenous responsibilities as Northwest correspondent
for the paper, the prospect of a full-time job at the *NME* was too much to
resist. Wilson's annoyance, his attitude that I was turning my back on the
world that had given me my big break, wasn't enough to keep me in
Manchester. To an extent, I felt that a part of what I had set out to achieve
had been done, and the rest of my ambitions could only be fulfilled by
working in London as a writer for the *NME* whose portfolio would now
be consistently larger than just Manchester and the surrounding districts.

A full-time job would lead to my photograph being printed above articles
that I had written, and the fulfilment of my teenage dream. Also, it must be
said, leaving Manchester, more specifically my dead, dark and degraded home
in Heaton Moor, Stockport, meant that I was leaving behind the smothering
shadows, and indeed the utter lack of his shadows, that my dad had
bequeathed his family. The living pop glamour of the *NME* versus the blasted
family life my dad had created with a single ecstatic act that intended to bury
all memory with it including mine – there was no competition.

And while I was in India chatting into the night with pop star Sting,
approximately the famous rock writer I'd set my heart on becoming, Joy
Division were now in London escaping some of the pressure that their life
and music career in Manchester had created for them. This pressure – a lot
of it so distressing it was best not to think of it too much, some of it simply
because they were assuming the speeding workload of two bands – and the
combination of such committed, disparate personalities would be given a

poetic dimension in the recording studio.

At the time it just seemed as if they came up with these songs with an invisible ease. The songs just suddenly existed, heartbreaking, steady and completely worked out, perhaps always on the verge of crashing to the floor, but somehow just stopping short, somehow representing lucidity and new beginnings even as a giant full stop loomed into view. No one was stopping for a moment to consider how it was happening. There was no sense as the process unfolded that the songs might be announcing to those in the immediate environment that all was not well, and that at least one member of the group needed the kind of steadying that more tours and more recording and more basic rock group work was not helping to supply. Even though the music was suffused with a kind of concentrated agony that helped make the record as theatrically uncanny as the first, it was conceived in a recording studio with a discipline that was almost mundane.

In a few short days, which decades later would result in perhaps one new hi-hat sound or a few electronic pulses buried deep in the ravishing centre of a song, Joy Division, stuck together in a very small corner of the world, came up with a complete and poised album, with a few songs left over for whatever eccentric promotional purposes Factory deemed necessary.

Nearly 30 years later I talked about the album with the three remaining members of the group. This means we do not have Ian Curtis' perspective, give or take that his complicated points of view of proceedings are all coiled up within the songs.

Also, because the story of Factory Records uses up at least a life every decade, eventually both record producer and group manager would die, as if being so close to such a rampant force of nature took so much out of them they were forced to withdraw early from their roles, and their lives. We do not have Martin Hannett's perspective, although you can possibly guess from the album that he was very calm about everything, whilst also in a numb, agitated state of panic. There are no words from Rob Gretton, but he never lost his faith in how the competitive chaos on the inside and near outside of Joy Division would always lead to, crudely speaking, a winning result.

I was commissioned by Warners to write the following sleeve notes for a repackaging of *Closer* that was to be released in the autumn of 2007. These reissues were timed to coincide with Anton Corbijn's film about the life and death of Ian Curtis, and a documentary directed by Grant Gee and written by Jon Savage about how Joy Division's music, image and history is remembered, and re-remembered. This schedule presented Joy Division, 30 years after they began, and 27 years after they finished, as a still significant contemporary phenomenon, as a mystery still requiring investigation, and as history needing to be properly analysed.

For my part, now that these 30 years, and these 27 years, and therefore the three years between the beginning and the end, leading to the history, mystery and continuing fascination with the music and image, connected with my own memories and efforts to estimate the impact the group has had on my life, and pop culture in general, it was another chance for me to explore just how much I now have to say about Joy Division.

I might have had it in me, somewhere, to write this much about the group from the very first moment I began writing about them. Then again, I wouldn't have known it, and there wasn't much to go on, in terms of my own response, before the group were called Joy Division, before my father had committed suicide, before Ian Curtis had committed suicide, before there were two albums, a series of singles, compilations, bootlegs, fan obsessions, and various other noise and thought, and before it became clear as the years passed that Joy Division were not going to fade away.

On this occasion, I was asked for 1500 words. It was also suggested that I might want to talk to the three surviving members of the group about their memories of *Closer*. I took this as an implicit request that I not disappear too far into my own personal memories and fantasies about what might or might not have happened, and that I introduce other perspectives into this particular version of history, and an amount of detail that might ground the story in some kind of reality, instead of some kind of fantasy, even if those details didn't necessarily make the whole episode seem especially realistic. I imagined that I was being asked to talk to the group, and introduce a certain amount of conventional reportage, as an implied recommendation that I did not write a poem, or try one of my impressionistic experiments in working out how to describe powerful music without ruining the surprise for those who haven't heard it, or even for those who have, and indeed without ruining the surprise I can still feel about music I've lived with for nearly 30 years.

Combining both my own recollections and speculations about what happened during the recording of *Closer*, and my need to clarify elements regarding time, date and background, if only temporarily, with the individual members' own thoughts meant that even though what follows is still only an introduction to what I could have written under the circumstances, it still was a little longer than the piece I had been asked for. About 10,000 words longer. When I delivered the piece, and expressed anxiety that it might be a little impractical, I was told, 'Peter Saville will make it work somehow.' This was somehow comforting. I considered perhaps writing a little more.

Talking to the three surviving members of the group over a quarter of a century after the events took place, it's obvious that all three, in their own different ways, are still trying to work out what happened. They will always be trying to work out what really happened in the few short months that led to an album and a death, months that produced a rich, coherent soundtrack to emotional chaos and an ultimate act of despair.

They talk as if there is a large part of who they are trapped in time, permanently held back inside the first few months of 1980, where everything was moving so fast, so fast it seemed as though time would never move on. They talk as if they're not yet quite ready to begin the rest of their life, which would involve always having to deal with the fact that what happened then, all around them, was something else altogether. They talk still in shock, still not convinced despite all the evidence that this has all happened, that they're being asked to remember a dream that they only recall a small part of.

Bernard is the most impatient at having to go over it again and again. He feels cornered, reacting like the subject of an investigation that might be trying to trick him into revealing more information than he's comfortable with. He'd rather talk about now, about what he's just done, is doing, will do with his life, about what makes him himself, an individual, not someone consigned to history, one mere player in a story that created a legend, or two, that to some extent overshadowed him. He talks slowly, as if this might be one way to control circumstances, a method of distancing himself from all this past, all this nosiness about this young man he used to be who he can barely remember, because of what happened, because there were other things on his mind at the time, and no one asks about any of that. He acts as if he's not really certain all of the fuss is merited. He makes it neutrally clear that he was a very near witness to what happened, an active participant, an involved insider, but pulls back from coming anywhere near to submitting to the idea that the essence of his life, all of its potential importance, is contained inside these turbulent few months. A single sigh expelled during the conversation between a question and answer about those times is all you need to hear to understand how irritated, and resigned, Barney is about being defined by his old group, and the suicide of their singer.

After all, given that there have been 27 or so years since most of this happened, most of what he has done as musician and performer has occurred in the years since. In the years since, he has tried to break away from that passage of time, even as that passage of time becomes more and more overwhelming, precisely because it is exactly that kind of thing that those involved in needed to break away from because it was so instantly cataclysmic.

For Stephen the only way to control it all is to still react with a stunned chuckle, and an appalled disbelief. He remembers the turbulent, tragic adventure of those few months with a comedian's timing as if it has only just happened, while being buried nice and safely in a remote past. He's more comfortable than Bernard at accepting where and how it places him, as a character in a story that has invented large amounts of his life for him. It was a time that furnished him with some fantastic anecdotes – it was a time that led to other times packed with potential to turn preposterous events into great, shocking, funny stories.

Peter is the most unashamedly and sentimentally proud of the achievements of Joy Division, and the most aggrieved, betrayed and confused by Ian's suicide. His bruises are taking the longest to fade away. He's the most brittle, even the most guilty, and the most confessional when it comes to remembering his friend, and how important Ian was in his life.

Bernard has evolved into a hypersensitive, self-consciously complicated artist reluctantly negotiating the reality of having once been in Joy Division. Stephen takes each day as it comes without ever losing sight that some days, once they come, are packed with terror, some are hilarious, some are uneventful, and one or two, like punchlines to a joke, are a combination of horror, banality and humour. He quite likes it like that. Peter has constructed an image of himself, almost a caricature, as the hard-living party animal driven by his appetites. He's spent the years working on protecting himself from the hurt and anguish he felt helplessly watching his friend self-destruct by creating a tough, apparently imperturbable personality made up of bonhomie and bravado, and even, as consistently represented by his bass playing, a kind of emotional brute force.

All three have become combinations of who they were at the time they made *Closer*, which led to quite intrusive chaos, and years of recovery, and who they have become since because they were involved in such an experience.

I talk to each of them separately. None of them have done much remembering together. Perhaps because they've just never found the time, or they can't be bothered, or they can't, as northern males, express such private, intimate thoughts with those that are, after all that, simply work colleagues.

Perhaps they've subconsciously decided amongst themselves that delaying the moment when they fully acknowledge what happened by agreeing amongst themselves on the version of events means postponing a little bit longer total acceptance of a terrible truth. After all, they formed a pop group together. They didn't do this to end up dragging death with them through the rest of their lives.

## XXIX

**A version of the sleeve notes to a repackaged version of Joy Division's second album, *Closer*.**

And then there was *Closer*, the second Joy Division LP, the very final Joy Division LP, give or take reissues and compilations and bootlegs, the follow-up to *Unknown Pleasures*, which was a seething vision of grand, decaying Manchester in the seventies, at the end of punk, a tense, stinging protest against an impure and tedious world. *Closer* soared above and beyond bleak, broken Manchester, beyond punk, and deeper into the ice and heat of a matter-of-fact nightmare. It was recorded between the eighteenth and 30th of March 1980, in London, and it seemed definitely connected sonically and emotionally to *Unknown Pleasures*. You could tell it was by the same group, that it referred to actions and stories set in the same city, as transformed by the same imagination, but it also seemed like something that existed entirely within its own space, its own story, its own fully developed integrity.

As it turned out, *Unknown Pleasures* was the start of a journey, the bloody, scratchy birth, and *Closer* was the end of a journey, the epic, unbelievable conclusion. As it turned out, Joy Division began making their second album, which has drawn such attention because of their lead singer's suicide six weeks after its weird, ordinary completion, by turning up at a recording studio. They turned up for work, and they remember the making of *Closer* as a piece of work they managed to finish just in time, as a few fast, furious days in their life that threw up a kind of still, dynamic eternity.

They, the survivors, because bodies fell during and after the making of this pop record, look back, to 1980, from 2006, still sort of stunned that they were somehow involved.

★

**Stephen Morris:** Making a record was a little simpler in those days. You didn't spend months on one song.

**Peter Hook:** In Joy Division, the songs came quite quickly – a song a fortnight, or even a week. It was so strange. We wrote the songs without ever recording them as we went along, because we had nothing to record them on. We couldn't afford anything. All the songs were in our heads, we just imagined them – perhaps we each had different ideas of what the song was, and we played our idea, our point of view, and somehow it all fitted together.

**SM:** *Closer* took longer than *Unknown Pleasures* to record, but it was only about twelve days. Nothing took a long time then. We got much more done back then in a much shorter period of time.

**PH:** Rob was determined to keep it all very boyish, very blokey, to make it like, this was work, this was our job, and there should be no wives and girlfriends. We had our girlfriends down one Saturday and all hell broke loose. Rob reckoned we needed to just be in it ourselves, boys together, on our own. He wanted us to concentrate on the group. Us against the world. That's what mattered.

**SM:** Strawberry Studios was Stockport, 10cc, and suddenly, it's Britannia Row, London, Pink Floyd! State of the art! A proper recording budget! This was the big league. Strawberry Studios had a crappy pool table. This had a full-size snooker table. We'd gone up in the world! We would get a basket of sandwiches. They'd make us cups of tea. Oh, the benefits of working at a posh studio.

**PH:** Recording at Britannia Row, down in London, it was also like a celebration of the fact that we'd all gone full time. It sounds really weird now – but we'd made this commitment to become full-time musicians, which seemed like an impossible dream.

It was much better technically than Strawberry Studios, where we'd made *Unknown Pleasures*. It was a great laugh, really. We were pretty happy. We had our own flat to stay in, we got £1.75 a day per diems for us to eat and drink. We were living the dream, I suppose.

**SM:** It all seemed so hi-tech, although I think Martin just chose it because some great albums had been recorded there, and he wanted to have that rub off. His attitude was you could only make a great album in a place where great albums had been made. Crap, but he believed it. What did we know?

**Bernard Sumner:** We worked nights. Martin's idea. We'd get back to the flat at nine in the morning and sleep all day. It seemed to be just why you'd become a musician – to have days like that, and all-nighters. You weren't a kid anymore being kicked out of bed by your parents. It was me and Hooky and Steve in one flat, being naughty and laddish, and Rob and Ian and

Martin in the other flat, which I suppose was a little more grown up.

*

There are some details, and certainly some facts, a few of which are believable. They might help piece together enough information to work out how, in the middle of the most ordinary, the most trying and the most tragic of circumstances, a bunch of screwed-up, self-obsessed, fresh, hostile and randy young northern men, on the run from just about everything, managed to come up with these songs, and this sound, as if they were all in control of their destiny.

On the other hand, after many years spent pursuing the facts, and the details, of the making of *Closer*, my considered opinion is that to get closer to any truth there might be about how this record came to be, it's best to take whatever facts, and details, and recollections there might be, and sort of fold them into a feverish dream about how a rock record of such concentrated agitation, dense calmness and seething precision got made. The stark facts are there, but many of the clues to best understanding how this remarkable work of desolate self-knowledge fell into place inside a couple of tense, banal and desperate weeks emerge when you accept that something remote and dreamlike was driving this story. The details and the facts put the protagonists together at the same time in the same buildings, driving down the same roads, and sleeping the same hours, usually eating the same meals. They drank sweet tea and ate readymade sandwiches and entered some sort of trance, separate but together. What absurd form of fate drew together such a preposterous collection of egos, talents, slobs, narcissists, technicians, hustlers, bullies, hedonists, motivators, pals, schemers, nihilists, romantics, nerds, advisers, musos and visionaries?

*

**PH:** Ian did start to bring Annik, and that changed the whole dynamic of everything. He wanted to impress Annik as being this arty, tortured soul, reading poetry, plumbing the depths, and me and Bernard really just wanted to act like what we were really, young lads, fucking about, living the rock and roll dream, playing jokes, having a laugh, reading dirty magazines. When Ian was with us, he would go along with that, become a bit of a lad himself – perhaps out of politeness – I don't know. But he didn't like to be like that in front of Annik. He was the sensitive artist in front of Annik, and we were the buffoons. Maybe he just went back to how he was with Debbie, quiet and unassuming. With us, he joined in the larking about. I don't know. Maybe that's what he was really like – and he just pretended with us that he was the bloke into wild bloke things. Or maybe he was pretending to Annik, to Debbie. That was the thing with Ian, he could be all things to all people. Keeping it all up, wearing the right mask in front of the right person, he could do it, but it was a problem for him. It added to the pressure. And then Annik started to say to Ian that she didn't like the keyboards, that it sounded like Genesis, and that made him panic.

*Closer* was really in the Hannett sense halfway between *Unknown Pleasures*, where he was in terms of mental health and drug intake pretty okay, and *Movement*, the first New Order album, when he was well out of it, to be honest. With *Closer*, he was on his way out there, but still just about in control. There wasn't much evidence of drug taking. That came later. To some extent the drugs were his key to excellence. And just who he was, and what he wanted sound to do. Perhaps the clue to *Closer* is that our drug of choice was speed and his drug of choice was heroin – somehow we had to meet in the middle, us rattling along, him sort of grinding to a blissful dead end.

**SM:** It was such a strange experience working with him. I suppose it had to be for the thing to end up sounding the way it did, like nothing else you'd ever heard, really. I suppose really that's what we wanted – to sound like nothing else, but because it sounded like nothing else, certainly not Genesis, we couldn't work out what it was.

**PH:** For me, making *Closer*, it was basically, this is our second album, let's get on with it. I didn't think of it in terms of, what do we do next, what are we as a group, I never got tortured about us being this strange, mysterious group. I was very much into the music, I took it very seriously, and I loved the lifestyle that went with it, even though we never had any money. It's interesting how it was all divorced from money – there was no thought that we'd make a load of money and buy our parents homes, there was none of that *X Factor* nonsense about being in it just for the money and fame. It wasn't about success really, it was about just doing it, being it, gigging. We did gig a lot actually, and really we were starting to make a lot of money – I found this out later. But we never saw it. Where did it all go? Perhaps Rob kept it back from us on purpose, to keep us hungry, to keep this intensity we had going. Keep 'em lean and mean. Rob and Tony were always keeping the rations back. Always leave them wanting more, that was their style.

**SM:** It just seemed like we were making a record. We were making our second record, it was very exciting, and if we did a good job we would get to make our third album. We didn't think about it being a follow-up to *Unknown Pleasures*, there was no pressure there, we just wanted to make the best album we could under the circumstances, and we just accepted the circumstances, which were rather wild, as being the circumstances under which we were making the record. In the end, because of those circumstances, it ended up being more than just a record.

★

There was singer Ian Curtis, who had less than two months to live, and sort of knew it, and who was having an affair with a Belgian girl who saw him as some kind of pop William Burroughs while his wife looked after his baby in a tiny house in damp, depleted Macclesfield and saw him as the odd, nice boy she'd known at school. Playing central parts in the drama that rapidly unfolded, and then imploded, were Ian's bandmates, ebullient bassist Peter Hook, peeved drummer Stephen Morris and pensive guitarist Bernard Sumner. On stage, they kept straight faces. Off stage, they tried to make each other laugh, as if to escape the fierce, degenerate and lost places their songs made them go to. Hook, Morris and Sumner kept coming back from where the songs were sending them. For a while, so did Curtis. Eventually, he found it harder and harder to return from the bracing, crushing never-never land of the songs, where he had created a reality that was so much more apocalyptically seductive than the one he was leaving behind.

★

**BS:** We just wanted something that sounded better than *Unknown Pleasures*. Closer to our target. I didn't get *Unknown Pleasures*. I thought, I'd better get it, because this is our LP, but it was just a mystery to me. It's the same with *Closer* – it's become a classic, but I'm still regretting that it didn't get close enough to what I wanted. I'm on the inside, I know what it was like to stand on stage and feel that power. It didn't get close to capturing that power. Perhaps it got close to liberating some other kind of power – something emotional, something introspective.

**PH:** Bernard and I hated the sound of *Unknown Pleasures*. Hated it. There just seemed to be so much missing from how we were live, and live we could be so heavy, it seemed odd that the record was not like that. Perhaps it was heavy in other ways, ways that people liked, because they didn't have the feeling we had, that it wasn't what we thought we sounded like. We were determined this time to have a bigger input into the sound, and because Martin had been teaching us about sound, even if he didn't know it, we were more aware of how we might get the sound we wanted, that represented us more, at least to ourselves. To some extent, no one else cared – if people loved it, they loved it for the sound, and if they didn't like us, it wasn't really because of the sound. But we were not too happy, and we wanted to see if we could make this LP sound closer to what we felt we were.

**BS:** Me and Hooky were determined that this time we would have more control. *Unknown Pleasures* seemed too . . . strangled, if that's the word . . . it's not the best term, but it was a time when they used to put carpet on the walls to deaden the sound, and then electronically recreate the echo and reverb, which obviously Martin was into. Eventually this would be the norm, but at the time the equipment just wasn't up to it. You just ended up with this very strangled sound with echo artificially added. Martin was ahead of his time, but the equipment wasn't up to his technological experimentation.

**PH:** Me and Bernard would be sat behind Hannett and Chris Nagle, the engineer, at the controls. He hated that. Bernard would whisper to me, 'The hi-hat is a bit quiet,' and I would say to Martin, 'The hi-hat is a bit quiet,' and Martin would groan. Then it would be Bernard's turn to say something. We were a lot pushier. We gave him a lot more grief than on *Unknown Pleasures*. He told us we didn't know shit. But we were learning.

**SM:** He did try to keep us out of the studio. But he couldn't get rid of us that easily. He tried. He really did. He'd threaten to give up, that he couldn't work under those circumstances, with us crowding around him. Then he'd carry on.

**BS:** Martin and Nagle would be sat at the mixing desk. Me and Hooky would be at either end of a sofa behind them. They were trying to freeze us out of the studio, literally – they had the air conditioning on so cold. We'd be sat there in our coats, you could see our breath, it was like a scene from *The Exorcist*. We refused to budge. He'd hate it. He'd say, 'You lot don't know what you're fucking talking about.' But we did.

*

Their producer, antagonistic techno-freak Martin Hannett, had worked in the Manchester music business for years, promoting gigs, buying and selling speakers, producing Buzzcocks' quick, cutting first record *Spiral Scratch*, becoming part of the Factory Records collective that had no leaders but which was crudely, creatively led by dandy local television personality Tony Wilson. Factory Records also included the group's droll, devilish manager Rob Gretton, and the suave, nervy graphic designer responsible for the group's wilfully cryptic artwork, Peter Saville. Gretton saw the group as toiling, ideologically pure working-class militants, Saville saw them as a vehicle to make provocative aesthetic points about the function and meaning of twentieth-century design, and Wilson expected them to be the most important rock group in the world since Led Zeppelin. The members of the group knew they were all up to something, potentially on their behalf, but they didn't know quite what.

They all gathered as Joy Division made their second album, which would contain elements of everyone's personal vision of what the group was, but would be dominated by a death, which gave the whole enterprise the ultimate seal of profundity, and dragged everything through the mud of myth. At the centre of it all, there was Ian Curtis, in love, overwhelmed by the potential consequences of his affair, ill, depressed, severely epileptic, wanting to die, but not wanting to let anyone down, wanting to live, but not wanting to let anyone down.

*

**PH:** Ian was always very easygoing with Martin. He would be sat in the front office with Annik, pissing around like young lovers do. He left it to me and Bernard and Stephen to keep at Martin so that he didn't make it more Hannett than Joy Division. Ian was more gentle really, he left us to it. So did Rob. Me, Bernard and Steve were the ones mithering Martin to make sure he didn't go too far. We nagged at him. It caused him pain. Maybe he took notice of the nagging, maybe he didn't. It seemed part of the process – him at the controls, us trying to break into his private space and remind him that all this was our private space.

**BS:** Obviously a lot of his ideas originated in his enormous consumption of drugs. But also, at his flat, he had these enormous speakers, really eccentric sounding, they were like five-foot-by-four-foot perforated metal panels, and he had a chair, and he would sit right in between these two speakers, and his sound would sound great on these speakers – but no one else in the world had those speakers. He was designing music that only sounded good on those speakers. There was no bottom end. Just all this top end.

**SM:** And of course, everyone was disappointed with the sound of *Closer* – just like they had been with *Unknown Pleasures*. We thought, oh, no, we'll have to remix it. But Martin was adamant that this was how it should sound. He was absolutely convinced. Some people didn't like that ornate side of the album, the keyboards, it wasn't very punk rock. I remember listening to the finished mixes on a cassette player – I've still got that cassette somewhere – and thinking, oh God, what have we done? Rob was adamant it had to be remixed. I think Martin just laughed at the thought. He was just as convinced it was right.

**BS:** It just didn't sound like we sounded live. We were far more bothered about it than Ian. We were the ones that had a go at Martin about it. We wanted the rawness of the live sound, the wildness. To our ears that's what we were. We couldn't understand why Martin was missing that. The records seemed more experimental, which worked well on things like 'She's Lost Control', but not on some of the other tracks.

I was happier with the sound of *Closer*. Not 100 per cent. The experience was better but I still wanted it to sound more walloping. I suppose we were getting closer to the sound we wanted. But only closer. We didn't make it. It was baffling when it was so liked by people, but they didn't have the same sense of the sound from the inside. We just felt a loss.

**PH:** We were wrong, I think, about what Martin was doing. He was making sense of what we were doing without us really knowing that's what he was doing. It takes a big man to admit it, and I'll admit it. At that moment, we really needed him to do what he did in the studio, and in a way we needed to react against it, and he needed us to be so begrudging. Later, well, once you can do it without working with someone who is such a pain in the ass, so difficult to work with, why not get rid of him? *Closer* was the time when the relationship was not yet too negative, where the dynamic between us as the group with such strong ideas and him as the producer thinking we were ignorant about recording yielded results.

**SM:** It sounds fine when you listen to it now. It's fantastic. Nothing wrong with it at all. You wonder what we were all worried about at the time. When did we realise that it was possibly a great album? When everyone else told us. Quite a while after, actually.

**BS:** I've no idea what Martin was listening to. Actually, we never really talked about music within the band. Which is really weird. Every group I've ever known talk about music, and their own music, and what direction they're going in. We never really got beyond saying, 'Have you heard the new Iggy album?' We never discussed it. We never analysed it. We just did it.

The sound we got on 'Atmosphere' a few months earlier was getting there, to how we wanted to sound. That was at Cargo in Rochdale – and when we arrived there Tony was having an argument with the owner, John. Tony had got a good deal on the studio as long as John produced it, typical Tony bullshit, but then our producer Martin Hannett turned up, and that wasn't in the deal. So Tony had to sort that out. The two of them worked on it, so it's not clear who got that sound – Martin or the Cargo guy.

*

Some of the things *Closer* is: it's about the end of a life, about feeling out of place in the universe, it's about how rock history changes because of the invention of a new drum sound, it's heavy going in charged pop disguise, and it's a collection of songs imagining all sorts of horrors, melodies and substances made by people who had been big fans of music by Can, Kraftwerk, the Doors, Love, the Velvet Underground, Black Sabbath, Neu!, Throbbing Gristle, the Sex Pistols, Bowie, Buzzcocks and Brian Eno. Martin Hannett also looked to Abba and Steely Dan for inspiration, and I suspect Fleetwood Mac, Captain Beefheart and Bonnie Raitt. He was a fan of Lou Reed's *Berlin*, not just for Reed's monstrous darkness, but for the way producer Bob Ezrin had marshalled the talents of great musicians to give the record rigour and permanence. Who would have thought that Manchester in the late 1970s would have had such a producer living just round the corner, above the newsagents, someone who was quite happy to treat the making of a record as a matter of life and death, even when it was?

Hannett had an early inkling that producing records could send you as mad as Phil Spector and Brian Wilson, and he decided to go with the flow. Essentially, he encouraged the flow in whatever way he could, whatever difficulties that caused both in terms of his relationship with the people he worked with and his relationship to reality. For him, the manipulation of sound, the production of noise to articulate the pressure of existence, became his reality, and on *Closer* especially you can hear someone literally compiling and considering sound as if it is the only thing in the world that makes any sense of who he is.

★

**BS:** The record has had such a long life and is so loved so he must have been doing something right. It's definitely got its own sound, but ultimately it's an acquired taste. It's not really the sound of the band, it's the sound of the band imagined by Martin, which is quite different. For me, from my position, in the band, I preferred the sound of the band, not Martin's version of the sound of the band.

**PH:** It's the only record I've been involved with where I can divorce myself from it, as if it is nothing to do with me. I can listen to what Martin was doing without feeling that he was fucking it up. I can appreciate the way he layered the keyboards, and pushed things back, and brought things forward, and it all had a lingering, ghostly feel, as it turns out it should have. At the time I didn't really appreciate that, I didn't have the distance he seemed to have, which was amazing considering all that was happening around us. He supplied a point of focus for all the ambition, emotion, craziness, arguments, tension that there was, and channelled it into the music. Having said that, on *Closer* we were a bit more co-producers, if that's the right word, than we were on *Unknown Pleasures*. We were a little bit out there with him.

**BS:** It felt like we were just beginning to get closer to the sound we wanted – and we were so keen on getting that live sound because we had put so much into getting that live sound to be what it was. It was disconcerting to make records that were not us as we were live. We had worked so hard, playing anywhere and everywhere for three years, we had even paid to play in horror pits in Huddersfield, terrible working men's clubs, just because we wanted a gig. After three years of that, we were stubborn about what we wanted.

**PH:** It's not that I feel separate from it, as if it was nothing to do with me. We put a lot of work into being Joy Division, a lot of physical work. It was less physical with New Order. It got to be more mental, in all sorts of ways. With Joy Division it was mental and physical at the same time, and you can hear it on those records. We were putting all our energy into those records, even if we had to go through and around Martin to get it in there. That's our energy on those records, however it got there. And it's a different kind of energy on *Closer* than on *Unknown Pleasures* because we were in a different state, and the core people around us were in a different state. Martin didn't make that up – the energy is our energy, and he was translating it into sound.

**BS:** I think we sounded the way we did because we couldn't copy other people's style. We weren't good enough, so we didn't bother. We didn't really take any notice of what was going on around us. We did when we started – but we couldn't do it very well, be punk or whatever, so that stuff sounds naff. We decided to be ourselves. From then on it just worked for us. We didn't play in any kind of style but our own. Martin managed to turn it into the music on the two LP's in a way that I can't hear. It's strange to have someone involved with your vision when they weren't involved at the writing stage.

★

It was a record made by a group that had been together for between two and three years and who were working incredibly hard to succeed. They were gigging relentlessly, rapidly becoming tremendously dramatic performers who played as if they were in complete control of their circumstances even as they were being crushed by them. They were recording non-stop, disappearing into basic little studios in Rochdale to produce sleek, haunted and ludicrously alert songs such as 'Atmosphere' and 'Dead Souls', which genuinely seemed to be songs that were testing the limits of reality, whilst also just being quite simply new additions to their repertoire, new songs to play. All this playing and recording meant they were rehearsing and writing day in day out as if the world around them was not as important as their music, as if rock music had actually delivered what it promised to when they were fans, something that was reality changing and even, perhaps, life saving.

Somehow they also managed to live lives, take the piss out of each other, and talk about the weather, and smile.

★

**PH:** It's weird, because as I remember it, we were suffering a lot of strife with Ian's illness, but most of it was happy. It was a happy time. We were happy making *Unknown Pleasures* and we were happier making *Closer*. Sounds weird now, sounds weird considering what the records sound like, what they're about. It was a happy experience, considering. And then it was an unhappy experience.

**BS:** You could see that he was really ill, but we didn't have a solution. You just have to accept that there are things you cannot change.

**SM:** He would go off to see Genesis P-Orridge. We'd tell him not to bother with that kind of shit, to stay with us and lark about, but he was very determined. It was a side of him we never really saw, but it was obviously there.

**PH:** The sad thing is, when he was well, he was the type of bloke that really didn't want to cause any trouble. And when he was ill, he wanted to hide it from you. He didn't want anyone to know how much trouble he was in, physically and mentally. He didn't want things to go wrong because of him. You'd ask him, 'Are you okay?' 'Definitely,' he'd say. In hindsight, it's obvious he was a people pleaser. He was more and more in a mess, emotionally, domestically, physically, but he seemed okay more or less to the end, in terms of how he acted in front of everyone. But really there was no one to give him the kind of care he needed.

**BS:** If we really thought about it, at the beginning of the year, because Ian was so ill, the band's future looked really bleak but we didn't want to acknowledge it because we were at a creative height and everything was starting to happen for us.

**SM:** We had no idea at the time it would be the last album Joy Division would make, even though in many ways it could have been the last Joy Division album even if Ian had lived.

★

*Closer* is a record by a group of young musicians who could only really play their own music because they couldn't really play. Because they couldn't as such play they had developed a whole new way of being simultaneously primitive and sophisticated. They were the ultimate experts at playing the music they played. No one else played music like this, because no one else had been put in the situation they had. In fact, early on, when they tried to play

133

punk music, by copying directly other groups, they were not particularly good. They sounded scruffy, obvious and a little wet, and you would never have believed they would end up achieving such genuine elegance and insight.

They became what they became by making up their own rules, and using these rules, by 1980 they had perfected a unique kind of elaborate simplicity, an intricate brutality. They became intoxicated by their own speeding sense of discovery, basically turned on by the way they were evolving as a group, both in terms of raw rock power and intimidating autobiographical intensity.

★

**PH:** To be truthful, I would just think Ian's lyrics were fantastic, not that they were really about anything to do with him, or his life. In the end I was so wrapped up in myself that I didn't notice he was desperately trying to say something to us that he didn't really say in everyday life. I just thought, well, that's his job, and he's delivering, and they're great, and they're about something, but not something real, and on we go.

**BS:** We never listened to his lyrics. I find that incredibly bizarre, that we didn't. He wrote them, and we thought, they sound right, but we were concentrating on our instruments. We were trying to get on with that, and that was enough to be going on with. They were his business, that's what I thought. That's what he wants to say, that's what he wants the public to know about him, and that was as far as it went.

**SM:** The titles were a clue that they weren't love songs, or ordinary rock songs, but on the other hand you would just think, well, 'Atrocity Exhibition', nice title, Ballard, good image, next. There was obviously a lot of feeling there, but at the time it was just a case of he was doing his job. He was the lyric writer. The fact lyrics have more consequence than the drumming was just part of the job.

**BS:** I felt that Ian was writing about extreme stuff but in the way a novelist would. I didn't think it was necessarily autobiographical, even as looking back you would think with everything happening it was obvious. It's only obvious in hindsight. He was an extreme thinker, he had extreme opinions, he liked extreme music – but you never think of that actually taking over a life. He might have been signalling to us, but we didn't take notice. We were producing our own signals.

**SM:** On *Unknown Pleasures*, I think that what Ian was doing was assuming characters, and he was writing from someone else's point of view. From what I could gather, he was writing from another perspective. I felt at the time that he was doing the same on *Closer* – it's only with hindsight you realise that that's not necessarily the case. It wasn't a character he was writing about anymore. It was all about him and his life.

Perhaps he was trying to say something to us, although God knows what we could have done about it. He was clearly bothered about things. Now, you think, well, why didn't you say anything at the time? Before the last few weeks, after we'd finished these songs, then you might have thought, well, he's having trouble. Life's getting on top of him. But not when he was singing these songs. He wouldn't talk to us about any problems he was having. Well, you don't, do you? Or you didn't. We didn't. Not then.

**PH:** 'Are you okay?' we'd say. 'Take it easy mate. Look after yourself.' We were right in the middle of it and we were making this music and we had no idea. You don't. He just seemed normal with us, as normal as someone with strong epilepsy could be, as normal as someone can be when they have a mistress and a wife, as normal as someone can be when they've tried to kill themselves by taking an overdose. All I can say is at the time, when he said he was alright, despite all that going on, we were convinced. And if the doctor said to him, 'Calm down, stop doing all this,' he would do the opposite.

**SM:** It's easy to say that Ian hid it all, but he did. He was very good at putting on a brave face, at pretending things were other than what they were. He would withdraw into himself, but in a way that made you think he was just being quiet, not deeply troubled. He could play along with all the japes and the antics, he could act like he was into all the boyish silliness. It could all seem very normal. Then he'd have a fit. Then it would be normal again.

That was the thing about Ian – he would tell you what he thought you wanted to hear. He would always tell you he was alright. You'd sort of believe him and get on with things. We had our own problems at the time, with the group, with our lives. Not like him, but we didn't know that at the time. He seemed fine most of the time. A bit down. Worn out with all the work. We all were.

**PH:** There was so much pressure on him. The American tour that was coming up was a ridiculous pressure, considering what he was going through – the gigging, the double life, the writing, the recording . . . we just believed it when he said he was up for it, and he was saying he was up for it because he didn't want to let us down. He wasn't up to it at all.

We had great strength as a group, but as individuals we were all in our ways prone to stress. My reaction to what happened was to become boorish and yobbish in a way. The thug in me was exaggerated, if you like. Being in such a situation sort of exaggerated what you were deep down, and I escaped the chaos in my way, which was to be loud and laddy.

\*

*Unknown Pleasures* had introduced this combination of musicians, the way the bass player played as if he was the obvious leader, and the drummer acted as if the floor would drop away from underneath him if he didn't keep up, and the guitarist introspectively analysed how he was going to deal with the mad, roaming and potentially stupid bass, and outmanoeuvre the sly, possessed drummer, and he decided to do so by dragging shadows of sound around in violent little circles until people noticed he was there. The singer had all three of them in sight, sort of, and used his fortunate proximity to these three adventurous individuals working out how to become musicians to transform his excessive sensitivity, extreme shyness and outrageous bitterness into something that made sense within his reading of the history of rock and roll.

If you imagine the four musicians inside a room, Hooky stood firm and defiant in the centre of the room, oblivious to everything except his own rampaging bass lust. Barney was rummaging around in the corner with his face to the wall, digging for secrets. Steve was on the ceiling, lashing out at time.

Ian's not really in the room, but he is, he's everywhere, inside and outside at the same time. They were all looking out of different windows. It was Hannett that managed to make it seem as if they were all looking out of – or into – the same window, and he managed to do this with his head in the clouds, his feet on the ground and his back to the wall. He got them to all look at the same view, piecing together their different perspectives into a coherent whole.

On *Closer*, this was something of a feat, not just because the band were confident enough as live musicians, as members of the now consistently acclaimed Joy Division, to be increasingly suspicious of Hannett's studio techniques, tactics and tantrums, but because Ian's life was racing to an end, and Hannett seemed more aware of this than the others, or more prepared to face up to the fact that in the songs Curtis was dropping huge, grim hints about his impending absence.

136

**SM:** It all seemed such a horrible coincidence, the photograph that we used for the cover. We went to see Saville, and it was Ian who was rather taken with the photograph. That was what he wanted. It obviously made sense to him in terms of what he was writing about. It was his idea – don't blame us.

**PH:** We chose the covers for *Closer* and 'Love Will Tear Us Apart' well before Ian died without any thought that when they appeared they would seem so inappropriate, and yet horribly appropriate – one was like a tombstone, one was like a funeral. We didn't know, for fuck's sake. Ian was at the meetings – he was ill, but he wasn't in bed or anything. Some of us might have been the walking wounded, but we could make the meetings. Maybe it was a sign that we were the walking wounded, that we made such decisions – but how were we to know? We just didn't want our pictures on the sleeve, it wasn't what we were about, and Saville was wherever he was, finding that picture by the French geezer, and it seemed to make sense to us, in the place we were at.

**BS:** The sleeve seemed like a horrible cash-in. That's what it seemed. That was obviously not the case. The sleeve was designed well before Ian died. It was like the title, we didn't think of the connotations until after it happened, because there were no connotations before it happened. We used to come up with titles and choose the one we liked. We liked *Closer*.

**PH:** We were rebelling against normal groups in every way that we could. We just didn't like being all over our sleeves. That seemed a bit Clash. We were shy and unsure, and we didn't want our faces and personalities shoved forward. Rob very much liked the idea that four ugly faces didn't ruin the record, and Saville was obviously not into showing our faces. It would have ruined his vision. We were happy to pull back, to let the music be a soundtrack to a work of art. In the long run it has meant that the music seems more timeless, that it isn't rooted in the late seventies, with four spotty Manc lads from the late seventies pinning it down in time.

**BS:** We just wanted something beautiful.

**SM:** Now it seems obvious, listening to the lyrics, why he would have thought that picture would make a good cover – even though it now seems like we thought of it after as some kind of exploitation of his death. At the time, the lyrics just seemed the lyrics, they didn't seem to be anything other than what he was contributing to the band, like I was drumming, and Hooky was playing the bass. It was only afterwards that we would think, fucking hell, what was he thinking? Maybe we were too close to it, and for us it was just a technical thing – the songs needed words, and these were the words, and they seemed to fit and sound right, so we have a song.

**PH:** It's amazing. It amazes me – the aura that surrounds the group. I just do not know where it came from, thinking of how we were so young and naïve at the time, even though we didn't want anyone to know. Maybe we were putting on this front, and that was something that made it into the music – we were trying so hard not to be found out, that we couldn't really play, or write, or make records, or look good, and somehow we convinced everyone, even if not ourselves. Perhaps that's part of the secret – we were trying so hard to convince ourselves, never making it from the inside, but on the outside it seemed so sure of itself, so complete.

**BS:** It hit us afterwards – what about the sleeve? Shit. It's a mourning. It's a tomb. We had been detached from that when we chose it. Then it was horribly obvious. But that's the way it happened, and we didn't think of changing it. We were sort of fatalists about it. Or just too stunned to do anything about it.

**PH:** Perhaps it was working because there was no way it should have been working – Ian was in a right state, we were in our own worlds, Tony was off being Tony, Martin was getting more and more obsessive, Rob was making up being a manager as he went along, and Saville probably had the biggest ego of us all. The graphic designer had the biggest ego!

★

Hooky and Bernard were nagging at Hannett to beef up the fundamental thump of the sound, the fist in the face, the turbulent Sabbath side of things, but Hannett was paying attention, one way or another, to how best to reflect, to shadow, the way Ian's words embraced or were embraced by a kind of hysterical control. To Hannett the essence of their music ultimately was insubstantiality, not pure urban force. This sometimes meant that he was more concerned with imagining a Joy Division where noise seemed to leak from inside songs like steam in a dream, where bones were cracking and skin was melting, where rhythm was snatched out of thin air, where trembling noises made on guitars and primitive synthesisers echoed the passive, paralysed, continually surfacing and fading consciousness of Curtis as he sank further and further into himself, and the songs, and the warm, numbing idea that it was all coming to an end. Sometimes, Hannett tried to make sound turn time around, as if that might halt the dreadful inevitable. Mostly, he was holding in one place the rival thoughts of these four individuals as they worked out what on earth they were doing.

★

**PH:** We were four, five lost boys – I include Rob. We didn't know where the fuck we were, and for a time Hannett guided us through this chaos, he helped us get to the other side. He knew how to make it all become a record, even if we didn't know that at the time. He just seemed a bastard going out of his way to make our life difficult.

We had loads of arguments with Martin about 'Love Will Tear Us Apart'. We were so determined that it should sound right because we knew instantly it was special, and Martin couldn't wait to get his hands on it. I remember Rob calling me at five in the morning because Martin was down at Strawberry mixing it. I had a car, so I could get down to the studio to see what the hell he was doing with it. I had to kick the door for ages before they let me in. They were going to get the police. I eventually get let in, and I say to Martin, 'Alright then, play me what you've done.' He was livid.

We wrote 'Love Will Tear Us Apart' in three hours. We found the riff one night, and Ian went, 'I've got an idea for that.' When he sang it us, we didn't think, oh that's about Debbie and Annik, we just thought, that is fucking great – 'Love Will Tear Us Apart', rock on. Ian's done it again.

**SM:** We made him remix 'Love Will Tear Us Apart', because we really wanted it to sound more like we thought the group should sound. One day, he got me back into the studio – it was 2am, I'd just gone home, gone to bed, he called me in to do more drums on 'Love Will Tear Us Apart'. He said, 'You made me re-mix the track, so I've got you to re-do the drums.' That's why the drums are so pissed off. You can hear my teeth grinding.

**PH:** It was always important to us that we were radical, that we were rebellious. All the other bands sold out, they put their singles on their albums. 'Love' didn't fit so it didn't go on.

**SM:** 'Transmission' wasn't on *Unknown Pleasures*. 'Love Will Tear Us Apart' wasn't on *Closer*. That was the thing – you didn't put singles on albums. They didn't belong. It goes back to the Beatles. It was a purity thing. We're right and you're shite. That was our attitude.

'Love Will Tear Us Apart' didn't fit on the album even though it came from the same session, and not just because of the lyrics. It was a pop song, and *Closer* seemed a cohesive album that fitted together rather than a collection of songs. 'Love Will Tear Us Apart' would have stuck out like a sore thumb. We were very stubborn about the things we believed in. Ian was very stubborn. There was never a question of changing things to make things easier.

**BS:** I don't know at which point he decided to go, whether he got the album out of the way, and the single, completed those tasks.

We took how he was and his behaviour for granted in a way – the fits, the intensity, the illness, the drama of it all, and so the big shock was that we didn't expect it. That was the real big shock. Perhaps we should have dealt with it all with a bit more calm. Stopped racing. But at the time it all seemed what it was, our normal, daily routine. It was all at bursting point, we should have said, 'Stop the world, we want to get off.' But who was going to say it? Who was going to say, 'Let's stop'?

He would suffer terrible mood swings because of his depression and the drugs. He was feeling intense guilt because of his marriage breakdown and what it would do to his baby daughter. He had an intense longing to be with Annik. He had really bad epilepsy. He didn't want to let the rest of the band down. Tremendous pressure and not a lot of solutions. I felt angry that he did it. He let me down. He let his wife down. He let his daughter down. He let the band down. But I cannot imagine going through what he was going through. He was in such a fix.

He stayed at my place for a couple of days and I tried to talk him out of it. I'd had a lot of death in my family. My granddad had just died from a stroke, my stepdad had died of cancer, I felt suicide was not a good way to go. I remember we took a short cut through a cemetery in Monton near Eccles after rehearsing. I said, 'You're lucky you're not in one of those graves.' He sort of politely agreed, but he had this determined look on his face. I think at this stage his mental state was loaded and ready to go. It was still a shock.

**SM:** Originally the album was due to be released almost to the day Ian died. The momentum had picked up so much by then that it just got delayed a little while, and then came out just weeks after he'd died. It was all like a steamroller that you couldn't stop.

**PH:** And then it was a complete blank. I remember going to tax my car at the tax office on Stretford Road near Old Trafford. I turned on the car radio and heard that 'Love Will Tear Us Apart' had gone into the charts at number eleven or something. I felt completely numb. I was cut off from it all.

He just seemed to go in an instant. And time went with it. The time after *Closer* was released, it's just gone. It's just missing after Ian's funeral in 1980, and then suddenly it's 1981 and New Order. I've got a part of my life that's just been rubbed away and I can't put it down to drink and drugs. It's like I've been robbed.

**BS:** You just had this feeling even as we were on the verge of going to America, even as we were becoming such a big live draw, that it was all on the verge of being snuffed out. And it was. But we couldn't see that what was going to snuff it out was Ian committing suicide.

**PH:** I sometimes think if Ian had lived, the band would not have lasted as long as it ultimately did, as New Order. There's no way he could keep up with the pace. That was the bloody problem – we were going too fast for him, and he couldn't keep up.

**BS:** I don't think if Ian had survived the group could have lasted much longer, not considering the state he was in. It would have all ended a long time ago. In a way his death extended the life of the group. His head couldn't take it. I mean, Hooky's always on to us to play more gigs, like we did back then, but Ian would have been the first to have stopped playing so many gigs if he could have done it without feeling he was letting us down. In a way he wanted a quieter life. He talked about owning a bookshop. If he had lived, in some ways I imagine him writing novels, not living the rock star life.

**SM:** In the end, it was all very intense, and *Closer* is very intense, which isn't surprising. More than *Unknown Pleasures*, it captured some of the intensity of which we were capable live, but in a subtly different way. I didn't really see that when I heard the records, it was only when the Factory CD's came out that I really listened to them and thought, this is fantastic!

★

Joy Division thought that Martin Hannett didn't appreciate how good they were. Hannett thought that Joy Division didn't appreciate how good they were. In a way, he was so out there, whether on drugs or simply by his obsession with the infinite possibility of sound, that he was the only person that could have controlled what appear to be completely uncontrollable circumstances. He outwitted the chaos of the circumstances through his own belligerent madness, and ensured that in the middle of all this profound and petty carnage, as a life, a group, a set of families disintegrated in frenetic slow motion, he gave it all structure and shape. He managed to float outside the emotional mayhem and mundane everydayness that crowded around him and stay focussed on the immediate task – to properly represent Ian's extreme, ecstatic exhaustion, his strangely sublime calm, his catastrophic acceptance of what lay just around the corner, and also just to make the kind of record Joy Division needed to make at that moment. The grave, grown-up follow-up to *Unknown Pleasures*, and an album that looked out over into the next decade, at the way studio technology would revolutionise the way records were made. Perhaps he somehow anticipated that it was to be the last Joy Division album – that it was destined to pull up at the edge of silence, and be part of posterity. He sequenced the songs as if it could be their final LP, even should be, both as the work of a writer blotting out a private reality that has become too much to bear, and as the conclusion to a brief, immense journey that sent the bravado and fury of punk spinning out into the commercial world, out into pop culture . . . . . . they weren't to know it, but coming along in the years after they released *Closer* were groups such as U2, the Cure, New Order, the Smiths, Depeche Mode, Nirvana and Radiohead, all of whom wore expressions, or disputed the facts of life, or gave advice, or thought deeply, or sentimentalised melancholy yearnings, or plunged indulgently into bracing sound, or dominated stadiums, or found ways to turn noisy self-appraisal into fame and naked neediness into song because of Joy Division.

★

**BS:** It's all made it difficult to listen to *Closer*. It seems so sad. In a word. So sad. I just wish it could have had a more positive outcome. I wish Ian could have experienced just a bit of the success we've had. It just seems so sad.

We thought, we'll carry on, but how the fuck do we do it? What's the answer to the puzzle? How do we carry on and be completely different but exactly the same, what we were but where we were going without our lead singer?

We carried on, we made *Movement*, the first New Order album, which I hated. I hated the process. I was very depressed. Martin was well into drugs by then, which didn't make it any easier. I felt lost. Not lost in the music, from it. I didn't feel any connection.

I haven't played *Closer* for a long time. It's hard to play your own stuff, unless you're learning it to play live. I don't like looking back. I want to be in the present looking forward. It's hard having been in this group with this story, but really for me once something is done, it's time to move forward. The past is like a dream, it's like it never existed. The present is something you can touch, feel, smell . . . It's nothing to do with the death of Ian . . . and Rob . . . and Martin . . . that I don't listen to *Closer*. By now I've dealt with whatever I needed to deal with, and it's gone. If you dwell on the past too much it stops you dealing with the present, where your life actually is.

★

Hannett's bold, ridiculous decision to let the sound, the atmosphere, follow Ian's perilous, unfathomable journey around the edges of the abyss, rather than just recreating the searing live sound of Joy Division, means that *Closer* is lifted out of time, out of 1980, and achieves rare timelessness. *Closer* is something more than just a great sounding rock group dramatically captured at the peak of their powers – that's in there, but also there's the story of one man's struggle for survival as he comes to terms with his appalling discovery that there is something rotten in the very fabric of the universe, as he realises that the songs have taken over his life, as he decides that after this last burst of acute self-awareness and glamorous liveliness, after making sure he leaves behind enough sense of who he was and what he wanted, he'll not bother anymore. With anything.

*Closer* is a soundtrack to distance. The distance between being far away and being incredibly close. The distance you travel in order to create something out of nothing. The distance between surviving and giving up. There's the distance between when and how it was made and now. The distance between people, and their lives, between the group's idea of what they should sound like, and their insistent producer, between live Joy Division and studio Joy Division, the distance between a first album, and a second one, the distance between making it all up as you go along, and knowing exactly what you are doing, between turning up for work, and dreaming of something else. It's a soundtrack to the distance between having all the time, ambition and energy in the world, and then suddenly not. Between concentrating on the moment, and thinking about what happens next. Between togetherness, and loneliness. Between violence, and peace. Between taking things incredibly seriously, and just getting on with your life.

★

**PH:** We were young, which helped. We were very single minded, excited to be getting the chance. That went away, to an extent, replaced by something else. If I'd been making the record in 1986 you'd never have got me out of the Groucho. It was before all the bollocks. We had this incredible purpose without really working out what it was. It just was. In 1990 cocaine would have got in the way. And so on. But at the time, we were alive with the idea of being this group, making this record.

**BS:** We went to America to get away from it all, to go where we were going to go before Ian killed himself. We got shown the club scene in New York, which was so much more extreme than in Britain. The music in the clubs was harder and stranger. I thought, wouldn't it be great to have our music played in a club like the ones in New York? I built a synthesiser from an electronic kit. I thought it would be great to make that dance music on electronic instruments and then play it live. No one else had thought of that. It gave us a sense of purpose. It lifted us out of the gloom. We started to get closer to the sound . . . 'Everything's Gone Green', 'Temptation', and 'Blue Monday'. We found the sound.

**SM:** We just carried on, I guess. We turned up for work on Monday. What do we do next? Whatever it takes.

**PH:** I've lived with Ian for 30 years. I've got posters of him all around my office. He's always been with me. I'm so proud of what we achieved – it's the platform that New Order rests on, the platform that we all built together.

**BS:** How did we do it? How did Joy Division happen? We booked the rehearsal space. We'd all turn up. We'd start to play. We'd come across a good bit. We would find another good bit. We'd put the two good bits together and then put those with another good bit. Ian would write some lyrics. And that was it.

**SM:** What were we thinking?

★

# XXX

Suddenly, as far as I can remember, it was time, for the first time, and yet again, to write a piece about Joy Division that had to deal in a very direct way with death, with a death. In fact, there needed to be a piece written, for the first time but as always, about Joy Division that touched, deeply, on suicide, so this was very serious indeed.

Although I had not made much of it, and talked about it with no one, I had my own experience with suicide, and so I knew enough to know that any experience you might have with it, however close a connection, doesn't lead to any real knowledge. You cannot as such become an expert – the real experts in suicide are not around in the long run to pass on what they have learned. The real experts succeed only in wiping away at the exact moment they attain it their hard-earned revolutionary suicide genius.

My experience with suicide at the time had in fact created almost the opposite of knowledge. There was an endless vacuum in place of any sensitivity towards the values and conditions of self-murder. I was still in shock following my father's suicide, and was doing all I could to build up some kind of version of myself that did not seem so closely attached to being someone whose father had killed himself. It was not unexpected that I would find myself in the position that I would be asked to help write a piece about Ian Curtis' death in the *NME*. I approached it, though, not as the son of a suicide but as a fan of Joy Division. I did not want to draw too close a comparison between the two worlds, even though I was in this case such a clean, isolated connection between one suicide and another.

I found the piece extremely difficult to write. I did not admit to myself at the time that this was because by writing about such an event, I was not only – not even – writing about my favourite rock band and the awful death of their singer, but about the suicide of my father, which I was trying too hard to leave behind. I wanted to leave the suicide so far behind me, so far off the planet, so far on the other side of the specific fabric of time that enveloped me and all of those around me, I could perhaps pretend that it had never actually happened.

I attempted to write about Ian's suicide very much in the context of the new role I was making up for myself as a rock writer with angry ideological motives, a rock writer you could say had been so emotionally damaged by events offscreen, never mentioned, that he was trying to repair himself by aggressively advocating a better, purer rock scene based around the variety of principles that punk, and then post-punk, had thrown up. Mixed up with the self-important rock writer using the occasion to compose some kind of post-punk manifesto would be flickering reflections of the buried urge there was within me to say something, in public, about what had happened to my father, and subsequently to me.

There had been rumours – Joy Division were entering a state where they were becoming all rumour, like a great rock group surrounded by glamorous myth and intriguing secrets – that Ian had attempted suicide once or twice in the preceding weeks. Stories were circulating about Factory boss Tony Wilson being at Ian's bedside after one attempt – Tony allegedly joking, laying on the mocking blackness with typical jolliness, that if Ian wanted to be a rock casualty he had better make a better job of slashing/overdosing/suffocating/jumping/shooting/drowning next time.

Ian was out of bed and back to work within a matter of days. This was where Tony Wilson, real-life boss of Factory Records, blurred into Tony Wilson, a post-modern fantasy of a Northwest Victorian factory boss, working his charges with increasing ferocity to fulfil orders in place. Rob Gretton was his eager, obedient (if slightly more caring) foreman, and together they ensured that whatever the health of their employees, all targets were met, all appointments kept. The physical and mental problems that Ian was having as 1980 raced away from everyone involved just added a twist of reality to the intensifying reputation of Joy Division.

It was like some grotesque equivalent of a pop promotional stunt. Look, said Factory, here is this incredibly serious, passionate group, and look how serious Ian Curtis is at careering closer and closer to absolute danger. This is for real. The participants went along with this, relishing the seriousness, the reality, the exhilarating chaos, never really believing it was that serious and that real, until it was too late to stop the momentum.

I remember that for days, as I began to write the tribute, I could think of nothing to say about what had happened. This was not, at that point, because I had nothing to say about Joy Division. It was possibly because I now had too much to say about the group, and, in fact, about my father. I didn't know where to start.

In fact, it may have been that at the time I could possibly have written everything I have subsequently written about the group. It was all available to me, pressed behind the place in my mind where future events flooded back and united with the past to produce the present. I just implicitly understood that it would take a lot of time to piece it all together, in something approaching the right order, in a way that would map onto how the rest of the world was discovering the group. It would take, I have since learned, about 25 years. At the time, 25 years seemed the time it would take to travel to the sun via the rings of Saturn.

Lost for words, knowing that I surely had access to them but unsure how to find them, I somehow knew that this piece of writing was important not just at that moment, not just as another deadline to complete as satisfactorily as possible, but also as a part of the story itself. It was premature and presumptuous to think like this. It was also the only way to think according to the rules of how the story had developed so far.

It was too early to make the grand claims that would help facilitate the group's cultural progression from local cult to international presence, but, on the other hand, without initial grand claims this movement could not begin. I understood all this without being able to articulate it to myself, knowing deep down that one day it would all make sense. Or, perhaps, continue to make no sense. But at the time, sitting down dumb and blank for days at my typewriter, trying to work out what to say about something that had actually mixed up pop music with suicide, the most obvious thing in the world would be for some kind of piece – a messy, magnificent memorial accurately reflecting the chaotic energy that had just imploded – to appear in the *NME*.

The group would be on the cover of the *NME* – a bleak and dramatic photograph by Anton Corbijn that itself seemed as set up as Saville's epic, theatrical covers for *Closer* and 'Love Will Tear Us Apart', with the group facing away with their backs to the camera, staring down a strange, unsettling tunnel, standing together under disturbing metal tubes and harsh glowing lights, with Curtis pulling back, as if he had just thought of some minor, or major, reason why he shouldn't be looking in the same direction as the rest of the group. He was, perhaps, about to walk away, towards an unseen exit and self-imposed exile.

It was my job at that moment to help write the piece that you turned to after you had seen that photograph, and got the message that Ian had died at 23, mangled in the collision between his private life and his life as singer. I didn't know where to start, perhaps because I felt the pressure of a destiny that it seemed too naïve to consider myself a part of, perhaps because I felt uncomfortable that the only words I could come up with made Ian seem too important and significant a figure. Perhaps I felt I was being abstractly encouraged by the metaphysical Factory publicity machine to produce exactly the right kind of elevated gossip to support their grotesque, exploitative campaign. Perhaps I couldn't begin to work out what the hell had happened here before I had worked out what on earth had happened with my father.

With the hours running out, I started to panic. The piece was due on a Monday. The *NME* went to press in Kettering on a Tuesday morning. I worked through the night on Saturday and Sunday and by Monday I still didn't know how I would begin. The piece was being written with my friend and *NME* colleague (and at the time flatmate) Adrian Thrills. He had recently interviewed the group for what was going to be the celebratory cover feature that accompanied the highly anticipated release of *Closer*.

The idea was to work together my comradely tribute with his conventional on-the-road report. Perhaps this was another reason I had trouble working out the beginning of the piece, and therefore the end – I had Adrian's words, which supplied a large amount of the middle, and I couldn't decide how to blend together his approach with mine so that the reader wouldn't see the join. My own ego wouldn't allow the piece to be all Adrian, to be written in a more traditional way. I knew that the information he was supplying was important, and for most people all they wanted to know. But I didn't think it was enough, either because I was being appropriately uncompromising, or selfishly perverse to a point that Factory would appreciate.

Adrian was supplying the kind of coverage I was always ambitiously committed to supplying an alternative to – so that there were the solid, reliable facts of the matter, but also the fiction, the dreaming, the unreliable speculation, the part of everything that made music, and musicians, more than just everyday.

Arrogantly, and nervously, I felt the occasion needed something flamboyant, something that celebrated the livid, futurist imagination of Joy Division, not just their fine, hardboiled everydayness. I felt the journalistic details captured and conveyed by Adrian needed to be embedded inside a grandiose analysis not of why or how Ian had died, why Joy Division were or were not so great, but why any of us bothered about anything in the first place. And therefore why now and then some of us decided, spectacularly, not to bother, to the extent that we gave up on everything and escaped into nothingness.

I missed my Monday deadline. An endless, painful Sunday night had essentially extended into Monday and seen off the day. This caused some consternation in the *NME* office. This was their cover story, and three emphatically blank pages awaited the delivery of the piece I was now in charge of, Adrian having long ago given me his parts.

Suddenly it was early Tuesday morning, just past Monday midnight, and in a few hours I would have to take my neatly typed twelve-page copy to St Pancras station, where the editors caught the train that took them to the printers. At 1am I still did not have any idea how I would begin, and how I would fit together all the fragments, notes and thoughts I had generated, as I sank further and further into despair that I would ever be able to begin this piece, let along complete it.

I remember that because it was summer it was warm at night. This didn't help. Writing about Joy Division really needed coldness. It didn't seem right to be doing this in the summer. It required winter, and greater darkness. This became just another excuse, although one that by 2am seemed to be strangling me. Having trouble breathing was not at all helpful under the circumstances.

By the time I was starting to have trouble seeing and hearing, I finally had to begin. I began. I started to write, knowing that I had only enough time to write what I had to write and then catch the tube to St Pancras. I wrote hoping that how I fused together different ideas and observations would blend naturally with Adrian's words, and that the fusion of different sentences, almost a series of opening lines to a hundred different pieces I was on the verge of writing about the group, would themselves blend together to take on the appearance of a complete piece. I hoped that one or two of the lines would lift themselves up out of the piece, and become a brief, evocative metaphor for everything I wanted to say. I was hoping that occasionally one line was strong enough, even brilliant enough, to do justice to the band, and the astonishing thing that happened to them. That, to some extent, was all I was after – that one line, even that one word, to summarise the harsh grace and nebulous fury of the group by being in the right place at the right time, even if all the surrounding words didn't seem to belong with each other.

I finished it, and successfully delivered it to the editors at the station. It appeared in that week's paper. The myth, naturally, was already beginning. After all, the *NME* and other national music papers had put Ian Curtis on their covers and written highly-strung articles in honour of his death. Some people falsely remember that I ended the *NME* piece with the line, 'This man died for you.' In fact, that was the last line of Dave McCullough's piece in *Sounds*, as though he was implying that what had happened was a miracle, if we define a miracle as an event that inspires faith. I can just imagine the pressure he was under with his deadline, desperate to come up with a last line that managed to do justice to the circumstances, trying hard to avoid appearing hysterical. It was exactly the kind of line I didn't want to come up with, even as I appeared to veer close, even as I groped through a fog of personal memory and rock writer panic, even as I struggled to complete an article that represented the oppressive seriousness of the occasion without sinking into a pit of adolescent melodrama.

I finished the piece because I knew that I had to finish it. I also knew that what I was trying to say, as I desperately dragged together my words and put them together with Adrian's, now and then managing to smooth the edges between mine and his, was something to do with love. Love not necessarily for music, or Joy Division, or Ian, or language, or my father. Just love, and the way it helps you find yourself, and lose yourself.

I finished the piece, ultimately, because, eventually, in the nick of time, flirting with danger, as much danger as there can be when you are a writer, in solitude, with nothing on his mind but deadlines, and death, I started it.

# XXXI

## 'Don't Walk Away in Silence': an Ian Curtis obituary by Paul Morley and Adrian Thrills —*New Musical Express*, 14 June 1980.

So why do we get so animated and enthralled by Joy Division?

Rock is such an infuriating thing: it's a marvel we get so consumed. Mostly rock is an unstable, stale slab of crudity and stupidity: an endless roll of superficiality and lies. Some people, though, achieve within it even more than the usual palatable, topical noise, and create something beautiful enough to sustain our faith. The rock music that is above and beyond the status quo and narcissism of the enduring rock tradition that reaches us through business channels, that doesn't set up as its restraining barrier the cynical elements of Good Time and consolation, can be broadly split in two.

Good rock music – the palatable, topical stuff – is an amusement and an entertainment, the perfect pastime for this current season of hell. The very best rock music is created by individuals and musicians obsessive and eloquent enough to inspect and judge destinies and systems with artistic totality and sometimes tragic necessity: music with laws of its own, a drama of its own. The face of rock music is changed by those who introduce to the language new tones, new tunes and new visions.

The very best rock music will frighten us as much as it will entertain us.

It will always be the rock music that reflects the enormity of our struggle and our unease, that achieves a language that you feel in your heart, your spine, your eyes, rather than that music which submits to fame, fortune and fashion, that supports our faith in rock music. It is a faith worth having. It is certainly not a problem.

Joy Division throw us out of balance. Their music is undoubtedly filled with the horror of the times – no cheap shocks, no rocky horror, no tricks with mirrors and clumsy guilt, but catastrophic images of compulsion, wonder, fear. The threatening nature of society hangs heavy; bleak death is never far away; each song is a mystery, a pursuit. The music is brutally sensual and melancholically tender. The songs never avoid loneliness, cruelty, suffering, they defy these things.

All this isn't out of a love for deep repressive seriousness. This isn't about celebrating gloom. It's about a loathing for mediocrity and hypocrisy and complacency, the deceptions rock often seems proud to mould. There can be nothing so silly as believing that rock is a saviour, and nothing as outrageous as accepting it as an artificial attractive network of trash and flash. People tend to take rock music for granted – and never think what it could be.

Joy Division never took it for granted and pushed its possibilities to the limits.

The very best rock music is art, and to say that is nothing to be ashamed of. Good rock music is entertaining and amusing, legitimate and intelligent, and from week to week, single to single, surprise to surprise, it keeps us going. The very best rock music – because of the roots, the hedonism, the delinquency and the screaming of the rock tradition – is dramatic, neurotic, private, intimate and draws out of us more than just admiration and enthusiasm.

Whether it is Joy Division or Jimi Hendrix it suggests infinity and confronts squalor. In direct opposition to the impersonal exploitation of the rock structure it miraculously comes from, it cares for the inner person.

It is rarely straightforward wit and intelligence that produces the very best rock music. It is dreams, naïvety, aspirations, intuition, exuberance . . . there are dreams that shout for a better world and a deeper understanding. These are the dreams of the very best rock music.

Joy Division make art. The prejudice that hangs around the word 'art' puts people off, makes them think of the untouchable, the unreachable and the unrealistic. Joy Division put reality into rock. Yet for all the intensity and violence of their images, the music never relinquishes a classic accessibility: rhythm, melody, atmosphere are awesomely sophisticated.

Joy Division make art. Joy Division make the very best rock music.

This is heavy stuff, and why not? Joy Division achieve something unique. Joy Division are not merely a hot new wave group on a fashionable new wave label. Oh no!

The month before what were to be their first American gigs, Joy Division completed an impromptu set of British dates. In keeping with their corporate aversion to regulation and routine, the gigs hardly qualified as a tour proper.

Spread through April, they followed hot on the heels of the fortnight spent in Islington's Britannia Row studios on the new *Closer* album. The London dates took in venues as diverse as the Rainbow, where they supported the Stranglers, to three nights at the Moonlight Club. Out of town, they went largely unannounced or were advertised only locally. Though a few of the dates were cancelled as Ian Curtis fell ill, it was a period of hectic and intense activity for the group.

The last of the gigs was in the University of Birmingham's High Hall on

Friday May 2nd. It was also, fatefully, the last public appearance Ian Curtis made as vocalist in Joy Division.

Four days before the Birmingham gig, a video was filmed in Manchester for the forthcoming 'Love Will Tear Us Apart' single. The location – a disused, windswept Dickensian warehouse converted into a rehearsal studio – seemed the ideal place for a Joy Division video. But the band's attitude to proceedings was withdrawn and disinterested. Even on camera, they seemed to have little time for such promotional niceties.

Such lethargy could hardly have been further removed from the mood in the university dressing room later that week as the band prepared for the Birmingham gig. Joy Division, despite their reputation as sober individuals, despite the myth of romanticised gloom, that seemed to extend way beyond their vivid musical imagery, despite the cryptic humour of manager Rob Gretton, were earthy and easygoing people.

As Tony Wilson says: 'To people they seemed a very gloomy band, but as human beings they were the absolute opposite.'

The absolute opposite. Indulging in the customary dressing room horseplay and practical joking, beer swilling and football talk – Ian Curtis was a Manchester City supporter. Just because they painted graphic musical landscapes of unprecedented power in their work didn't mean that Joy Division never joked or didn't smile in their quieter moments.

Or even split their sides laughing, as when 'Tinny', their red headed roadie in chief, managed to shatter the dressing room window as he tried to sneak a couple of fans into the gig and then lied brazenly to the gig promoters when they came to investigate the rumpus.

But the earthy offstage demeanours – the blunt, wary Peter Hook, the mischievous Bernie Albrecht, the quiet, easygoing Stephen Morris and the shy, fragile, polite Ian Curtis – were transformed the minute the group stepped out into the misty blue and green glare of the stage spotlights.

Though a reticent student audience were sluggish in warming to them, Joy Division's power and purity was immediately apparent in the undiluted vigour of their music.

Their ultimate live set characteristically made few concessions to rockbiz tradition, the opening track being an unfamiliar, untitled instrumental built around a revolving drum motif, one of two new songs already written and rehearsed in the few weeks since the completion of the LP.

A couple of cheers greet a feedback-ridden, faster than usual 'Shadowplay'. But Joy Division never stooped to play easy games, and follow the familiar song with two choppy, strident ones from the new album, 'Means to an End' and 'Passover'. Indeed, it is only with the end of the slow, mournful 'New Dawn Fades' that Ian Curtis acknowledges the audience verbally for the first time with a curt 'hello'.

But the crowd, surprisingly, stand transfixed, their feet taking all of five numbers to warm to the dark dance music as the swirling, shifting guitar and drum patterns of the hypnotic '24 Hours' give way to the pulse beat of the throbbing bass introduction to 'Transmission'. The band's third single suddenly seems to have taken on the aura of the hit it should have been as the audience finally begin to respond with any real vigour for the first time during the entire gig, their reticence melting in the face of the frightening intensity of Joy Division's performance.

The euphoria rises through 'Disorder', Curtis' flailing robotic juggle dance taking on almost violent proportions as Morris and Hook hold down the back beat with precision and power and Albrecht studiously picks out the purest improvised guitar solos.

The guitarist takes over on synthesiser for the two closers, both again from the new LP, the translucent 'Isolation' and the serene 'Decades', a track, like the awesome 'Atmosphere' or 'Love Will Tear Us Apart', that accentuates the delicate side of the group and provides a sharp counterpoint to the more physical hard rock that comprises most of their set.

Curtis, however, stumbles from the stage before the end of the song, totally exhausted and obviously showing signs of strain. The band, despite demands for more, return only for a sharp one-song encore, a re-vamped version of the 1978 *Factory Sampler* track 'Digital'.

It doesn't really need saying, but Ian Curtis was highly emotional, deeply romantic and acutely sensitive. It was these qualities, plus an irrational willingness to take the blame for things, combined with a set of problems it's not relevant to reveal, that made him decide to leave us. A change of scenery. For him, perhaps, freedom.

On Saturday, May 17, four days before Joy Division were to fly to America, he had visited his old house in Macclesfield to watch the televised film *Stroszek* by his favourite director, Werner Herzog. Hours later, in the early hours of the Sunday morning, he hung himself. He was 23.

That a myth will develop is inevitable, if only because of the 'type' of group Joy Division seem to be, the passions they arouse. Ian Curtis' words are vivid and dramatic. They omit links and open up new perspectives: they are set deep in unfenced, untamed darkness. He confronted himself with ultimate realities.

However it's written, this piece contributes to the myth. Things need to be said, things that would have been said anyway, without perhaps so much unconstrained emotion. Ian's leaving gives his words and his images a final desperate, sad edge of clarity. It's a perverse way for Joy Division to get their deserved attention.

When we listen to future and past Joy Division records the myth takes on a new shape and stature. Our memories add to the myth. Ian Curtis' myth, the myths he dragged up from the deep and turned into our reality, inspire it.

The myth gets stronger . . . we might as well get on with it. Ian would love this myth. Ian Curtis was young, but he had already seen the depths. His death is a waste, but he had already given us more than we dare hope from anyone.

We were looking towards him.

And he was no longer there.


Joy Division played their first gig at the Electric Circus supporting Buzzcocks and Penetration in May 1977 after many months' excited preparation. Their name then was Warsaw, having rejected the Pete Shelley suggestion of Stiff Kittens. The Warsaw name was derived from 'Warzawa', a song on Bowie's *Low*.

Warsaw were undistinguished, but there was a great belief and romance guiding them. Slowly, the noises formed. In the first months of their existence it was mundane business problems that hindered their natural growth. They recorded a four-track single *An Ideal for Living* and planned to release the EP using their new name Joy Division – joy division being the prostitutes' wing of a concentration camp. Poor sound quality postponed the release, and even when it was put out, both as seven-inch and twelve-inch, it created no stir although something was obviously forming.

In 1978, Joy Division felt isolated, played few gigs, met their manager Rob Gretton, who took away their cumbersome organising duties, and concentrated on developing their music. Producer Martin Hannett took an active interest in the group, and he and Gretton became fifth and sixth members.

There was no great plan behind Joy Division linking up so neatly with Factory Records. It was just a series of circumstances that eventually developed into a funny logic. Joy Division had a quarter of the *Factory Sampler*, contributing two Martin Hannett produced songs. These two tracks were the first indication that Joy Division had a special understanding.

Following the *Factory Sampler*, it was never certain that Factory could afford to put out another record. And Joy Division, after early silly mistakes, were taking their time before committing themselves to a record contract. Finally, Factory took the plunge – and just in time as Joy Division had seriously considered signing to a Martin Rushent run subsidiary of Radar Records.

'There was a point when we were thinking about signing, but we weren't rushing anything,' Ian Curtis said. 'We went down to London to see what kind of working relationship we would have, but by that time we had already agreed to do the first LP with Factory. So we decided to wait and see how that went. It started to sell well so we realised that there was no need to go to a major.'

The progress of Joy Division's music could logically be followed from record to record, but still the completeness and strength of *Unknown Pleasures* was unnerving. From the rough contribution to Virgin's *Short Circuit* recording of the last night of the Electric Circus – the naïve, overstretched 'Ideal for Living' – to what seemed like the shocking transformation of 'Digital' and 'Glass', it was clear the group had discovered their own potential. They had quietly, effectively travelled from one extreme to another. And on the sleeve of *An Ideal for Living* they were coyly boasting that 'this is not a concept it is an enigma.' With the sleeve of *Unknown Pleasures* they were offering no clues at all.

Every word counted, every line had a chilling penetration. Somewhere between *An Ideal for Living* and the few months later when *Pleasures* was recorded, a radical change had taken place. Everything had shifted into place.

An audience began to look their way, but Joy Division never let go of doing things their way. They relished Factory's uncomplicated flexibility, contributing two extra songs from the *Pleasures* sessions to Fast Records' *Earcom 2*, recorded two new songs for a Sordide Sentimental single, and found the time to record a thrilling single for Factory called 'Transmission'.

They quietly established their independence, prolifically and ambitiously expanded upon their already considerable originality, and unpretentiously discovered the capacity there is in rock for truly traumatic and radical developments. They played scores of gigs but never made it seem like they were merely promoting product. They created their own pace. They made it look so easy. 'It' being something like an ultimate lack of compromise.

Joy Division matched the haunting intensity of their music with a pragmatic, unfussy way of presenting it, using just a bit of self-conscious Factory art.

Only the cruellest blow could shatter Joy Division's brilliant, confident development. Really, they show what is possible. They never dared wonder aloud what effect they were having. They never asked to be treated special. They never shouted for attention. They just got on with the job.

Joy Division's powerful work will naturally persist and live on. The name Joy Division will not be used by Hook, Albrecht and Morris. The group had decided a long time back that if anyone of the quartet should, for whatever reason, depart, the rest would, in cautious recognition of the fact Joy Division were making something special, change the name of the group.

There are no set plans for the future, but it must be said that Ian Curtis was not the major force in the group. He wrote the words and offered contributions to the make up of the music. Hook and Albrecht wrote the melodies. Morris composed the rhythms. Curtis was a dazzling focus, but the music is unique in itself. Each contribution was equal.

Hook, Albrecht and Morris are for obvious reasons impatient for the release of remaining Joy Division songs. There are many to come. Within a matter of days a maxi-single including a slow and a quick version of the penultimate rock song of our times is released – 'Love Will Tear Us Apart' (a song they had traumas in mixing.) The LP *Closer* (hard 's', as in closer to the centre) is suffering production problems, but should be out within six weeks. Without being insensitive we can thank whoever that it was completed in time. It is something you will never forget.

(Factory Records hurry to point out that the LP cover – a gothic portrayal of dead Jesus – was decided upon months ago. A photocopy of the sleeve pinned on an *NME* wall for weeks does confirm this.)

Ironically, because it probably would have happened anyway, there's a possibility *Closer* will chart. So too the single. The name Joy Division now means something more than it did a few months ago, due to both Curtis' departure and growing recognition of their magic. Curtis always anticipated commercial success, but felt it was more likely to happen first in Europe and America. All that is swept out of the way now.

There's enough songs for perhaps half an LP, with live stuff making up the other half, that may somehow, somewhere surface. For those despairing that they weren't one of the thousand-odd who found a copy of the Sordide Sentimental single 'Atmosphere'/'Dead Souls', 'Atmosphere' will be the b-side of a readily available twelve-inch re-recording of 'She's Lost Control' (a song incidentally on the b-side of Grace Jones' next single). 'Dead Souls' will turn up somewhere, somehow. And the flexi-single 'Incubation', a track from the *Closer* sessions, which you can get just by walking into a record shop and asking for, is not a limited edition release and will continue to be re-pressed until everyone who wants one will have one.

Joy Division's innate suspicion of the established music industry and their dissatisfaction with numbing routine extended to their dealings with the music press.

Though it landed them a reputation among many journalists as awkward customers, their distrust of the standardised rock interview procedures was genuine and largely valid. The original plan for a Joy Division feature had been for a journalist to spend a day with the band, with an interview of sorts only a vague possibility. In the event, the formalised question and answer type interview in the dressing room was ruled out, largely by manager Rob, although the band themselves had differing opinions on the subject.

While Morris and Albrecht seem relatively unconcerned about interviews, Curtis was against too formalised a set-up. Peter Hook is the most hostile in his objections to the procedure.

'To me personally, it is redundant. I don't read interviews. I read the music papers but I can't read a question and answer interview. One of the best things I've ever read was Lester Bangs' article on the Clash in *NME* 'cause it wasn't actually an interview, but it was full of stories and things about the tour. That was interesting but interviews as such I don't find interesting.'

But doesn't a refusal to do interviews put up an unnecessary barrier around the band?

'The way we look at it is that any interview is a bit forced. The only reason a journalist wants to do an interview is that it makes it easier for him to write his piece. But to me it's obvious that if you spend a bit of time with people and get to know them in a very informal way, you'll get a lot more out of them.'

Ian almost begs to differ.

'I can see the point of interviews. People want to know why things are the way they are. If they buy a new car, they want to know how it works. Why does it do this? Why can this car go faster than this car? Why does it look better than that one?'

Rob Gretton interjects to make wider, perhaps not so valid, points about the media in general.

'I can understand that journalists are just doing their job. What I don't agree with is the job they are sent out to do. I think it's a very stylised, outmoded way of doing things. The average guy in the street tends to read his paper and takes what he reads as the truth. I think they don't analyse it enough. The average guy in the street just takes it in. I think the fault lies in the press, 'cause they don't make it clear that any article is just a purely personal opinion.'

The impact of Joy Division can only grow stronger, more importantly so than any myth. Joy Division cannot clean away the trivia and delusion of mass based rock, but they throw a shadow over it all. They emphasise the vanity and vulgarity of the rock music so recklessly publicised and glorified by industry and media, the plain mundanity of the majority of pop, and their own complete lack of conceit or ego indicates the uselessness of pretending rock is some sort of weapon of change. The very best rock is part of a fight, part of a larger decision, a widespread perception, something that can actively remove prejudice and restriction.

Rock's greatness is its emotional impact on the individual. Joy Division's worth is immense to every individual who relishes their strange awareness, who does not mock the lack of explanation of artistic endeavours. The struggle and the conflict never ceases. There is no real safety, no consolation, and often the evil, futile boundaries of existence become too claustrophobic.

Ian Curtis decided to leave us, and yet he leaves behind words of such strength they urge us to fight, seek and reconcile. Joy Division will not change The World. But there is value: there has to be.

The effect of Joy Division, the unknown pleasures each individual fully tuned into Joy Division ultimately discovers, can only be guessed at. But the moods and the insight must inspire us, excite us, challenge us . . .

The value of Joy Division is the value of love.

# XXXII

**From an interview with Tony Wilson conducted in 1991 for a documentary about New Order/in long coat sat in his ghostly looking Haçienda club/during the day/smiling at some secret punchline/smirking even/already anticipating that this story is to involve a sequence of flashbacks.**

Wilson: The phrase, 'you bastard' did come to my lips in the sense that, 'You left us to deal with all this stuff – you just got out.' A kind of easy way out – there's the line from the album, 'You take my place in the showdown, and observe with a pitiless ease,' or something, and yes, we took his place in the showdown, and he got out, and there were a lot of nightmares to come – particularly with this bloody place, the Haçienda . . . and he should have shared it all with us. He started the whole thing . . . he should have gone through all this shit with us . . . he copped out of quite a trip.

Wilson: Yeah, people die – blame me!

Wilson: Ian was the most charismatic singer of his generation . . . Bono always used to say to me, 'He was the best. I was always number two . . . but I'll do it anyway now he's gone.' And I think Bono did do it. I've never been a massive U2 fan, but when I saw that performance at Live Aid, I thought, well, there you are. But Ian would have been even better . . .

## XXXIII

A short time after Ian Curtis died, the ruthless, scheming Tony Wilson was working as hard as ever at keeping energy levels up, naturally choosing himself to take on the role of maintaining the momentum of Joy Division – the ambitious provincial group now abruptly a provisional legend needing to be nursed and nurtured – at a moment when everything had surely collapsed. I have a memory of everyone moving really slowly at the time, picking their unsteady way through the ruins that now surrounded them, except for Tony who, if anything, was moving even faster than ever, leaping across the chaos with an unsettling expression on his face that suggested, surprisingly, he was having the time of his life. It's no wonder that sometimes people were scared of Tony Wilson, or at least intimidated by the way he was always charging forward with such ferocious, radiant self-confidence regardless of who he might be upsetting or annoying.

Looking like he knew exactly what he was doing, he opened a door inside a building in Macclesfield, and ushered me in. All I can say is, I didn't have the power to resist him. What happened next was a crafty, breathtaking slab of show-business high jinks beyond the realms of the reasonable, a completely unexpected transaction, a startling act of impertinence, an uncanny piece of documentary planning, a questionable publicity stunt, possibly a moment of deviant tenderness. What happened next was a garish, incomprehensible example of how Tony decided without any consultation with those around him what would happen next, knowing all along that eventually, after a period of confusion, and a certain amount of chaos, it would make, more or less, sense. He acted as though he was accountable to no-one.

There was something about the way he was operating at the time that I could not put my finger on. A quarter of a century later I can only explain it as being like he alone knew the script that was being followed, as if he had travelled to the very end of the story and then returned knowing how to motivate and influence anyone directly and indirectly involved, to ensure that it unravelled in the correct sequence. He knew exactly where to move, and how, whenever any obstacles fell in his way, so that they ended up not as obstacles but as signs telling him which way to go next. He would cover up this talent, this power, by often pursuing a course of action that led to failure, to mayhem, to disarray, but even this near nihilism was part of his plan to ensure everything moved forward just as it should.

I was a minor player in the continuing drama, my roles in the films that were to be made of this story would be just above the level of extra, but his attention to detail was such that he even arranged to open this door in Macclesfield, and escort me in. Before leaving me alone in the room, to fall into my thoughts, he stood next to me with a furtive look on his face that was somewhere between incongruous pride and uncanny professionalism, and seemed very sure that one day I would be writing exactly these words, the words that follow, and many others just like them.

## XXXIV

**The opening section to *Nothing*, a northern memoir concerning Stockport, the self and suicide, published by Faber in 2000.**

I have only seen one dead body in my life.

It didn't look dead and it didn't look alive and it didn't look anything in between. Significantly, it was positioned inside an open coffin, dressed for an occasion, and cushioned against reality by white satin-covered padding. The coffin was resting on a wooden table or a slab of concrete covered with drapes. It looked as if it was floating, suspended in the air as it seemed suspended in time. The body looked very quiet, as if it had made enough noise for now, as if it was just thinking, not of something to say, but of how thinking was a thing of the past, and in the future there would be no thinking, and no past. It was very thoughtful looking. It was perhaps thinking that it would have to do an awful lot of not thinking. Or I was thinking that on its behalf. Or perhaps it was not thinking that it would in the futureless future have to do an awful lot of not thinking. For all of the ways the body had this thoughtful bearing there was also something very thoughtless about its general demeanour.

I have only ever seen one dead body in my life. I could tell just by looking at it that not only was this once a human being but in some ways, for all its stillness, it still was. The body, the dead thing I was there to see for some living reason, had all the features and angles and curves of a living thing, and it even had an expression you might want to associate with a living thing. It was quite a composed expression for someone who was only putting decomposition on hold. For someone who was about to become some thing, transformed brutally quickly sometime during the past few days from a somebody into a nobody, the expression was acceptably dignified. At the time, I was doing the accepting. Perhaps somebody else doing the accepting might interpret the expression in another way. Someone else might see a hint of terror. Or a dark suggestion of desperate resignation. Or a chilled sparkle of odd joy. From where I was standing, a couple of vast intimate yards away from the body, I would stick to my conclusion that, under the circumstances, you could say that the expression on the faint face of the solidly dead body was approaching the serene, even the blissful, for all its understandable seriousness. A smile would have been very inappropriate. A smile fixed for anywhere between ten seconds and eternity always looks a little sinister, and the last thing you want on a dead body laid out for friends and loved ones to pay their final respects is anything transparently sinister.

The body kept a classically straight face to match the general level of its immediate ambition. The body was very still indeed, but it was presented in such a way that you felt any split second there might be a flicker, a twitch, a breath, some movement that would actually stop my breath and bring my own flickering and twitching to an instant, revolting halt. It was a shocking sight, this thing that was a dead body checking my sense of reality, and I was directly connected to a liquid state of shock. But through it all the body was lifelike enough to make you think that at any moment it might blink. Or burp. Or break into song. What would it sing? 'This is the end, my friend.' Or a love song with a sad ending. Or something about dead souls. 'Heaven Knows I'm Miserable Now'? What about 'Fly Me to the Moon'?

Perhaps it could mime – badly – to the words, 'This is the way, step inside.' Drums would be pummelled with detached precision, bass guitar would rumble up from deep out of the ground and a guitar, as if it were an electronically charged knife, would cut through the atmosphere. Because this was atmosphere you could cut with a knife: cut into shreds. The voice the body was miming to would croon with a kind of objectless longing, an urgent aimlessness. It would sound like a voice that demanded to be heard. A voice that was young and old at the same time, weak and strong. It would be inviting the listener into a void, or emptiness, or infinity, to watch the basic adventure of man's metaphysical self as it tears itself from life to death. Either that or it was moaning melodically that it was too cold where it was, or too hot, and there didn't seem to be any natural distance between itself and its surroundings.

A host of angels would ritualistically dance like disordered demons and the body, drained of all spirit, a kind of spent arrow, would continue to mime. Terribly. Its lips were surely not moving at all. It would mime the words, 'This is the way, step inside' as if it might continue to do so forever, as a guitar cut everything in sight into metallic shreds while some drums rolled over the present and a fat bass broke up the past.

But the body had had enough of singing.

It was covered up to the neck, for somebody's convenience, and it had been delicately made up, no doubt to tactfully hide the last marks and traces made on its mortal body before it stopped thinking. There was not a hair out of place. Then again, all of its hair was out of place – hair on a dead body is pretty much a definition of being out of place. The body was close to being handsome, in a desolate and dead sort of way. Perhaps it was just that it seemed so settled, so confident in its position, so committed to its final position of complete rest and epic listlessness that gave it this appearance of senseless attractiveness. Or perhaps it was just the way the dead body had been disguised, as if it was an actor, to appear alive. The actor seemed to be sleeping. And breathing very slowly.

Sleeping is a very appropriate way of presenting death, perfect for occasions when the body is lacking its life but for certain social reasons requires the appearance of life. Sleeping is, on the long stretched-out surface of things, a quite close approximation of the look of death. When a dead body needs to be looked at, for someone's convenience, for reasons of comfort and assurance, it is an advantage that there is this apparently coincidental link between the dead body and the sleeping body. It is better for the dead body to look as if it is sleeping rather than for it to look as if it is writing a cheque.

I have only ever seen one dead body in my life. I wondered what I was doing in this room of goodbyes and awakenings looking at something that was pretty dead but which retained the shape and size of life. I'm not sure who had more on their plate as we contemplated each other in this small grey room, a little larger than a coffin, that someone had taken the trouble to decorate. For something that was dead the body had presence. For all its intense muteness it clearly communicated that death was larger than life. As a young man in his early twenties giving this stiff and vivid dead body a stunned once over, I couldn't help but begin to think that the experience didn't make death any realer or unrealer but it definitely made life a little bit more strange.

The body didn't smell of anything. It smelt of nothing. I wondered when the last time the body as a moving person had cleaned its teeth. I wondered whether when the teeth were cleaned the person doing the brushing had an epiphany about the absurdity of cleaning their teeth at such a momentous time. If you are going to die any moment and you have a vague notion that you are going to die, or a very specific idea, an idea so specific it puts you in absolute control of your own immediate fate, do you prepare for death by carrying on some of the well-established hygienic routines of modern living? Or are other thoughts a priority? What would those thoughts be? I looked at the body but it didn't want to say even by using sign language what it was thinking in the hours before its death. Unless it was thinking absolutely nothing. Unless its mind was dreadfully blank as it – he – went through the slow, irresistible motions of turning with such will and might and exhaustion from life to death.

I wondered if anyone had cleaned the body's teeth after it was dead in the way that they had applied powder to the body's face, in the way that someone had certainly straightened its hair. Actually that's not quite true. I didn't wonder that at the time. But I wonder it now. At the time I didn't consider at all the process that had creatively held the body in this limbo state of deathly lifelikeness. I took for granted that the dead body bore a striking resemblance to the body when it was alive. I didn't think to think what the body would look like without the crude yet subtle rot-stalling cosmetic support. Now I can't help wondering if there was a notice attached to the door of this waiting room – and what a wait you can have in such a room – explaining the face-saving particulars of embalming.

## NOTICE

*Embalming disinfects and temporarily preserves and restores, to an acceptable physical appearance, a dead human body. As human remains begin to decompose almost immediately after death, thereby offering an ideal environment for microbial growth, untreated remains pose a public health concern. While embalming sanitises the body, it also retards decomposition, thus temporarily preserving the body. Embalming restores the body to an acceptable physical appearance following a traumatic death or devastating illness.*

*Many bereavement experts agree that viewing the deceased confirms the reality of death and helps survivors take an important step towards recovering from their loss.*

*The embalming process begins with thorough washing and disinfection of the body. The mouth, nose and other openings are closed to prevent excretions which could be a source of disease or infection. Embalming chemicals are then injected into the body through the more accessible arteries while body fluids are then drained through corresponding veins.*

*Embalming fluids kill bacteria and temporarily preserve the body by altering the physical structure of the body's proteins. A latticework of inert firm proteins is created that can no longer serve as a host for bacteria or be acted upon by enzymes. Thus the decomposition process is retarded and the body is sanitised and temporarily preserved.*

*Thank you for your attention.*

Such a note on the door would give the game away, shatter the illusion of the perfectly presented dead body, undermine the magic trick, the minor miracle. The fact that I cannot recall whether there was such a notice pinned to the door isn't because of faulty remembering but because there wasn't such a notice. It didn't say exit on the door, either.

I have only ever seen one dead body in my life. The dead body I saw might have thought that it was dreaming. As far as I knew, it was dreaming. Or it wasn't dreaming. Or it wouldn't remember its dreams. Maybe I would remember them on its behalf. It was dreaming that it had been alive, once. It was dreaming its life. Or it was dreaming its death. Or both. The dead body gives little away, when it's been dressed, made up and elegantly posed, about its dreams, forgotten or remembered. I looked hard at the well-mannered body for what seemed like less than a second and more than forever. Sometimes the body appears in my dreams, floating from some engagement to another, as handsome as ever, and as inscrutable. I wonder if I ever appear in its dreams, looking for clues, thinking of something to say. Mostly, I think, I never find a clue, and I never think of anything to say. I couldn't think of anything to say as I looked at the body, which had died so recently it still looked as if it could wake up at any moment. It would wake up and wonder what the intensely black little marks criss-crossing its neck were. It would wake up and it wouldn't be an it anymore. It would be a he. A he that would be at a loss to explain what on earth was going on.

I think of the body as an it rather than a he. Whatever made it a he had dissolved somewhere between the moment of his death and the moment when he became a memory, a feeling, to those he knew, stronger than the presence of the body that remained. The memory becomes the he, the life that is remembered was lived by a he. The body is an it, separated from the he that it was.

It lies in front of me like something that belongs in a dream. A dead body in front of you, all dressed up with nowhere to go, will heavily remind you that, if you are looking for *it*, then a good place to search is a dead body, which is and has and was and will be nothing but it. A dead body is it incarnate. It is it no more, no less. It is it dead stop. It is where all things end. It is.

It really is.

As I looked at it, this big bag of it, laid out in front of me dead to the world, reeking of it, stiffened to an ultimate point of absurdity, it beyond it, I realised, in a second that had been split into infinity, that the truth is, I have only seen one dead body *in the flesh*. In the flesh, so to speak. The breathless, bloodless it-hammered flesh. This dead body that I saw in front of me, decadently showing off its magnificent deadness, an unlined glowing deadness no living body could ever hope to duplicate without achieving something deeply drastic, was and is then and now the only dead body that I have ever seen. The only dead body that I have seen for real, as dreamlike as the occasion seemed. It was real, very real, in the way only it can be. And, as far as the eye could see, it was in the flesh. It was three-dimensional, with in some senses a fourth, even a fifth, ominously hovering near.

I could see the skin on its face and it looked very fleshy to me, if slightly clownish, due to the makeup applied to bring a little natural colour into its unnatural cheeks. The makeup failed to be perfectly natural, to be perfectly honest. There is a big, mysterious difference between flesh colour and flesh itself. The body was a long, lonely way from being in the pink.

The flesh colour was a curdled blend of pink and yellow, a yellowish pink, a pinkish yellow, a strained colour only the dead could look relatively good in. It was a broken colour that had not yet made its mind up whether to be a colour, as such, or just a shadow, a shadow of death, in hopeless disguise. It was the kind of colour you couldn't believe was going to be still for very long. The kind of colour that didn't suit being static. It was what happens to living colour when there is lack of oxygen and lack of blood. It was, generally speaking, a lack of colour. A colour that was at its best on the move, melting, dissolving, changing its tone, changing its appearance. A colour that was never an absolute colour, but a colour in transit, a colour on the way to something else, to somewhere else. It was the colour of changing places, a colour on its way to another place, a colour at a loss in this world that would come into its own in another world. It was a rotten colour that didn't belong to the living, a colour giving lost last cover to flesh that was close to life but closer, much closer, to death. It was an off colour for an off body. You could call this colour *forlorn yink*, although I think the technical term is 'zombie yuk'.

The body was an arrested, emptied blend of doomed flesh and gloomy flesh colour. For something that didn't exist it was very much in the here and now, sharing space with some objects and fabrics that did exist and the quiet, wary me, nervously representing the pale colours of existence. I was not so in the pink myself, but I was, I'm sure, the colour of something in the room that was lively enough to be breathing. There was warm fluid me, living on the edge of my nerves, and there was cold cadaverous it, having fantastically and infallibly charged over the edge of its nerves into considerable abruptness. It was as if it always had been nerveless, careless, doubtless, less than less, and now it was well on the way to being fleshless, having died in the arms of an urgent abyss. The body stretched out in front of me, the exact frozen shape of the past. It represented then. It represented the moment that had passed. It staked a claim for all moments that had passed. Moments that reached so far back into the forever past they met up with a returning future. No wonder the face of the body was a peculiar colour.

For now, a now that was having trouble becoming a then, its flesh was not so much human flesh as something beyond flesh. Something that, in this dream-edged reality biased towards the living, was drowsily approaching the spirit of flesh. It conspired to have the distant look of flesh, the smooth ways of flesh if not quite the rough means. I can't say what was hidden away from the face, if there was any flesh elsewhere, apart from the discreetly messed-up neck. And I could see the hands, the hands of it, the hands with nothing left to hold, the hands with nothing left to do. The hands were arranged in such a manner that if this was a person actually asleep you might think that it was a very unlikely, but very peaceful, way of being asleep. You would think they could be faking that they were asleep. They were posing. The flesh of the hands was set into such a position you might consider for a fleet moment that death is such a pose. The ultimate pose. The hands looked very beautiful. All in all, it was a good pose. A pose poised right on the cusp between mortal possibility and impossible immortality. A very glamorous pose, drawn up with such sullen assurance by a mischievous power that was using this body to play around with the endlessness of the end. I'm sure that the he that once livened up this body would have been pleased with the pose and the shadow of death that grazed it. Film stars and pop stars and models work hard to create such a cold and splendid pose. Working too hard to achieve such poses can often lead, what with one thing and another, to an early, controversial death. The earlier the death, the better, the more tragic, this final pose. The neat black marks crossing the neck of the body of the man who died early and was truly in front of me only succeeded in increasing the depressed glory of the final pose. The black marks that danced on the body's neck like some gothically extravagant beauty spot drew attention to the damned flawlessness of everything else, emphasising with sick, magnificent force that this was indeed – as he would have wanted, if he had to choose – a good-looking corpse.

This was a dead body in the flesh, it was no photograph, it was no processed image, but the flesh had stopped, or was stopping being flesh. The body was in a state of having been flesh. I was looking, towards and then away, at the flesh of the dead. I was looking, out of politeness, out of courtesy, out of time, at the skin of a dead body that had been made up with due care and attention to be lifelike. It seemed to me – if not at the time, but later, when I had left the room with a view of the dead, the room of colours dead that was part of a church that feebly stretched to the sky – it seemed to me – later, when I was remembering the dead body rather than looking at it as if I should say something – it seemed to me, eventually, that its skin was bad skin. It was wrong flesh. I didn't think this at the time, as I shared this cold room with a dead body and acted as if I too was wearing thick makeup and had no feelings in my fingers, because I didn't think anything other than wonder what I was doing there and what it was doing there and what should I say? What should I do? I didn't think this like there were words in my head. The room compelled me to be profoundly wordless. There were no words in my mind. There was just a wash of slowed sensation and a sense that my mind was somehow holding its breath. Or a sense that my mind was being held by distorting outside forces, and the overall feeling struck me as being something that might make me sob or might make me giggle.

But I felt that once I had left the room and words (the words of thoughts, the thought that is talking to oneself) had returned, the kind of words that would emerge, they would be to do with awkwardness and dull confusion, and with details of life and death, of the still stillness of the body as an it. And they were. They formed, words and thoughts, found by my mind, little by little, over the years that have passed over my life since I looked in a state of suspended animation at the body locked in a dead weight of cancelled animation. While I was in that dead room I stored in code the thoughts about what I was doing and going through, and bit by bit my mind has cracked the code. My mind has turned brief minutes of extraordinary experience and totalled numbness into thoughts, into words. I wasn't thinking clearly as it was happening as to what was happening but gradually it has all become clearer. For instance, I didn't think about it at the time, but I remember now – my mind has just deciphered another fragment of the code – that neither of us, me playing Life and it easing through the early stages of Death, were worried about the time. And both of us felt in our own equally dramatic ways that there was nothing much to say. I think, also, that I was in this life-soaked hurry to leave the room of death, but it, the body, the dead one, was in no hurry at all. Its grand lack of hurry gave the body a fine sense of bludgeoned elegance, but then most of what had made the it a he had already hurried away. To wherever. Whenever.

Forever and ever.

I felt funny looking at what flesh was on show, and filed away for future decoding some muzzled confusion about just what this flesh actually was. It used to be flesh, not that long ago, so you could still call it flesh and get away with it. Everyone would know what you meant. But now it is flesh at some stopped dead place between being and non-being. It's ex-flesh but at the same time it is existing flesh. After death, using this body hanging around in front of me as my research, the body's flesh remains for a little while. It doesn't disappear as instantly as say the soul. The body's had it wrapped around its little finger for long enough, and meanwhile there are still a few steady moments to go before the flesh is finally forced to accept, perhaps through burning, that it is, ultimately, nothing. It has no right to even pretend that it was something. It's nothing without a soul, the word used here to describe whatever it is that makes you a he, she or whatever above and beyond being a basic hollow, bone-stretched vessel leaking eerie essence. Without life and soul, flesh has a bleak future.

It was fleshless flesh, or lifeless flesh, or flesh kept flesh for a final few days thanks to science and compassion, flesh that had been flesh and was now hanging on for dear life, or should that be dear death? It was flesh of sorts, anyway. So even though I have seen many dead bodies in fact and fiction through film and television, seen people shot and stabbed in fake ways and real ways, this was the only dead body that I have seen in my life in real life. The only dead body I have seen that wasn't on the other side of a screen, dreamt up, glassed off, made of light, as removed as yesterday. The only dead body that, if I was so disposed, I could touch.

I suppose I saw my first dead body on television when I was six or seven. I have a feeling that the first dead body I saw was probably the body of a cat. A cartoon cat. Tom. I saw him smashed and mangled by a plump little cartoon mouse pumped up with frivolous malice. Frankly, I saw him destroyed to death. Tom fluttered up towards the sky, and heaven, as an angel, a transparent cat with angel wings and an expression of benign acceptance. Seconds later, he was alive again. Tom and Jerry didn't make death seem so fatal, in the same way that they didn't make violence seem so violent. They made death as funny as violence. I watched Tom and Jerry flirt famously with death and torture, and I laughed at it all. I laughed in the face of death.

I estimate that by the time I was eight I had seen a couple of hundred dead bodies on television, a few on film, of which only about ten were cartoons. It wasn't just the cartoon characters who died only to live again. The numbers of screened-off dead bodies piled up in my life, but the way I saw it death was just part of a game. Part of a war game or a space game or a cartoon game. The dead bodies looked like they were sleeping, dreaming, waiting. They looked like they'd lost the game. Then another game would begin. Sometimes, the dead bodies would go to heaven, which was like earth but fluffier and whiter. Then they would come back to earth, as if nothing had happened. Death was just another part of life, it was enclosed by life, you could die and still be alive. There was a sense that something stopped, but it certainly wasn't life that stopped. At eight, even as I watched cowboys killed in front of my eyes and heard the screams of soldiers as they were halted in their tracks, even as I watched coyotes flattened to the width of paper, even as I vaguely registered that people died and death was dark, darker than night, I hadn't yet begun to believe that death stopped everything. I had no reason yet to suspect that death was anything other than a funny thing that happened on the way to another adventure. The biggest, realest deaths I remember were the ones of J. F. Kennedy and the Scottish racing car driver Jim Clarke. TV told me very clearly about both deaths. I was sad about Kennedy when I was six because everyone else seemed upset. I was angry about Jim Clarke when I was eight or nine because he was my favourite and I realised that he would never race again and never win again. It was the end of the game, the end of the race, and there wouldn't be any others. His death made me feel a bit sick in the stomach, and was perhaps the first, above the world-changing Kennedy's, that prompted me to consider death as a rather unsettling disappearing act.

As the body count mounted, and after Clarke's crash, I got a little suspicious. I don't know if there was necessarily a connection between the dead bodies I was vaguely watching on television and my own growing feeling that death wasn't so funny and wasn't as such the end of a game, but I was soon asking my mother what happened to you when you die. I couldn't imagine what the answer could be. At first, my mother didn't have much of an answer. I think she also had difficulty imagining one. Her initial answer suggested that the route Tom the cat took to heaven and the wings that materialised on his back were, for a cartoon, incredibly realistic. I imagined in a rough, rushed way Jim Clarke racing about a fuzzy heaven with little wings on his back. I clung to the notion that somehow, somewhere, really, there was still a Jim Clarke being a Jim Clarke even if he wasn't racing cars and winning races and being exotic and, if I only but knew it, damned near erotic. To be honest, in my heart of hearts I didn't trust this image of Clarke in heaven much, and I left behind the confusing death of Jim Clarke, the way it interfered with my wishes and dreams, and found other sports to obsess about, other sportsmen to adore. After the initial shock faded away, I didn't want to think about it too much. Or think about it at all. Deep down in my mind I knew for bumpy sure that there was no such thing as Jim Clarke anymore, as silly as this seemed. And there was little chance of John Edrich, the opening batsman for the Surrey cricket team, disappearing as suddenly and unfathomably as Jim Clarke. There would always be John Edrich playing his game and so everything was alright with the world. Or it was when the sun shined.

Dead bodies continued to be screened and stocked up for me as I grew up. By the time I was thirteen, all knees, navel and fumble, I must have seen thousands of dead bodies. In the film *Zulu* alone I must have seen 2,356 dead bodies. They littered my life. One or two seen on the news might even have been the dead bodies of people who had actually lived. Chasing dumb entertainment so as to help further numb my growing appreciation that death led not nowhere in particular but nowhere at all, and I do mean all, meant that I was coming across dead bodies by the day by the handful. I might have looked stupid, and pretty vacant, by the time I was thirteen, but I was sensitive enough to know that all those dead bodies being paraded in front of me weren't actually dead. They were as dead as a cartoon cat. Actually, they weren't as dead as a cartoon cat, because a cartoon cat is deader than dead. It's the deadest. A cartoon cat hasn't really lived and in that sense it's dead in the first place – in the second place, the third place, the fourth place and so on, through all the places from here to eternity. This is why it's difficult to take the killing of a cartoon cat seriously even when you're six or seven. The cat was never alive. How can it be dead in the sense of having once lived? How can it even be playing at being dead? It's just dead by great virtue of the fact that it never lived. Everything else is just an illusion, what with one thing or another.

The dead bodies taking their rehearsed position in various screen dramas and thrillers were about as dead as me. They were as dead as me with my eyes shut. As dead as me lying down and dreaming of something else. As dead as me pretending to be dead. Any war victim that I might have seen in the news who was actually as dead as a pre-existing cartoon cat, really dead, as lifeless as a drawing that's never been drawn, seemed as unreal and unimpressive as any actor playing dead by being as still as possible for a few seconds. The screened dead bodies tended to show that death was everywhere, it was all around, it was on top of us and right round the corner, but fiction and make-believe could keep it in its place. Fantasy's job was to control death. To place it right in front of our faces but to wrap it up in cotton wool. To draw constant attention to it and yet at the same time deflect attention by pretending it was no big deal and no one gets hurt, as such. It's nothing, really, and quite easy to get over.

I went to no funerals. All through my teens, none of my family died. None of my friends died. I had a friend whose father died. He was told about it one day at school. When he arrived back in class after being told by the headmaster about his father he didn't seem that bothered. He shrugged his shoulders and sort of smiled and got on with the day. I was vaguely puzzled but just assumed that's how death was. A bit of news. A change in routine for a while. Me and my friend never talked about his father's death. I never asked if he ever saw his father's body.

I remember when I was twelve or thirteen our next-door neighbour's wife died. He must have seen his wife's body because he discovered it. I remember him being a bit shattered for a few days, chatting aimlessly, or maybe with perfect aim, to my mother about this and that and death. But I didn't really think about it. I didn't want to think about it. I made a decision not to pay too much attention to what I distantly felt was an immensely difficult situation. The neighbour helplessly drifting in and out of my vision swapping small talk and then abruptly not so small talk with my mother made me feel very awkward. I felt awkward enough as it was, as an unkissed and unscintillating thirteen-year-old feeling far too hemmed in by his skin. (As for his bones.) The neighbour, who had been married to his wife for about twice the length of my young and flimsy life, made me and my bones feel uncomfortable just looking at him and the way that grief hugged his shoulders. He didn't seem to have the faintest idea what to do next, which way to turn, how to smile in a way that wasn't thin and forced. How can you smile brightly when your lips are trapped by unhappiness? I have no idea, and I didn't even contemplate such a thing at the time.

Then, overnight, as far as I could tell from where I was, lodged within my blank carelessness, he got on with the rest of his life, a life changed into a very different shape because he had seen his wife as a dead body. I wonder how long it was before he too was a dead body someone was looking at with the result that their life was a little more shaded than it had been. I didn't wonder that at the time. I was wondering if and when and how I would ever be kissed.

I wasn't well versed in the art and craft of death. None of my sporting heroes died anymore. I became a fan of Jim Morrison and Jimi Hendrix after they had died. My teen years were mostly a deathless motion, while on the screens all around me images of dead bodies multiplied in the scenic abstract. Death did make a cameo appearance in my life when I was fourteen. I wanted to kill myself. After some dark thought, as I adolescently abandoned myself in a great dark pit of worked-up helplessness and scorching self-pity, I realised that I couldn't think how to do it. This only increased my misery, and confirmed my sore and sunken sense of failure. I also ended up focussing hard and clear on an interesting understanding – if I did kill myself I wouldn't be around anymore. This understanding, which has increased in interest as I've grown older, didn't particularly help me on the suicidal planning front. I wonder now if I had already seen the dead body that eventually I would get to see it might have offered up some neat black criss-crossed clues about how to go about killing yourself. But I wasn't to see this dead body for a good, bad and indifferent few years yet. The dead bodies planted onto the television, the dead bodies strewn over the imaginative wasteland of films, they offered absolutely no clues about how to kill yourself. They supplied a load of fairly unwanted advice about how to play dead.

After I had failed to kill myself and resigned myself to an immediate future full of life and other things equally tentative and uncertain, there was during my teenage years not much death to write home about. Mine wasn't so much a suicide attempt as a suicide fumble. I frightened myself before I could kill myself. I believe I reached the very last stage you can before you actually get down to business, and although this was life-changing enough for death to make a big move in on my life and eat away some of its charm, death and the dead still remained active and alive only in fiction and fables and films. I was aware that death was following me around, and a lonely melodramatic part of me was repelled and attracted by its creeping absent presence. But death was apart from me. It had not entered me. It had not twisted my brain or chilled the very heart of me, except abstractly. The woodwork teacher at my school died, but, largely due to the chisels he liked to hurl at boys who were behind in their woodwork exercises, that was a cause for unsuppressed and quite open celebration. Death could be OK.

In the end, the first funeral I ever went to was that of my father. Which made death very much a part of me. But his wasn't the dead body that I saw. I have only ever seen one dead body in my life and I saw it a few years after my father died. I saw the dead body of someone who had hanged himself. The dead body of a young man who had savagely succeeded at suicide even as he felt useless and hopeless and pointless. I saw the dead body of someone who was about my age. The dead body of someone who I was not related to and only barely knew. It was the dead body of Ian Curtis, the lead singer of the rock group Joy Division.

I don't really know what I was doing there, staring at him when he was at his most exposed and most crestfallen. He certainly didn't know what I was doing there. But one thing I did know for sure. He was dead. I could see that. The best way to know for sure, to really believe, that someone is dead and gone is to see their body with all the life and character and personality and essence scooped and seized right out of it. You see the patched-up shell of a whole lifetime. You see cancelled existence. You see terrible peace. You reach a hard but inevitable conclusion. That's that, then. That's it. Life, and death, goes on.

I have only seen one dead body in my life and it wasn't the body of my father.

## XXXV

From an interview with Rob Gretton/conducted in 1991/who died eight years later at 46/for a documentary about New Order/Rob is as amused as ever by the idea he is on camera/elsewhere in the documentary/Neil Tennant of the Pet Shop Boys explains that Rob's role as manager is never to smooth things over but to make things difficult/so that the group never forget how they began/fighting for their right/Peter Hook would always say that he felt Rob Gretton had a technique whereby he would withhold money from the group/he perhaps not intentionally/perhaps intentionally/kept them poor/to keep them hungry/to keep them angry/to keep them in the same state they were when they began/when they were fighting for their lives/for a bit of attention/with a cagey, psyched up twinkle in his eye/tickled to death by his role as manager.

Rob: We've all got our idiosyncrasies.

# PART TWO:

## After/Life

## XXXVI

For a while, I stopped writing about Joy Division. I carried on making myself up in ways that moved me further away from dead bodies, shattered families, northern towns and decaying atmospheres. Now and then I would continue the moving away by travelling back to the North to write about the northern groups following in the wake of Joy Division. If I had been asked until recently when I wrote the following *NME* interviews, I would have said in the following year or two after Curtis' suicide. It's only now I note that they were all written a few months after he died.

This also means they were written not long after Tony Wilson had shown me Ian's dead body, although I don't remember thinking about that at all in those following few months. There was no obvious way to proceed with such senseless information, so I decided to ignore that particular episode. I had quickly put the experience away somewhere, possibly in some remote mental place very near the effectively buried memories of my father, and his useless breathless deadness.

The following three articles demonstrate how, following the end of Joy Division, it was business as usual, for their label, for groups associated with them, groups who had played shows with them, and for me. Somewhere else, off the page, out of vision, Joy Division, along with the time and substance that surrounded them, had shattered into a million pieces. The cultural, emotional and industrial process that would eventually put them back together was only just beginning.

First of all this meant that everything carried on as normal, whilst wounds were licked, thoughts were hidden, wires were crossed, and energised feelings transferred to other areas of concern. Those of us near to the original point of impact were quick to turn to other things that might be on our mind, not aware at the time that this would be in the long run part of the process that would put the idea, the presence, of Joy Division back together again. Instantly, initially, the group was a shocking shadow of their former selves. Gradually, while the world busied itself with itself elsewhere, flesh and blood and power returned.

Within a few months of being shown into that remarkable and unremarkable Macclesfield room by Tony Wilson I wrote three pieces for the *NME* about two groups who had been on Factory, and one group that was still part of the label. Of the two groups no longer on Factory, one was signed to a major label in London, and one was earnestly exploring post-Factory independence. The group remaining on Factory were, on the quiet, being set up as a new Joy Division, by their label, and their managers, who happened to be their label.

The three pieces written in the post-Joy Division landscape that was quickly forming were like the interviews with Joy Division that I never got to do, with a Joy Division that moodily articulated the pressurised oddness of their position as Factory guinea pigs, that relished the space given to them to map out an adventure in radical entertainment, that were working out how comfortable they were with pop success. They were the kind of interviews people assumed I had done with Joy Division: they were the kind of interviews I assumed I had done with Joy Division. Interviews with serious, sometimes funny, mostly mild mannered, if occasionally exasperated, even bitter, young men in dark clothing carefully working out strategies in the particular area of their existence, young men who were gradually relying on each other for a sense of purpose.

Each of the groups I covered had in their own way the same intensity, youthful zeal and uncompromising spirit. Each of them was where they were to a large extent because of punk, Factory and the North, and because of Joy Division.

A Certain Ratio represented the surly, defensive, defiant and insular Joy Division, the one looked after, sometimes a little too firmly, a bit too flamboyantly, by Wilson and Gretton, as if they were a kind of avant-garde boy band. They had a laugh, they sulked, they grumbled about money and Wilson's bossiness, they got on with things in their own close, secret way.

Cabaret Voltaire represented the open-minded, experimental and thoroughly dedicated Joy Division, the group fighting for art in a world smothered by commerce. A group fundamentally opposed to music business hype. They were not frightened by the idea of obscurity – they just wanted to make their music, as purely as they could, locked away in sad, unswept rooms empty but for machines, microphones, chairs and chipped mugs, pushing primitive electronic equipment as far as it would go in the isolated, perfectionist search for new sounds and rhythms.

Orchestral Manoeuvres in the Dark represented the serious, successful, eccentric pop group dealing with new commercial realities, the group who wrote atmospheric and enigmatic songs about unusual subjects that still belonged in the top 40, the group destined for American success, the group settling down to a long career. They had achieved their unlikely ambition to have pop hits inspired by the Velvets and Kraftwerk and were playing large British theatres standing proudly on a surreal pop set designed by Peter Saville.

Mix the three groups up, and you could find, if not exactly Joy Division, then certainly a suggestion of the group that Joy Division were to become.

A Certain Ratio were put on the cover of the *NME*, largely because they were so specifically from the same factory as the now known and notorious Joy Division, part of the same manufacturing process. Possibly, it was too early for such exposure.

And, for some reason, I was still calling Alan Erasmus a 'tramp'. This is particularly strange, because I had been to his house on Palatine Road in Didsbury – the home of Factory Records well into the 1980s – and it was a fine home. Perhaps it was because of the tatty flat cap he would shove down on top of his unruly curls – the flat cap of a clichéd North he was dedicated to overturning. Perhaps it was because he always seemed quite content to just hang around, as if he'd come from nowhere, and was quite cheerfully going straight back there. Maybe I was thinking of the tramps in *Waiting for Godot* – Wilson and Erasmus as two tramps standing underneath a tree, waiting for someone, but they are not sure who he is or what he looks like.

## XXXVII

**Article on A Certain Ratio – *New Musical Express*, 6 September 1980.**

We leave the grubby Hulme human hutch where some members of A Certain Ratio live. The view from this particular section of hutches is not completely derelict, but neither is it splendid.

I stare out from the fourth floor landing into the miserable spread of concrete, scrap, brick, wire and wasteland, imagine in my mind A Certain Ratio's next single 'Flight', and the logic of the relationship between the entertainment and the environment makes my hands clammy.

Logic! In this world – today! I don't know.

A Certain Ratio are a crazed Mancunian unit who spent their wild youth doing some heady, posey nightclubbing at Manchester's more decadent clubs. The members gathered together to make music almost out of spite.

Their sound is a derisive, decisive contemporary coalition of abnormal rhyme, the recession and no distinct reason; where funk's smouldering exuberance has been coarsened by lack of money, lack of future and a certain neurosis, and twisted viciously by an impatient post-Ubu/Pop Group spirit. It's a wretched, wrenching doppelgänger to the sensual funk that reached a creative peak a couple of years back, the darkest, deepest side of disco imaginable.

And if truth be known ACR play not art-rock but failed CSE rock.

A Certain Ratio's attitude is that 'we can do better' – than anything or anyone. Singer/trumpeter Simon Topping once said to Chris Bohn that in all the two years he went to the Factory and Rafters he only saw two groups he liked – and they played on the same night. As soon as I read that I knew he meant Pere Ubu and the Pop Group. They were noisy and kinky, you could dance to them or collapse to them, they weren't out to do any whitewashing. They weren't normal! I was going to ask ACR what they thought of the Pop Group these days, but decided I didn't have to. In the middle of the tiny living quarters of the Ratio hutch there was a twelve-inch copy of the Pop Group's greatest hit 'Beyond Good and Evil'; two cigarettes had been dissected on it. Chopping up cigarettes and scattering the crumbs over records is a strange thing to do.

But A Certain Ratio like to do strange things.

★

We walk down darkened stairs to the ground level of the precinct. I mock bass player Jeremy Kerr's black plastic hold-all. Very Dexy's. ACR have already been accused of being the 'genuine' young soul rebels – whatever that actually signified – but Kerr's not into that line of thought at all. He makes sure that he always has the holdall slung over his shoulder, never gripped in his right hand as a symbol of dejection. When the group are being photographed he even gives me the bag to hold, so that silly links between the two 'moody' post-punk soul boys are not even remotely seen to be there.

I ask Topping what he feels about the Dexy's current campaign.

'What am I supposed to feel about it?' he snaps back reasonably.

The Ratios have less than nothing to say about other groups and their attitudes; and only slightly more to say about their own group and attitude. They are not keen chatterers.

We wander along the darkening precinct. Always curious about what others think about the group and their occasional tricks, Topping asks whether I'd seen them play in khaki shorts. The time when fake tan could be seen coursing down their usually pale bodies? (A no-doubt discreet reference to their manager's prediction that ACR will soon be cruising round Bel Air in Cadillacs.)

'Yeah, we got some girls to rub in that stuff, but afterwards they wouldn't take it off.'

I can't say I'm surprised.

'Did you think wearing those shorts was funny?'

Within reason. Is that why you did it?

'Not really. Tony [Wilson, Factory boss] got us them. They were only two quid. They're really practical, it gets very hot on stage.'

We drift towards a 'phone box, a dirty red shadow amidst the great concrete shapes all around us, to call a couple of taxis. Ratio's cute guitarist Peter Terrell, whose cheeky grin should easily snap away any fear of their music, tells me that sometimes when he strolls through this part of the hellish Hulme structure young kids probably not much smaller than himself hurl stones and abuse at him.

'They're instant stiffs as soon as they're born,' he scoffs, 'stiffs' being the ultimate insult. 'They've got to fall in with the rest of them, they grow up like their parents. They don't even think about being different.'

As the group collects around the 'phone box and various Ratios attempt to get through to a taxi firm, the temperature's so low a different kind of stiffdom beckons. I'm close to being frozen on the spot in a lost corner of Hulme.

It's the middle of the evening, and in a few hours' time ACR play Manchester Rafters. This hanging around, shivering into space, doesn't seem the ideal preparation.

'Is this going to be a page interview?' asks Terrell.

'Or a double-page spread?' crows Topping, snidely.

'Do you think it'll get on the cover?' wonders Terrell.

Automatically – if I had my way. Terrell half-heartedly pulls a face.

Would a front cover mean much to him?

'They'd probably stop our dole. I don't know. I suppose it'd be quite nice. Something to show your parents,' he chuckles.

Jolly drummer Donald Johnson fails to get a taxi, but trumpeter/guitarist Martin Moscrop fares better. Taxis should be on their way. We wait, freezing into the pavement. Four fifths of Ratio look the part for this sort of dreary street corner lingering. Johnson, tubby form not very well hidden by a large-ish yellow and black tracksuit, wearing an ever-present jockey cap, looks like a Central Park jogger. The others, who could all be described as quiet, have a baggy, anti-chic chic Jarrow March look.

A taxi arrives, takes Moscrop and Kerr into the city centre a couple of miles away. The rest of us wait some more. The second taxi doesn't turn up, so we have to wait even longer for Johnson's girl to come along in his new car. We move along the pavement a few yards to be more noticeable, wait some more. 45 minutes in Hulme open air is not recommended. No wonder ACR always look so grim on stage if this is their usual preparation.

'It's always something that has gone wrong, some bad luck during the evening,' shrugs Johnson, shaking his head, perking up to exclaim that he's having trouble getting accustomed to Topping's new and startling short back and sides.

'My Grace Jones look,' says Topping, defensively. A sleek, shiny hatchback motor pulls up. I whistle. Not an expected ACR vehicle! It's Donald's.

'He works at the airport and earns £75 a week,' marvels Terrell with an unexpected blast of total awe.

We drive off to the centre of the city, Topping perched on Johnson's knee in the front seat.

★

When a journalist writes a piece on a Factory group he is inevitably met at Manchester's Piccadilly station by Factory's wizard Tony Wilson (to Hannett's mad professor, Gretton's hooligan, Erasmus' tramp and Saville's executive). And sure enough as I burst through the ticket barrier of platform nine there's the grinning Wilson, pushing loose hair out of his face, striding towards us in pathetic khaki balloons, happily sockless. He's skiving off more time from Granada Television.

Taking such time off has meant that Wilson by mutual agreement has been taken off the *World in Action* team. Too fast, youthful, unpredictable within that context, he once hitchhiked to an important interview with Sir Keith Joseph and turned up dishevelled and disorientated, with a minute to spare.

Granada's respect for him as an onscreen personality – the man who grannies used to love, who still gets recognised in Manchester streets by teenage girls shoving each other in delight – has meant that he's to front an upcoming Granada pop show, *The World of Pop*, the inevitable attempt to visualise *Smash Hits*.

The probable success of this, combined with the phenomenal and significant success of Factory Records, suggests what the more flexible amongst us have always thought: that *So It Goes* was more perceptive and brilliant than merely being erratically entertaining. Wilson's understanding of rock's volatile inner tension, its crude art and its ace style, is unimpeachable. Factory Records is a success because it perceives what is wanted and needed in 1980's pop.

By not limiting eccentricity, extremity or indulgence, Factory – along with labels like Ze and Fetish – define where pop is and where it's going as a reflection of today's turmoil. They are dragging rock forward.

Who else but Factory would have discovered and patiently encouraged A Certain Ratio, a group who in their early days were unhelpfully primitive? And what a loss it would have been if no one had!

By totally lacking general rock expectations, Factory are more likely to spot inner coherence in a superficially messy group like ACR than in the restricted code of an average tidy rock band. By saying that commercialism can be anything, not just this and that, Factory's definition – rather lack of it – is best.

It allows ACR to be. They're continuing punk spirit rather than the letter of the law. Listen to them and you know what's going on all around.

★

Tony Wilson is ACR's manager. As such he is ruthless, ever watchful and scurrilously protective. The first time I ever saw Ratio was in May '79, the London debut of Factory groups at Acklam Hall (along with Joy Division and Orchestral Manoeuvres when there were less than 100 in the audience). They were drummerless and I thought cumbersome. I didn't like them.

'We thought we'd played really well,' comments Topping wryly. 'But

Tony thought we were drunk and he gave us a right bollocking because people like you didn't like us.'

ACR are not too sure how honest to be about their manager. They like to have it their way at all times. Equally they are not too sure about their position of relative acceptance, but try to take it in their stride.

'I think the reason that we are accepted has something to do with Factory Records. Yeah, it's only because we're a Factory band that we get a lot of the attention that we do. Factory bands do get a lot of attention. Tony knows how to do things right.'

There's a quiet respect for Wilson mixed with a tinge of suspicion. ACR have gained a lot of attention through the Factory packages, packages that now become slightly predictable and restrictive.

'We don't want to do that anymore. We're going to stop doing them after America. That's where arguments have started . . . Tony thinks that we're being arrogant. We can't understand in what way.'

Wilson's side of it is that he hears Ratio developing the type of crusty aloofness of latterday Pop Group. This so-called arrogance could be rooted in Ratio's intense desire to keep everything as personal as possible.

'Well, it's just we want to do things our way and they want to do things their way. It's mainly that Tony's ideas are so different from ours because of his age and everything, and he used to say that we could do what we wanted but now he's trying to control us – not the music, just the other things. It's become less of a family, Factory. It's more of a major record company. It's definitely gone up a stage since six weeks ago. Some things have changed. Since Joy Division. Since the money started coming in.'

To some extent ACR are being mollycoddled as the next Factory superstars: right now they're elitist press darlings, in the shadow of JD but ready to leap into the glare . . . they skirt around any such pressure there may be to be the next year's successful Factory band.

'If there is that sort of pressure we can leave. We are not chained to Factory Records.'

Mildly controversial stuff. Their pragmatic attitude to the organisation that gave them everything is typical.

At one point whilst Ratio are mutely discussing Factory flaws, happy Donald Johnson, a faithful Factory man, puts things into perspective.

'Where would we be without Factory? No equipment, no records, no gigs . . . no money.'

The less convinced are not too sure about 'no money'. But then there's a continual ration of uncertainty in ACR's make-up. This uncertainty, thinly disguised, is what makes ACR's whirl go round.

We drive over to the other side of Manchester to pick up ACR at their rehearsal room. They hardly acknowledge me, but I wasn't really expecting them to. As we drive back into Manchester for the soundcheck at Rafters, Wilson and ACR work out some vague plan for sleeping accommodation when Factory invade New York this month.

Being caught up in Factory has meant that Ratio will spend some weeks in New York, gigging and recording. They're not exactly tickled ecstatic by the prospect.

'The original reason we were going over was that some record company was interested in us.'

Ze?

'Antilles, the Eno thing. But when Tony went over there for a week to see them he said they were stupid. But we're going over anyway.'

Inside Rafters, people rush here and there. Musicians seem to be turning up minute by minute looking to soundcheck. Four groups are to play: Swamp Children, Blurt, Durutti Column and Ratio. Wilson lectures Invisible Girls' Steve Hopkins about some important date he must remember.

'There's always some excuse. One minute it's working with Pauline Murray, the next it's being interviewed by the bloody *NME*.'

186

The bloody *NME* withdraw into a dark corner to watch ACR soundcheck. A wacky house light show is set in motion by Eric Random. Everyone present seems to be in their recession/military togs. This is beginning to become an Era. Johnson soundchecks for a couple of songs he'll be doing with Vini Reilly (bassist Kerr has also been doing some work with Reilly, his soft voice more suiting Reilly than Ratio, and Moscrop will play drums with the disconcerting Swamp Children) and then we leave.

Moscrop, Terrell, Kerr and Topping walk from Rafters to the Hulme hutch. By now we're talking, but closer to sulking than plotting a conspiracy. Terrell and Topping buy some toffees. Moscrop gets a Mexican take away. We head for the Hulme hole. Topping chucking me toffees, Terrell pointing to the underside of an overpass scrawled with punky slogans.

'If we were a punk band that's where we would have our photos taken.'

Somebody remarks that in Hulme someone has sprayed A Certain Ratio on a wall.

'Should we have our pictures taken in front of that?' suggests Terrell. The group groan. One of them burps. One of them asks if there are any eggs in the hutch.

Like I say, ACR are not keen chatterers.

★

Before I set the tape in motion, Kerr sits next to me and runs his fingers up and down his bass strings. Two are new and he's slackening them. 'Tina Weymouth taught me how to do this,' he mock-gloats. 'She taught me everything I know about bass guitars!'

ACR finished 1979 by supporting Talking Heads on their short British tour, last-minute replacements for Human League whose non-human film idea was not up to T. Heads standards. ACR did the Heads tour, and look where they are today! (That will make more sense when you hear 'Flight', which took more time to craft than 'Love Will Tear Us Apart' – and if it doesn't freak you out you must be very cold.)

Their first Factory single 'All Night Party' is a representation of their sound when they were drummerless and all but formless. At the time, I played it a few times and just thought Wilson was being a perverse little toad for flirting with them. Playing it recently and joining in with its ache, I realised that it's one of the best 2,000 singles ever made.

ACR's development can be definitely split pre-Johnson and post-Johnson (and then pre-trumpets and post-trumpets). Pre-Johnson they gravitated towards surly abstraction, laboriously and grumpily constructing hard death-drones; somewhere between 'No Pussyfooting' and 'Sister Ray'.

Post-Johnson – by which time Ratio had spent some months learning their way around their instruments – the sound became very much a dance music, still undecorative and devious and in many ways non-epically daunting; somewhere between Pere Ubu and the end of a dream.

At one point Topping asks me (I think ACR for all their apparent reserve asked me more questions than I asked them) what I thought ACR were going to sound like once Wilson had uncovered Johnson and eased him into the fray. I did hope it would become more a dance music.

'Mmmm,' he ponders, 'it's just that some groups sound like we did when we didn't have a drummer even when they do.' A savage indictment?

The first chance the people had to purchase post-Johnson stuff was *The Graveyard and The Ballroom* cassette-in-a-purse. A sweet Factory idea, typically creating their own trendiness, it wasn't really much to do with ACR. One side was recorded on the Heads tour at London's Electric Ballroom, the other side is some demos recorded at Prestwich's Graveyard studio by that man Hannett.

*Graveyard and the Ballroom* is horror music, elegiac in a strange way, violently contemporary, nervy, pugnacious. Black comedy, white noise, nightmares and phobias. It was music of fear – but for all that, a compelling communication of enjoyment.

Free of the perverse shackles a lack of rhythm had placed on their music, ACR had stretched out, were translating their own lacerating language.

The songs were a lonely, longing statement. ACR didn't want to make the world a nicer place. They just wanted to make it out. The feeling isn't dismal but stimulating. When I ask if they feel their music is emotional, the question is so dumb they don't even bother answering.

ACR are not afraid of playing live (although Johnson said he got a bit scared playing those large places with Talking Heads: 'I couldn't see the faces of the people'). In a way they're playing too many gigs.

'We're not as enthusiastic about what we do as we were at the start. We still like what we're playing, but we play it all the time. We've been on the road for two years now playing . . . it doesn't make a difference when you're playing the same old things over and over again. I think we're in a dilemma at the moment because Donald's often working and we don't get a chance to rehearse.'

*

What ACR are working towards will remain vague. Probably just the day it all disintegrates. They just are and that's very much how they operate. They place all the emphasis on their music, that spilling over into how it's presented. There's a constant, unquenchable thirst for the mythical change. With dry submission they maintain that there is nothing they can do to change rock's web of deceit, and so commit themselves to retaining their own purity, their own particular creativity. Dancing down the tunnel to dystopia.

They continue for their own enjoyment. 'And the development of our ideas. To play music how we feel it should be played.'

How should it be played?

'The way we play it.'

Sometimes they say their music's not that good, other times they imply it's the only music. I ask myself if they think they're not as good as they can be because they're dominated by influences.

'No.'

They must have learnt from something else.

'You use what you can. You can't be totally original. What we're playing is like everything we've ever heard recycled, how we'd like to hear it done. Sometimes it works, sometimes it doesn't. What is good about our music is that we try new ways. We try to be different. It's just like a combination of all the things we like.'

ACR say they want things to change and yet they say nothing can be achieved. When I say this, they feel threatened.

'What we're trying to achieve we're achieving through the music we play. Is that alright? I don't think the music's very important. It's just what we do. A way of expressing ideas, feelings.'

To start the interview I had sat down in front of the tobacco-covered copy of 'Beyond Good and Evil', Ratio spread around me in a semicircle, and asked the group if they wanted to be rich. A daft, abrupt way to start an interview, but I felt in a stupid mood.

'No. That's just a snide shot,' murmurs a voice. Ratio's subdued voices blend into one another on tape, and it's impossible to separate who said what. I remember Terrell did the most talking, Topping was the most sarky, Johnson didn't say a thing while the tape was humming, but that they all agreed with whatever was being said (apart from minor details like who first saw them – Wilson or Gretton).

What's the good thing about playing music?

'Playing what you like.'

What don't you like about other music?

'It's safe.'

Aren't ACR?

'Yeah, in a way. We used to play to annoy people but now people don't get annoyed anymore. Which isn't what we want!'

What fun did they get out of annoying people?

'Just the fact that it was different. We were trying to annoy people into thinking about other things, instead of just accepting the same old things. But we don't think it's very easy to get through to people. We don't think there are many things you can do to change how people feel.'

Tight! ACR reckon it's commercialism that has diluted groups like Buzzcocks. It could happen to them.

'There doesn't seem to be any way around it. It'll just be interesting to see how we can deal with it.'

Are they in the middle of it now, in a slightly less fundamental way because of Factory's support?

'We don't feel that we are. We've got no benefit from it. No financial benefit . . . that is the thing that does change people. Lots of money. But if we have more money we'll be able to do more things.'

Although it is the money that's likely to compromise Ratio.

'Yeah. The whole thing's a contradiction. The whole thing about rock music – it's a contradiction.'

Maybe in their understated way ACR quite relish that. But they tend to talk about their essence in such a dreary way it is a wonder they continue. This is because what they do is intensely private – they live in their own heads, where that becomes negative who knows – that a stranger like me is hardly likely to penetrate. Ultimately they have no choice; they play music, they continue.

I say to them after being worn down by a confusing mixture of acceptance and assertion, pessimism and confidence, that they must want to have some effect. They must have aspirations.

'Yeah. Personal ones.'

But aren't they making a public statement?

'No, I'm not telling it you now am I?'

Making it public by going on stage?

'If the statement is going on stage and making records and that we like making music and like making it in a certain way, then that's the statement. As far as personal things go it's not really more important than what anyone else says really.'

Pretty humble. In some ways ACR are pretty things. In other ways they're pretty vacant. Essentially, in their own way, they're pretty sharp. Eventually I feel like I'm being bricked up, so the bastard tape recorder gets tucked away. Things tangibly relax. We drink some tea. They ask about that oddly edited review of their Belgian single 'Shack Up', and say they didn't understand the retraction in T-Zers. Neither did I. They ask why they're appearing in the *NME* indie charts when only 1,000 of the singles were released here.

Sheer elitism, I say.

Just before we're due to leave to get those taxis, Kerr and I play electronic tennis on one of two large TVs dominating the room. He slaughters me fifteen-eight, fifteen-seven, fifteen-seven.

Now that's reason not to show my face in public again.

*

The gig at Rafters was heavily under-publicised. Although Factory reckoned proceeds were only likely to be £350 they, with ritualistic cheeriness, spent £300 printing up a full-colour Jon Savage-designed poster. ACR didn't have much to say about that. The poster didn't overshadow their performance, but that's the sort of thing Factory are always trying to do.

The rabid mafia who do Manchester's fly-posting conveniently pasted up only a handful of the posters. That's about all the advertising there was. It looked like hardly anyone was going to turn up. A couple of hundred did.

The gig is not nostalgic, regretful or impeccable. It is either a precise statement or it is blather. On one level it is the best new dance music around. For ACR fanatics – and ACR are the type of group who attract hordes of those – it's getting cosy; merely attractive. Not even the dual trumpets bawling like bad tempered babies over the mutilated funk make it shocking for those convinced. In terms of the mainstream it is no doubt a tyranny of unconformity. Only with Factory's inventive help will ACR reach into the mainstream to shock.

That's not too important. What is important is that ACR linger in the shadows, offending people and callow notions. That they are around to genuinely and progressively document reaction to the apocalyptic landscape. ACR carry meaning in their very confusion and their irrational commitment. Their mood, however ambivalent, is one of real curiosity. They are for everyone who is interested.

I leave Rafters thinking that ACR have it in them to make some of the most cosmic and militant music of the eighties, or that they could fall into a self-deluding cul-de-sac.

We'll find out which way it's going to be very soon.

At the end of The Interview Topping finally lost patience with my nagging. I'd asked if they intended their music to be depressing or stimulating. He didn't want to know about that. He made a wild attempt to put the whole ACR thing into perspective.

'Our music . . . it's like a mother, she has a baby and everybody thinks that it's really ugly . . . but she absolutely loves it and thinks that it's beautiful.

'That's like us with our music.'

Donald Johnson bursts out laughing, the only sound he made during the taped interview. ACR laugh so hard they cry. They cry so hard they laugh. I turn off the tape recorder, go outside for a brief breath of Hulme air, come back inside and drink my tea.

In a few minutes we'll leave the grubby Hulme hutch where some members of A Certain Ratio live.

## XXXVIII

**Article on Orchestral Manoeuvres in the Dark – *New Musical Express*, 22 November 1980.**

Andy McCluskey and I are the last two of the Orchestral Manoeuvres in the Dark party left in the Edinburgh hotel bar.

It's the early hours of a Wednesday morning: four hours after Orchestral Manoeuvres had played a sell-out show at the Edinburgh Odeon, with the takings second to Wings for the year. McCluskey, Paul Humphreys, Malcolm Holmes, Martin Cooper (OMD) and Paul Collister (OMD manager, currently on a three-way split with founder members McCluskey and Humphreys) had each received a charming presentation mirror – the sort you see on market-stalls, usually with Travolta or Debbie etched in – to mark their achievement. Pure kitsch.

OMD appreciated that; the tackiness seemed more realistic than the fact they'd sold out a major city hall.

Earlier in the afternoon McCluskey and I had sat at the back of the Odeon's empty rows, and slowly looked around at its mock ornate grandeur.

'Y'know, I used to come to halls like this when I was young,' McCluskey sighed in wonder, 'and see people on a stage like that, and I used to think they were famous!'

McCluskey's pleasant openness, combined with the newness of what's happening, can make him seem fey and prosaic. He is a very puzzled 21-year-old.

'It doesn't sink in,' he tells me as we order one more nightcap in the Edinburgh hotel bar, 'that I'm playing venues like that.'

McCluskey and I are last up in the bar to discuss the importance of OMD being earnest.

I'd spent two days with OMD, getting to know their idiosyncrasies, sensing the walls closing in, appreciating their complete confusion at their raving new success. I'd got to know things like when McCluskey laughs he clasps his usually gloved hands together and brings them up under his chin, a representation of an odd humility. I'd also realised that he likes talking. He talks plenty trying to sort things out. Right now, he's remembering . . . the A-Level schoolboy who wanted to be an archaeologist, then wanted to be an artist, and ended up if not a 'musician' then someone trapped in all the trappings.

'We started because Paul and I had been writing songs out of our own personal interest. We'd been doing it for two years and we'd never heard them on stage played how we wanted them to be. That's the only reason we got up at Eric's and did it. Everything since there has just been a bonus really.

'That's what is the hardest part. We never intended to make money. We never thought we could. I know it sounds a cliché, but we just seemed like the ultimate no-hopers, we had a stupid name – the first time I ever rang up *Sounds* to get us in the gig guide they said, "You'll never get anywhere with a name like that, sunshine."

'We had everything stacked against us. There we were, two guys with a tape recorder and a stupid name playing songs that apparently no one seemed interested in – there was no way we could try and pretend to be rock 'n' roll stars . . . and now we find ourselves in that position . . . in this country at least.

'It hasn't done me any good. I was confused enough a person anyway.'

## II

It could be premature to call OMD pop stars, yet they have reached a level none of their post-punk contemporaries have. They have not just had a run of medium hit singles, and an album in the charts for a month; their first LP lingered in the charts for six months. Their second LP *Organisation* seems to be embedding itself in the Abba/Police/Streisand heavens. What started off almost as an experiment is reaching a complex and traditional state.

Their audience is, surprisingly, teen orientated and predominantly female. Their following isn't yet Oldfield/Genesis rejects.

At Glasgow they were forced back for a handful of encores; were moved to tears; spent 90 minutes after the show signing autographs.

At Edinburgh the response wasn't as wild, but it was still loud and long enough to challenge McCluskey's experience and capability as front man. Again there was another 90 minutes signing autographs for lines of under-eighteens. The group went through the showbiz procedures in a state of shock, but seemingly in total control, even if McCluskey feels he is not.

'I've got a whole paranoia about rock 'n' roll. Like in Glasgow when we got all those encores, I hate going off saying that, "You've been really great." But there's nothing else to say.'

Their show is unexpectedly spectacular, even disturbingly grand. It commands. It's as if OMD have owned up that to break through they have to look as if they mean . . . something.

A large back-up team and tons of technology are required to set this show in motion. 40-foot articulated lorries have become dubious symbols of their new status. Yet these symbols are necessary if there is to be decent competition for Abba, Wings etc. But when they left Tony Wilson's Factory Records, a year ago, joined Carol Wilson's new hopeful DinDisc label and toured with Gary Numan they were a clumsy two-piece who all but disappeared onstage.

Now, they are a four-piece – as permanent as that can ever be. Both keyboardist Martin Cooper and drummer Malcolm Holmes used to guest with the group – and they both played on the first LP.

Plucked from a two year non-drumming, beefburger-cooking commitment by his old friends, Holmes is baffled that he just has to turn up at the gig now and his kit is already set up. He only has to 'bash away'. Simple.

From group and equipment travelling in a transit to a mighty circus within months. It's close to the syndrome McCluskey loathes.

Can he defend the glaring rock 'n' roll aspects of the new show?

'I don't know really. There are real clichés conjured up that I don't like to be associated with us . . . I like to think we think! And those big, big lights are old and it's a sign to me that this band hasn't thought about their lights.

'But there's only so much effort that you can put into one tour. We flogged ourselves before this one teaching Martin to play the songs. We involve ourselves with all sides of a tour, so we say there are things wrong with this tour, but actually to put your finger out to do something about them it seems like climbing a mountain. We seem to have done so many things.

'Some of the objects of the trade do seem to be rock 'n' roll clichés, but you have to realise that it's the only way to do it. Our attitudes have changed.'

### III

For a group with minimum obvious visual sparkle, who not long ago looked so drab, their impact now is fantastic.

This new super-enticing, theatrical OMD, its intoxicating blend of richness and economy, harsh light and shadow, the sharp creases in the boys' trousers, the narrow ties, the astro turf, the layout of the stage . . . it all comes from the ideas of Peter Saville.

Saville is a Factory director and salaried DinDisc designer. His work is clear and cool, not afraid of going over the top, or round strange corners, and is supremely anti-vulgarity. Already he is being widely imitated; but his self-consciousness is inimitable, his precision incomparable.

I ask Paul Humphreys whether Saville's ideas have been a major contribution to OMD.

'Oh definitely. When we first met him we looked awful, we dressed really badly, looked scruffy and dirty. He said to us, "Well, listen, you're getting on now, you can't keep up that really scruffy image. If you don't want to do anything really outrageous, at least look smart and tidy." Which is what we did. He didn't really tell us what clothes to wear, we just wore what we felt comfortable in.'

It's Saville's contributions that lessen the rock 'n' roll effects of the OMD show: props that seek to enhance, not dominate. The flashing, blushing light show and its gaudy reds, blues and greens are nothing to do with Saville or OMD – but another era.

OMD have released two LPs this year. The first was definite and dandy electro-pop, a group who loved Kraftwerk and whisked that love into something almost burlesque. OMD were disciplining themselves, out of a vague duty, to compose electronic music using coy pop mannerisms. It is a great singles LP.

This LP, the anthemic properties of 'Electricity', and the tour with Numan instigated an electro-phobia within the group. They didn't want to be tagged and trapped.

Their second LP *Organisation*, released months later (a group discipline), is more mood than melody. The production is smooth and precise next to the first's rawness, and after that first LP's unabashed pop, flirts with MOR. Saville packaged it in silver grey, with a sombre highland landscape on the front cover, and a small picture of Humphreys and McCluskey all sad and shadowy on the back cover. An attempt at seriousness.

Within a year, OMD had glided from one extreme to another – and were uncomfortable with both.

McCluskey tells me that in the early summer he spent a lot of time driving around with Saville, who was constantly playing a cassette of *Closer*. This heavily influenced McCluskey's feelings for the second LP. He says he regrets that with *Organisation* OMD have lost some of the 'naïve brashness' of the first, is unsure about the smoothness of the sound. Yet the *Closer* influence is noticeable. There are atmospheres that correspond – a smoothness may have been necessary.

'Yes, it was. I like variety. I like too much variety for my own good. The thing about Joy Division, it began right from the time we started to play with them, years ago. I'd liked the music, and once I'd started to hear it recorded, it had such an effect on me. I really began to think, well, this is what music is all about. And that's when we started to move away from Kraftwerk and disregard the synthesiser image, and get much more emotion into our music. We try to emphasise that on this album.

'Plus we were pretty pissed off this summer, and I think that's come out. You can't write happy songs when you're not feeling too chuffed.

'I think Joy Division will be remembered longer than we will be remembered. That scares me to death. Whilst I like playing pop music, when it's all over and done with I would like to be remembered for something that has artistic shape to it, that changes the course of western civilisation or whatever

– which Joy Division will be remembered for. They will leave their mark.'

Are you disappointed with *Organisation* because you feel you've failed to achieve that artistic shape?

'We tried to . . . no we were not trying to be epic and artistic. There's only so much you can try; once you start to write a song, it just comes out naturally. You can manipulate those pieces, but where you get those pieces from . . . it's a combination of thinking them up, selecting them. It's a big part of your personality. We couldn't hope to emulate Joy Division.'

(This kind of honesty has their record company slightly alarmed. 'We get criticised for being honest, in terms of record company and management. Whilst it is refreshing for journalists to have reasonable conversations with people who are not just trying to sell their product, it's the thing of undermining people's confidence in you. Well, the band don't like the record, why should I?')

## IV

The OMD show starts slowly, and moves slowly until the end: mercilessly leaving the hits until the end. 'Electricity' (McCluskey cannot conceal his feelings for this gem – 'I think it's a pop classic'), 'Red Frame White Light', 'Enola Gay' and then the inevitably excruciating encore 'Waiting for the Man'.

The show is still artful and powerful, full of far more subtlety than average pop shows, but doing 'Red Frame' – a song Humphreys and McCluskey openly despise – is a cop out.

'Yes, it's very much a sweetie. It's guaranteed to make 70 per cent of the audience party. It's one of the few songs we do though that is there for that reason . . . really . . . apart from "Waiting for the Man".'

I'm shocked they still drag that one out.

'Yeah, I don't want to do that anymore.'

How can you put commitment into such songs?

'Because you have to keep the audience going. Or maybe you don't.

'It's a good question. Maybe we're fooling ourselves. They're in there because they're fast numbers and we were worried that the set was short of fast tempo numbers. They're a cheat in a way. We shouldn't be doing them.'

So you're seduced by aspects of the fame?

'We are. We play "Red Frame" and "Man", it's part of the game . . .'

Could you be seduced into repeating a formula simply to maintain success? Everyone says no and then goes and does it.

'It could happen. But our one saving grace is that every time we try and repeat a formula it fails abysmally. Our best songs are always when we don't give a shit.'

The show is a gorgeous first move towards the compromise OMD want to make between pop, MOR and avant-garde. It needs to be more dissonant, harsher and harder. OMD are more aware of that than anyone. For many, the show is probably revolutionary in that it is guitarless. That is one of its pleasing parts.

After the success of the Glasgow performance, McCluskey sits proudly in the dressing room and catches my eye. 'I wish Tony Wilson had been here tonight to see that.'

He desperately wants to impress Wilson.

In Edinburgh I ask him if he considers OMD to be a Factory band.

'Yes. I really do. I'm sure people like A Certain Ratio would loathe us to be considered a Factory band. Tony told us that we were going to make hit singles – we didn't believe him. It always seemed we were on Factory to move away from Factory, and I think everyone realised that. We did feel the black sheep of the Factory family at the time. We needed a DinDisc to push us, Factory couldn't do that. All those things you need to sell singles, we need that. If you don't get on radio stations, it's very hard.'

Being on Factory meant that OMD were never effectively a Liverpool band.

'Yeah, we were glad we were in Manchester . . . the Zoo thing . . . Zoo turned us down. We sent "Electricity" and "Almost" and they turned us down. We would have been very Liverpool then. I'm glad they turned us down.'

## V

OMD seemed destined to be one of those groups who sell enough LPs to the same people to make the top 30 for one week – and that's it; a cult response for a shady, shadowy, white European dance music. Simple Minds, Human League, Magazine; all these groups should have broken through, but are perhaps now doomed forever to pale half-anonymity. Without even trying OMD have surged through into the mainstream.

That's something to cheer. Their two LPs are the two most exciting in the charts this year.

Does McCluskey now feel that people are looking towards OMD in the same way they always do to 'experimental' pop groups: to mock the showbiz company that they've inadvertently joined?

'Eyes focussed upon us! I don't feel that onus at all. I don't think people have been interested in us. The large proportion who are the interested elite don't give a shit about Orchestral Manoeuvres; they think we're like electric Mike Oldfields.

'So it doesn't matter to them. I want to be in the top ten, I want to do it my way, with things that push people . . . I don't want to play a set full of "Electricitys" every night, just because I know that's what's wanted.'

McCluskey tells me that the development from small clubs and transits to city halls and 40-foot lorries seems very natural. Their manager Paul Collister said that if their LP went straight into the chart at number one, and the concerts sold out within two days, then he'd accept that OMD had broken through.

McCluskey: 'The novelty only lasts three minutes with us, then we have to go and do something else.

'We're also perennially depressed about things; that's reflected in *Organisation*, the witticism's dropped out, there's much more depression, because I think we now realise we're beginning to play the game. The first album wasn't, we had nothing to prove. Now we have people like you coming along and telling us we're successful, and that makes it a bit harder. We don't consider ourselves successful.

'I can't really get off on our major gigs and the over-the-top reaction because I remember when I was a kid I used to go over the top on people who I can't remember now . . . I don't like the idea of fading away.'

The rest of the group don't share McCluskey's caution towards the next few months, his feel for the pressure of following 'Enola Gay'.

Holmes is fully aware that he came from nowhere and is quite willing to go back there again.

'I would be prepared to drop back into obscurity again,' Humphreys also says. 'I don't know about Andy. I might get married and settle down in a few years.' (The plain man OMD image – stretching un-rock 'n' roll to its limits.)

McCluskey had told me that if the second LP had failed, he would have quit.

'Yeah. When we recorded this album we were beginning to be aware that we were playing the game, and that if we failed then there was no point in carrying on – or in carrying on in that format. We would have had to go back to the garage. We would have decided that people didn't want our music, that we weren't going to be a pop group, that we should stop doing *TOTP*. It's not that now we're successful it's "I'm alright Jack, we don't care anymore, we've got money in the bank." I would give up being a pop star, I would give up going on *TOTP*, and I would return to Factory, I would quit the routine . . .

'I say that now, that I wouldn't hang on, but maybe I'll be conned into thinking maybe the next one will be a hit. I strike myself as being a prime candidate for a scared old man rock 'n' roller. I strike myself as being an archetype Steve Harley. I hope I avoid that. I dunno . . .'

The tape runs out. We finish our drinks and go to bed. 'I'm more confused than ever now,' says McCluskey.

## VI

Audiences will easily and willingly set up a huge distance between themselves and OMD. That distance is badly unwanted. But the group still employ enigmatic synthesisers. The stage show is performed with a concentration that looks like severely cool reserve. A sense of mystery pervades the group that has nothing to do with what they think – more ordinary than mysterious. Humphreys blames photographs of himself and McCluskey for a lot of this.

'I think the photos we've got are far too posed and mysterious for us . . . you just can't not look posed, because that's what you're doing – posing.'

McCluskey agrees: 'And there's nothing more contrived than trying to look uncontrived in a photo.'

During the show the four formal un-heroes look nearly intimidating. As 'Stanlow' slumbers into place, a heavy hanging taped drone, picking up its melody and atmosphere, Humphreys, Cooper and Holmes stare passively out over their instruments into the audience, perfectly composed and content looking. McCluskey has his back turned to the audience, ready to casually spin round and sing the vocal.

What are they thinking, these fearless hearts, as 3,000 expectant eyes train on them? At Glasgow, McCluskey spins round and almost reels at the sight of the massive auditorium. His eyes show his nerves. He admits that during some of his performance he can feel embarrassed more than intimidated. Humphreys and Cooper are praying during the taped intro; as they stand with folded elbows above their consoles, they won't know until it's too late that all the leads are connected, that everything is going to work.

Dry ice seeps out into the front rows. The music swells profoundly. There's a tongue in a cheek somewhere, but it's not easy to spot where. Holmes sits morosely behind his kit, looking ultra-smart in short-sleeved white cotton shirt and thin tie, seemingly unaffected by anything.

What is he thinking as he sits in open view for minutes, doing nothing, before he starts to drum? As the dry ice swirls under his riser, the lights collide all around him, the music rises and rises . . .

'I feel like a right prick, like, y'know . . .'

And the crowd roars!

## XXXIX

**Article on Cabaret Voltaire –** *New Musical Express***, 29 November 1980.**

Catch a train into the dark depths of the North again. Flee the wonderland. A million miles away from London town, the conditioning centre where all is lost, into the hills and the drizzle and the places where 'rock 'n' roll' doesn't have quite such a death grip.

I am on a journey to demystify and mythologise: to dispel the tedious untruths that clog up Cabaret Voltaire, that turn them into ugly monsters, and replace them with the plain truths, and turn them into sleek heroes.

As the train rolls into ghostly Sheffield, a profound greyness descends. Grey – the colour of the City, the colour of depression. Imagine a musical soundtrack for a November Sheffield, for a decaying symbol of crumbling capitalism, for the lonely hearts and lost hopes of the city dwellers, for reason . . . imagine the turbulent, tense, obsessive Cabaret Voltaire sound. An integration and aggregation of stern rhythm, rigid sound, unexpected noises, ghostly bumps, newsreels, snatches of conversation, screams, wails, unspecified signals . . . a sound of our times. The sound for our times.

The room is cluttered up with audio and video tape equipment, papers, chairs, electric fires, the three Cabaret Voltaire men and the interviewer. Posters and bits of paper cover up the bare walls. Everyone's smiling! We're talking about the stereotype that dictates a group such as Cabaret Voltaire are all groan, grim and despair . . . 'Maybe it's just the way we are. Maybe we're really grim people.'

They're not. They can be serious now and then . . . 'Maybe we have that image because we're not an over-escapist band.' They laugh at the thought of people imagining them to be dour and difficult. 'I feel so grim!' one of them bursts out in mock horror. 'Well, just look out there.' He points out of the solitary window at a small square of Sheffield. Doomy, heavy clouds ganging up, a fine sheet of drizzle, jagged corners of derelict buildings. 'If you lived here you'd be grim.' As grim as Amos Brearley.

Sheffield is grey: a grey place full of greyness, frayed but friendly. Cabaret

Voltaire make a grey music. But it's not just grey. It's also red – the colour of anger. It's black and blue and purple. It's elating and disturbing. It's one hell of a response. It's not rock 'n' roll the way the London leeches still want rock 'n' roll to be: light, frothy, frisky, bland, controllable. It reinterprets past pop to fit the times and contemporary predicament. It doesn't wish to cover up flaws, it rips away the covers. It's close to being the most natural culmination in rock, a progression from Chuck Berry accounting for the rock musics that have emerged since James Brown, Velvet Underground, Sex Pistols, Faust, Can, Joy Division. It's an active pop music that hugs experience and isn't stuck in fantasy or the past or an idealised present or a make-believe future or the middle of nowhere.

The definition of rock 'n' roll has not changed with the times. Rock 'n' roll shouldn't describe a sound, but an attitude, a feeling. 'Rock 'n' roll is not about regurgitating Chuck Berry riffs, rock 'n' roll is breaking traditions, attacking the establishment, and we're more in that vein than most groups who consider themselves to be rock.'

Cabaret Voltaire make a desperate music. It's a music of gestures, shock, a constant enquiry into the nature of things. Cabaret Voltaire is eighties pop music like the Velvets were late sixties pop music. They churn up the emotions like the Stones must have in those sixties years, they blast aside surrounding mediocrity and banality like the Sex Pistols did. They don't reject the attraction and attractiveness of rock and pop, don't want to drown in the coarse new underground. They have to avoid manipulating and being manipulated.

Cabaret Voltaire are probably Malcolm McLaren's depressing, soppy frowns in heavy great coats, yet in a perverse way they're both on the same side. Both want to cut up the establishment, mock and disrupt. Cabaret Voltaire want to bring a freshness, excitement and spontaneity back to live shows, and they refuse to exploit fashionable grimness. 'We don't play that up at all, like some bands . . . We're just here. What did McLaren say? The war poet look! That was quite funny. In a way we are going about the same sort of thing, but in different ways. With us it boils down to being more realistic.'

They also painstakingly stay clear of any hype. They don't boast about being modern thinkers, playing the most outrageously modern music. They just get on with it. It's not that teenagers couldn't relate to Cabaret Voltaire;

simply that Cabaret Voltaire aren't allowed through the dense blanket of propaganda. These days, music like theirs is denied its natural audience. Too many idiots with old-fashioned, stubborn, over-smiley ideas stand in the way, running music papers, the record companies, the TV and radio stations. In a way, Cabaret Voltaire scare the controllers by refusing to negotiate the expected curves and corridors of the pop fantasy, by advancing, alarming, even by working so independently.

Cabaret Voltaire are entertainers and wouldn't mock the word. But they also confront, decipher, dissect the problems of their times. They want their music to be something special, but not unapproachable or inaccessible. They think it more indulgent to borrow blandly from the past and sing about your girlfriend than to violently cut up the past and sing of boredom, chance, despair, violence, isolation. Their music captures the confusion of a generation. It stimulates and generates like all great music and is concerned with more things than just being a one-dimensional means to a career-success end.

Cabaret Voltaire's music is grey. But it's not just grey. It's as important to its time as Joy Division's. No words, no radio DJs, no hyped up pseudo-moderns, should be allowed to get in its way.

The room is one part of Cabaret Voltaire's Western Works recording studio. The interview has just begun, and we're talking about the working situation and environment of the group.

Watson: 'We had a strange conversation with our accountant yesterday. He was talking to us about the possibility of the group forming a limited company, and saying you need to be earning about £50,000 a year gross to actually justify it for tax reasons, but he was sure that in the next twelve months something big was going to happen. It was quite difficult to explain to him that we weren't anticipating that, that that wasn't what we were trying to do. Because he thought, as we were a rock group . . . well obviously one record was going to do it, and then we were going to be in business moneywise. We had to explain that it was more a steady progression than an explosion and TV adverts and world tours . . .'

Kirk: 'You get your fifteen minutes and then everybody forgets.'

Mallinder: 'That's intrinsic in what we've done, that the idea of being an overnight success is totally opposite to what we want. We've never had a masterplan, never really known what we would be doing in the next twelve months. The whole thing is that we've been able to bring records out and communicate something, that is quite an end in itself. It's not part of a plan. I don't know that we've got any idea what we're going to do in the next six months. I don't want to know really.'

★

Cabaret Voltaire are at the station to meet the writer and photographer. It's the first *NME* piece on the group for two and a half years, but it's not that they won't talk. 'A lot of the things we do tend to get glossed over. We'll talk to anyone. We do loads of interviews with fanzines.'

Christopher R. Watson (electronics, tapes) Richard H. Kirk (guitar, wind instruments), Stephen 'Mal' Mallinder (bass, electronic percussion, lead vocals) are receptive, informative, even talkative, and have no pretence that to speak freely will destroy some vague mystery about their music. 'We never go overboard to sell ourselves, though.' They are impressively down to earth about what they do: see it as part of something, not 'the' something. I ask them if they think their music is important.

'First and foremost it's important to me,' answers Watson. 'It's important to my life and, if you like, that's enough. It is important to me, so I'm the person who's got to answer for it. It's something that I truly believe in, if that's not such a gross statement to make.'

'I think it's important to me,' decides Kirk, 'to be creative in one way or another. If I couldn't release my emotions in a creative way I'd probably go and kill someone or something. Everybody's got something to let out.'

Watson: 'In some ways it's like animal urges. You've got to get it out. It's fortunate for me that I've found two people to work with who have similar feelings. That's it. I don't think it needs any more justification than that . . . if you can go and make records and sell them and earn money then that's even better.'

'But it's not simply a case of making records and making money,' adds Mallinder, 'there's also the thing that people do relate to us, because I think that the feelings in Cabaret Voltaire are within a lot of people.'

The group are not scruffy. They dress well, care about their appearance. Watson and Kirk have disconcertingly pronounced Yorkshire accents. The three are close friends. Because of media ignorance, it often appears that the group is inactive. Out of choice, they don't often tour. They like every show they perform to be different, and see no point in disappearing into a touring routine. But they're just back from a short visit to America, and not long ago toured Europe, reaping the benefits of an audience uncontaminated by media propaganda.

'It may appear that we do little, but we probably work as hard or harder than any other band. We work six days a week, it's just that we put our energies into things that people don't regard as being normal for a group. Whereas most groups fit into a pattern the way they work, we don't strictly fit into that pattern. But we work hard.'

Through Rough Trade's new American operations, Cabaret Voltaire played five shows in San Francisco and Los Angeles. 'It was definitely worthwhile,' they say. 'We played to nearly a thousand in San Francisco, on the same night as Talking Heads, which is pretty good, 'cos we were headlining . . . not so sure about the people who came, it was a case of playing to a thousand bombed-out-of-their head lunatics. But we even made a bit of money.'

For all their independence – because of their independence – the group live well, almost to the point of leisure. Whilst contemporaries are trapped by record company deadlines, managerial limitations and almost have to beg for pocket money, Kirk, Watson and Mallinder have carefully reached a state where they're totally in control and make enough money to more than exist. They limit themselves to £45 a week each, and turn all their royalties back into buying equipment. Their eight-track studio is primitive but eminently functional. They received a £3,000 advance for their last LP *The Voice of America*, and talk of being due £10,000 royalties. This doesn't make them rich, but they owe nothing to anybody. Most groups signed to labels are forever in debt – groups more commercially successful than Cabaret Voltaire.

Voltaire are supreme examples of post-punk enterprise. An original punk group made good. Lack of greed and patience have set them in an enviable position. There is no pandering to an imaginary audience, no hurrying and harrying for success. They have no manager, although Buzzcocks/New Hormones' Richard Boon and Joy Division/Factory's Rob Gretton occasionally help, and Rough Trade coordinate from London. It is a classically un-rock 'n' roll way of working. In many ways they exist on the periphery of New Hormones and Factory (Mal has recently produced the excellent Eric Random New Hormones twelve-inch, and recently they all did some exploratory work with New Order at Western Works) but are embedded in the grubby Rough Trade manor: which has neither the style of Factory nor the (he)art of New Hormones.

Mallinder: 'I think one thing we've got in relation to a lot of groups is that we still work on the principle of repetition. It's intrinsic to our music, and a lot of people connect with that. Repetition has got an annoyance factor, but it's also got a hypnotic factor that appeals to people on a gut level. It may not be a traditional form of repetition, but it is repetition . . .'

Kirk: 'I think repetition is used in all music anyway, western or eastern, it's a key factor, no matter what.'

Do you theorise about your music?

Kirk: 'In odd ways.'

Not like Philip Glass and Steve Reich.

Mallinder: 'No, we try to be very spontaneous, because that's the way people listen to music. We try to be as immediate as possible, and not just try out some all-engrossing philosophy and concept. I think music always falls flat if you conceptualise about it too much.'

Watson: 'I think there's a lot of music where the ideas are more interesting than the end product.'

Mallinder: 'I think we conceptualise after the record has come out. A lot of the things that we've done make a lot more sense after we've done them. Once they're recorded I can maybe look at them in a theoretical light . . .'

Making music that deals with oppression and repression, it's easy for that music to be oppressive and therefore useless.

Mallinder: 'I think we avoid that. We like music that doesn't just shock but also appeals, and I think our music can appeal. I think it's quite easy to get into. There is humour in our music, it's not a joke, but that's part of it. I can't see how something like "Obsession" is grim or a song of impending doom . . .'

Kirk: 'I think we proved that when we played in Europe. A lot of people didn't understand the lyrics but there were a lot of people out there dancing and enjoying it. They're not conditioned to act in a particular way to Cabaret Voltaire.'

Cabaret Voltaire live at the moment is very much 'an experience'.

Mallinder: 'Hopefully it is. We're working towards that. But we've got to be aware of taking it too far and taking away the simplicity. We like to keep it crude and basic, and if it begins to get slick, that's the time to move on. The light show we use, and the slides, I don't think they're particularly grim! I think they're quite funny really . . .'

I had great difficulty explaining to non-believers how much your last London show was dance music, and about the kids dancing on the stage at the end . . .

Kirk: 'Actually I was surprised by that!'

Mallinder: 'The fact people won't believe what we're like live sums it up . . . people won't find out for themselves.'

Are people scared of Cabaret Voltaire?

Kirk: 'I hope so! I hope they respect us, not so much scared . . .'

Not intimidated, but frightened of the themes and intensity of Voltaire attack.

Mallinder: 'I think yes, because that's something they've got to get to terms with. Not so much with us, but with things that they shy away from in everyday life. And if they shy away from us, they're shying away from those things. Our music particularly antagonises them in that way, because they're totally conditioned into believing music is just entertainment, music is just fun . . . That's it, you use the term "grim", but the thing is, grim is an emotion, and I think if you take it to that very basic level, our music is emotional.'

You've never felt a need to move towards an audience?

Mallinder: 'I think it's a two-way thing. I don't think we would ever go to an audience to the extent of pandering to them, to give an audience what it expects of us. But I think it's a natural progression: you move in a way that communicates a lot more and, through time, the audience you're trying to reach has gradually become more open. The audience gradually move towards you and you move towards an audience.'

Watson: 'It would be very nice for us to have a record in the top ten, but we can't actually play! We're not very competent musicians.'

Mallinder: 'Maybe that's what Cabaret Voltaire is all about . . . three people who've spent seven years trying to play and still can't do it. Maybe that's where our appeal lies. But I'd love a top ten hit!'

Kirk: 'As long as it was on our own terms. As long as we didn't put out this really slick single, really well packaged, just for the sake of it – we just couldn't go through with that.'

Watson: 'We've always been interested in the facetious side of contradictions, and it would be quite funny if we had a hit single. It would be bloody funny! Cabaret Voltaire in the charts, taking it back to what Cabaret Voltaire were originally, that would be hilarious.'

Cabaret Voltaire have worked together since 1973. 'We had no intentions of playing live when we got together. We simply got together in an intense but elusive way and made tapes in a little loft, listened to them ourselves, and literally just experimented with ideas.'

Their first live performance was on May 13th, 1975.

Watson: 'We conned our way on to the bill. It was an organisation called Science For The People who had a disco every week at Sheffield University, and they were looking for something to liven it up, and I happened to be working with one of the organisers, and he said, "Hey you're in a group, can you play rock music?" So I said, "Yeah, sure, anything you like," and he said, "Great, we'll get you on halfway through the disco." We were advertised as rock and electronic music. It's hard to give you an idea of what was going on. We had like a tape loop of a recording of a steamhammer as percussion, and Richard was playing clarinet with a rubberised jacket on it covered with flashing fairylights, and it just ended with the audience invading the stage and beating us up.'

Kirk: 'A lot of people who came were our friends, but a lot of people got really pissed off and it got really violent. We were lucky lots of people we knew were there, otherwise we would have been dead.'

Watson: 'Mal fell off the stage and broke a bone in his back, the equipment was smashed . . . Richard was using his clarinet as a club.'

Mallinder: 'That was the only thing that stopped it, Richard flinging his guitar into the audience.'

Watson: 'I think to be fair that did actually incite a lot of people, Richard throwing his guitar into the audience. I don't think that helped calm people down. The organisers came on stage, nearly in tears, shouting, "For fuck's sake get off the stage, you've ruined our reputation, we're totally discredited." They weren't allowed to use the university for any purpose again.'

Punk's arrival briefly opened things up for the group. General expectations of what a group should be were momentarily broken up. Punk actually left certain areas where a self-consciously experimental group like Cabaret Voltaire could work. It became easier for Cabaret Voltaire to play live. More people became involved in putting on shows that audaciously opposed the old traditions of rock.

'Which is why we conned our way into things. When we played at that time people expected us to be the Sheffield Sex Pistols. The thing is that basically we tried to do the same thing as punk originally in that we did specifically go out to upset people, and to provoke reactions, although our intentions were different from punk. But that climate enabled us to work live more, and eventually to make a record.'

Before their first record, they recorded an extremely limited edition of cassettes – twenty to 30 – sending them to every record label in the country. 'We got rejection slips from every one.' Cassettes sent to more aware and interested individuals did stir the first, perhaps most positive, Voltaire publicity. Jon Savage, then at *Sounds*, responded loudly in the paper to the group's aggressive, ambitious collage technique. At the time it proved the power of the cassette communication. 'Although that's been bastardised, just like the synthesiser has.'

Do they consider themselves an important symbol of the possibilities of using electronic equipment distinctively and productively, and of being non-musicians making coherent statements through sound?

'I hope so. We seem to inspire people to go out and do things for themselves. We get a lot of tapes from people, some are appalling, some are good. Geoff Travis at Rough Trade says that each week they get tapes of ten or twelve Falls, and ten or twelve Cabaret Voltaires. That'll never work though, because whatever it is we do, good or bad, it is Cabaret Voltaire, and that can never be equalled.'

After a first single on Rough Trade, they played one of the four opening shows at Manchester's the Factory. The Peter Saville-designed black and white poster for their October 28th 1978 performance with Joy Division and the Tiller Boys (Eric Random and, on that day, Peter Shelley) is Fac 1. From this they appeared on Fac 2 – *The Factory Sampler* – with two flawed, fluid pieces, 'Baader-Meinhof' and 'Sex in Secret'.

'It would have been nice in some ways to have stayed with Factory. We didn't know what we were going to do at that time. We wanted to do an album though and Rough Trade asked us. It's quite popular to knock Rough Trade at the moment, but basically I don't think we'd be better off with anybody else. The people within the organisation are certainly okay, and we're able to do things with other people – we're doing a single for Benelux in Belgium, and a tape for Industrial.'

Cabaret Voltaire make their music unlike anyone else. They don't fuss over it. They layer and construct, striving to re-capture a primitive language that cuts through to the heart of matters. They tell stories that have no middle, no end and odd beginnings. The moving and discomforting *The Voice of America* proved that Cabaret Voltaire are much more than elitist doodlers. They are saying something to us. Something that is different and deranged.

It doesn't fit in for most people. It's the way they're brought up. It's who brings them up. Cabaret Voltaire are out to clarify, not confuse. The Voltaire process is like keeping a diary. Their records are thoughts, essays, jottings, expressions of feeling, transmissions of understanding. It's product and it's not product.

*The Voice of America* is a challenging, struggling, fascinating development upon the musics of the Velvet Underground and Faust, a radical hybrid of pop economy and avant-garde freedom. Cabaret Voltaire have matured their sound so that it is one of the most unsettling and effective distortions of pop music: that is parody and paean, violent and vivid.

Kirk: 'I should hope we reflect what's going on around us. In a way we're like journalists, we're taking things in and reporting in different ways . . . this is going on, what are you going to do about it?'

Mallinder: 'I don't think we shun away from anything. We don't shun away from politics, from sex, from anything, but we don't try and put our views forward in an overbearing way. We comment, let people make their own minds up, and I think that is more realistic than most things.'

What themes are there running through *The Voice of America*?

Kirk: 'Oppression, control, the general state of what's happening in a lot of western countries. It's always been happening, it's happening in Britain right now, especially under this government.'

Watson: 'I think the main theme running through *America* is control used as a weapon, and, if you like, it's a question of bringing thoughts like that into people's minds. The idea that you are under so much control, that is ignored to a large extent.'

You think it's important that you make these comments, drop these hints?

Watson: 'I think it's part of our job actually, going back to that rock 'n' roll thing. We've got the facilities through this recording studio, and we've got the access to distribution . . .'

Mallinder: 'People seem to think that music that contains the themes we're dealing with is self-indulgent, but I think it's far more indulgent to sing about your girlfriends . . .'

You readily associate yourselves with 'rock' – some would imagine that you would want to associate with the 'avant-garde'.

Kirk: 'When we started we had a load of tape recorders and we could have gone two ways. We would have gone the Philip Glass way, like you say, the intellectual theorising way, but we chose to buy electric guitars as well.'

Mallinder: 'If we had tried to go the Glass/Stockhausen way, that would have been really pretentious. The thing is, we've grown up on Tamla, ska, James Brown, pop music, you name it, and really all that is the basis of what we do even though we try and break it up a lot. It's just that we don't want to listen to that music and regurgitate it straightforwardly.'

Watson: 'That's not to say that people like John Cage and Maurice Kagel haven't had interesting ideas, but it's the ideas that are interesting, not the music.'

But you wouldn't admit to any intellectualisation?

Kirk: 'Well, yes and no. There are certain levels . . . I wouldn't like people to think all we do is sit around and theorise, because that's not true.'

Mallinder: 'You learn all the time and you educate yourself. Any avant-garde music we've picked up on is a secondary thing, and we realised the parallels between them and us, but it hasn't been a conscious decision where our music is supposed to parallel that. We've only realised it in retrospect, and in retrospect we've come to appreciate people like Cage.'

And that appreciation has enabled you to break up pop noise in interesting ways?

Mallinder: 'You realise that music isn't simply making noises on guitars and drums and whatever. It's a reflection of a hell of a lot of your environment, social conditions, economic structures, and although I don't think we put too much of an emphasis on that in our music, you realise how much music is a reflection of the times you live in. You can't take the music away as a little entity, a little satellite, it relates very much to politics, to social strata, and everything. You can say music's wonderful, but it's not "just" wonderful. It relates to everything that's happening. I think our music appeals on different levels and in different circumstances. I don't think music should solely satisfy one feeling, one emotion, I don't think you can listen to it and react in a certain, set way. There should be a whole cross section of people who can listen to it.'

Catch a train back to the wonderland. Cabaret Voltaire's industry seems a million miles away. They get on with their job. 'When you consider how much money is ploughed into the industry, and how much is spent conditioning people if you like, then there's no way that we're going to alter that ourselves. I think you've got to accept that. Maybe we've lost. There's no way we're going to break all that, but at least we feel we've knocked a dent into it. I think we've helped. It's not just our responsibility though. It's up to everybody who's interested.'

A room with a disturbing view. This is entertainment, this is fun. It's a show business. It's a little bit more. A sound for our times. The sound of our times. I want to hear it more than just about anything else. Where does it fit in?

Anywhere . . . Celebration and damnation, determination and reconciliation. Dance in the new fashioned way.

This is my Cabaret Voltaire. It should be yours. Their music is great. But it's not just great.

## XL

I wrote about Joy Division in different ways during the 1980s, none of them especially part of my everyday life. I didn't think of them as being a major factor in what I was doing throughout the 1980s, but in truth, even though I never acknowledged it, they were never far away from my thoughts.

I wrote very little about pop music for over a decade. Most of what I did write tended to be about Joy Division. One way and another they were coming back to life again after death. They were not fading away. In some ways they hadn't yet happened.

By the mid-1980s I had stopped writing about pop music full-time, having become part of the Zang Tuum Tumb record label. I had been hired by the record producer Trevor Horn, after his work with ABC and Malcolm McLaren. Horn, surprisingly twisting out of the pop middle of the road, had created the extreme, supreme entertainment soundtracks for the way ABC had dreamt themselves up as a surreal Sheffield Motown act and the way McLaren had discovered on his pioneering travels a distant primitive hip hop world that would one day be less distant and less rudimentary. At the end of 1982, when Trevor approached me, this classically eccentric English pop mind, after novelty hits with Buggles and a startling period as a member of Yes, was at the centre of the British pop universe.

Horn's exact words to me when he called asking if I wanted to be involved were: 'Would you like to invent a record label?' These were totally the right words. If he had asked me to do some A and R, which to some extent I ended up doing, I would have immediately declined. A and R seemed to me like it would mean working in an office and making decisions about how to delay making decisions.

I still wanted to dream, in fact to still write, even if that meant writing notes and lists that I would give to Horn as he worked on various records for the label. I would stop working as a rock writer, but commit myself to a different kind of writing – one that literally forced new narratives into position, that wrote pop history into place not from the outside but from the inside.

I wanted to work with Horn the way ABC and McLaren had, supplying manifestos, schemes, proposals, methods, codes and miscellaneous cultural guesswork for Horn to react to with an original musical soundtrack. I imagined making up potential stories and scandals that Horn could turn into pop music.

My contribution to the label – concepts, publicity, marketing, theories, energy, designs, various amounts of ranting and raving, cataloguing, myth making – was directly inspired by everything I had learned watching how Factory Records operated. (And, it must be noted, other resourceful cult labels distinctively designed with personality and adventure in mind such as Fast, Mute, Fetish, Ze and Postcard.) I wanted to do what Factory had done – not respond, as I had been doing as a writer, after the event, after the fact, but help generate the events and facts. Factory had shown that a record label could be a shifting, dazzling combination of poetry, theatre, art, design, politics and philosophy, that a commercial enterprise need not be mundane and predictable.

For a month or two, or a year or two, Zang Tuum Tumb somehow worked as an excessive and absurd testimonial to the unruly ideals of Factory. Horn struggled to invent whole new realities through the manifestation of new drum sounds. He existed in, for, because of the recording studio, with access to the most advanced technological equipment available in the world at that time, and the most skilful technicians. For a while during 1983 and 1984 he fused together sounds with song in a way that took the rest of the world decades to catch up with. (Up north, Martin Hannett was stunned that Factory had decided to invest their money in a nightclub, like Peter Stringfellow or something, and not in the kind of advanced studio equipment that Horn was flying through space with. Hannett was convinced given the right machinery that he could fly further and faster and at the same time slower than Horn.)

While Horn fussed around trying to make electronic music sound like it had not been made using computers, or make acoustic music sound as though it had, I was bringing to Zang Tuum Tumb all the abstract analytical zeal I had expressed at the *NME* about how pop music should be better, stranger, purer, smarter and more beautiful. I transformed my speculative, furious editorials about post-punk purpose into elaborate record sleeves and music advertisements that told stories about their own existence and quoted entire literary and philosophical histories. I tried to make a full-page advertisement in a music paper for a ZTT record seem as provocative and entertaining as I had tried to make one of my articles. I paid as much attention to the label on a seven-inch single, inspired by Factory, as I did to one of my concert reviews.

The combination of my worked-up freelance post-punk attitude and Horn's fanatical commitment to having hits with brand new sounds – the binding together of two neurotic forces in love with pop, aiming for the same result from different directions – led to 1984 being very much in my head, and to an extent for the rest of the pop world, the year of Frankie Goes To Hollywood. They were our boy band in the way that A Certain Ratio were Factory's boy band – although our boy band was, for better or worse, more successful. Because I was influenced by Factory, our boy band was built not merely to soothe, or aggravate, the flaming nerves of horny teenage fans, but also to leave behind certain irresistible and hopefully discomforting cultural traces.

Two of the singles we released on Zang Tuum Tumb in 1984, 'Relax' and 'Two Tribes', ended up as the biggest selling singles of the 1980s. Not a week went by during 1984 when the label didn't have a single in the top 40. Another group that we manufactured at the label, Art of Noise, the house band, represented more deliriously the crusading spirit of the label as I imagined it, and I had high hopes for Propaganda to rival Depeche Mode as arena-level electro-gothic pop champions.

But we were best known for Frankie Goes To Hollywood, and this quickly made ZTT a more tabloid enterprise than Factory, its post-punk, idealistic foundations, as laid mostly by me, rapidly hidden under a towering skyscraper of scandal, sales figures and ordinary music business hype. By 1985, Zang Tuum Tumb, as the kind of post-Factory record label I had hoped for, had more or less collapsed. It had risen to the conventional top, breaking some long-held chart records of the Beatles in a matter of months, and then crashed to the floor as those who worked for the label fought with the groups they had signed, over rights and money, and with each other, over the direction of the label.

As all this was happening, among many other things that I was thinking, as I acted, with grating, inflating Wilsonian pomp, as though all of the success, if not the failure, might actually have something to do with me and my manifestos, I thought that I would not be writing about pop music again. I hardly wrote about pop during the first successful years of the label, and then for many years after, as I recovered from this unexpected adventure in the heartland of pop culture, and made erratic attempts to rescue the label, or at least the battered parts of it I thought belonged to me, from its ignoble decline.

I wrote about Joy Division if I was asked to, and as soon as I was asked I wanted to write about them. In 1984, just about the only thing I wrote directly about pop music was to contribute to a book that was being compiled about Joy Division, and Warsaw, by someone who, as far as I know, had nothing to do with Factory, or the group. An American called Mark Johnson appeared out of nowhere with the first plan to publish a book about Joy Division.

You can tell from what I wrote that I had other things on my mind. You can tell that I am assuming that Joy Division seemed to have happened a long time ago, and it was not yet time, if it ever would be, to talk about them as though the shattered pieces had been put back together again. It was too early to think back, it was too early to work out what the truth was going to be, it wasn't time to consider something that hadn't yet found its way into history, the kind of history that works its way into the present. The shattered pieces of the group hadn't yet fallen to the floor, where we could pick our way through them, and work out what kind of solution we were going to create out of the puzzle. The shattered pieces were still flying through the air, and from the way I wrote, I couldn't quite make them out.

You should also be able to tell, if I'm not giving too much away, that I was still determined to keep the idea of the group secret, either because I felt, or knew, that it was too early – would it always be too early? – for them to be seriously promoted as rock legends, or because I wanted to keep them to myself, and a few others, where they would not be spoilt by mass sharing and petty communal analysis. I didn't want to obliterate the uncanny by reducing everything to insipid reminiscence and scratchy celebration.

Before Joy Division could cross over, from ancient history to contemporary relevance, or vice versa, I still clearly – or not so clearly – felt that the group needed more coatings of wonder and mystery. I didn't feel inclined to remember dates and details – there were others doing that, and that was guaranteed to ruin the surprise which I was convinced had to be protected – concerned as ever that this made the group seem ordinary, as if what they had been up to was merely a case of chronology, one day followed by another, the everyday singing of songs, and the unexceptional passing of time. I was now talking about the group by not even mentioning their name, by mentioning barely anything about them, by tossing theories about that might accidentally connect with what they had done. I was stripping everything back to nothing, to fiction and make believe, before the truth could be written, trying to postpone until the time was right – like I knew when that would be – to reintroduce Joy Division into the real world. At that point, deep in the centre of the 1980s, I decided that the best way to remember a group that had become another group, and whose singer had killed himself, which made no sense, whose dead body I'd seen, which bordered on the obscene, was with a kind of cavalier formlessness – searching for reason, or a reason, by reflecting the fragmentation of the story with fragments, some of which may be part of the final story once it's all pieced back together again, some of which might be a help in anticipating what that final shape might be.

I was happy to keep them a little less real, a distant memory, a recent catastrophe we didn't talk about too directly, a punishing puzzle, a source of strangeness, a rustle of whispers, a subject for a poem written in the guise of a few essays about a pop group that may or may not have existed and that may or may not have had more meaning than most.

At the beginning of the first essay written for Johnson's book, I mention that I had made a plan with Warsaw to produce their first record. To some extent, there is some truth in this story, although because only about five or six people can vouch for this, one or two who are not with us anymore, there is also, to some extent, very little truth in this story. We'd made the plan, perhaps, a mere seven years before. The group had not yet been pulled out of the past by history, so those seven years seemed a lot longer than they actually were. It's hard to remember the immediate past, unless you invent a lot of it. The distant past can be easier to remember sometimes. The distant past can seem closer the more you leave it behind.

## XLI

**'Pre-Face' – from *An Ideal for Living*, a book of dates and photographs published in 1984.**

I left my memory to play its tricks, rather than fight it. It's only recently that I've been reminded that Warsaw were waiting for me in the Manchester city centre before they drove off to an underground bunker in the mourning Pennine wilder/ness, to record some songs. Today's exaggeration considers that they waited four hours for my baby blue presence, but they probably paused for minutes before hissing open cans and hitting the silver road. I think that they wanted me to produce – a loose term covering four bald sins, I expect – their first recording, seriously called *An Ideal for Living*. Who knows how my life would have been changed if I'd managed to squabble through a hangover out of my bed and keep that Sunday appointment. (How drunk could I have been when I made the promise to them, suggesting I could conjure up the crystalline mystique of Spector, Brod, Eno and Czukay combined? How stoned could Martin Hannett have been when he, at some later date, made the same promise, or one like it, one in his own words, one that was actually a little more . . . true.)

A change in my life? Probably none at all: things were blinking in and blanking out lazily and fast in those '77-heaven days, causing no effect that would stick fast. We were all pale hysterical ghosts of anything we were to become. I would have produced Warsaw, the record would have sounded no different because if the time isn't right the trees don't joke, and it didn't sound like too much, it sounded like a producer was missing, and it would have been as important in my life as a stone in a date, and for Joy Division my association would have settled into social blandness. You see, and I knew this the time we all sprang up in our places at the Free Trade Hall to see Buzzcocks and Sex Pistols, it was all predestined what we were going to get up to. I was the writer. They were the group. It was not written in the stars that I produce them, that they be produced by me. Even if I'd started out as a Stiff Kitten I would still have threaded my way into the position as top pop writer of the post-modernist times: and nothing except a real fine joke would have stopped Joy Division alighting on that empty space which stretches between person and person, between ignorance and knowledge, between one hand and another, and shocking those who were awake with what it was they did.

What it was they did . . . all those creeping inside here hoping to embrace the essence, the essential sinful pleasure, of what it was they did – a minute or a century past *An Ideal for Living* – should fade away: Back Off Boogaloo! as Ringo said, aptly. No *such* luck: not much luck is left. All the luck of the century is greedily snatched at and soaked up by young people like Joy Division, searching for nothing to do so that they might do something. Joy Division were drunk on luck before anything else, Pernod or bitter. Joy Division were lucky, lucky that they turned the damned whore rock language back into a virgin, lucky that out of their common sense blossomed a peculiar beauty, lucky that amidst it all they were quite stupid, lucky if you assume that what they wanted to do was create something rich and better than some fucking decorative abbreviation. And we should thank our lucky stars that they were *so* lucky, if not think about what it was they did every other minute of the day. To look straight at luck, head on into the glare, is to have it disappear, twitch away, like a black spot on the eyeball: it hovers, in vision but out of it, irritating and enthralling, restless and nowhere, here and then. Luck; just *like* Joy Division, in vision but out of it. A *grasp* that can be found even in our artificial and fearful times.

In a way, and I say this a lot to myself as my memory plays its tricks, my connection with Joy Division and their particular halo is that of a minor character in a minor Beatles biography. I tell my story to a dim researcher, I went to school at fourteen with Pete Best, I once almost asked out George Harrison's cousin or, in this case, I talked with Ian in ranches, circuses and factories about gluing our personalities to the world through words and pauses. Nothing much, I wasn't there, but in the end I wasn't far away.

Somehow, reminding us how much the pop writer can be celebrated disproportionately, I gained small time fame as the one who took a torch to this dark Division: shined a light on this . . . un-usual commitment to living. People will approach me at Rainbows and Odeons to say that if it hadn't been for you and what you wrote and how you wrote it . . . I blush, I might even boast, because I don't tell good jokes. My small talk is tiny. But my contribution, it was slight – what else? I was there as it happened. I saw and heard certain things. I stood around as they were photographed in the snow. I mentioned Joy Division often enough for everyone nearby to know of them, and maybe look for themselves. I never said *anything* directly about the group: I did little more than talk about the weather, hoping that readers knew their Oscar Wilde and would be certain that I meant something else.

(This also applies to the best ever interview with a member of Joy Division when I asked their guitarist what he wanted to drink.) I was as quiet as I possibly could be allowing for my former urge to be bouncily awestruck given the flimsiest encouragement, because what I felt about Joy Division is no business of yours. What New Order mean to me is nothing, really, to do with you. What I let leak out may give you a clue, it may be a joke; when I use the word 'impatience' I might be showing you a glimpse of one of my biggest secrets.

So, they won't name any streets after Joy Division. At least the group never tried to help *anyone*. They just took their chance, as everyone can, to reinvent the things around them. Until they stopped, half way through a sentence, at the start of the road, at the edge of a moment, in the middle of the night, in a tiny living room, while no one was looking. I think we're all aware in our own private ways that we can only respond, in public, to what spun out from what they did and what surrounds what it is they do. The Division, the order, is all guessing, luck, wishing, indifference, impatience . . . to reach past that point we're forced to disentangle and wipe away habitual conceptions of reality. We can never talk sensibly in public of 'the inside'. No words reach that deep. I've often felt that those on whom the group's effect would be most beneficial are repelled, and on those on whom they most fascinate their effect may be dangerous, even harmful. And then, when I reach this far in, somewhere between patterned leaking and plain spilling the beans, I just have to tell a joke. Heard the one about the tragic Jew and the lucky scholar . . . ?

I am inclined to believe that one should only listen to Joy Division when one is in a euphoric state of physical and mental health and, in consequence, tempted to dismiss any scrupulous heartsearching as a morbid fuss. When one is in low spirits, one should possibly keep away from them, for, unless introspection is accompanied, as it always is with New Order, by an equal passion for the good life, it all too easily degenerates into spineless narcissistic fascination with one's own sins and weaknesses. We wouldn't want that, would we?

# XLII

## 'About-Face'

Now we turn from transplantation to acclimatisation. A group – oh, any group, hip or square, hard boiled or hysterical – became The Noise.

Not any noise.

The Noise settle and unsettles around the fundamental disorientation of being which Conrad speaks of as 'the heart of darkness' or Bettelheim as 'the extreme situation'. What Ringo, talking to Russell Harty, called 'madness'.

The group – we call such things 'groups' but four young boys teaming up together, why, it's almost a little gang – were as threatening as a spilt drink. It's no use crying. But The Noise *is the threat*: a little hell after my own heart.

The group rocked, in the antique sense of the word. They were snapped into place like a white Lego brick. The Noise – anti-Platonic – sees art not as an imitation of 'the real' BUT MORE REAL. The Noise is homeless and proud of it: it's no accident.

The group's ambition was to use up as little space as possible, and here make various experiments, folding their arms and crossing their legs, huddling close together. (It is for them and their kind, the unfinished and the bunglers, that there is hope.)

The Noise keeps its distance but moves inside, has an ambition to, say, recreate the sensation of fright, extend mild flirtations, a violent temper, a lonely craving, a dreadful shyness into a restlessness on the other side of time and outside history. I do not claim that the ambition is a conscious one, but it is bound to be present: it is The Noise's reason of state.

How do we explain the sense of this Noise, or the true (literal) non-sense? Perhaps we imagine something, anything, connected to the sentence: 'the outbreaks of rage are timed to the tickings of the seconds to which the melancholy man is slave.' Perhaps we pay tribute to the stupidity of the broad masses. Perhaps The Noise is only fit to throw away. Is it enough to announce that The Noise is infinitely new and uncanny? Does it enact the dialectical reciprocity of closure and radiance? The Noise – mood for thought? It is not known if Ringo has any thoughts on this.

So – is The Noise, perhaps, Ideal?

Not particularly.

# XLIII

## 'De-Face'

1. Ringo has always said the group would never get back together again. They would just remain friends.
2. Ringo had toothache. Ahab lost his leg in the fight with the white whale. Molloy gradually became paralysed from the foot up. Physical misfortune only corrupts what is corruptible.
3. The condition of man, says Martin Heidegger, is to be there. To not be there suggests that one is in no condition to sing for one's supper.
4. We have curious ideas of ourselves. Think of the muddle we get into when we consider the weather.
5. Right and wrong is an instinct: and, again, indistinctive.
6. We get ideas in our head of what we mean by life. For Ringo, life was eating beans and seeking cash, and he had a point. And he farted ferociously. For politicians and rock critics life is there to be sliced and wrapped; it's as pointless as firing bombs into people who are neither your enemies nor your friends but there it all goes. For some, life is here one moment, gone the next, but the word of The Lord shall last forever. Some don't mind being drugged in their life, and dragged nowhere in particular. There are those who believe that life ends at the finger-tips. D. H. Lawrence decided that nothing was important but life.
7. No things come to nothing.
8. And then there are a lot of stupid people who are 'dead' but not dead, *the dead man in life.*
9. The Noise, supremely, can help you not be the dead man in life. It shakes the ribbon from your hair. Refreshes you with a bracing awareness of your own finitude.
10. The grounds of incompletion lie at the heart of The Noise's undertaking.
11. Ringo, a meaningless mule, rolled over and died. He will be remembered for a wide passiveness and a long tail. The cause of death appeared to be a portion of gingerbread stuffed with darkness.
12. The demiurge is an hermaphrodite.

## XLIV

Once I had made it as far as discussing hermaphrodites in the context of Joy Division, using whatever help I could find to get my bearings, I stayed silent on the subject of the group, and the group they had then become, for a few more years. The conclusion of my writing about Joy Division, and associated events, could have been that final sentence to the 'De-Face', the ultimate example of a fan's defensive hyperbole, the extreme enthusiasm for a private pleasure that both wants to attract attention to and repel attention from something you want the world to know about but don't want to ruin. I had ended up as quiet on the subject of Joy Division as I had been on my father, transferring all that I had to say about Joy Division – it was welling up inside me – into a place where I was lost for words, where shock and a distant death, or two, and a body, or something, had made me wonder if words were all they were cracked up to be.

Factory, as part of their contribution to the piecing together of Joy Division, to the maintenance of myth and the organisation of legacy, continued to release Joy Division albums, in various forms and formats. To mark ten years of Factory activity they released a four-disc box set of hits and un-hits. They asked various fans, participants, friends and colleagues to contribute impressions about some of the songs for the sleeve. I chose three Joy Division songs. I seem relieved that I had made it past Ringo Starr and the hermaphrodite, or that Ringo and his pal had made it easier for me to just say what I felt.

I seem relieved that I have a chance to express some feelings about some songs I hadn't had much of a chance to talk about, both because I hadn't been asked, and because when I was asked I tended to race through doors and down long corridors towards what I thought might be safety in lack of numbers. I hid in the dark just in case I revealed too much about what I was feeling before I had properly worked it out for myself.

I said something else about Joy Division, and couldn't help but notice as I did so that the group were not at all fading away, even as they had become another group. Their songs were making a move from where they had been, at the back and beyond of memory, and invisibly slipping alongside the mess and momentum of pop culture, searching for a position somewhere in the atomised, atemporal pop future when they would seem even more modern than they ever had.

They were coming back, gaining in mystery, gaining in appeal and intrigue, using their time away to ensure that when the rest of the world was ready for their reappearance, they would be ready as well, as if it was meant all along.

## XLV

**From the sleeve notes to the Factory sampler *Palatine*.**

### On 'Transmission'

I remember leaving a Secret Affair concert at the London Rainbow, oh, during some month or other in 1979, or was it '80? Anyway, I'd left early, being an *NME* critic and all that, and some skinheads attacked me, thinking for some crooked reasons that I was a 'mod'. They slashed my mouth with a Stanley knife. I remember crying out, 'I am not a mod, I am a brave, rigorous and austerely clad fan of Joy Division,' but they took no notice, and just kicked me a bit in the ribs before smartly leaving me to feel sorry for myself. I really did struggle home, and as the blood poured out of me, I spent hours playing and replaying this track, taking it seriously, cursing every ignoramus and ass in the world that didn't. By morning I'd played it, oh, 50 times, and found that I was writing about Joy Division using words a little like the following: 'With instinctive unanimity, they hate all firmitas, because it bears witness to a healthiness quite different from theirs, and seek to throw suspicion on firmitas, on conciseness, whilst celebrating a fiery energy of movement, on abundant and delicate play of the muscles. Joy Division have agreed together to invert the nature and names of things and henceforth to speak of health when we see weakness, of sickness and tension when we encounter true health. Why the fuck aren't they being played ten times a day on Radio One?' I don't know why, but people started to say that I took Joy Division just a little too seriously. So what! I had the scars, I felt the holy wrath, and even today when I play this track anywhere up to 50 times a day, I still feel, after everything and after all that, that any number of astonishing things are possible. The greatest song ever written.

## XLVI

### On 'Love Will Tear Us Apart'

I remember a disc jockey called Ray Teret, a sickly slick Mancunian reduction of Sir Jimmy Saville, introducing the video on some late seventies Saturday morning kids' show called *Go Stupid Fun!* or something. 'You know about Joy Division,' he slickly sicked, 'I know about Joy Division . . .' I wondered what on earth he meant, looking so happy and hale and hearty, and I couldn't begin to work out how differently he and I knew about Joy Division, although I suppose in our own far apart far-fetched ways we both thought they were magic. 'Here they are at number fourteen in the charts with "Love Will Tear Us Apart".' I remember thinking I really do about the ghostly afocussed indifferent video, the extravagant introspection of a song where everything had been remembered in the just cold light of day, the way the confused past was interpreted using the intelligence of the future, the way an exalted lack of understanding was channelled through a system of opening and closings that this lack of understanding alone set into motion and kept in motion, about the whole relation between absence and presence, between too many things and never enough things . . . I remember thinking so much that I just knew some people would say I was taking it all too seriously. So what! So what did they know, the fucking Philistines? It is no small thing to make a game out of human time, and I'm not joking that this is what I assumed Joy Division to be doing. Ray Teret assumed them to be in the pop charts, the hot parade. After the video had finished, somebody hit somebody else over the head with a water-filled balloon. The greatest song ever written.

## XLVII

### On 'Atmosphere'

The *NME* banned me from ever writing about this song. I remember thinking that it seemed like the whole world was telling me that I took it all too seriously. Funnily enough, I never really thought I took it seriously at all, well, not seriously enough. I don't think I take this song, or anything else for that matter, really seriously. For now, for then, for whenever, sound and movement and thought can only rarely sound and move and think the way this does. When I play it, I'm quite happy to imagine that nothing else is ever going to happen, and I quite seriously take the song to be the best ever written. The *NME* banned me from writing words more or less vaguely and vainly much like those I'm writing now, because they said I would send people to sleep, or worse, to another paper. I told them to fuck off. This song helped me define myself, to find the most comfortable place between 'here' and 'nowhere', to almost come to terms with the suicide of my father, to learn how to cheer up in the eyes of the world. Seriously though, it's nice, isn't it?

## XLVIII

I wrote a fourth essay for Mark Johnson's book about the group Joy Division would apparently become, had become, presuming, in parts, that it was next to impossible that this one group could become any kind of another, even if change does happen, at least until the story had taken on the kind of shape it needed to for there to be any kind of progress.

'Sur-Face' imagines small parts of a world there would have been if a group had existed because Joy Division stopped existing and then carried on without themselves. This group could have had any number of names, although some would have been a bit more Warsaw than others, and who knows if their name had not been what it was whether they would have been the group that they were.

## XLIX

### 'Sur-Face'

The bastards – the little horrors more like, all things considered – won't go on *Top of the Pops*. Here we see how silly New Order can be, how small. Why, it's a wonder they even leave their cork-lined room! If we accept how the group with their Noise celebrate the strength in mystery, show to us through nonchalance and naivety that mystery is nothing to be ashamed of, then it must be that they shouldn't be ashamed that they are entertainers. There are meaner things to be. One can be obvious and yet still be a radiant object in the path of obviousness. The trick is to be obvious and alarming: for the obviousness to be ambiguous. More people have ears than those who jostle in the margin. Now is the time to push beyond the alternative, to enlarge the details of the spectacle. There can surely be nothing to fear.

The Noise is fearless and cannot be harmed by wrecked pen pushers and soulless fusspots. The Noise cannot be hurt by being sold. Nothing can distract from The Noise's impersonal purpose. The Noise has never heard of false teeth.

Maybe New Order should grip the hand of commerciality, let the hot glow of their appeal and their accessibility burn away the duff suspicions of archaic merrimen and wet broken 'radicals'. The Noise must hurt. Constant mobility is necessary to support the combat, mobility includes opening up to the worlds of numbness, numbers and masses. New Order must face The Noise, accept responsibility, acknowledge how they hurt, move in closer. Pissed wry detachment is of small-ish use.

The Noise hurts horribly: why else have it?

Maybe New Order should move away from the field of commerciality, withdraw further into themselves, rub at the surface details so that they're even muddier. Perhaps disappear completely behind The Noise, beneath its mystery, create a serious isolation. After all, The Noise is unforgettable. Their apparent irresponsibility, this seeming indifference, would be but a slight tickle of triviality next to the sublime concentration of The Noise, a hover of fluff in comparison to the something that lies outside knowledge, outside order.

Remember, Ringo is dead.

In 1964, Susan Sontag was arguing against interpretation: 'In most modern instances, interpretation amounts to the philistine refusal to leave the work of art alone. Real art has the capacity to make us nervous. By reducing the work of art to its contents and then interpreting *that*, one tames the work of art. Interpretation makes art manageable, comfortable.'

Denis Donoghue in the 1982 Reith Lectures deplored the zealots of explanation: 'One of the strongest motives in modern life is to explain everything, and preferably explain it away. The typical mark of modern critics is that they are zealots of explanation, they want to deny to the arts their mystery, and to degrade mystery into a succession of problems . . . . The removal of mystery from the arts is one of the ways in which our society tries to tame the occult and its offence . . . . If we want to live without the sense of mystery, we can of course, but we should be very suspicious of the feeling that everything coheres and that the arts, like everything else, fit comfortably into our lives.'

We can make our fuss about The Noise: we will be fond. Beyond that we cannot expect anything that floats from it to connect with the conventional, the convenient. Let it 'be there'. The Noise becomes clearer and clearer until nothing is understood. When nothing is understood, we can, for the first time, sense the extraordinary murmurs of freedom.

**L**

Another ten years passed by, until it was 1997, and the past, this past, where this story began, and continued, seemed to move closer all the time, as if it was due all along to appear in full at some point in the near future. Rock was now more something to remember than look forward to, a soundtrack to lifestyle, mass-produced sounds readily available to copy and catalogue and recycle. Music had led to more music, which had led to more music. Within a few years all eras and generations of rock music would exist simultaneously, and the pose and noise of rock, its attitude and gesture, would be at the absolute vivid centre of commercial culture. Joy Division ghosted through all these changes, reacting to whatever technological and consumer alterations there had been in music, unperturbed by new genres, new styles, new innovations, a law unto themselves. Their astonishing show-business comeback was actually being helped by all the change and redirection.

Jon Savage asked me to write some notes for a Joy Division compilation, to be packaged by Peter Saville as a deluxe reference book, another addition to the strategic list that began with his Fac 1 poster twenty years before. I hadn't written much about pop music since the last time I had written some sleeve notes for a Factory compilation, but whenever anyone offered me a chance to write about Joy Division, I did not refuse. After all, it gave me a chance to find out what I was thinking, not just about Joy Division, but about other things, some to do with music, and the writing about music, some to do with thinking, and some to do with what I guessed had happened in this story, and what might happen next.

When I did write about pop music, I noticed that even though there were now many more words written about pop music than there had been fifteen years before, this didn't mean that the articles, essays and reviews could be long, and more expansive, and more exploratory. It meant, in fact, that they needed to be smaller, and tighter, and more compressed, and you were now required to mark records and gigs, give them stars, and ticks, break them down into pockets of product, line them up and pat them on the head or slap them on the hand, say they were brilliant, or awful, without really explaining how or why you had come to that decision. There was no room whatsoever for investigations of inner worlds, or suggestions that there were hundreds of different ways of writing about music, some a little more farfetched than others, some of which involved rhymes and puzzles and, possibly, an avoidance of any detail that on the surface of things implied you were not as such tackling the music as you were meant to be, but working out what on earth was inside your own head, and how words on a page might go a little way to reaching a conclusion. Commas were frowned upon.

Suggestions that the bass guitar sounded as though it were surrounded in death's foam would cause magazine editors to assume you had lost your mind back in the punk rock wars of '77. If you wrote a few thousand words on your chosen subject, the attitude was you had written yourself to oblivion decades ago, unless you were prepared to write a kind of autopsy of a certain allegedly classic artist, to bury songs and careers in a kind of grave that would be well tended and politely observed, on the way to being largely forgotten.

Writing sleeve notes for a Joy Division album, even though it was now released on a major label, embedded in a world filled with more music and more consumers chasing, and destroying, secrets and cool, it still felt as though Factory was alive and well and a living brand. They were still selling style and beauty above and beyond, prepared to accept and liberate other kinds of thinking, and the kind of writing that didn't necessarily begin at the beginning and then assume there was, exactly where it should be, an end.

Then again, who's to say I wasn't beginning at the beginning, even if I wasn't necessarily heading straight for the end but simply another beginning?

## LI

**'Listen to the Silence:' – an extract from a permanently unfinished manuscript entitled** *Out There is still moving but I'm still in here.*

*23/10/97*

And so, here.

And so, to make some promises that cannot be kept.

And so, to speak.

And so, wonder.

I am wondering what to write about Joy Division or, to be exact, what exactly to write about Joy Division this time. How exact can I be? How exact should I be? I've been writing about Joy Division all my adult life: all my writing life: all my life. In many ways (and this is one way) everything I've ever written has been about Joy Division. (Let me explain, eventually . . . if I can . . . if I should . . .)

Everything they make me feel – or suggest I feel – is a central metaphor for everything I feel, about myself, the world, music, emotion, love, death, time, God, and so on. And so, now I come to think about it, this is how exact I am going to be . . .

And so, in the ways (count the ways) that pop music opens you up and explains things (and t/fore closes you down and unexplains things, which is so part of the still moving thrill that pop zips and unzips in its own time and space) then shall we say for the sake of argument that when I was fourteen Marc Bolan with a wave of his magic wand showed me the light and then at another age Joy Division – they were only my age, the fuckers, so what did they know of this world let alone any others? – showed me with a dizzying dip of the mind the dark.

And so here are the extremes of pop: the masking of the world of appearances, and the unmasking . . . The glittering surfaces, and the shattering depths. Marc Bolan stuck stars onto his skin, and that was pretty exciting. Joy Division pierced their skin – put a hole in their being – with their cracked and cracking obsessiveness, and that was pretty exciting as well. Twenty years on, Marc Bolan reminds me of my past. He is, alas, behind me. Joy Division still point me towards my future. In many ways (entertain the ways) they're still to come.

And so, what? I could say (count the coulds) speaking as a damned virtual rock critic that Joy Division as a rock group are an interesting case, if not the most interesting case. This is speaking historically (whoever does the speaking, metaphorically speaking) and so does go some way (watch the way) towards creating some kind of shape to rock things, some order, but please feel free to remove the traces as soon as they seem to appear. In no time at all, just a sliver of no-time at the no-end of the seventies, which in many ways (discount the ways) is as far away as the sixties, the sick boy band eventually named Joy Division after an auntie or something – boy oh boy – made up quite a myth with the help of themselves and a vain desire for purity.

The myth of the group quickly ghost-rolled hip-deep around their music: you thought that you could never see through this spilling myth, and yet somehow (count the somehows) you could see all the way through. To (the other side.) They had only been going a few months before the evidence was plain to see and hear: here was a strange out of nowhere out of place out of it rock group who were opaque and transparent, visible and invisible, straightforward and dissident. They changed all the time. They shed all manner of inner and outer skins monthly, some disconcerting musical menstruation saw them change inside a couple of seasons from chubby punk babes to mean rock 'n' roll cockroaches implicated in some absurdly grand mission to take over the world, or bits of it.

And so they did it all – all of what they did – with two LPs, a handful of singles and some shows. (Shows that showed how fast they were going however steep the corners were. Occasionally they slowed down, but that was only for some blood shedding.) And talking of blood, there was a suicide (count it, you cannot miss it, it's just around the corner) that manufactured for the group the ultimate end, a sudden stop to what had begun so unsuddenly, and so slovenly, and this sheer shiny pointed end at the opposite end to their ragged quite pointless beginning created this great shape (count the shapes), this missile, and we can now see and hear how this missile was launched into the light and then within a matter of time it exploded into the dark and so the story of Joy Division had the perfect twentieth-century (leg) ending.

And so, the myth so soon, so scandalously, was neck high and climbing. And tightening.

And so, speaking my mind, as I see it. The Interesting Case of Joy Division, to be defined as a rock group (or, as we shall see, in this order of things, The Interesting Case of Joy Division, to be defined as THE rock group). For a start, they had these values, this stubborn need not to sully their worth. They took themselves very seriously, which suggested that deep down they might be comedians as much as tragedians. The two LPs they made didn't contain any of their singles so there was no over-familiarity to back-pollute the complete and separate works that the albums were. The singles were from different worlds. Joy Division defied commercial conventions with such shrugging care and inattention because they knew, really, that in the long run – and perhaps they were always in it for the long run, the steep climb – it would pay off. The deliberate distinction they wanted to maintain between their two albums (the two energised masterpieces *Closer*, with its soft and hard s, *Unknown Pleasures*, with its spaced-out s and s, different but connected, one icy and jumpy, the other thawed and graceful, one out of the womb, the other into the tomb) and their irresistibly overemotional singles was their way of achieving the aloof splendour enjoyed by the likes of Led Zeppelin and Pink Floyd. Groups far too grand and superior to fret about the grubby worlds of hard sell and instant gratification: their glamour came from their anti-commercial perversity, a wonderful mixture of laziness, arrogance and self-confidence. Some antisocial need to preserve integrity, to play on reclusiveness, to back into the limelight. (They were independent but never 'indie'.) This was for Joy Division a matter of long-term style not short-term fashion. From the very beginning, they thought big.

And so, their music had to be big too, and rebellious, and they had a lot to go on: in many ways (keep counting) they had as much to go on as any group twenty years later. With Joy Division, you hear a group with a great record collection, who have great discrimination, and whose intention was to absorb and dominate those influences, to equal and surpass. Their music has this balanced European detachment – arted, parted, departed, stop and started separateness, music that oozed out of the great European cities – that they picked up from the likes of Can and Kraftwerk. When they started to get so good, they started to rub noises together, to blend temperatures, to mix rude rock directness with shy nervy avant-garde indirectness. They drifted even as they shifted. They glanced as they flashed. They floated as they attacked.

There was this sarcastic alternative American thing about them that they nicked in their bedrooms from the Doors, the Stooges and the Velvet Underground – the way they used their guitars as an abuse, melodies as a sign of bittersweet intelligence, beat to beat up beat, the way hate was as great a subject as love, the secrecy of thought as sexy a subject as sex. These surly, sacrificial Americans revealed to them the edgy. Then they even had this deadpan sensation-seeking camp outsider thing snatched out of the studded back pocket of the smart, aplombish Eno, Roxy Music and Bowie. The sleek, bleak and S&M-bruised Roxy of *For Your Pleasure*, the colder, fishier, tenser Bowie of *The Man Who Sold the World* and *Low*, the allusive Las Vagueness playfulness of Eno the singer-songwriter. In the wet dead Northwest such delectable subversive stuff was the surreal thing; there was a way out over the grey walls and through the sharp and hostile things of everyday.

And so, all these distant decadent musicians banked up in the lives of the four impressionable young men shared this thing about 'not belonging' and not wanting to belong and they had this flamboyant and tenacious urge to tell the truth about the world around them through magnificent and liberating lies.

And so, as if the world could be a better place . . . and why not?

And so, at just the right time in this order of things, came punk rock (turning private emergencies into public urgency), named after somebody's uncle or something (still counting), and this fitted in just right with all that other stuff. The Sex Pistols, vomited out of the mouth of the Stooges, harassed the group that would be Joy Division into action, and they adapted to and pretty soon transcended this frenzied coincidence of the Sex Pistols, Kraftwerk, Brian Eno and the Doors. (And you never know, Peter Hammill, Nick Drake and Black Sabbath. And you never know more, J. G. Ballard, Mary Shelley and Albert Camus. And you never know more than Kafka and Dostoyevsky. )

And so, there was more to help this transcendence, this disorderly magic.

There was the Manchester damp and the shadows and omens called into dread being by the hills and moors that lurked at the edge of their vision. It wasn't soft, where they lived. It was stained green and unpleasant. It seemed to be at the edge of the edge of the world. You had to dream your way out of such a tranquilised, inert stretch of land/mindscape. You had to use your imagination to believe that there was anything else than nothing else. In these slow suburbs, your mind would ache for release. And so would your body.

There was sexual frustration battering the air from all directions. There was godless depthless nightclub music desperately seducing these serious young men with remorseless promises per minute; the adventure of art and the chaos of the mind versus the mindless temptations of the rhythms of the moment, and eventually as New Order, the remains of Joy Division would solve this absurd dichotomy without compromise, introducing northern lights to northern darks.

And so, anyway, circus-minded glam pop, with all its bump and grind, something of the comedy meat of this stuff (count the stuffing) made it into the JD pot, into the wilderness of the familiar and the freshly compelling, this atmosphere of futuristic cataclysm.

So they happened.

And so, rage lurked beneath the taut surfaces of their worlds.

And so, they thought.

And so, they had the daring of the timid.

And so, they knew what they were doing.

And so, they did.

And so, things happened to them.

And so, there was tension and a release of tension.

And so, all hell broke loose.

And so, they didn't know what they were doing.

And so, it came from somewhere and nowhere and the group didn't like to think about it too much just in case it stopped coming.

And so, they just let it happen.

And so, they blanketed the skies with orange sheets that turned to a diaphanous white chiffon before sweeping upward into instant oblivion.

And so, time and time again reality burnt through to the surface of this wicked and deep adventure.

(And so, what about their record company, Factory, not so much a record company, more a state of mind, or a state with a mind, who pushed them and pulled them? And so, who encouraged them. And helped them. And hindered them. And indulged them. In some ways, they drove Joy Division, and in some ways, Joy Division were very driven. Sometimes, Joy Division drove Factory. They drove each other up the wall. Together they erratically defied the banal rock gravity of following certain rules of promotion and presentation.)

Since when has a record company – not so much a record company, more an existential minder – been a combination of villain, pantomime dame, benefactor, wicked stepmother, clown, lover and butler? Factory and Joy Division are the perverse proof of that old chocolate pudding of a saying that there is no business like show business. (And that old banana split of a saying that there are more quests than panthers.)

(And so, also, they had a manager, Rob Gretton, who loved them, like a child, like a brother, like a friend, like a fan, and who also watched over them with such belief and commitment. He followed them to the ends of the earth and then, funnily enough, beyond.)

And so, all of this bled fed wed and headed dead or alive into the drastic mind and body of Joy Division (who were outgrowing their mind and body and packing more time into the time they had than they had time for) and all of this, all these coincidences and transmissions and transitions and (r)apt moments and exotic settings and mild distortions, it all added up, and put them into this unique position where they were both the last ever great rock group (after the Velvet Underground, the Stooges, MC5, the Doors, Television, the Sex Pistols) and the first ever great rock band (before the

Pixies, My Bloody Valentine, Nine Inch Nails, Nirvana, Smashing Pumpkins, Radiohead) . . . they were some twisted turning point, some tunnel of light and dark and love and hate that you must journey through from one era to the next if you are to make any new sense . . . Joy Division summoned up in a rock shell in their time and place all the great rock – surface and substance, pose and power – that there ever was and ever will be.

And so, somehow (and what are the odds of this happening?) they drew into themselves all the greatness of rock's past and rock's future and received all this interference and information from fact and fiction, absence and presence, that transformed their music into an epic of timelessness. Say what you want, time never seems to corrupt the music of Joy Division; the actions, sensations, images, movement all seem to fit into the next moment, the noises and agitation, the courage and diligence, always seem to be happening for the first time. Their music so feverishly conjures up insecurity, malign gods, moral chaos, human lostness, caged energy, loss, shifting meaning and danger that it could never slip back into some cosy version of itself. It could never be stripped of its harrowing power because its crystallisation of moody form and seething content is so classic and universal.

And so, where was I?

Joy Division are in this order of things the centre of the (rock) universe. They even ended up being as dug up and compiled and recompiled and remastered as Hendrix – and so, here we are finding even more ways to extend the brief moment(ousness), to spin it out, to hold on, searching for clues in the outtakes and bootlegs for how this might have happened, knowing all along that it's a mystery, and within that it's accidental, and within that it's futile, and within that it's over.

And so, there was a death in the family. And rock and roll, the very real greedy myth of it, the sly shifting life of it, loves early death and gaudy sacrifice. The rock and roll myth, the sensation of it, loves death as the lions loved Christians. Death in rock and roll chronically cosmically represents rock's vain mad mock mocking danger. As if there is such a thing after all. It makes it seem worthwhile, all the effort and frenzy, all the lust and collapse. All the fucking fantasy. True, tried outsiders – pretenders and contenders – can find a place to live and die inside rock and roll. At the extremes of desire, death proves rock and roll, certifies its acts of rebellion. And death proved Joy

Division, it set them up. Death rams home into amplified eternity the essential black glamour rock and roll aspires to, instantly, brutally creates the kind of immortality that all entertainers – even the frail, unformed and boyishly, conscientiously alienated Ian Curtis – desperately crave.

And so, Ian Curtis, dead name, dead stop, dead mysterious, dead success, dead all the same, dead at the moment, a close relation of the unknown, as withdrawn as it gets.

And so, how romantic can you get?

And so, how accidental is life and death.

And so, fatalism.

And so, Joy Division, dead cool, as made up as history, as mad as rock and roll history, had seriousness thrust upon them overnight – that's overnight, that's serious, that's boys becoming men, that's their music coming true, the fictions becoming facts, overnight, seriously.

And so, Joy Division, who'd perhaps played at being out of this world, were hurled out of this world.

And so, overnight.

And so, they played at taking themselves seriously.

And so, in the middle of one martyring night, it worked for them.

And so, seriousness.

And so, who could deny it?

This was some meaning.

And so, Joy Division, as lovely as a dream in stone, just as their record sleeves always cried and whispered, had it all going for them as rock and roll myths.

A great short fast fractured life rendered psychedelic by a messy midnight death.

And so, their seriousness was left hanging in space.

And so, that is something.

Else.

And so, what might have been was viciously disturbed.

And so, all along they were glorying in their fate.

Oh, and so, the death of their producer Martin Hannett – more mischievous myth, more (disjointed) history, more incidental insubordination, more violence, more degenerate heroism and indecipherable cowardice, all in all adding to the serious components of Joy Division as big deal rock and roll illusion inside their very own infinitely variable endlessly interpreted mystery melodrama. They were bigger than they seemed, bigger than they seem, on the quiet as big as they come. Their myth is noisy and quiet, dazzling and hidden, static and dynamic . . . and/because so is their music.

And so, seriously, Joy Division, after their overnight stop, neither exist nor do not exist.

And so, as specimens, as living things, as boys, as innovators, as brats, as fuckers, as feelers, as dreamers, as ghosts, as petulant bleeders, as occultists, as neurotics, as heroes, as narcissists, as dead things, as commodity, as history, as future, as ageless punks, as sceptics, as forever young, as practical jokers, as autodidactics, as deceivers, as a touch inflated, as vapours, as liars, as chaos, as northerners, as Englanders, as Europeans, as futurists, as the inspired, as the inspirers, as metaphysicians, as sentimentalists, as next-door neighbours, as sell-outs, as swines, as artists, as borrowers, as lenders, as drinkers, as addicts, as cults, as confessors, as back catalogue, as weirdos, as adulterers, as fathers, as sons, as images, as details, as nutters, as musicians, as Joy Division, as survivors, as far as it goes, we can say that they are like group zero.

Out of the group, all that they are and sound like and did and had done to them, you could find traces of all the great 'not/non-belonging' rock music that there has been and ever will be. Their myth is the myth of rock, they're a compression of all the obscure and commercial, wild and inexplicable dynamics that makes – made – rock such a force in our face and in our lives.

They are the end, the beginning and the middle all at once.

And so, they never belonged.

They never got bogged down.

They never repeated themselves.

They were always in the process of discovering themselves, in the process of thinking, in the process of processing their influences.

They had it easy in the sense that for them it was all over after three years – and the rest was history – and they never reached the point where they might get assimilated or jaded, but then again (and again) they had it hard in the other sense that there was something about them that knew they had an awful lot to do in such a short time. You can hear in their music that they knew some kind of crash was coming: the end of the century or just the end of their dawning noise.

And so, that was an order.

And so, far so good.

And so, selfish.

(And so, when one is doing rock criticism one gets to the point where one would just like to emit an inarticulate sound.)

And so, I could place Joy Division in that order.

And so, I could not.

And so, I could write – with intention – about Joy Division's central role in it all, the it all of rock et al, and yet how they are also so off-centre; but then to be so central to the story they have to be off-centre as well, because the central beauty of pure rock is that it is off-centre. If they were just central they would not actually be central. That would be too banal for words. They must be off-centre to be central, to be properly obvious and mysterious, to be (in the skipped beat of a missing moment) enigmatic.

And so, they are.

And so, good.

And so, moving on from the centre where we have placed them off-centre in the history of (rock) things, the myth still rises, and obscures, and provokes.

And so, I was just thinking.

And so, their music could form a soundtrack to Godard or Bergman or Fassbinder or Wenders or ( ... ) Herzog. It could worm through the worlds of Sterling or Gibson, and it could buzz around the up-sense and down-data of Ballard or Burroughs. And it could be called cyberpunk or cyberphunk, perhaps their one true location is to be lost in cyberspace, they're scattered, vastly out there, intimately in here, and they're as hyperreal as the next hyperreal thing and image – how hyperreal that is – and girl oh girl are they ever hypersensitive. There was something (the way they got the human spirit dancing on the end of pins and needles, the way they didn't smile much in public, the way they could evoke derangement with such cool clarity, the way they wore their second-hand clothes, the way there was something cruel lurking behind the beauty) about them that was so ancient, and so gothic (1548 and all that). They were post-modern (post-modern as something atmospheric, something bored and fanatical, a volatile mix of this, that and the approximate other, fraught with an eerie, brittle significance) from the moment – if not the moment before, but let's not get too date-specific at a time like this – they facelessly if not namelessly produced *Unknown Pleasures* and said that they were waiting for some guide to come and take them by the hand, and there were these gulping black noises and squirming off-white sub-noises going on way out beyond their realish rock that sound like they were giving birth or operating on themselves, and yes, Joy Division's music could form a soundtrack for Lynch but not Tarantino, oh no, that's the point.

Joy Division never had any intention of wanting to cut The Universe down to size. They love – and hate, but with respect – the size of The Universe. The size of The Universe is everything.

And so, the size is in the details.

And so, one of the great things (count the things) about Joy Division is their

246

appreciation of size and their attention to detail.

And so, I suppose. And so, believe me it was as if, whether they intended this or not, they were trying to warn us about dangers to avoid.

And so, according to Joy Division whether they knew it or not, nothing is neutral, nothing is impotent in the universe, an atom may ruin all, an atom may ransom all.

And so, you awake frightened with the sensation of having overslept.

And so, Joy Division made us think of another separate world that maniacs and exiles invent when the normal everyday world seems impossible.

And so, the mood shifts again.

And so, then there were the writings of Ian Curtis, who was underground by the time he was 23, and he wrote these overloaded and penetrating autobiographical fragments, these notes and notices from the aboveground underground, these tensings of the senses, that seem to come from someone who has lived so much more than twenty years and a bit. Something was concentrating his mind dramatically. It was like he suspected it – the all embracing it, the it of all its – was coming to an end one way or another sooner rather than later. Even without having all that I've mentioned – their off-centred centrality, their essence-ness, the zero matrix, symbolic status – Ian Curtis' impressions and depressions would have lifted Joy Division into greatness.

He sang from the knife edge with a kind of suave sordid middle of the road disconnectedness. He sang suffering with an almost tender listlessness. He put this awkward but handsome spin on despair. He crooned anguish. He delivered sullen commotion. He expressed his restlessness and soul-sickness with a damaged insouciance. Even when he was charged, and brutal, he seemed resigned. He sang his sharply apprehensive songs in the spirit of:

I'll get this off my chest.
And then get my chest off me.

This music that rocked – that could go the distance, from here to there and beyond – hung inside a sense of sadness and waste and emptiness.

And so, more and more, a mental and physical exhaustion, as if Curtis was transferring himself into the very body of the music, slipping over the line from where the music was for him to where he was for the music. The music was taking him away. Taking him over. Needing the drama of his life.

And so, more drama.

And so, more.

And so, the sin always rises.

And so, Ian lived his (rock and roll) life intensely to such depths.

And so, the love and alarm of 'Love Will Tear Us Apart'.

And so, you can tell exactly – around an unknown centre – when his life started to end. (And, somewhere else, where it started to begin. You can even hear when he started to really believe in death. It's right there in the way his voice forms and reforms.)

And so, there was Ian Curtis leading the band who were all playing their instruments as if they were leading. Three lead instruments – the glassy and capering Sumner guitars, the cold and anxious Morris drums, the iron and lurid Hook bass – plus spare and marooned noises off and noises in that acted as if they had an (ectoplasmic) ego all of their own and were themselves leading . . . and Ian with his tragic voice and his antic dancing and the way he was leading the group and us into . . .

His space.

A space that hung around the music like a tarnished halo, a space that seemed to fill the music out from within, a space that kept itself buttoned up even as it spilled the beans and lost its marbles.

The space in Joy Division's music has always been intriguing. Somehow (one more time) the group could leave such emptiness in the middle – and at the edges of their music – without weakening it. In fact, it added to the strength, the resonance. Perhaps it came out of the space they were all leaving around themselves – even as they came together to make this music they kept themselves to themselves, they stayed trapped inside their own splendid isolation, stuck inside their own young minds. They all played and sung inside their own worlds. Privacy times four – and beyond.

And so, their music is, sure enough, about isolation, and the difficulties of keeping in touch with other human beings as we create for safety's sake a reality around us, that works for us as much as it can. It's about the mind – as far as my mind is concerned – and the tricks it plays on itself. It's about the way (one way) the mind can find all sorts of ways (link the ways) to prise apart illusion and reality and then cobble them back together and then start all over again and so on.

And so, to the songs, again and again because they just do not wear out whatever you take from them, wherever you take them. Somewhere in there, amidst other more secretive and even more catastrophic narratives, you can just make out Ian's battle for self preservation, a battle he was winning, because of the band, and then he was losing, because of the band. These songs were lifted beyond themselves by being somehow – as far as it can go, if this isn't being too farfetched – set inside the enclosed, abstract and echoing space of a mind which enveloped the songs from all sides like a prison. This is some illusion.

And so, some reality. Ian's mind somehow – how this is so is on the tip of my mind's tongue – held the songs in volatile place.

And so, I suppose, this time, what I am saying is that, with the music, we can see inside his mind. And we see him begin to think ideas he only has so much time to formulate, ideas and thoughts that are about, with such boyish bravado, everything, and then nothing.

And so, he re-enters the shadows of his living night, the overnight that strangled his everything, and then, so, nothing.

And so, ideas, forgotten, abandoned, miscarried.

And so, Ian Curtis. He gave Joy Division their life and their death. He gave Joy Division his life and his death. He gave them their specialness. He actually risked his neck.

And so, what was the fucking point of that? (The point: not the point.) He was under crisis and he passed this sense of crisis – real and imagined – right into the bloody unstable mood of the music. He was fighting mad, and you can feel that in the turbulence of the music. He was frightened, and the music is frightening. He was in love.

And so, he was lonely. That he and his friends – who were just as lonely in their own ways – could turn these thoughts and confusions so magically into sounds – gentle, pure, heartbreaking and lacerating sounds – is but a hint of the alchemical extravagance of this strangely intelligent, ridiculously burdened, youthfully defiant, glooming and blooming, magnificently doomed, old style, avant-garde, anonymous and famous rock and roll group.

And, so?

What.

Exactly.

And so, if I may be so bold at such an exact time as to say the following: Joy Division locate us in the gently smouldering nowhere solid hell* of communal remembering, of mutual awareness, never exact, never erased.

And, so, mind you, there. **

---

*The word 'hell' stems from the Germanic root meaning 'concealed', and originally, like Hades or Sheol, had less to do with punishment than simple, bleak survival in a vague netherworld.
**Another end, another day, another doldrum, another beginning, another way of seeing things where there is nothing and everything to see. And so, on.

## LII

Wilson explained to me, at the time, or a little, or a lot, later, that he thought it right that he show me the body of Ian Curtis because I was the one who was meant to write the Joy Division book. I would need that stupefying detail to help with the end – or the very beginning – of the book. He was playing the role of some kind of hyperactive assistant to me, helping me with my research. Perhaps he intended ghosting it for me.

I resisted the book notion for a long time – until now, I suppose – perhaps because it was Wilson who was suggesting it, and for all of the eighties he was part of something that I was escaping, a part of a past I had to get far away from before I could even begin to consider it. I wasn't ready to write the Joy Division book, however much Tony kept circling me, confronting me, with the idea, with the inevitability.

I didn't consider that the world was ready for a Joy Division book – or Joy Division weren't ready, not yet in any kind of pieced-together shape. This was still some years before the first sighting of mood-and-melancholy groups directly influenced by Joy Division, by their costume, riffs and darkness, by their bass and drum and the way they extracted reality from reality. 'Love Will Tear Us Apart' was not yet a pop standard.

In the early nineties, now in full spreading colour, the late seventies world of Manchester had shifted back in time, buried under the young drugged Manchester of Stone Roses and Happy Mondays, sent so far back there seemed no way it would ever make any kind of cultural comeback. Joy Division hadn't yet recovered from the fact that another group, containing three members of Joy Division, had throughout the 1980s deflected attention away from their history, even as they reminded people of it.

I wasn't sure that a book about Joy Division was a good thing, a book that couldn't help but give things away, or make hasty decisions about how the truth should be obtained, as if there was such a thing as obvious truth. I thought a Joy Division book – a biography, a pasting together of facts and figures – would do little other than drain away the strangeness, and that any book that attempted to examine, even enhance the strangeness, assuming that was the word, would be just as useless, at least while the pop world began the final run-in to the end of the century.

Ultimately I wasn't ready to write a Joy Division book because I needed to write about my father first. The chronological order for me as far as this story went consisted of, very much first of all, the suicide of my father. As I started to search for a subject for a book I might write that wasn't directly about pop music, now having buried my past behind me, behind the past itself, I didn't immediately think that my father, in an act that was positively Wilsonian, had through an extreme act of self-sacrifice given me, as a writer, the gift of some exceptional material.

By the end of the 1990s, a magazine editor asked me to write about my father's suicide. The material I had available to write about revealed itself, as if it had something to do with me and at the same time nothing. I started to think about this, about why I hadn't been thinking about it for nearly twenty years. And then, slowly, I started to write about it.

Acknowledging that this suicide had got tangled up in my imagination, and my life, with the suicide of Ian Curtis, I began the book I wrote about my father, *Nothing*, as if it was going to be the book about Joy Division that Tony Wilson had always wanted me to write.

The book began with a dead body. In fact, to get to the actual story, you had to first get past a dead body. Some suggested that this was commercial suicide, pointing out that the dead body would put people off.

The more this was pointed out, the more it seemed quite fitting, and was therefore something I was not going to change. This stubbornness also seemed appropriate, representing as it did not just the attitude of my father – what is suicide, after all, but an extremely exaggerated form of stubbornness? – but also the anarchic approach to art and business of Factory.

And so the book began with a dead body, and then it seemed to be a book about Joy Division, but just as the reader, having made it around the dead body, settled into the idea that it was going to be a book about Joy Division, it changed into being a book about my father, which surely had nothing at all to do with Joy Division. For me though, the way things had turned out, a book about my father was still a book about Joy Division.

While it was temporarily playing the role of being a book about Joy Division, I included an updated version of the sleeve notes I had written for *Heart and Soul*. There had been complaints, I was aware, that whilst not being entirely bogged down in the hermaphrodite quagmire, the notes were still a little . . . withdrawn, if not – to those not paying attention, or paying too much attention, or looking for some simple information about the group – downright annoying. Actually, they were fragments, notes for a possible work, a series of abrupt shifts that still, I hoped, managed to sustain a moving sense. I wanted the words to be faithful to the jostling movement of thought. It seemed more appropriate in the context to write about Joy Division in fragments, as the group themselves had been broken up into pieces and flung into space.

I had not written them as being a general introduction to Joy Division. They were more of an introduction to the Joy Division that exist uniquely for me – there I was, still committed, after all these years, to ensuring that writing about Joy Division didn't all end up the same, packed with the usual repeated history, dates, details, anecdotes, statistics and quotes. I was still pursuing an alternative to that kind of writing, knowing that it existed, and had its place, but still wanting to find the one word, in conjunction with the right collections of words places around it, or the one sentence, linking one particular sentence to another, that might communicate some of the force and immensity of the group, rather than just spelling our their influences, hard work, song titles and career highs. I made changes to the *Heart and Soul* piece, but not because I regretted not supplying the introduction – or the more balanced analysis – that some wanted.

The *Heart and Soul* writing was another piece I viewed as the beginning of something that over time would turn into something completely different. At each stage of the transformation from one state to another I wanted the writing to represent the way Joy Division's music changes form and shape, and how each song has a different impact each time you hear it, wherever you are, and whatever the time. Each line in the piece has a potential alternative. Gradually over time, each line would change, sometimes just one line at a time. Thousands of pieces could exist, lines and words and meaning and thinking merging in with each other, filtering themselves, creating a kind of response to the music that accepted how words lead to mistakes, however certain they seem, or they are too strong, and clumsy, and indecisive, however carefully they are put together.

The piece was in that sense a way of trying to describe through the fixed use of printed words a sense of the infinite – this was the latest attempt using language, feeling and the material of the story to represent something of what happened, somewhere between 1977 and 1980, and then between 1980 and the present day, and then in a past always changing as it fell away from our lives, and beyond that, between the present day and the rest of the future.

In a way, the piece was the same piece about Joy Division that I had written when they were Warsaw and there were only a few words available. Twenty years later, because more had happened, all over the place, there was more to say, on the way to saying more, on the way to reaching as far as possible into the story without interfering with its energy and freshness. It's all the same piece. It became part of the book about my father that in another light was a book about Joy Division. It existed inside the book in a state that was only a little different from how it was in *Heart and Soul*; the first change on the way to other changes leading eventually to the perfect last line to a piece about Joy Division, the perfect end.

This meant that to get to the story of my father you had to get past a dead body and then climb over the body of Joy Division, or, to find the book on Joy Division, you had to deal with the death of my dad. You can imagine how much of a problem this was to those people who like their rock journalism not to in any way involve the personal life of the writer. I always thought it was impossible to write about music without revealing something about your personal life, even if you were trying to hide behind the bland sweep of objectivity, even if you pretended to remove yourself from the writing.

I decided early on as a writer that I might as well be honest about it – that it was not possible to have opinions, and make judgements, and decide value, without all that being filtered through who you were, and how you'd lived, and how you had ended up having the attitude that you have. And so, I would not write about Joy Division, or any music, in the way that I would if I was not the person that I was.

I could hide behind the words, as is often done, and as I sometimes do. Or I could be right alongside the words, right in front of the words, watching them as they collected together, in an order that I decided at that moment was exactly the order I wanted. In a few seconds, I might have changed my mind. For now, they were fixed in place. There was no going back. I was the words. Here they were. There they are. The same words. Different words. Words helping memory to assume its ultimate shape.

## LIII

And so, here.

And, so to make some promises that cannot be kept.

And, so I reveal a few secrets and keep a few others.

And so, wonder. I am wondering what to write about Joy Division, or, to be exact, what exactly to write about Joy Division this time. How exact can I be? How exact should I be? I've been writing about Joy Division all my adult life, all my writing life, all my living life. In many ways (and this is one way) everything I've ever written has been about Joy Division, what with one thing and another. Their music has followed me out of my teens into my twenties, escorted me into my thirties, and is still with me as I drift clear into middle age. Whatever age I am, at whatever state of optimism or pessimism, hope or despair, if I'm in love or out of love, facing death or denying it, feeling young or feeling old, their music, their mental metal music, their solid liquid music, always has meaning for me. It is a music I can always turn to, music that can elevate my soul or calm my nerves or liberate my senses. Their dark, brooding, ecstatically thoughtful music, rock 'n' roll played in the shadows of life and death, consistently manages to connect with my moods, to fix my feelings, to turn me on. The music of Joy Division sounds like it belongs to the darkness and exuberance of my youth, but it also sounds like it belongs to the peace and fear of my middle age. It suited me when my future stretched out as a shape that resembled forever, a forever that it seemed I would live to see. It suits me now my future has shrunk in one way, but in another grown to exactly resemble forever, a forever I will miss through some inevitability or other. The music was a soundtrack to the curiosity of youth, and it is a soundtrack to the experience of age.

Everything the music of Joy Division makes me feel – or suggests I feel – is a central metaphor for everything I feel about me, the world, music, emotion, love, death, time, God. As exact as I can feel about things, so their music is exact, as exact as pain, as exact as the present. And their music is as inexact as I can feel about things, as inexact as pleasure, as inexact as the future. It's as inexact as life and as exact as death, and so it's as inexact as death and as exact as life, and so it changes shape and dynamic to reflect the mood of the moment. It's my favourite kind of music: it never sounds like it's stopped or that its meaning has stopped. It moves with time. It moves through time. If I was trying to be exact about things, I would say it's the noise of time and it will never sound dated or old or wrong. I suppose Joy Division are like my Elvis Presley.

And so, in the ways that pop music opens you up and helps explain things, how it cleans you out and clears a way forward, let me say for the sake of the promise I might have made about how pop opens you up and explains things that when I was fourteen Marc Bolan with a wave of his magic wand and a rhythm that rhymed with sex, space and time, showed me the light. And Joy Division, with a dizzying swoop into the unknown and a rhythm that rhymed with thought, showed me the dark.

For me they were both the absolute peak of pop. Bolan stuck stars onto his skin, and that was pretty exciting. Joy Division pierced their skin – put a hole in their being – with their cracked and cracking obsessiveness. That was oddly exciting. I think, because Bolan slickly skated over the surface of life with a mischievous smile and made a pop that went with life all the way, and because Joy Division dived under the surface and made a pop that sometimes turned back on life, that Bolan seems to belong to my past. Listening to him now I'm reminded of the faint young teenager who was cracking open the world, and using Bolan as a kind of cosmic key. He is, alas, behind me, a fabulous fling, the star I lost my virginity to, the pop prince of innuendo. Joy Division still point me towards the future. They wrote songs on a journey towards a place and a world of imagination that is like a journey that I'm still on. It wasn't music that only meant something to me as a teenager. Their music is a soundtrack to an adventure that I'm still following. Their music is the soundtrack to the end of this adventure, it is a soundtrack to how you see and sense this end, how you deny it, how you deal with it. It's a soundtrack to how life goes in different directions, and around odd corners, and under itself, towards its end. It's a soundtrack to how the end is as near as anything and as far away as a dream. It's a soundtrack to the question: where *will* it end? It's a soundtrack to the following paragraph:

' . . . and if it is the living, existential experience of the individual that matters and has precedence over any abstract concepts it may elicit, then the very act of confronting the void or continuing to confront it is an act of affirmation. The blacker the situation and the deeper the background of despair against which this act of affirmation is made, the more complete and the more triumphant must be the victory that it constitutes. The uglier the reality that is confronted, the more exhilarating will be its sublimation into symmetry, rhythm, movement and noise.'

2/

With Joy Division, apart from the unearthly elements, apart from the unholy drive, you hear a group with a brilliant record collection, who have great discrimination, and whose intention was to absorb and dominate these influences, to equal and surpass. When they started to get good, they started to rub all these noises together, to blend temperatures, to mix blatant antic rock directness with shy, nervy avant-garde indirectness. They drifted even as they shifted. The glanced as they stabbed. They floated as they stung.

They took their influences and fumbled and twisted them into something original. They took the gaunt tick-tock motion and frosty deadpan adroitness of Kraftwerk. They inherited the hyperactive and gormless artistry of Iggy and the Stooges. They gingerly stalked space and intimately scratched time because they had heard the jelled indulgence of Can. They gnashed and flashed with their guitars and drums as abrasively as MC5.

There was this sarcastic, alternative thing about them that they nicked in their bedrooms from the likes of the Stooges, the Doors and the Velvet Underground. The way they used guitars as bursting abuse, melodies as a ripe sign of bittersweet intelligence, beat to beat up time, the way hate was as great a subject as love, the secrecy and hardcore drama of thought as sexy a subject as sex, the way fear and loathing was as great a pop subject as love. These surly, self-sacrificial Americans revealed to them the edgy, and many potential edges to hurl themselves over.

They wanted to be as fishy and theatrical as the green-skinned Bowie and as randomly precise as the Velvet Underground.

They were touched up by the sleek and bleak Roxy Music of *For Your Pleasure*. They loved how Bowie lost himself to himself in the tall and tense songs on *Station to Station* and they loved the becalmed insanity of Brian Eno on *Another Green World*. They loved it when Eno and Bowie worked together on *Low* and *'Heroes'* and worked up a tender, fractured sound that was at once angelic and diabolical.

They fancied being as unsentimentally epic as Pink Floyd and as sentimentally violent as Led Zeppelin. They would be as male and as pale as Nick Drake and as blunt and infernal as the Sex Pistols.

In the wet, dead Northwest, with its low-slung dirty blue sky, such delectably subversive stuff was the surreal thing; it showed there was a way out over the grey walls and through the sharp and hostile everydayness of things.

And so all these distant and not so distant decadent musicians banking up in the lives of the four impressionable young men shared this thing about 'not belonging' and not wanting to belong, and they had this flamboyant and tenacious urge to tell the truth about the world through great, sly and liberating lies.

And so it was as if the world could be a better place because of the imagination, and why not?

And so just at the right time in this history of things along came punk rock (turning private emergencies into public urgency) and that fitted right in with all this other stuff, not least because a lot of what punk was had slipped and slithered out of all this other stuff.

It was the Sex Pistols tonguing out of the mouths of the Stooges that harassed the group that became Joy Division into galactic Northwest technological rock and roll action, and they adapted to and pretty quickly transcended this frenzied coincidence of the Sex Pistols, Kraftwerk, the Doors, Brian Eno and Television (and you never know, Peter Hammill and Black Sabbath, or J. G. Ballard and Albert Camus, or Franz Kafka and Chic, or Neu and Isaac Asimov, or Mott the Hoople and Dostoyevsky . . .)

3/

All this, and they ended up their own creation, their own creatures, wandering through their own shadows. Perhaps it was because the words of Ian Curtis came only from his brain, only from his life. His lonely, tormented images and restless stories were generated by acute self-consciousness and they low-lit the songs with their own dead level uniqueness, and polluted them with barely suppressed, terribly sourceless and ultimately exhilarating dread.

And so there was more that helped the group be mysteriously more than the sum of their influences. There was the Manchester damp, and the phantoms and omens called into empty being by the hills and moors that lurked at the edges of their vision. It wasn't soft, where they lived. It was stained green and unpleasant. There were times when it seemed to be at the edge of the edge of the world, buried under a grievous history. You really had to dream your way out of such a tranquilised, inert land/mindscape. You really had to use your imagination to make believe that there was anything else but nothing else. In this slowed and woeful land your mind would ache for release. And so would your body.

There was sexual frustration battering the air from all directions.

And so there was godless, depthless nightclub music easily seducing these serious young men, music with remorseless promises per minute: there developed a tension between the adventure of art, the chaos of the mind, and the mindless temptations of the rhythms of the exact moment – and eventually as New Order, the remaining members of Joy Division would somehow solve this daft little dichotomy without compromise, cunningly introducing northern dark to northern lights.

4/

(And so, what about their record company, Factory, not so much a record company as a state of mind, an organisation in constant graceful disarray, and a company of freethinking sub-maniacs who were responsible for pushing and pulling Joy Division through their short, frantic career. Factory encouraged them and guided them and held them tight to their chest. They helped them and hindered them. They indulged them and spoilt them and disciplined them. In some ways, Factory drove Joy Division. In other ways, the group drove the record company. They certainly drove each other up the walls of their mutual adventure. Together they erratically defied the boring rock gravity of following certain rules of presentation and promotion. Factory helped wrap the darkness of Joy Division in darkness – they wrapped a shroud of provocative anti-glamour around the group, either for protection or to expose even more dramatically the enriched drama of the music.)

Factory Records were unusual. Since when has a record company – not so much a record company, more an existential bodyguard – been a combination of villain, pantomime dame, benefactor, wicked stepmother, clown, love, butler, coach, pervert and performance artist? Joy Division could only have been the Joy Division they became because they were a big part of the Factory family.

Factory was a mad, maddening male communion of Northwest television presenter Tony Wilson, a sort of cross between Jerry Springer and Malcolm McLaren, actor and will o' the wisp Alan Erasmus, record producer Martin Hannett and Joy Division's manager, Rob Gretton. Joy Division couldn't have become the Joy Division they became without Gretton, the quiet fanatic who managed them like he was on a quest for some rock and roll holy grail. He loved the group like a child, like a brother, like a father, like a friend, like a fan, and he watched over them with such belief and commitment. He followed them to the ends of the earth and then, oddly enough, beyond.

It was Wilson who had a zealous need to create rock history using Joy

Division as his tool. He was a seedy idealist, a vulnerable creep, a loveable rogue. He loved the rock myths of Hendrix, the Doors, the Pistols, myths made up of death and danger and cultural derring-do. He loved the idea of his beloved Manchester being the home of a fantastic new rock and roll cult, a massive new youth myth based around the life, and then the death, of Joy Division. He had the lead-lined conceit and the whipped-up energy of a fan who wanted to make rock and roll history. It's always the fans of rock and roll history, the fans who believe in it religiously, who make rock and roll history. He was greedy for the thrill of being associated with a bona fide cultural event. When Ian Curtis was alive, and so therefore were Joy Division, he hustled hard and shamelessly to ensure the group were destined to fulfil a rock and roll fate that would see them as notorious, as known, as classic as the Doors, or the Velvet Underground. He wanted to be part of something that sold the noise of dreams to the whole world, something that changed the very nature of pop culture.

While Ian was living, and Joy Division were more and more communicating the details of Ian's careering life, Wilson was convinced that they could be a British group as massive and as iconic as the Stones, the Who, Led Zeppelin. A group that could create the images and moods of a decade, a generation, even a century. A group that could get into the minds of the whole world.

Curtis' death didn't stop Wilson in his tracks. It whetted his appetite even more. The violent suicide of the lead singer gave Wilson strong raw material to play with. He wasn't the type to play down such an episode, and as far as he was concerned it didn't mean that any myth that was growing around the music of Joy Division died with the singer. Such a death was a massive shot in the arm to the myth, and he was determined to use the black energy of the suicide to maintain his belief that Joy Division had cultural and iconic importance. What this importance was could be made up along the way. Rock and roll history is always made up of spontaneous and unpredicted moments that are then rationalised in comparatively comfortable hindsight.

Curtis had made earlier attempts to commit suicide, and these failures perhaps encouraged Wilson to consider the possibilities of what could happen to the reputation of the group if their singer destroyed himself. After all, the group made a music that seemed to point towards suicide. The later songs that Joy Division were writing were the increasingly sensitive Curtis' autobiographical way of dealing with his depressive struggles to live, his struggle with love, they were songs about the burden of the future, and the death of sensation, and death itself. They were the songs of someone losing touch with the conditions of everyday reality, songs about someone slipping into something else, someone discovering new levels to reality. The songs of somebody drugged by his own predicament.

A suicide would certainly suggest that this doom-laden, energetically exhausted and gracefully self-obsessed music wasn't any kind of fake. The intensity of the music would be sealed into permanent myth by the suicide of the singer – the utter reality of such an action could only succeed in spotlighting the darkness of the songs and confirm that the songs were made up of dense and packed truth.

Wilson felt before Curtis died that he had a modern post-punk Pink Floyd on his hands. He saw Joy Division as a potential supergroup, taking out their uncompromising view of madness and desperation into the commercial world and developing into rock greats who were serious and artistic about what they did. He felt that the group were good enough and powerful enough to dominate the nineties and beyond with their sonic drama and imageless image. Eventually, he would claim that Joy Division set up the territory and cleared the way for the success of U2. He considered that U2 became what Joy Division would have become without the suicide of their singer. Legends in their own rock and roll lifetime.

At the time, once Curtis had died, Wilson, fascinated by the shape of rock and roll history, was convinced that the suicide could help Joy Division become a modern post-punk Doors, and Curtis as mythically malleable, as posthumously iconic, as Jim Morrison. Curtis killed himself on the eve of a tour Joy Division were about to make of America, a tour Wilson and comrades were hoping would be an integral part of the plan to establish Joy Division as the first real post-punk supergroup. The abrupt disintegration of the group, the shocked and melodramatic response of a small but influential number of fans and critics, meant that instead of an American tour propelling the group towards anti-superstar status, it was a suicide. Wilson, with amoral glee, playing a slippy game of manipulation and fantasising endlessly about creating some hard-edged Northwest equivalent of the Sex Pistols, set to work. Rumours, lies, facts, fictions, hypes, all started to develop around the ex-group and their ex-singer. Within a matter of weeks after Curtis' death, the group had their first hit single. 'Love Will Tear Us Apart' contained in its lyric and melody and weary dynamic all the information you might require about why Ian Curtis killed himself, in the way that a seed contains everything that eventually becomes a tree. The song was his agony and desperation compressed into the irresistible shape of a great, moving pop song. It probably would have been a hit even if Curtis hadn't killed himself. Already the rumours about his suicide attempts and his horribly random epileptic fits were adding to a fever that was spreading in pop circles regarding the nature and commitment of the group.

As it was, Joy Division began their first few weeks of unintentional non-existence with a hit single, and the strange facts of the strange fate of Ian Curtis ensured that Joy Division were destined to find a place in any list of rock and roll weirdness and rock and roll greats. Just how high their position would be in such arbitrary lists would be down to the to-ing and fro-ing, the egging and fretting of Wilson and his cohorts. And down to how writers would respond to the suicide and Factory's creative and commercial exploitation of it . . .

5/

And so I responded, and continue to respond . . . surrounded by fallout . . . from one thing and another.

6/

And so all of this, all of this before and after, all of this makeup and varnish, all of these coincidences, and transmissions, and transitions, and (r)apt moments, and exotic settings, and wild distortions, it all added up, and multiplied, and put the group, what with one thing and a bloody other, into this unique position where they were both the last ever great rock and roll group (after the Velvet Underground, the Stooges, the MC5, the Doors, Television, the Sex Pistols) and the first ever great rock and roll band (before Sonic Youth, the Pixies, My Bloody Valentine, Nine Inch Nails, Nirvana, Smashing Pumpkins, Radiohead . . . ), and so somehow they were some twisting turning point, some tunnel of light and dark and love and heart that you must journey through from one era to the next, from one noise to another, if you are to make any sense of the urgency and desire of great rock music . . . Joy Division summoned up in their time and place, summed up in their local way, with such certainty and uncertainty, with such chilling heat, all the great rock and roll that there ever was and ever will be.

7/

Joy Division are, in my order of things, which is pretty correct all things considered, the dead centre of the rock universe. They sounded like the greatest rock group of all time, and they ended up all mangled and martyred like a great rock and roll group. They just kept going faster and faster until they suddenly stopped, slammed into themselves by the force of love and the temptation of some other life.

8/

Or death. Because, and so, there was this death in the family. And rock and roll, the greedy bastard, loves early death and gaudy sacrifice. The myth of rock and roll loves death as the lions loved the Christians. Death in rock and roll, and there just isn't enough of it, chronically, cosmically represents the ideal levels in rock of madness, danger, self-belief and self-deception. At the extremes of desire, death proves rock and roll, certifies its acts of rebellion. It's not all playacting. And death proved Joy Division weren't playing with all those extreme, surreal, eerie themes. Death – general, individual – rammed home into amplified eternity the essential black-hearted glamour that rock and roll aspires to, instantly, brutally creates the kind of immortality that all entertainers – even the frail, unformed and boyishly, conscientiously alienated Ian Curtis – desperately crave. Immortality without death might be preferable, and mid-song, mid-ecstatic moment, soul deep in modern fame, caught in the glare of awed attention, an entertainer might glimpse a sort of immortality. But it needs a messy, publicised mixture of show business and death to achieve an authentic immortality, a rock and roll immortality. In Ian's case, there was the show business, there was the death, and there was the fact that the dreams written into his songs, the life-suffering death-dreaming songs, tragically came true. It was immortality garlanded with death, an extra special kind of immortality.

9/

And so Ian Curtis, dead name, dead stop, dead mysterious, dead success, dead at the moment, dead all the time, a close relation of the unknown, as withdrawn as it gets, yet in some ways more alive than when he was alive.

And so how romantic can you get?

And so how accidental or intentional is life and death?

And so, fatalism.

And so Joy Division, dead cool, as made up as history, as insane as rock and roll history, had flawless seriousness thrust upon them overnight – that's overnight, that's serious, that's boys becoming men, that's their far-out music becoming true in the time it takes to stop breathing forever, that's the fiction of their songs becoming fact in the ultimate instant it takes for the lights to go out. Overnight. Seriously.

And so Joy Division, who perhaps played at being out of this world, who just played and sang what came naturally however supernatural it sounded, were hurled out of this world.

And so, overnight, they played at taking themselves seriously. In the collapsed, dense middle of one martyring night, seriousness worked for them. Who could deny the seriousness of it all? This had some meaning. This had the kind of meaning the spirited Wilson was ready for. He was ready to suck out all the goodness. All of the badness. He was ready to suck on the seriousness of the situation for all it was worth. To suck on the fallout.

10/

And so, Joy Division, as lovely as a dream in stone, had everything going for them as rock and roll myths. It was just as their record sleeves always cried and whispered, as if they were implicitly predicting in their abstraction the fate of the group and their singer. A fate that was beyond everyone's wildest dreams, even those of the extra-dreamy Wilson at the dreamy Factory. His dreams, though, were pretty wild. Dreams based on thought. The thought of a wonderful tomorrow.

He thought in the extra time Curtis' death gave this once upon a time group; 'a myth of myths can be built upon this short, fast, fractured life that was rendered psychedelically breathless by a messy midnight death.' He thought exactly those words, whether he knew it or not. He thought this as a fan of rock and roll corniness, as a fan of rock and roll seriousness, as a fan of fans and the power of their worship.

11/

And so, the seriousness of Joy Division was left hanging in space, and violently rocking.

12/

And so what might have been was left viciously disturbed.

And so all along they were glorying in their fate.

And so now Joy Division were disturbing the future because a suicide, whatever the circumstance, whatever the pointlessness, must never be forgotten. Because a suicide is two incredible things. It's the waste of a life and it's the making of a life. Suicide is where the point of life gets all mixed up with the pointlessness of it, and there's a shiver that races down the spine of the universe, and beyond, out into eternity, creating shock waves that never ever stop vibrating from one end of the end to another. And when you think about it a suicide is unforgettable. Oh, and so, there was the death of the man who produced, with an ear that could hear the moon circle the earth, all of the songs of Joy Division. His name was Martin Hannett, and apart from anything else I remember that he was the first person I ever saw smoke a joint. Sometime in the mid-seventies, somewhere in an office down Manchester's Oxford Road, near the university. I don't remember what I was doing there or why I was meeting him but I remember this man talking to me as if he knew all about the reasons Captain Beefheart and Tim Buckley and Iggy Pop made the music the way they made it, as if he'd been to their world, and back. And there was something about the way he smoked the thing he held loosely in his hand that suggested it was the secret to visiting the worlds of Frank Zappa and Neil Young and Love. I remember feeling a little unnerved in his presence, not because he was scary, but because he seemed to know things I only knew that I didn't know, and as he smoked the thing in his hand he sank further and further into his own brand of knowledge, further and further away from me. Eventually, he got so far away from me he appeared quite motionless. I guess he was motionless in relation to the stars.

His knowledge as inspired by the thing he held seriously but lethargically in his hand seemed more romantic and unreasonable than any knowledge of mine. Eventually I would get to hear a soundtrack to his reality-curling knowledge, when I heard the music of Joy Division. I would hear a hint of his take on reality, a take that could be taken as ever so slightly, but prettily, mistaken, with how he framed, and softened, and toughened, the songs of Joy Division. He set them into landscapes he'd learnt about by visiting imagined other worlds. He created sound effects copied from sounds he'd heard experiencing the weather in imagined other worlds. I suppose you could say he sort of stoned the songs.

And so Martin Hannett died too. Another death in the Factory family, although by the time he died he was pretty much the black sheep in the family. Or maybe he was the white sheep in a family of black sheep. He didn't kill himself directly. He died from heart failure. His heart broke.

But who's to say that someone who so willingly and regularly visited other worlds – worlds artificially created and/or worlds as real as this one – in the name of discovery, of escape, of courage, of cowardice, wasn't slowly killing himself, and perhaps in the end not so much committing suicide as deciding to visit permanently some other world. A world with new and different possibilities. A world which consisted of sounds and shadows, some of which he'd already laid into the close background of some of Joy Division's songs. Sounds which sounded like nothing else but otherness. Sounds that sounded like ghosts sounding out other worlds.

The death of Hannett added more mischief to the myth of Joy Division, more fun and games, more disjointed history, more incidental insubordination, more violence, more degenerate heroism, more seriousness. All in all another death added to the gathering components making up Joy Division, with one foot in this world and one foot someplace else, as this big-deal, rock and roll illusion trapped inside their very own infinitely variable, endlessly interpreted mystery-melodrama. For a fairly obscure northern rock act with a badly botched-up life, they were getting bigger than they seemed, on the quiet as big as they come. Their death-festooned myth was becoming noisy and quiet, dazzling and hidden, static and dynamic . . . not quite reaching the level of the Doors, but then the Doors myth is not quite as intriguing as that of Joy Division. And for Wilson, there was always the hope of the book, the film, the commercially maximised publicity to help propel Joy Division up another iconic division and into another mythical dimension.

13/

And so, seriously, Joy Division, after their overnight stop, their collision with fate, neither exist nor do not exist. With the help of a shattered Curtis, the tangle he got his marriage into, the crush his mind squashed into, and a lethal length of clothesline, the group plummeted a few feet or a few million light years into a rainy limbo where they hang around somewhere between myth and Myth. They hang around somewhere between giants and insects, for everyone to inspect. And sometimes quite a queue builds up. A queue of inspectors expecting this group as they sway in breezy limbo to supply them with something you tend to expect from insects and giants.

14/

Wonder.

15/

And so I could write – with the intention of a rock writer showered by fallout – about Joy Division's central role in it all, the it all of rock and roll et al, and yet how they are also so off-centre. But then, to be so central to the story they have to be off-centre as well, because the central beauty of rock and roll is that it is off-centre. It must never be at the centre. Joy Division had to be off-centre to be at the centre of rock and roll, but even when they were at the centre, they were outside the centre. Anything else would be too banal for words. They had to be off-centre to be central, to be central in a place that has no centre. At this place, the centre of no centre, the central place in a centreless place, they could be properly obvious, mysterious, and (in the skipped beat of a missing moment) enigmatic. Here, at this centre that was no centre at all, they would exist in a non-existing way as the greatest rock and roll group ever to be found and ever to go missing.

16/

And so moving on from where we have placed them off-centre (to the point of anti-centrality) in the history of rock things, the myth still rises, and obscures and provokes.

17/

And so they said that some guide was going to come and take them by the hand, and there were these gulping black noises, and these squirming off-white sub-noises, that sounded like they were giving birth or operating on themselves. Noises that had travelled from other worlds and which hovered around the realish-sounding rock like vultures surrounding a body they weren't sure was alive or dead. *Unknown Pleasures* began with music that sounded like it was inside your head, nibbling away at your nerve endings and crunching through bone.

And so yes, Joy Division's music could form the soundtrack for something very David Lynch-like. It would be no good in a Tarantino setting. That's the point, really. Joy Division, like Lynch, never had any intention of wanting to cut the universe down to size. They loved – and hated, but with respect – the size of the universe. The size of the universe is everything.* And the size is in the details. Each detail in the universe carries within it a map of the universe, sometimes to scale. One of the great things about Joy Division was their appreciation of size and their attention to detail, and when to use a map, and when to trust their own instincts about where things were.

And so, believe me, it was as if, whether they intended this or not, they were trying to warn us about dangers to avoid. In doing this they of course alerted us to dangers we may not previously have been aware of.

And so, according to Joy Division, whether they knew it or not, nothing is neutral, nothing is impotent, nothing is next to nothing, nothing comes first, nothing comes last, nothing is at the centre and an atom may ruin all, an atom may ransom us all.

And so you wake up frightened with the feeling of having overslept.

And so they made us think of another separate world that maniacs and exiles invent when the normal everyday world seems impossible.

18/

And so the mood shifts again.

19/

And so there were the writings of Ian Curtis, who was underground by the time he was 23. He wrote these tranquil and delirious autobiographical fragments, these notes and notices from an aboveground underground, images that leapt out of language, and it sounded as if all his senses were being tensed. The words seemed to come from someone who had lived so much more than twenty-odd years. Something was concentrating his mind wonderfully. It was exactly as if he suspected, consciously or not, that it – the all embracing it, the it of all its, the it you can see in the eyes of a dying man – was coming to an end one way or another sooner rather than later. Even without having all that I've mentioned – their off-centred centrality, their essence-ness, their post-punk zeal, their book of contacts – Curtis' impressions and depressions, his fast decaying urgency, would have lifted Joy Division into greatness.

He sang from the knife edge of doubt with a kind of suave, sordid, middle-of-the-road disconnectedness. He sang about defeat, and a defeated mind, with a dissolved glory, as if there was a kind of triumph in the difficulties of life. He sang suffering with an almost tender listlessness. He put the perfect voice to strangled thoughts. He put this awkward but handsome spin on despair. He crooned anxiety as if he was flirting with the grim reaper. He delivered sullen commotion. He expressed his restlessness and soul-sickness with a damaged insouciance. Even when he was charged, and confrontational, he seemed resigned. He sang his sharply apprehensive songs in the spirit of . . .

I'll get this off my chest. And then get this chest off me.

And so this music that rocked – that could go the distance and bash your brains in – hung inside a sense of sadness and waste and emptiness. And, as more and more of Curtis' life spun through its complications, the music was embraced by a physical and mental exhaustion. It was as if Curtis was transferring himself into the very body of the music, stumbling over the line from where the music was for him to where he was for the music. The songs weren't helping him deal with or recover from the traumas of his life, they were encouraging a fascination with the speed and danger of the drama. They weren't an escape from the madness; they sent him right into the madness. The music was taking him away, from himself, from others, from life. It was taking him over. It needed the drama of his life.

And so there was more drama. And more madness.

And so the sin always rises.

And so Ian Curtis – depressed, epileptic, unfaithful, artistic, pressured – was using his songs and being used by his songs to create a map of despair at the end of a life. The map was perfectly in scale. Of course, he didn't have to follow the map. But he'd lost his bearings.

20/

And so Ian Curtis lived his life intensely to such depths. It became a rock and roll life. A poet's life. A madman's life. A sick life. Formerly a real life. You can hear the depth and intensity on the deep, intense pop song 'Love Will Tear Us Apart'. Listening to the song you can tell exactly – around an unknown hard centre – when his life started to end. (And you get a hint of when it started to begin. You can even hear when he started to believe in death. It's all there in the details of his voice, as it forms and reforms, as it swells and fades, and in the way it's coated thickly with memory, and regret.)

21/

And so there was Ian Curtis leading the group who were all playing their instruments as if they were leading. As if there were three lead instruments. The glass-smashing and capering Bernard Sumner guitars, the cold and splendidly alert Steve Morris drums, the iron-tough and lurid Peter Hook bass. Even the spare and marooned noises off, the phantom implants drafted in from some other blue world by Martin Hannett to gee up, or down, proceedings, these noises acted as if they had an (ectoplasmic) ego all of their own, as if they were actually leading. The circle completed itself with Curtis and his tragic voice and antic gee-ed up, or down, dancing – he moved to the music as if he wanted to run on the spot faster than the planet was spinning – and he was leading the group, and us, into his . . .

. . . space.

The space that exists in the music of Joy Division has always been intriguing. Somehow – everything still stretched around somehow, stretched as tight as the rope that squeezed the life out of Curtis – the group could leave such emptiness in the middle of their music, and at the edges, without weakening it. It added to the strength, the resonance. Perhaps it came out of the space they were leaving around each other – even as they came together to make this music, and sort of fell in love with each other, they kept themselves to themselves. They stayed trapped inside their own splendid isolation, stuck inside their own young minds. They all played and sang from deep inside their own detailed worlds. Joy Divison was privacy times four.

And so their music is about, finally, isolation. It is about the difficulty of keeping in touch with other human beings as we create for safety's sake a reality around us that works for us as much as it can. A reality we can trust. It's about the mind, as far as my mind is concerned, and the tricks that it plays on itself, the harm it can do itself as it struggles to float in a world containing so much water it can drown you in a second. The songs are about the way the mind can find all sorts of ways to prise apart illusion and reality and then cobble them back together in a way that makes sense if only for the moment.

24/

And so to the songs, again and again, because they just do not wear out whatever you take from them, wherever you take them. Somewhere in there, amidst other more secretive and even more catastrophic narratives, you can make out Ian's feisty, frail battle for self-preservation, a battle he was winning and then he was losing. Perhaps if he hadn't have got drunk that night, and hadn't listened to Iggy Pop shrieking for mercy, and hadn't watched a Herzog film, and hadn't thought he'd fucked up his life, he wouldn't have killed himself. Until the next week, or the next month. Perhaps he might have found his bearings and done away with the map.

Even if he had survived, there would still be these songs, and they're not great because he died, they're great because he sung about how close life can be to death. He sang about how the difference between life and death is never more than an instant, a moment, a thought, and he sang about what it's like to get closer and closer to that moment, that thought. He could have got this close to the moment and survived. But the closer you get to such a moment, the more lethal emotions become. Emotions can kill. Emotions kill more people than anything else, one way or another.

25/

These songs were lifted beyond themselves by being – as far as it can go, if this isn't too farfetched – set inside the enclosed, abstract and echoing space of a mind which enveloped the songs from all directions. This is some illusion. And some reality. Ian Curtis' mind somehow – how this is so is always on the tip of my tongue – held the songs in shivering space.

And so I suppose I'm saying, this time, that with the music of Joy Division we can see inside a mind. And we hear him beginning to think ideas he only has so much time to formulate, ideas and thoughts that are, with such boyish bravado and such adult cynicism, about everything and then nothing. He was beginning to think and his early thoughts were the end. The thoughts were just too good. And too bad.

26/

And so he re-enters the shadows of living night, disappears into the overnight that strangled his everything and then nothing.

And so his ideas, they're forgotten, abandoned, miscarried, before he ever really knew he was having them. Carried away by the twists and turns of his own life, startled by responsibility, adrift in the turmoil of extended adolescence, he thought for a moment he could escape. He thought he could fly. But he didn't fly. He slumped with a vicious snap into the infinitely miniscule gap between life and death. A life that had weakened him beyond measure also conspired to give him the uncanny strength, so that he could lift life right out of his body and hurl it into the dark side of the dark.

27/

His empty and empty-handed body survived him a few days and was laid to rest one afternoon in a chapel in his hometown, Macclesfield, for friends and relatives to pay their respects.

28/

And so Ian Curtis. He gave Joy Division their life and their death. He gave Joy Division his life and his death. He gave them their perverted specialness. He actually risked his neck. He was under crisis and he passed this sense of crisis – real and imagined, and in the end what's the difference? – right into the bloody, unstable body of the music. Right into its heart and soul. He was fighting mad, he'd given up, and you can sense the tension between wanting life and wanting death in the turbulence of the music. You can hear the fight that went on between the steady common sense that stabilises this life in this time, and the ferocious senselessness that constantly threatens the balance of life, that wobbles life, and rocks it, and rolls it, until it shakes itself apart. The epilepsy that came late in his life seemed to symbolise the way his life was shaking itself to bits, pulling itself apart at the seams, dragging Curtis and his very being into another state of mind, a sleepless unconsciousness. He danced with controlled uncontrollability as if he wanted to outstrip the speed of the planet. His epileptic fits sickly emphasised his need to move faster than the world. His emotions moved him faster than the earth as it hurtles through space. His soul was vibrating like a demonic hummingbird. It all added up to an acceleration, a momentum, that saw him leave the third planet from the sun far, far behind.

29/

He was frightened, and his music was frightening. He was in love with the wrong woman at the wrong time. He was hurtling down a tunnel of love and hate wondering why there was no light at the end. He was a father a lifetime before he was ready. He was depressed because he was sick. He was sick because he was depressed.

And so he was lonely. That he and his friends – who were just as lonely in their own lost ways – could turn these thoughts and confusions so magically into sounds – gentle, pure, heartbreaking and lacerating sounds – is but a hint of the alchemical extravagance of the strangely intelligent, ridiculously burdened, youthfully defiant, magnificently doomed, glooming and blooming, old-style, avant-garde, anonymous and famous rock and roll group.

30/

And so if I may be so bold at such an exact time, covered with the fallout of a series of big and little explosions in my past, to say the following: Joy Division locate us in the gently smouldering nowhere solid hell** of communal remembering, of mutual awareness, never exact, never erased.

And so, mind you, there we have it. ★★★

★And nothing.
★★The word 'hell' stems from the Germanic root meaning 'concealed' and originally, like Hades or Sheol, had less to do with punishment than simple, bleak survival in a vague netherworld.
★★★Another end, another day, another doldrum, another beginning, another way of seeing things when there is nothing and everything to see. And so, on. And on. And so on.

## LIV

Because of Hooky's bass lines, the journeys they embark on

because of 'Love Will Tear Us Apart'

because of the showmanship of Wilson, and Gretton, and Hannett, and Erasmus, and Saville

because they wanted to dazzle the world regardless of profit, Factory's comedy brothers crossing the ocean in a bathtub, shooting people out of cannons

because of the suicide, the chaos, the internal feuds, the love affairs, the brief moments of glory, and the sordid exploitation of young men's natural urges

because of 'Atmosphere'

because of the relationship between the Factory Club and the Haçienda, between the Sex Pistols and the Happy Mondays

because of the relationship between memory and the unfolding of time

because of the connection between the order of things and the strange intersection of events in the world

because of the great health and the utter bankruptcy

because Manchester is in Europe

because some things are remembered with clarity and some things are not

because we are all egotists who allow our feelings to dominate our lives

because we pay more attention to some things than to others

because memory is deceptive

because it is coloured by the events of today

because of 'Transmission' and the turning of knowledge into ideas and convictions

because of Curtis' last days and Wilson's exaggerated preoccupation with social position

because Gretton supplied a note or two of comic irresponsibility

because Joy Division never made it to New York until they were something else altogether, in fact a sort of New York group

because of the sudden visions about the value of life that Curtis had during epileptic fits

because of the relationship between the world of the imagination and the real world

because of the tortured, self-torturing souls and the hair-raising pessimists

because of the gentle souls and the tremendous hedonists

because high art had gone public

because Curtis knew as well as Saville and Hannett how and why shadows decompose

because of the cranky, cornered drumming of Stephen Morris

because of the optimism and opportunity

because Hannett combined intense inwardness with a proliferation of sensual data

because Hannett emptied the space of a song in order to let the listener inhabit it

because their air seemed to disappear and there was nothing to breathe

because Wilson decided that since we shall never know why we are alive he must select an arbitrary purpose and stick to it

because we can't see other people's thoughts

because Hannett sued Factory

because Saville was late, a slave to the depth beneath surface

because Gretton smoked for Manchester, until Manchester became Madchester

because freedom which on this earth can only be bought with a thousand of the hardest sacrifices must be enjoyed unrestrictedly in its fullness without any kind of programmatic calculation as long as it lasts

because the thriving city is just a few miles away from an almost barren landscape

because a group of locals all helped each other and got in each other's way

because time damages the memory and memory burns into time

because Joy Division's music was not as such interested in the shape of the universe as it was but in the shape it would become

because Wilson was a little older than everyone else

because poetry overlapped with comedy and clowns clashed with revolutionaries

because rock history took shape around Wilson's definite intention to make rock history

because people looked back at the way things happened as if they had happened exactly as remembered

because the modernist impulse of unrestraint had taken over popular thought and style

because Wilson was financially useless

because he was always midway between himself and another thing

because all this happened in and around Manchester between punk and rave, putting up big brackets of nonsense, love and perception around the grim, disconcerting Thatcher era

because Wilson acted like he always knew the whole thing was going to become a film, as if he was already in a film, and it was all about him

because some of this in some way had to be provisionally explained so that it might not dwell forever in the distant margins of fading appreciation, then eventually the story became a film.

The story, for all its messed-up messing with reality and associated factors, became real, or as real as art and/or entertainment ever is, lodged into the memories of those who watch films for some assistance with their memory.

With true Factory precision, and imprecision, it became a film about itself, a made-up true story, a collision of anecdotes and speculations turned into dubious documentary. A character broadly based on me is played by the comic actor Simon Pegg. Steve Coogan as a comedy Tony Wilson wants to show Simon Pegg as an unformed and reluctant me the dead body of Ian Curtis, and perhaps it's just one of the many absurd punchlines that Wilson anticipated – that this eccentric moment, the time he helped me out with some dubious but dramatic material for a book I'd never write, would one day somehow be an odd little part of the chaotic texture of a film history that sorted out the truth by making everything up.

The film explained only that there was a large amount of activity and information concerning the creation and collapse of Factory Records that needed to be explained and one day possibly would be. For the moment, one of many, it made do with making an exquisitely English entertainment out of a fascinating search for a definition of the creative imagination, or an exposure of glorious, occasionally dangerous idiocy.

## LV

**Article for *The Guardian* about the filming of Michael Winterbottom's *24 Hour Party People*.**

001

As I sit in a Manchester hotel bar a young man walks slowly across the room. He's quite tall and very slim, stooped inside slightly ill-fitting dark clothes that might have been bought at Oxfam, and he wears an expression of distracted sadness. For a stunning moment, I swear that it is Ian Curtis, the Joy Division singer who killed himself twenty years ago. He disappears through a door, vanishes like a ghost.

002

I'm in Manchester to watch the filming of *24 Hour Party People*, a story about the Manchester music scene from the punk of 1976 to the post-acid of 1992, a story about the suicide of Ian Curtis, a story about the artful dodging of Shaun Ryder, a story about a city that changed its face inside a decade, a story about the Haçienda nightclub, and most of all, a story about Tony Wilson, hero, villain, intellectual, slimeball, charlatan, loser, eccentric, drama queen, ultimate northern romantic.

003

The film features *Human Traffic*'s John Simm, *The Royle Family*'s Ralf Little, *Human Remains*' Rob Brydon, *Snatch*'s Lenny James, *A Room for Romeo Brass*'s Paddy Considine, and comedians Peter Kay, Keith Allen, John Thompson, and Dave Gorman.

004

And then there's Steve Coogan as the brilliant, infuriating Tony Wilson, the man who soaks up the sacred Manchester air as if it is a drug that will speed him up and spin him around until he glimpses God, or becomes God, or perhaps just gets to boss God around. Coogan as Wilson! Only in Manchester. It may be a story about art, love, death, ambition, betrayal, vanity, sex, drugs, rock 'n' roll and more death, but you've got to laugh.

005

John Simm is driving in from Manchester airport to begin work on the film. He is, to his sheer delight, playing Bernard Sumner, the Joy Division/New Order guitarist. Simm's cab driver recognises him. He asks him what he's in town for. Simm tells him he's got a part in *24 Hour Party People*. 'What's that?' asks the cabbie. He will at best know Wilson as the annoying man off the telly, the one with the poncey clothes, not the rock 'n' roll games player. You know, Simm explains, it's the story of Factory Records, and the Haçienda, and Tony Wilson. The cab driver cannot believe his ears. 'Hang on,' he shouts, 'you're telling me they're making a fucking movie about that wanker Tony Wilson, and he's the main part? Oh, he's going to fucking love that, isn't he?'

006

If you live outside the Granada television area, and can't quite place Tony Wilson, imagine TV's silky, sickly smooth John Stapleton, but as well as smiling on the TV, reading autocues and twinkling from the eye, make believe he also runs Fatboy Slim's label. Or think Richard Madeley of *Richard and Judy* blended with Archer, Attenborough, Hefner, Branson, Don Quixote and Umberto Eco.

007

Steve Coogan was ten when he first saw Wilson in the flesh. It was 1975 and Wilson the local TV celebrity was visiting Coogan's house for a birthday party. He seemed so exotic, even though he was just the local equivalent of the weatherman. Coogan worked with Wilson for a while in the late 1980s on a late night Granada show, and got to know him semi-socially. 'And I used to do an impression of him,' Coogan tells me after a hard day being Wilson. 'Easy day, actually, although I probably shouldn't say that. But Tony Wilson has done all the work for me. I just turn up and put on the wig and clothes, and off I go.' He does a bit of Wilson for me, and he's as camp and as breathless as the real thing. 'It's that sort of foppish, self-conscious thing he has, it's quite effeminate actually, and you can't work out whether he's being incredibly eloquent or just bullshitting, and it's sort of in the middle.'

008

'It's all untrue,' Wilson bellows down the phone when I call him about the movie. He takes himself very seriously, and laughs at himself constantly. He's all mixed up and dead sure of himself.

009

The film sets him midway between local hero who helped drag Manchester into a bright 21st century and an almost psychedelic figure of fun. 'It's all made up. Which is good! I always quote Howard Hawks – that between legend and truth always choose the legend. Well, that's what's happening with this film. They've gone for the legend. I tried hard to get them to make the film about the two really great stories, Curtis and Ryder, but I gave up when I realised where Coogan was going to go with it. And that's fine. It's his gig. I'm sort of like the Rovers Return in it, you know, everything in *Coronation Street* revolves around the pub, and that's me. I'm the pub. And they're going to take the piss out of me. They have to. How else can they make it? But I'm at ease with it. You probably think I'm a fucking idiot for letting them do it, but I'm at ease. Flattered, embarrassed and at ease.'

010

39-year-old director Michael Winterbottom told writer Frank Cottrell-Boyce that he was thinking of making a film about Factory Records. Frank told Winterbottom that if he got anyone else to write it, he would kill him. He's a Liverpudlian, but he appreciated what set Manchester apart: the sheer madness and self-belief that seemed to be passed from the Sex Pistols to an audience of about 50 Mancunians the night they played the Lesser Free Trade Hall in 1976.

011

'At first you think it's the story of Ian Curtis, a rock 'n' roll suicide, or that of Shaun Ryder, classic rock 'n' roll excess, but actually, it's more than that; there are loads of other stories to tell about Manchester during that time. And the best way to tell them is through Wilson, because somehow he was always at the middle of it all. And if you grew up in the Northwest during the 1970s, then Wilson was an absolutely riveting character. Because he read the news, and he did stupid local news stories with ducks and sheep, but he also presented a punk rock programme and had a really hip record label. He was like your uncle, but he was totally rock 'n' roll. And all this mad stuff happened because of him, and in spite of him. And whereas artists seem to have a skin missing, entrepreneurs like Wilson seem to have this extra skin. You can never seem to upset Wilson. He knows people think he's a wanker, but it doesn't bother him. I sent him a copy of the script, which is affectionate but also has a go, and I thought he'd send out a hit man to kill me. But he rang me up, and said, "Love, it's fabulous, do you fancy a drink?"'

012

Coogan, as intensely serious as only an off-duty comedian can be, worries away at who and what Wilson might be, an impossible task, because as soon as you think you've pinned him down, he's changed shape, he's changed his mind. 'It's like he's not sure if he's Melvyn Bragg or Malcolm McLaren, and in a way he's more interesting than either of them, and the fact he's never achieved as much as those two is also interesting. Joy Division could have been U2, Haçienda could have become Cream or the Ministry of Sound, but somehow the wild energy that went into setting everything up caused its collapse, and nothing ever went corporate or boring. It's like Wilson would rather have disaster than obviousness. As long as it causes a reaction.'

013

The film's producer Andrew Eaton explains how hard it was to raise money for the film; and how hard it was to get all the proud, uncompromising characters involved to agree to their lives being stretched and shredded into this substitute reality. 'It was hard to get backers to appreciate why anyone would be interested in these characters. They didn't think anyone would know who they were. But it doesn't matter whether you know who these characters are or not. It's such a great story. You couldn't make up stuff that was funnier, or sadder. And everyone who we've featured is willing for it to work. Because as funny, or as sad, as it is, it's a celebration of a great movement, and the people who made it happen.'

014

We're talking in a nightclub in Manchester that's doubling for the working man's club in Hulme that Wilson and co used in 1977 to launch their Factory night. Coogan as Wilson is persuading Peter Kay as the club owner to let them use his venue. I catch my first sight of Coogan camped out in a

1970s Wilson wig, and my mind boggles in sympathy, respect, and the kind of love you can feel around Wilson that sometimes bleeds over into less than love. (When you hate Wilson you think you're being too harsh: when you love him you wonder if you've been conned.) Later on, the opening night of the Factory club will be recreated, with frail ambient guitarist Vini Reilly and Joy Division. I can't wait. Joy Division are the greatest rock group I have ever seen on stage. I was there at the opening of the Factory club 23 years ago, and I'm here to see what kind of mess, or what kind of strangeness, there will be in trying to mock up such a past. A past that has its own particular mess and strangeness.

015

When people hear that Coogan is playing Wilson, there's a gasp. But in a way it's not Coogan playing Wilson. It's Alan Partridge. There was always a bit of Wilson, the pedantic, pushy, self-centred Wilson, in Partridge.

016

'Tony Wilson is like a leftwing, avant-garde Alan Partridge, although Partridge is a much bigger idiot and isn't trying to push the frontiers of anything. And I like Wilson for many of the same reasons I liked Alan Partridge. Wilson is very flawed, but very human, and there is something brave and amateurish about what he does.'

017

'Yes,' sweet-talks Wilson, his speech gathering pace as he talks down his mobile phone. I have caught him searching Manchester bookshops for a photograph for a Joy Division album sleeve. I imagine him marching – no, swanning – around the streets of his beloved Manchester as he talks to me. Coat flaring out behind him, him and his shadow larger than real or film life. 'Yes, it's the past and it's fun and it's entertaining . . . but it's all over. Who gives a fuck about the past? The film seems very irrelevant to me. I'm interested in now, the future, in moving on . . . I'm about to sign the best rock 'n' roll band in the world, I'm setting up an internet company, I'm doing a new Factory with a new name . . .' He begins to talk even faster, as if he's running away from a past and a self that this film celebrates, and satirises, and fixes in time, The film may be his monument, until they build a statue in Albert Square. A sad, stupid, lovely tribute that proves he was right all along – he knows what he's talking about – and yet wrong – he didn't have a clue what he was doing. I ask him if he feels the film is sort of like a lifetime award and means that, as far as his adventures are concerned, it's all over bar the nostalgia. 'Absolutely not,' he snaps heatedly, 'no, no, no . . .' There might be a note of panic in his voice, there might not be. Who can ever tell with Wilson?

018

Keith Allen tells Winterbottom that if he's not in the film, he's going to kill him. He gets a part in the film.

019

Rob Brydon, punked up for the day, hasn't got a clue what's going on. 'I missed the Sex Pistols,' he admits, 'I was dancing to Shakin' Stevens in 1977. It was all disco and cheesecloth for me.' He represents all those people who know very little about the rise and farce of Factory Records, who know nothing about the extreme mood music of Joy Division, or the artistic vision of the label, or their belief in the rights of the artists, or their magnificent failure. He doesn't know anything about the Haçienda club, opened as a prize for Manchester people using money made by Joy Division and New Order, because Wilson and his collaborators were committed to giving something back to the city they loved. He knows nothing about the shootings and stabbings that shut the club down. He ended up in the film because he's close to Coogan.

020

He's playing a local journalist, and I am pleased to put on the record that Brydon – known for playing perverts, misfits and nutters, often with a vicious streak – is not playing a character based on me. A vague, nervy writer played by Simon Pegg, from the TV series *Spaced*, is reluctantly dragged by Wilson to see the dead body of Ian Curtis lying in his coffin, and somewhere in that scene is a small part of my messy, strange past turned into film. The script tells it all wrong, yet sort of right, and I suppose the whole film will wrongly translate the near reality of what happened with an underlying rightness that will be as real or unreal as anything.

021

Brydon plays a niggly character always trying, and always failing, to wrong-step Wilson. 'I'm sure there will be people like you saying this is wrong, that's wrong, that wouldn't have happened then. But most people like me aren't an expert on any of this. For me, it's just a great story, like some twisted love letter to Tony Wilson, and I saw the recreation of the Sex Pistols concert the other day, and they looked great to me. They were the Sex Pistols as far as I was concerned. I don't know any better, like most people. The thing about these kind of biopics, they can be terrible, but in the end it's not about the period detail, it's about getting the spirit across.'

022

I tell him that the Sex Pistols T-shirt he's wearing at a 1978 concert wouldn't have actually appeared in Manchester for about another seven and a half months. He gives me a right Welsh look that shrivels me to Manchester drizzle, and I shut up. 'I hate these fucking punk clothes . . . what is the point of wearing clothes that make you look less attractive?'

023

He all but gobs on me.

024

Just to piss people off, the man known as Tony Wilson to a generation or three of Northwest people changed his name. He became Anthony Wilson. And then, to wind people up even more, Anthony H. Wilson. 'I never liked Tony. I was always Anthony to my mum, at university. I just wanted to be Anthony again.' The H stands for hopeless, hardcore, high falutin', hippy, hype, hard sell, high brow, hubris . . .

025

Anthony H. Wilson is entering his office in Manchester when he sees a terrible sight. He sees himself 23 years ago. 'There I was,' laughs Coogan, 'in full Wilson makeup, in the long coat, with the scarf he always wears, and there he was, the 2001 version, with the 2001 version of the coat, and the scarf.' Wilson took one look at Coogan, and scampered . . . Coogan shouted after him: 'It's 1977 again, Tony!' You feel that if they had touched, like the Patrick Troughton Dr Who touching the Tom Baker Dr Who, the universe would have imploded. Right now there are two Wilsons with all the ego and appetite that involves time travelling across the city of their dreams. Scary.

026

Mostly, Wilson tries to stay away from wherever they're filming. Worried, perhaps, that it will be too inaccurate. Or too accurate.

027

I interview Joy Division for the first time in twenty years. I once thought by the time I interviewed Joy Division for *The Guardian* in 2001 they would be bigger than Led Zeppelin. Instead, because of an enforced change in style and pace, they became New Order, and changed music history on the loud quiet, influencing the 1980s change from punk to rave.

028

Sean Harris has perhaps the most difficult job of all the actors in the film. He's playing Ian Curtis, representing physically and mentally the sharp tragedy that is at the heart of this broad comedy. I interview the film's Joy Division. They're like a tribute band: Joyless Division. Ralf Little – born in 1980, the year Curtis died – is freaked how little he resembles the man he's playing, Peter Hook. I bet he wishes they were still as faceless as back in the days when they hid behind the bleakly glamorous Peter Saville artwork.

029

Little races around the set in a state of extreme panic. 'Paddy's great at Rob, John's got Barney, you should see Martin Hannett, but me – I have no fucking idea what I'm doing.' John Simm seems as compact, wiped-out and wry as his target, Barney. The film's Hooky and Barney banter like the real-life couple and tell me that Harris is extraordinary as Curtis. He's apparently unbelievable at doing the possessed Curtis dance, where the quietest of men would suddenly explode into compressed derangement. Shyness transported into a kind of flight. I can't wait to see it.

030

Harris slumps next to me in an exhausted Ian Curtis pose he's copied from a particularly dramatic Anton Corbijn photograph. The resemblance to Curtis seems to be on the right side of right and wrong. He appears to be in character, although the character of the tortured artist Ian actually wasn't, at least not in public. He mumbles: 'I feel very obligated to doing this well . . . there's a lot of pressure . . . I met his daughter the other day. She's an extra on the film. She's about twenty now. She came up to me and said, "You're playing my dad." I just apologised. It was the first thing that came into my head. She just stared at me. I just stared at her. What can I do? I ain't going to get it right. I'll get it as right as I can.'

031

I can't shut Wilson up. Who can? 'I had a drink with the two actors playing two of my best friends who are now dead, Rob Gretton and Martin Hannett, and that was shocking. They're so much like them. Very, very disturbing. I was extraordinarily moved and confused.'

032

Characters from real-life Manchester played by actors in film-life Manchester get a chance to appear in small roles. Wilson himself will appear in the film as a Granada TV studio director. Shaun Ryder plays his own father. Howard Devoto, the man who could be said to have started it all by arranging for the Sex Pistols to play at the Lesser Free Trade Hall, appears in the film as a toilet cleaner. There is so much and so little that can be read into that.

033

While I wait for the film Joy Division to mime to the real Joy Division, Howard is filming his cameo. He's blissfully unaware that the actor playing him, Martin Hancock, is best known for the role of Spider in *Coronation Street*. Howard doesn't watch *Coronation Street*.

034

Howard's cameo finds a way for today's Devoto to question whether an episode attributed to yesterday's Devoto – sex in the Factory club toilets with Wilson's wife Lindsey – actually happened. The thing about this film is that everyone involved in the Manchester past being trapped and caricatured remembers things differently, and the film is just another version. Sometimes it changes things to how perhaps they should have been rather than how they were. 'Martin pogos when he's performing as me. I never pogoed. Perhaps I should have done.' Devoto adds his own detail, wearing bright yellow rubber gloves with the words love and hate written across them. Now that is very wrong, and yet, somehow, quite right.

035

Hancock cannot believe that he is playing Devoto. He unpeels a huge Spidery grin. 'We were both just smirking at each other. I was smirking because I was working on the Howard Devoto smirk and he was smirking because he could see that I was working on the Howard Devoto smirk. We just had a massive smirk at each other.'

036

In the end, I never get to see the four actors play at being Joy Division. Time runs out. I do see a pretty right Vini Reilly play delicate electric guitar as a sound rippling from the gods to the gutter, and note Sean Harris doing what Ian Curtis used to do, sit at the front of the stage and let the loveliness of Vini's music rinse away whatever ugliness or sadness Ian felt was darkening his world. He sits exactly like Ian used to sit, and amongst a lot of cartoon spooky things that had happened during my day on set, revisiting a past as rightly and wrongly farfetched as this recreation, this sight is the most authentically eerie.

037

I decide it's a good thing that I don't see Sean try to capture Ian's incandescent dance. It's absolutely vital to the making of the film that Sean doesn't look like a twit performing as Curtis, and not important at all. Coogan's three Wilson wigs will make the thing look like *Confessions of a Pop Svengali* and ruin everything, or just add to the general anarchic gaiety.

038

In the directing distance, way out of my set-visiting range, Michael Winterbottom, with the deep trust of his excellent cast, juggles a real Manchester and an unreal Manchester, a real art versus commerce battle, and an unreal one. He's making it all up as he goes along in true Factory spirit, basing everything on a vague plan wrapped around an impossible dream. I'm told the original idea was a Mancunian *Boogie Nights,* and now the aim is a sort of rock 'n' roll *Natural Born Killers.* It's up to Winterbottom to make sure that the film is more Oliver Stone than *Carry On,* or at least a kind of *Stoned Carry On.* 'The worst thing that this film can be,' says Coogan, 'is dull.'

039

It is a chance to tell a modern story about modern Britain in a modern way, something that is absurdly rare.

040

Anthony H. Wilson leaves a message on my answer machine. He's been fretting at the idea that the film will signify the end of his journey. He's keen to explain that, as always, he's actually only just beginning. 'There's the things I'm doing now that just make the movie irrelevant to me . . . big development projects in Liverpool, lots of things in Manchester to do with moving the city on . . . I just want to get it over that just because they make a movie about your life, it doesn't mean that it's all over. Life does go on. Okay, God bless, bye, love.'

041

On the way to the station the next morning a solitary figure in grey passes right by me, a million miles away. He's apparently concentrating on something beyond comprehension. For a moment I swear it's Ian Curtis. Walking once more the streets of the city Wilson built, a city that made and destroyed him. Looking for home.

## LVI

**Notes on the release of *24 Hour Party People*.**

It all began at the beginning of time, it all began in the twelfth century, it all began in the 1800s, it all began after the war, it all began in the 1960s . . . and then it all began again with the Sex Pistols, who came, once or twice or more, to Manchester in 1976 . . . It was a hell of an adventure, and the rest is local history, the rest is everyday hysteria, the rest is story upon story about music, and life, and love, and the night, and the morning after.

The madness involved in making a film about music, about a city, about a group of individuals who all felt that they were at the centre of the universe, about a movement, about a series of dreams that came true and/or turned into nightmares, is itself in the spirit of a Manchester madness that has given the city a mythical quality ever since Johnny Rotten stared, with sheer nerve, at a few self-chosen representatives at the exact moment the story began. Whatever it was that he meant, man, meant a lot to those representatives, these anti-disciples, and they went out and they spread, they savaged, they screamed, they smashed, they beat, they timed, they sold, they drank, they snorted, they wired, they reworded the word. Everything that has happened in the Manchester music scene this last quarter of a century can all be traced back to the time Johnny Rotten raced out of nowhere to announce, with volume, that there was a world out there, a world that needed to be changed, a world that could be changed. And so some people tried to turn the rest of the world into Manchester, and they almost pulled it off.

The story of Manchester from the Rotten moment to the moment when the stories he inspired came to an end – even as other stories began, because Rotten's energy will transmit to the end of time, or at least pop time – should not be filmed. Therefore it has to be filmed. Too much happened. Too much to collect, to store, to control in a mere movie. Therefore it has to be turned into a movie. Too much chaos and story telling and self-examination and too many moments for a film to even begin to interpret. Therefore a film has to be made to begin to interpret all this chaos and all these stories and all those moments. People discovered themselves, and created themselves, and turned dreams and love and hate into music, all in the space of a 'Manchester' that was outside itself and inside itself and beside itself. The space of 'Manchester' slips from view as soon as it becomes visible. 'Manchester' is a rumour that can only be glimpsed the other side of the music. It is impossible to film the music, and the movement, and the movement of the music. It is impossible to film a rumour.

So film the impossible, and what happens around the edges of the impossible, in the darkness, and the light, and the next day. Turn the film into a rumour. Manchester was about a madness that you cannot ever capture in a film: so try and capture it in a film. Capture the way Buzzcocks said it all – ALL – inside three minutes. The way the Fall still can't stay still. The way Jon the Postman was raving not drowning. The way Joy Division put life and death to music. The way Vini Reilly turned tears and dreams into chords. The way Martin Hannett piloted a recording studio through the space of 'Manchester'. The way A Certain Ratio put the blood into funk. The way Happy Mondays made every day seem like a happy Monday. The way Factory Records mixed anarchy and business and crisis. The way Tony Wilson put the space of 'Manchester' in between every word he spoke. It can't be done, there is no way a film can be made that gets across the sound, the suicide, the intoxication, the drama, the merchandise, the obscenity, the stress, the rain, the ego, the trousers, the designs, the lust, the landscape, the business, the silliness, the gossip, the catalogue numbers, the art, the dancing, the dawn, the drinks, the heat, the building, the mayhem, the murder, the haunting . . . the fucking philosophy, the doomed heroes and the final beauty. You can't make a film about a geographical location, a chunk of the planet, a space called 'Manchester' that was all in the mind.

So there has to be a film. The film has to be made. This stuff really happened, these people lived, those people died, that music was written, long fast nights were beaten up and the next day just kept coming. So turn it into a film. Turn it into fiction. Turn it into myth. Into costume comedy about collective consciousness. You cannot be nostalgic about something that fought against nostalgia. So turn yesterday into tomorrow. Make them laugh. Make them cry. Make believe. Make it as real as it never was. Manchester the myth is absurd. Making a film about the myth is absurd. It won't work. It can't fail. All that can go wrong is that they get it wrong. Which, in a Manchester way, would be kind of getting it right.

This is the film that should never have been made so it had to be made about a post-punk Manchester music scene that was as close to hallucination as reality can get. Viva the North. Viva the stupid magnificent dream. Viva the freedom to act. Viva the impossible.

## LVII

The Factory Story could be filmed from any number of points of view and each story would be completely different than the other and yet end up telling the same story. Following the faking frenzy of *24 Hour Party People*, you could view the development from say June 1977 to the Haçienda heights over a decade later through the life, eyes, shirts, mouth and shoes of Rob Gretton, Martin Hannett, Alan Erasmus or Peter Saville, and that's just the Factory Collective. Each member of Joy Division could be at the centre of their own film universe. A story told from Vini Reilly's point of view, or the point of view of his guitar, would be particularly absorbing. A story based around those who never became part of Factory – Mark E. Smith of the Fall, Howard Devoto of Magazine, Pete Shelley of Buzzcocks, Ian Brown of the Stone Roses, one Gallagher or the other from Oasis – could still be told from the point of view of Factory's contribution to Manchester, to music, and the idea of ideas, and the whole principle of making your way through life with a high, or low, opinion of yourself while everyone around you passes judgement. The film telling this story from the point of view of Peter Saville would be one of the saddest, and funniest, of the series, a film about a worried, gregarious loner whose sensitivity to the appearance of his surroundings actually causes him pain. He was concerned, from a very young age, that the world should look better, and more beautiful, and be practically different the next time you look at it from how you remember it. He took the packaging of records, or product, so seriously it seemed his whole universe relied on such objects for its structure. The film would be about how a lonely, narcissistic young boy with grave dark hair and an eye for the girls attempted to correct grubby reality through a fixation with type, and it would be a plaintive, occasionally uplifting musical.

Saville was responsible for disguising Joy Division, for closing them up and slicing them open. He was responsible for visually capturing and defining their essential qualities – which had something to do with a most careful weighing up of the whole universe. He took it upon himself to reach out beyond flatness, shape and colour into a world where it's possible to discover meanings, to hide the group behind deep, beguiling fantasy, to lift them up out of the time and space where they found themselves, to take it for granted that it was possible to refer to the eternal through the fastidious execution of commercial artwork. He was as important to the group as the physical bass, the feverish guitar, the rushing, reflective drums, the singer's obsession with suffering and the (let's face it) sickly horror of his own existence.

Saville was an important part of Joy Division, who were the four musicians separate and together, directly responsible for content, and also those argumentative, self-assured thinkers, hustlers and technicians around the edges who busied themselves with proposing, if only to themselves, exactly how the group should sound and appear in front of, and behind, the world.

The position of a 'fifth member' is a well known phenomenon with rock groups. It is usually the manager of a group that becomes known as the fifth member – Brian Epstein with the Beatles and Paul McGuinness with U2 are prime examples of where a group could not have become all that they did without a guiding hand that is all at once fraternal, paternal, psychological, conceptual and financial. Joy Division certainly had a classic traditional fifth member in their magnificently down-to-earth manager, Gretton. He contributed not only guidance and protection, and an overall force field made up of smirking humour, unshakable frankness and a kind of bored, aggressive reticence, but also made a world of difference to how the group perceived themselves, and how others perceived them. From very early on he encouraged an exemplary northern 'us against the world' attitude, and believed more than anyone, just about before anyone, that there was something special about the group.

But Gretton wasn't the only 'fifth member'. There was producer Martin Hannett, the mumbling mystic Manc pottering around in the studio, making sure the group sounded exactly like they should – rumbling and echoing to the ends of time – even if for a while he was the only person in the world who thought they should sound like they did. There was Tony Wilson, imagining Colonel Tom Parker as a Situationist, plotting how to make the esoteric have mainstream appeal, perpetually gathering information to ensure his plan for the group succeeded, even if he hadn't completed it yet.

And there was Saville, a handsome young man born in the mid-fifties with a thing for Bryan Ferry, as sure as anyone within the collective that we were approaching a new era in which there would be a spiritual awakening and it would be a joy to live. Design, he was sure, could help supply directions. Design was, pretty much, the actual destination, a reduction, or an intensification, of existence to the level of pure sorted pleasure. Design was everything. Without design, the design of objects leading to the design of emotion, nothing fitted together, everything and everyone was separated from each other.

At a Patti Smith gig at the Manchester Appollo, Saville nervously approached the increasingly visible and volatile Wilson for some work, noting that the new Factory Club probably required some promotional material. Saville's school friend and art college colleague Malcolm Garrett was already working in a professional capacity for Buzzcocks, designing sleeves and full-page music ads. To establish its difference, to represent the abrupt announcement of change and a fundamental realism, the punk movement had rapidly incorporated inciting images and inventive typography into its artwork. There was a role for graphic designers to play in underlining the ideological attack of punk, in helping new music break free of rock clichés and general literalness in the way it was presented and promoted. Punk offered great freedom to those who were keen on the potential social purpose and function of art and entertainment, and anticipated, and satirised, the increasing amount of visual information that was dominating and directing our lives. For Saville, intrigued by the power of good, uncompromising design to actually change the world, to invest it with positive, progressive value, punk was an immediate opening into an arena where he could experiment with the aesthetic and social potential of design.

Saville was desperate to catch up with Garrett, who was revelling in his role as Buzzcocks designer and exploiting the opportunity to develop a brand new visual grammar for pop music by incorporating techniques borrowed from art, advertising and architecture, as well as the whole untapped history of graphic design. He was transferring a history of visual ideas and design theories learnt at college into his work.

As soon as Saville was given his chance by Wilson, he began his own, more aloof and self-absorbed history, charting a steady course through twentieth-century design, every idea and image he adapted or stole taking on a startling freshness in the new context of what was, by the time he delivered his first flamboyantly subtle designs, post-punk. Saville's novel method of combining typography and imagery appropriated from non-rock worlds mapped onto the way post-punk, in the pursuit of originality, was lashing together ideas taken from other more experimental musical genres, and from art, politics, literature, marketing and film. The methodology was to exploit largely ignored and unused techniques and experiments from the progressive, aggressively radical past in order to race into the future. The intention was to look and sound as new as possible, to make it clear that the draining past was over, and change was all that mattered. Change meant that tomorrow would be different, and therefore worth seeing, and hearing.

Perhaps Wilson gave Saville a very specific brief for the first Factory posters. Perhaps he simply gave him the bare information that Saville just barely organised on the page. Perhaps Saville just cleverly noted his client's own pretensions and supplied exactly the kind of severe, rather grand design that flattered Wilson's intellectual conceit. They might coincidentally have had the same plan, something to do with giving rock music a more glamorous, intellectual and inspiring look, and getting as far away as possible from the crude, the scruffy and the vulgar, from the kind of dull, repetitive images and commercial complacency that kept people in their place and underestimated their craving for the unexpected and imaginative.

It did seem as though Wilson had been waiting for Saville, even though he had no idea there was such a thing as a Saville, at least not more or less living round the corner. It was another part of Wilson's chaotic plan that at just the right moment a youthful, neurotic, self-assured design groupie obsessed with the symbols, fonts and legends of international graphic design turns up and establishes a coherent and influential brand identity for your fledgling fantasy company. From the very start, when Factory was just a mad gleam in Wilson and Erasmus' stoned late-night eyes, Saville fantasised that he was developing the corporate identity for a major commercial brand, one that had its roots in Bauhaus, Dada and surrealism, one that had a particularly sly, slightly insane, proudly inconsistent and vaguely decadent personality to express. Some of this personality was actually his own, as within weeks he was not just working for Factory, he actually was a part of Factory – practically hiring himself, giving himself a brief to follow, and, inevitably, an unlimited budget and a distant, possibly non-existent deadline.

He would often express this personality by pretending to hide it behind soaring beauty, ironic impassiveness, artistic economy and various crisply overblown, pseudo-impressive solutions to various design conundrums. He also detected in Wilson's fascinating manner a hint of tragic destiny – maybe he noticed it in Erasmus as well, and even, once he was confronted with it, sensed it in himself - and he made sure he represented this destiny in all sorts of cryptic code embedded into every piece of artwork he produced for Factory.

The first Factory club poster – Fac 1, as unexpectedly yellow and blinding as life – might have just been a good private joke: a classic looking, glossy, clean and spare poster advertising a rock show held in a dirty, greasy working men's club. It eventually supplied the base aesthetic for the whole of Factory itself, as a liberating flash of smart minimalist modern potential in a city apparently in gloomy and terminal post-industrial decline. It was obvious, just from the few words that Saville laid out with the ritualistic precision underneath a favourite stolen image, that Factory had to be more than just a club. It had to be active in other areas, if only so Saville could extend his journey into type and establish his very own radical design traditions. To some extent Factory was constructed around Saville's narcissistic need to have a place where he could indulge in his dreams of design without being hindered by mundane financial, practical and marketing restrictions. Factory was designed as a home to design, design as a practical sign of intellectual freedom, as much as it came into being to release music, provoke reactions or sponsor liberating nightlife.

Within months, Saville was designing extravagant, elegant and expensive record sleeves, and they looked, and felt, like no other record sleeves, and yet seemed entirely familiar. They were objects that emerged from a delicious reality, one running parallel to this one, and they got to the heart of why vinyl records containing pop songs were so intensely potent. They celebrated the way they slipped in and out of their case, revealing and at the same time concealing the source of their magic, thin, shiny, glossy fragments of the imagination, protected inside sleeves that were like windows that connected one universe to another. Whatever else Saville's sleeves did, whatever games they were playing with the idea of design, and the idea of pop music, they passionately and romantically honoured the love a fan could feel for their favourite disc, even if it was just mere infatuation. Saville took very seriously the belief pop music fans had in the objects of their desire, and dedicated himself to making a record look, and feel, as gorgeous and irresistible as it could possibly be, considering it was all paper, ink and cardboard. The material that wrapped music could make the music seem as magical as it was meant to be. It could be a part of the music.

A couple of Saville's early records – the rubbery, metallic, delightfully sombre *Factory Sampler* silver pouch, and the austerely playful 'Electricity' for Orchestral Manoeuvres in the Dark – had already fulfilled any initial aims there were to produce pop product without precedent. They appeared to be made, individually, by hand, for a few people in the know. But as much as they seemed painstakingly carved and hand-stitched, you didn't think of them as having been designed but somehow imagined into existence. They had emerged out of Saville's dreams, and took their solid place in reality with a fluid sense that at any moment they could wink out of existence, leaving behind ghostly traces of something that was only meant to last for a few special moments.

By the time Saville was given the debut Joy Division album to design he had already established a house style for the label, and given limits for the packaging of Factory product that involved having no limits. Because it was felt that Factory Records might never actually have an audience beyond the few people who were standing very close by, the visual volume could be turned down incredibly low. The label could whisper, and anyone who wanted to hear would be able to because they were already close enough. Beyond that, to conceive of millions of people, of a mysterious potential audience who might be interested, meant that you were allowing thoughts of accessibility, or mass appeal, to interfere with the pure idea of creating what it should be if the thing wasn't to be sold, but merely appreciated. To factor in a wider audience, to make decisions based on potential sales, was allowing the design to be influenced by others. The sleeve would in fact be designed by thousands of people, and look like something that was trying to please too many people at the same time. Saville had the opportunity to design something that would, in fact, please only one person at a time. It didn't need to shout.

He would be the first person it had to please. He might be the only person that it ever pleased. His confidence, though, was already extremely high, and he was convinced that if he was pleased, then one by one other people would be pleased and something would have been allowed into the world that didn't resemble other sleeves, or other products. It would be something that might even be original, because it was not based on thousands of people's idea of what a record sleeve should look like.

The product did not have to appear as if it was for sale, only that it now existed and was itself. It did not have to draw attention to itself in the old fashioned way, with photographs and large blatant type and a general attitude of commercial neediness. It could be a symbol, a thought, a passing idea, a moment in flux, a fleeting mood. It could be a graphic way of representing how Ian Curtis' dancing bruised the air around him. It could be a sign of the little explosions in Martin Hannett's head when he found a sound that perfectly captured the natural gravity of expanding consciousness. It could be Peter Saville's heartbeat or his libido turned into a thin piece of sculpture. It could be a brief revelation Saville had experienced about the randomness of existence. It could be an attack on cold, commercial simplification committed in the guise of faceless but enlightened minimalism.

It was decided in Factory discussions that might have had the disciplined atmosphere of a get-together of writers working on a sitcom pilot, or just lacked discipline altogether, that ultimately, because we are all going to die and the sun will eventually burn out, it didn't particularly matter whether the album actually had the title on the front. It might be that no one would ever see it that didn't know what it was anyway, so why ruin a wonderfully calm if violent image by printing the title?

It was not necessary to put the name of the group on the cover either. The black, the white, the blankness, the whiteness, the texture, the diffidence, the aggression, the significant hybrid of noise and quiet: this would say to those that knew, and those that knew always did know, that this meant *Unknown Pleasures* by Joy Division. Any further clues as to the nature of the product would seem a little obvious, and to Saville, given the licence to avoid obviousness at all cost – because obviousness leads to the mundane, and the mundane leads to an increase in obviousness – the tiniest hint of the obvious was, under the circumstances, an appalling failure of nerve.

The absence of literal information might then create the kind of curiosity that itself leads to supplying information about what the record actually is. The amount of people who understood what this combination of black and white and blank meant would grow, and those who did not know what it meant were not the type of people who would like the record even if it said on the cover who it was by and what it was called. The absence of information, of conventional labelling, also made the announcement that this was not a mundanely commercial product, even though it was for sale. This was very enticing for those people who were looking for their music to emerge outside of a dreary, soul-destroying mechanical process.

The absence of literal information might just have led to obscurity and general indifference. It didn't. The music carried on the work that the sleeve had begun, in the general area of producing something that was in a world of its own. The music would ensure that gradually more and more people would find out that the detailed black and white sleeve explained without giving much away that the album was *Unknown Pleasures* by Joy Division.

The music immediately sounded as if it was a continuation of the black and white of the sleeve – the cover was the first sound you heard, in a way – and then it sounded as subtle, and mysterious, as the sleeve. The music had the kind of power that meant it did not need a sleeve packed with distractions, a sleeve that appeared to be conning you into believing things about the music that were not true. The sleeve could simply tell you the time – even if the time was always changing – mark out the position of the music, signify where it belonged, be a detail on a metaphysical map, an abstract form of protection between the still, emphatic music and the churning rest of reality. It could perform a series of functions, none of which directly had much to do with the apparent ordinary function of a record sleeve, which was to sell you a world you were familiar with and confirm ideas you already had about what a record sleeve should look like.

The music was as timeless as the sleeve; it belonged inside the sleeve. The sleeve belonged on the outside of the music. In a way the sleeve was the last sound you heard after the album had finished.

One by one, beginning with the group and the Factory workers, everyone agreed with Peter Saville – who had only imagined what the record would sound like – that this was the best way for *Unknown Pleasures* to be packaged. Over time, the sleeve has protected the group, and the music, from the wear and tear of time. Instead of looking like 1979, it looks like all of the twentieth century, boxed in and squared off and yet on the outside of time, and it isn't fixed as a punk record, or a post-punk record, or even a rock record, so that the music – even as it might be, in some discussions and some lists, punk, post-punk or rock – never disappears inside a diminishing label. The sleeve somehow constantly feeds the music new life, and helps power Joy Division further and further into the future. Even the way it has been shrunk and squashed inside a vulgar plastic case, the absolute dignified twelve-inch-ness of it, the insolent vinyl majesty, worn down into discount CD cheapness, has not completely compromised its energy and effectiveness. Repeated commercial use, years of over explaining, and numerous everyday sightings have lessened the shock of its impact, but contributed to the continuing knowledge that this basic, lavish combination of black and white stands for *Unknown Pleasures* by Joy

Division. This is not an *Unknown Pleasures* by Joy Division as stuck in the quaint past inside a specific tourist-friendly Manchester, as a commodified emblem of a rock star casualty, but an *Unknown Pleasures* by Joy Division that still manages to exist inside its own space and time, making up its own rules about the cold, forbidding universe it is describing and resisting.

Precisely because it had been designed with the disconnected idea that few people beyond an eccentrically cultured elite would ever see it, there was an instant ready-made audience for a record that came inside such a sleeve. For an idea, and a sound, to be eventually distributed out into the wider world, there is always going to be an initial number of people who discover it, treasure it, and understand, even without really thinking about it, the wider implications. They help create the set of circumstances that lead to the momentum that slowly leaks thoughts with an initially limited appeal out into the mainstream. A first few fans set the ball rolling. Sometimes this distribution can happen very quickly. Other times, the distribution takes a little longer.

Saville and company's uncluttered, cerebral sleeve drew the attention of the first post-punk fans to a new kind of music that linked together the American Stooges with the German Kraftwerk, English punk rock and pathological Manchester anxiety. It said, in an almost indifferent way, here is a different combination of influences pounded together to produce something quite different. Take it or leave it.

The sleeve was stunningly contemporary, connected to punk and the prevailing independent spirit, but also connected to a whole history of intellectual ideas. It appealed to those music fans who knew too much to be chased down and conned by the usual record company clichés, who didn't want to be treated as consumers and customers. The idea that a small independent label could release a record without printing the name of group or album on the cover seemed fantastically anti-corporate, and also entirely reasonable. Its oblique approach succeeded in advertising its discreet specialness to those who appreciated the care and thought involved in the production of something so emphatic, and yet at the same time so withdrawn.

Those first fans felt that they had stumbled across a startling secret, and felt the pride, joy and intoxication you feel when you find something first, before the crowd, before it is ruined by overexposure. You have it all to yourself, you are ahead of the world, you are in the know, you are out on your own, with your very own understanding of the best, most fantastic things in life. Everyone else is stupid for not knowing this, although you are not going to go out of your way to let it slip. *Unknown Pleasures* was one of the most sublime examples ever of the kind of secret that all fans of rock and pop are eternally searching for. The kind of secret that makes them feel like a new kind of individual, smarter, quicker, less ordinary than everyone else. These secrets supply a kind of personal power to music fans, a key to some kind of understanding of the universe, a feeling that they have their own super-power, based around the ability to identify and decipher a secret that, for a brief, tantalising period of time, seems to be all their own. The perpetual need for newness, for difference, for the next thing, that has driven the constant changes pop has gone through over the last 50 years, is because of this search for secrets. As soon as one secret is made public, made ordinary, commercialised and commodified, tamed and controlled, other secrets take its place. These secrets allow those in the know to maintain the illusion that they can make their way through life without having to follow the banal rules and regulations handed down to them by their fearful, fearsome elders and leaders. The best, most unique secret can give you the power to resist authority, to evade the restrictions of the establishment, to reject the blandishments of corporate power, to allow you to live purely by the laws of the imagination. You can stay on the outside of routine and never become part of the mindless herd. Rebellion is all about locating and maintaining your very own distinct set of personal secrets.

So secretive was this Joy Division secret, so gloriously hidden behind vivid blankness, behind a kind of pristine carelessness, it seemed as if it would be kept by a precious few forever, never to be ruined by blanket mainstream knowledge. The peculiar thinking behind Factory, as turned into imagery by Saville, was that what they were doing was so important and so innovative that the whole world should know about it, but it didn't really matter if no-one ever heard about it, because the next release, the next product, was the most important. That would be the one that mattered, until it was done, and then all attention would be given to the next one, and so on. Factory loved the idea of making the world a better place, but their way of achieving it was to make up secrets, and then do everything they could to keep them secret, even as they worked hard to make their secrets so beautiful and persuasive the world surely had to pay attention.

In the end, Factory Records was a combination of their secretiveness, the way they played to an audience of themselves, even when they were actively selling themselves, with the occasional flash of incredibly good or bad luck that enabled their secrets to take on a commercial life without it looking as if the label had done anything as vulgar as blatant self-promoting. Good luck involved the support and space given to them by journalists or disc jockeys, how they responded to the way the music itself often wasn't so secretive. Sometimes the music was the absolute opposite of secretive, even if Saville wrapped it up inside a secret or two. Good luck could arrive in surprising ways from the outside world, events and happenings forcing Factory in the direction of success against their apparent will.

Bad luck involved the kind of spectacular matters of life and death it's hard to keep secret, especially when they lead to suicide. Wilson, being the least secretive person imaginable, thrived on both the good and the bad luck. He could seem secretive, presenting Factory as a kind of philanthropic non-commercial modesty, even as he encouraged and exploited and ultimately demanded the clicking, snagging noise of publicity.

Factory acted as if their only interest was in enabling work and art to exist in the purest and most imaginative way possible, regardless of whether it was financially practical or not. For a while, even their eventually famous nightclub, the Haçienda, operated as a secret known only to a select few who could treat it as a private drinking club.

The remote, diligent Saville kept up the front, the straight face, the unflappable commitment to pure reason, to calm content, to a mysterious awareness of quality and beauty, even as everything around him was in various states of paranoia, failure and catastrophe. Saville kept up the illusion of method. He gave coherent visual shape to the endless, almost slapstick improvisation. He produced a pattern, giving a private order to public mayhem. When the Haçienda did trip backwards into success, it was accidental, and yet it all seemed part of Wilson and company's plan of reaction because Saville's designs and strategies looked as though they were always heading towards such a happening, and such a conclusion. Without Saville and his eye for detail, Factory would have been far less conceptually definite. Without his numbered version of what Factory was, it would have been much harder to have explained in hindsight that history happened the way that it did because Factory set it all in motion from the moment, even the moment before, there was a Fac 1.

Meanwhile, Saville somehow knew that all eyes were on Joy Division, even when they weren't. He knew that eventually, one way or another, they might be. Or that it was worth believing that they would be. He treated Factory as though it was IBM, BMW or Nike. And he treated Joy Division from the very beginning, when they were only known to hundreds, even tens, as though they were Led Zeppelin or Pink Floyd. Apart from anything else, he made Joy Division believe they were as great as their artwork claimed they were, so great that they were capable of writing 'Atmosphere' and 'Love Will Tear Us Apart'. He did this all without ever giving away the secret.

Eventually, to his surprise and disappointment, the world of design he adored, the world of design he took out of the library and gracefully slid into the pop-culture future, was appropriated by a corporate world who loved the decorative side of his work, if not the idealistic and metaphorical side. The world became filled with the kind of design that Saville's initially obscure work with Factory had drawn out of the avant-garde, but by the time it made it to the high street and onto television screens, the poetic implication, the philosophical resonance, the romantic adventure had been eradicated. In a way, a similar thing happened to the music of Joy Division – by the time other groups had ransacked the sound, the image, the commanding sense of inscrutable urgency and turned it into chart music, which took about 25 years to achieve, the original sting and purpose had disintegrated. Those that followed Saville and Joy Division had taken what they did as merely attractive patterns to copy, not changing, restless, mysterious signs that indicated where to go next, and what was over the next horizon, and how the imagination can rewire reality.

## LVIII

**An essay written for *Designed by Peter Saville*, edited by Emily King, published by Frieze, 2003**

There [1] was [2] a [3] time [4] when [5] the [6] only [7] art [8] I [9] had [10] on [11] my [12] walls [13] was [14] by [15] Peter Saville [16].

1.

The work of Peter Saville that I like best is the work that really places you there, there where you should be, there inside the work, inside the work that the designs, the thoughts, the decisions, are wrapping, interpreting, enhancing, positioning. When his designs put you right there, a there where ideas are smart, bold, old and new, a there where a mind meets the outside world on the inside, where art meets commerce, where space meets time, where there and then meet there and now, then you are exactly where you should be, in the centre of the there that there is whenever form embraces content and vice versa, wherever the visual collapses into the linguistic, whatever there is where text, type and technology are made to spatially coordinate, the there where Saville actually removes himself from the act of designing and doesn't really do anything at all.

2.

What was so great about the early work of Saville, when he was working for Factory, and DinDisc, even Ultravox, hardly Wham though (I think around here there should be a !), that period that was between say 1978 and 1985, when he was mostly a designer of record sleeves that you were tempted to applaud whenever you saw them, was that his designs were so entertaining and eclectic they were simply unlike anything else in the pop world, and he was himself using these sleeves to develop a narrative that was his own personal history of graphic design. As he drew out this narrative, he added to the history, and took the history down new twists and turns. He was part of design history, and he was outside design history. He was academic and aesthete. Student and guru. Peter Saville, for a time, was a genius, which is not to say he isn't one now, just that you only really notice that he was a genius because of the way his twenty-year-old work does not look twenty years old but somehow a hundred years old and/or a day old, and yet something out of now or tomorrow. He was great because the designs that are now 'was' still have considerable power beyond the product they were promoting, packaging, branding, disguising, revealing. What was relevant at the time now has a modern relevance as a sign of mental sophistication that had little to do with the fashion of the times. His work has crossed the abyss of time, and remains interesting to look at and think about. The passage often makes commercial work wither into the time of its origination. Saville's work never belonged fully to the time it apparently appeared and represented, so it has never really been required to stick there. It was in the past, but it connected to other periods, some in the future, or *a* future, which perhaps accounted for why at the time it seemed so unique. He was capturing essence, which went beyond the time and space of any particular fashion. What was originating back in the seventies, the eighties, the period where he was obviously classic, was not itself the destination, it was the means of travel.

3.

Until Peter Saville I had never really considered the kind of mental energy, the poetic vividness, the balanced exuberance that there could be simply in fashioning, positioning, isolating, imagining, worshipping, neglecting, manipulating, loving the letter 'a', let alone the 25 or so other letters in the alphabet. Saville could take the letter 'a' and in a matter of time, with the help of a little space and surface, produce a piece of work that said quite a lot about the fragile, preposterous dynamics of existence. With just one use of an 'a' Saville was confirming what he believed in – the fact that faced with the difficulty of believing in anything we have to believe in something so we might as well believe in the letter 'a', without which language is only a fraction of what it could be. It was also always exciting seeing him put 'a' with 'b' just for the sake of going from a to b. Sometimes he would borrow an 'a' and borrow a 'b' but the way he mixed the 'a' with the 'b' was totally original. And then there was his ability to mix an 'a' with a 'b' using different typefaces altogether. With Peter Gabriel's *So* he was able and willing to make an erotic corporate logo out of a two-letter word while using conflicting typefaces, something I've always felt was the graphic design equivalent of a great, richly minimal Miles Davis solo. Saville's technique or trick of estimating the exact distance necessary between a letter and some white space was always very impressive.

4.

We can detect from Saville's relationship to time just what his relationship is to reality. He considers reality something that must be improved at all cost, and oddly enough this is how he perceives time – as something that isn't all that it seems, as something that can actually be improved. He treats time very seriously, as you can see from his work, which is all about time. He treats time so seriously that he makes up his own version of time. He reproduces time in two-dimensional form. He understands time only too well, which is why he tends to be in time, if not on time.

5.

I remember when I first saw the sleeve for Joy Division's *Unknown Pleasures*. With such a sleeve there was no way that the music could not be important. Whatever group of people had come to the conclusion that the album sleeve was going to be so symbolic, secretive and madly composed were clearly involved in something strangely new. It was a surrealistically sensible and deeply appropriate design, the last thing you might have imagined at the time, thinking of what else was around, thinking even of the Bowie/Kraftwerk/Roxy things that had inspired the group, but as soon as you saw it, it was absolutely the only sleeve possible. It was visual sound, processed memory, static movement, collapsed space, smooth friction, tuned time, detailed nothing, and it helped create the reality whereby the group could be perceived as truly great.

6.

Saville never really worked well with groups or products that began with 'the'. He worked best when there was a space where 'the' might have been, in a time before and after 'the', for reasons that have something to do with a sentence that begins with 'the'.

7.

Only time will tell if Saville will ever actually finish what he started. The

Factory list, the collection he inspired, the order he made happen, the catalogue he imagined, the art and the numbers, the philosophy and foolishness, the play and avoidance, were like his *Citizen Kane*; he did so much so early, and along the way, obviously, there have been his *F for Fake*, and his *Macbeth*, and his *Touch of Evil*, and there have been voiceovers, hackwork and ad work, but you tend to wonder if he'll ever get a chance to produce his *Don Quixote*, if he'll ever get to finish his history – or did he finish it when no one was looking? – and after all that appearance, that manipulation of appearance, the thing he has achieved is a disappearance, as part of his history, his imaginative history of design history. He changed everything to such an extent there was no room left for anything else. He changed the look of things so that he could find somewhere to hide.

8.

a/ The art of seeing things that are invisible.
b/ The art of seeing that rescues the existence of things.

9.

For Saville there is only one 'I' in the Universe, and it is his 'I', the 'I' of the form, the 'I' in the ego, the 'I' for an 'I', the 'I' which everything revolves around, the 'I' of Saville, the 'I' in his smile, which is an 'I' for a story, the story of 'I', the designing of a designed world he wants his 'I' to occupy and patrol.

10.

I'm not sure if Wham had Saville or if Saville had Wham, but either way this sentence finishes with a !

11.

On reflection it is a shame that Benetton or Nike or Mercedes-Benz didn't turn out to be the Factory of Saville's later life.

12.

My feeling is that Saville found ways to work for other people and create something that was all about him whilst also being representative of his client, so that he created a series of portraits that capture both the illusion of the subject, their different stages, as well as the illusion of his own personality, his own shifting moods, emotional needs, and changing skills. There are also various grades and shades of reality connecting him to the illusion of his work, a lot of them to do with his sense of history, his sense of humour, his nerve, and basically his taste, which controls him.

13.

In fact, I don't usually like having art on my walls, and at the moment, I have no art on my walls. They are bare. They are waiting for Godot. They are biding their time. But once upon a time, I had some Saville-designed posters on my wall, and as far as I was concerned, they were art, and Saville was an artist. I had two posters on my wall, a black and white poster advertising a gig at the Factory Club in Manchester, and a yellow and white poster advertising another gig at the same place. They were in fact just a list of names and words, an arrangement of type, text and space reminding me of a time to come, or a time that had passed, actually the time of an event, but even though they as such lacked an image, lacked any kind of imagery, they seemed to me to be art. They were the beginning of Saville's history, and it was a history that began very calmly, and with an unbelievable belief in simplicity, and the future, and indeed the past and the present. Somehow, these two posters said – next.

14.

See number two. Note also that the device used in the writing of this essay was first employed by J. G. Ballard in the seventies, and I have appropriated it in much the same way that Saville would take an image or a style or a theory from the past and change it by applying it elsewhere, in another time zone, in another context, in another sense, as if to say, nothing is new, unless you say that it is, and you really believe in what you say, up to a point.

15.

Each piece of design by Peter Saville that makes up the idea of what it is that he is designing is really a part of his ongoing search as to what exactly a graphic designer is. Every design by Peter Saville is a question about itself that supplies a kind of answer. Anything by Peter Saville is a particular solution to a specific question that he then turns into a new question, a question usually to do with himself, and his own value to himself, and the outside world.

16.

Peter Saville has always been designed by Peter Saville.

## LIX

**In answer to the question posed in 2003 by Manchester magazine
*City Life*, 'Who Was Manchester's Greatest Ever Front Man?'**

If rock and roll is serious, and it's all about being serious about the serious
things that happen to you as you grow up, and get old, and deal with life,
and death, and falling in love, and falling apart, then Ian Curtis is the
greatest front man etc, because he was very serious, he took things very
seriously, his life was serious, the love in his life was very serious, his death
was serious, and he showed us things through his songs about how serious
life can get, up to the point it falls apart. He did all this in less than a few
years, he did all this in less than a few songs. He did all this with the world
dragging him underwater, underground, under pressure, under life. He did
this because he had to, because he knew how to, because he could see that
when Iggy sang 'no fun' it was serious, and when Lou Reed sang 'rock 'n'
roll' it was serious, and the world is no fun without rock 'n' roll.

If rock 'n' roll is Manchester, Manchester being rock 'n' roll, rock 'n' roll
being how you mix music up with pleasure, sex with love, thought with
feeling, ego with despair, privacy with publicity, etc, and Manchester has
produced Devoto, Shelley, Smith, Morrissey, Brown, Gallagher, then Curtis
is the greatest etc, because he sang deeper harder louder wilder sweeter
quicker than any of them, to a point of desperate sensational entertainment.

If rock 'n' roll is having your own dance, dancing in your own world,
dancing for an audience to know just how much you're in control of being
out of control, dancing on top of your dreams, dancing through your
nightmares, then Ian Curtis is the greatest etc.

If rock 'n' roll is pop, then Ian Curtis is the greatest etc, because even as
he was going over the top, going under, going stranger, he had a pop thing
going, that was bloody glamorous in a way that got darker and darker until
there was nothing left but the light of the universe passed through a melody
and traced with rhythm.

If rock 'n' roll is whatever you want to call it, but we might as well still
call it rock 'n' roll, then Ian Curtis is the greatest etc, because he tore
through the whole business of being a rock 'n' roll star without ever
knowing how much of a rock 'n' roll star he was going to become, once it
was all over, once he'd been torn apart by this, that and the serious other.

If rock 'n' roll is a matter of life and death, and it has been known to be
so, then Ian Curtis is the greatest etc, because when you think of a list with

Hendrix, Cobain, Morrison, Lennon in it, a list of big fucking myths, serious legends, his name fits, and it fits for a reason, the reason being, he was serious about belonging on that list even when he was just a singer in a local Manchester rock band called Warsaw. Early days, when he sang coming off the back of the Sex Pistols and Buzzcocks, off the chaos of his own life, he seemed to know something about how great he could be, how his quiet local modesty mixed with a loud universal madness was producing something dangerously special.

If rock 'n' roll is loneliness fired into belonging, Ian Curtis is the greatest front man in the heaven and hell of a fictional, galactic, everyday Manchester.

If rock 'n' roll needs to be listed and framed and indexed and counted and themed, then Ian Curtis is the greatest etc, not because he died, but because he lived, and packed that life into song, as if he knew that the songs would last longer than he would.

If rock 'n' roll is a look, then Ian Curtis wins whatever this battle is, because he looked inside everything, which takes some doing, and he had a hell of a look. And, look, he was the singer in one of the greatest rock 'n' roll groups of all time, and afterwards, once he'd gone, they carried on as if nothing was wrong, which takes some doing.

If rock 'n' roll is what I think it is, then Ian Curtis was the greatest etc, because when he was on form on a stage on his toes on his edge, he was as out there as anyone has ever been.

If rock 'n' roll is a drama, then Ian Curtis is, etc, because of all the infernal drama inside and outside the songs.

## LX

**From an interview with Tony Wilson conducted in 1991 for a New Order documentary/Tony rolling his eyes/his patient impatience/and shaking his head, amused and disconcerted at how his part in the story is taking shape/alongside all the others/Alan Erasmus lurks nearby/briefly showing his face/checking on things/but refuses to do an interview/hands out Factory badges/and then fades away/when you have nothing to say/say nothing.**

Question: Who is Alan Erasmus?
Wilson: The spiritual presence . . .
Question: Have you upset him?
Wilson: Yes.
Question: Do you upset a lot of people?
Wilson: Yes, I do . . . I don't know why though. I'm a nice guy really.

Question: Is this Rob's story as much as anyone's?
Wilson: Yes. But he isn't on TV. So no-one really knows.

## LXI

Just as I was getting to the point in this book where I had planned to write about Tony Wilson – sooner or later he had to be approached directly, pulled to the front of the stage, given his own spotlight, handed the microphone – he died.

If this was the novel of the film of the truth based around selective memories, I might be able to get away with writing that the news came through of his death at the exact moment I was working out what shape his chapter, his section, should take. If this was a novel, the fiction it often seems to be, the reader might be convinced that at just the moment I was working out exactly how to explain his charisma, mark his contribution, explain his role, summarise his presence, news came through of his death.

Perhaps it appears as if I am trying to play into the idea that in this story there is something a little occult around the edges, by suggesting that I heard he had died as I reached the section I had prepared for his appearance. There was white space in front of me, waiting for news about Wilson, waiting for me to work out just how to properly position him in this story, how to sift the truth and lies into some sort of acceptable shape, how much freedom he should get. I was working out how much space to give him.

Perhaps he would just get a paragraph, a couple of ridiculous, almost exasperating anecdotes, because he shouldn't distract too much from what, after all, is the story of Joy Division. No more than a page, perhaps. Then again, one of the things about the story of Joy Division that makes it so endlessly fascinating is that formidable characters and self-martyring loudmouths like Tony Wilson were a major force in the rush of events. His enthusiasm, his obsession, was a major factor in the way the story of Joy Division developed, and his determination to pull and push me towards the very book I am writing is in the end the very reason that I am writing it.

He created many of the circumstances that meant the story turned out like it did and I ended up writing it the way that I am. The story of Joy Division is told time and time again not just because there is the mystery of the group, and the suicide which solved nothing, but also because there is Tony Wilson, bringing together at the right time in the right city a group of thinkers, dreamers and operators all extremely capable of doing their allocated job. It worked the other way as well – without Joy Division, their size and might, there would not have been at the centre of Wilson's life this sense of an authentic, unprecedented achievement, the fact that he was associated so intimately with such an extraordinary affair.

More, then, than a page. A way, perhaps, of explaining how you had to let him talk, talk about everything, and try to isolate the dazzling things that escaped from him. A few words pointing us in the direction of: what attracts us is his pride, his marvellous insolence, his lack of equity, of proportion, and occasionally of decency. If he did not constantly irritate us, would he have got anything done? And again – I mustn't ignore the fact that he relished the uneasiness that he inspired. Yes, and he must have had a plan, as revealed by the sequence of his failures as much as any success.

Perhaps I can use the article printed in *The Independent* on 31 August 2003 that explained how we met, just to confirm that, in this saga, the reality is, more or less, he had his position, and I had mine, and we found ourselves in the same novel, a story of love and hate, hyperbole and scandal, mystery and music, work and play, and sometimes he was writing it, and sometime I was writing it, and sometimes what was happening in the novel took on the texture of something real. All of this is to some extent actually happening, just so that we can listen to some songs, and marvel at them, and observe how they enter the world, at different points, at different speeds, with different intentions.

**Tony Wilson**

*We met in 1976, in a basement or dive somewhere. It wasn't the Ranch, the social club of punk, because I never went. So it was probably Rafters. Certainly, our first conversation was to do with* Out There, *one of his fanzines.*

*Unless you lived through the horror and boredom of the early 1970s, it is unimaginable how bad it was. The idea that there was some music, some expression, that was going to destroy all this Rick Wakeman bollocks and bring back the reality was the cause that united us all around whatever this punk thing was.*

*No, Paul and I weren't mates. Then again, in the music business, you're emotionally close to the people you work with, but if you're not working with them you don't see them. So, you're not friends, but you're aware that you're comrades-in-arms. There is a cause, however ill-defined, and you know that you share it.*

*It's like Ian Curtis. I loved him, but I was kind of a business partner, and a comrade-in-arms, and slightly in awe. It's the same with Morley. I don't see us as similar people. We overlap, but he's a real artist. His writing goes beyond journalism, and I've kind of been conscious of that most of my life. I feel no jealousy of Paul. It's like being jealous of Shaun Ryder [of Happy Mondays]. There's no point, it's just wonderful that one is privileged to know people with that talent.*

*The night of Ian Curtis's lying-in-state in Macclesfield, I knowingly shoved Paul and his girlfriend in the car and drove them up there. Unlike in* 24 Hour Party

People, *I didn't take Paul in to see the body. I wasn't so crass, I had some respect —
but I wanted him to be part of it. I knew one day he would have to write the story.*

*I'm aware that it's self-consciously Machiavellian. I almost feel guilty about
thinking, at that moment, 'Paul is the writer of our generation. One day, if our story
gets written, he's the one who needs to write it,' but I put that down to my respect
for Paul's writing, and the fact that I'm proved right. The bits about Joy Division in
Paul's book,* Nothing, *are fantastic.*

*Because of the way he writes about me, my children and my girlfriend think
Paul's a tosser. But I don't take offence. I just say, 'No, you don't understand, that's
how we do it.' It's a Manchester thing. And a little bit of punk.*

*One of my favourite things was the* Newsnight Review *where they dealt with
24 Hour Party People. Paul was wonderfully praising of it — in Manchester, you
knock each other and you're competitive, but you don't take the piss out of great stuff
— and someone said something about America. Suddenly, Paul went, 'Oh my God, the
Americans are going to fall for this Wilson shit too.' The look of amused horror on his
face was perhaps the best moment in that whole time. It made me laugh enormously.*

### Paul Morley

*The first time I remember Tony talking to me, I'd just done a fanzine called* Out
There, *and he was very nice about it. This was before Factory Records, in an era
when everybody regarded Tony with suspicion. It was like, 'What's he doing here?',
because he was a local celeb, he was Richard Madeley, and he just looked too old. So,
when he started talking to me about the fanzine, I was actually very touched.*

*There wasn't much small talk. It was about . . . changing the world sounds too
pompous . . . winning over people who didn't get it, I guess. We were fighting for
ideas. I felt like he was a political colleague. In the same party, but there'd be argy-
bargy about tactics and manifestos.*

*I remember when they did the beautiful Factory Records sampler.* NME
*wouldn't let me review it. And Tony did what he does rather well, he was on the
phone saying, 'The entire future of what I'm doing rests on you, you must get me
that review.' Which I did. I worked hard because of Tony's charm and his flattery.*

*Moving to London was a big betrayal, almost like he was a relative. I stopped
writing about Factory and, in his eyes, started writing about Kim Wilde and Dollar.
Tony's never mentioned ZTT or Frankie to me. We did* The Tube *together, live,
when 'Relax' had just got to number one. Tony wouldn't mention it at all.*

*He was thick-skinned, you'd always have a go at him. The Alan Partridge
'Tony's such a prat' side to him, which came out of his anarchic lust for impact,
brought that out in a lot of people. I'd have a go at him — at times I thought I*

*loathed him. But then I realised that I liked him an awful lot. In* Nothing *I wasn't nice to him at all. I was going through a period of 'What's he up to?' But he liked the book, and I think that's fascinating.*

*In the end, you form a union because you believe in the same things. I think the liberal things that have happened over the past 50 years have come from popular and alternative culture, that they're an important antidote to business and Western conservative politics. And I think Tony shares that.*

*Whenever you do things, there's people on your mind, and Tony's definitely one of them. He might hate* Words and Music, *my book about pop music and celebrity – it's an area he didn't follow. But then it's all based on the same thing: ideas and thinking. We've always been passionate about ideas as aggressive things. Sometimes you need to feel there's an ally somewhere, otherwise you feel like you've lost yourself.*

People might think I made that up, but what the hell. Note the method Wilson uses to flatter me into considering that I do his bidding, not at this stage by needling me, but by building up my role, by making me feel I belong more substantially in the story. Also, the way that there is still debate about whether he did or did not – as it implies in films and books, one of which I wrote based on my very own experience – unveil to me, as rash, trespassing illusionist, the deceased body of Ian Curtis. Shocked by his own audacity, his own dedication to messing around with reality, he himself begins to doubt that he actually did it.

In fact, he is responding to how I ended my book *Nothing*. I began the book by explaining that I did not see the dead body of my father. I had not been asked to identify the body and therefore, for at least two decades, without this definitive evidence continued to dream that he had not died and that at any point he might return from some unbelievable adventure, having faked his own death. By the end of the book, having built up an image of my dead father in words and memories, a body of experience and investigation, I imagine that the truth was that I had seen the body of my father, and not of the lead singer of Joy Division. I could then accept that he had indeed died. I had made him up so that I could mourn him.

Perhaps it was the lead singer of Joy Division that had not died, and certainly there was greater evidence, in the images and songs and stories that survived, that he lived on more than my father. My father had more comprehensively disappeared, to the extent that even his name seemed to be disappearing with him. Only by giving him life, if alongside death as well, in a book, an official report, would his name be known, just so that there be no doubt that he had lived.

This fantasy sequence at the conclusion of *Nothing* allowed Wilson to reconfigure his recollection of events. He could tamper with the past, and adjust the truth so as not to appear too much the master of ceremonies. He could lead me up to the door, but then, not quite the extreme master manipulator, suddenly taken by an unaccustomed shyness, pull back, and not throw back the dense blood-red curtains for the sake of shock and biography.

Perhaps this promotional item from *The Independent* is all I need to use in the Wilson chapter – have us fight it out in a battle of egos, leave us jostling to see who would in the end be the one in charge of building up the myth, have Wilson briefly appear in comradely conflict with me, currently the author in charge of events.

And then, circumstances changed.

It would be too much, a lapse in taste perhaps, but one Wilson might have appreciated, for me to pretend that, as I stared at the white space, not sure yet how to cram him into the space he had been allocated, it was the last day of his life. Only in a novel could I somehow make the case that, in this story, the one where I decide where the centre of the universe is, Tony departs in the most thorough way possible, vanishes into white space, and leaves me with the perfect opportunity to literally sum up his life as part of a book that is about life and death and the way order gives way to chaos as much as it is about pop music, memory, the accumulation of truth, and the manipulation of image.

He gives me something to write about, at exactly the right moment, and with an extraordinary flourish ensures that his place in the book has a terrible grandness about it – that is, a stunning, incredibly specific climax, not merely a fragmented series of fiascos, more drug-fuelled damage, biased towards the idea that he is a megalomaniac, charlatan and charmer rather than a confrontational genius dashing toward his destiny. If this was all made up, there would be a great case for making it clear that, just when Tony was completely on my mind, right at the front of my thoughts, late afternoon on a Friday (and for a lot of the time I do not think of Tony Wilson), just as I looked at some white space on a screen that needed some of his life on it, I heard that he was dying, and then that he was dead.

I must have made that up. He must have made that up.

He had been ill for months, and was clearly in a great amount of physical trouble, slowly slipping away, his voice getting shaky, his whirling dynamic presence rapidly wearing down. But I did not consider it feasible that someone so remarkable should actually die, certainly not now, surely just as the plan he had made up moments before and after he executed it

316

was achieving the greatest momentum of all. Films, books, television documentaries, contemporary Saville-engineered re-releases of the Joy Division albums – even though this was the kind of sentimental nostalgia that made him uncomfortable, that seemed to interfere with his desire for progress, it was also further proof that he had helped make things happen, that as he charged into the future he left behind clear signs that he had made the world around him different and, you would think, better.

Of course, it might always have been in the plan that he should also die before his time, keep the myth burning in the old fashioned way, drop out of sight leaving an overwhelming absence that in itself was as loud, as demanding, as absolute as his presence. He wouldn't have wanted to make it happen with as much deliberate, desolate force as Ian Curtis, but, given the circumstances, he wasn't going to pass up the chance to ensure that his departure could be, with Wilsonian reason, looked upon in hindsight as having showboating elements.

The day I heard he'd died had begun with what can now be seen as a few preliminary clues – minor interference leading to an abrupt burst of clarity. A few emails and phone messages had come through, all concerning Joy Division and Factory Records. This wasn't anything to do with this book, but simply because the momentum that began at Rafters in early 1978, or with Fac 1, or Fac 10, or around the time Bernard first played his 'Transmission' intro, or because there was such a disintegration in May 1980, had now built up to such an extent I find that, whereas fifteen years ago I would receive maybe one fact-checking or commissioning call a year about Joy Division, I now receive at least one a week.

The director of a BBC4 documentary on Factory Records that I had appeared in, Chris Rodley, left a message asking me a question about how I wanted to be credited in the programme. The photographer Kevin Cummins passed on a message from BBC Manchester about a documentary they were making on Joy Division to coincide with the October release of Anton Corbijn's film, *Control*. I did a phone interview with *Music Week* for a special they were doing on Joy Division to be published the week *Unknown Pleasures*, *Closer* and the *Still* compilation were re-released, again in the light of Corbijn's *Control*. I raced through the facts and fiction, knowing that out of my half-hour the writer might find a couple of quotes that he could use to confirm the shape of his particular version of events.

The Pistols came and gave blood, basic, pasty Warsaw, revelatory third drummer, nazi nonsense, dramatic name change, the livid third gig at Rafters, teasing manager Gretton, unreserved patron Wilson, gnostic producer

Hannett, font fan Saville, madcap Factory Records, the diabolically understated *Unknown Pleasures*, the chaotic conviction, the epilepsy, the tearing apart, the bleakness and havoc, the wounded wound-up pop songs, the revolting finale, the cover of *Closer*, the charting of 'Love Will Tear Us Apart', the icy waste of 'Atmosphere' over which the group grimly marched from one end of their life to the other, the influence, the timelessness, the corrupt cultural route from suicide to Madchester, more Wilson, and a bit more Wilson, always Wilson, winging it, wanting to stun the world with his claims.

Late afternoon, having satisfied myself with my own ability to now compress the story into a hasty, chatty 30 minutes, Kirsty Wark calls me from BBC2's *Newsnight* to tell me that Tony Wilson is very close to dying. (I am a regular contributor to *Newsnight's* arts review programme.) Will I be ready to come into the studio and appear on *Newsnight* just in case he does die? I don't for a moment believe that he actually will, and simply note how flattered Tony would be that BBC2's flagship news programme are ready to pay tribute to him. Is that the kind of conclusion we expected, spotting Wilson sticking out like a groomed television presenter at those first Sex Pistols concerts – earnest, slightly choked tributes on *Newsnight* for the man who made up a new Manchester?

If I was making this up I would say that I carried on writing this book. I could claim that it was due that day, with just the Wilson part, and a couple others to complete, but that would be pushing the coincidences too far, into a realm of fantasy too preposterous even for a story containing the life's work of Wilson. And so, one way or another, perhaps I am just checking the section written the day before that leads to the *Closer* sleeve notes, and I am just – wouldn't you believe it? – looking at the line about there being a Factory death every decade or so.

And then I hear the news that means I could, if I wanted to put an asterisk next to that line and then a little further down the page, write:

* The day after I wrote this, Tony Wilson died – not necessarily to confirm that this story continues to be a matter of life and death, and those involved tend to give most of what is essentially their all, until there is no more all to give, or take, but it certainly made me think about where I was in my world, about his life as a participant in the making and remaking of Joy Division, about Tony's timing, and his unerring, self-publicising genius for ensuring he is not underestimated when I come to figuring out his role in all of this. After all, he might not have featured too much in, say, the next part of this story, as related here, if he didn't pass away with such a flourish right in front of me, just at a point in the book where I hadn't mentioned him for a while.

And so the story, which ended, and then began, with the sensational suicide of Ian Curtis leads to the early deaths of Martin Hannett, and Rob Gretton, and Tony Wilson, and amazing regular reminders that this story exists because of the combination of such extraordinary adventurers, their lives, and egos. Many of these lives have been cut short because of the kind of commitment it took to be a wholehearted participant in what is part lively pop music story, and part merciless journey into darkness.

Now that Tony has died – for now, for the sake of dramatic effect, and to ensure this story maintains its merciless momentum, at the exact moment in this book that I write these words – I have outside help to fill in the white space reserved for him. People begin to call, asking me for words about Wilson, words that I had been thinking about anyway, because I was at the point where Wilson arrives.

Kirsty calls back to confirm that I will be needed on *Newsnight* later on. A car will come and collect me in an hour. The next phone call is from *The Guardian*, asking if I will write the formal obituary of Tony Wilson, needed by Sunday. Then the editor of *The Observer* calls to ask if I will write a personal tribute, needed the next day. A few minutes before my car arrives to take me to the BBC, *The Guardian* calls again. This time it is a different department – the news section, asking for a couple of hundred words, needed immediately. I have half an hour to write it before I am driven off to live television to talk about someone.

The Tony Wilson section of this book will now have the kind of urgency that suits his mercurial, unflagging personality. It will be written to a series of deadlines that creates a situation where, essentially, I have no safety net. I will have to rely on first thoughts.

It reminds me of the night when I had to deliver the Joy Division tribute to the *NME*, and I had nothing to say because, in a way, I had too much to say. 27 years after that deadline, I am a little more prepared, and know that *The Observer* and *The Guardian* will not be as indulgent if they receive pieces of writing that contain a series of first lines to a number of essays, that consist of a number of fragments in search of completion. They will want the facts, however tricky that might be, considering that Tony's instinct was usually to change shape before the facts had a chance to settle, before they could turn him into dull, static caricature.

I have been thinking along these lines anyway, the lines of imagining how to tell plainly, which would approach perversity, the true story of Tony Wilson, the take-charge man who ran, and often threw against the wall and turned into dream, the record label of Joy Division. If this is fiction, and as

I begin my weekend's task it does seem as if I am now inhabiting the novelisation of a film where a man's life must be accurately summed up in a manner of hours with no second chances, then it makes perfect sense that, just before I appear on live television, I have a few minutes to write.

It reminds me that this whole story, and ultimately all life, is like this, made up of a series of deadlines – minute to minute, month to month, things have to be finished, on time or not, in order to give shape to proceedings, to existence, to ensure that from day to day there is movement, and change, and structure, and if things finish they must start, and if they start they must lead to something happening. And along the way, as we rush and dawdle, stressed and liberated, from deadline to deadline, sense and purpose is supplied by the way we edit our lives, and/or our lives are edited for us, until, eventually, there is a final edit.

It makes sense, for now, that it should be Tony Wilson who supplies the most dramatic demonstration of how this story is based around what happens because life can be so decisively edited by death.

### The Guardian – 11 August 2007
*a/*

*Tony Wilson was furious when I left Manchester and his beautiful North back in the late seventies. I was leaving for a new life and a new job down south at the* New Musical Express. *He felt this was a terrible betrayal of my responsibility to the city of Manchester, a city he had definite plans for. He wanted to find ways to connect where the city was going with where it had been, with its reformist, radical, pioneering industrial past. He wanted to work out how the nineteenth century visit to the city by Engels led to the 1976 visits of the Sex Pistols, and his absurd, splendid solution, Factory Records, including the Haçienda nightclub, became an emblem of the city's traditional belief in progress. Factory became the great Manchester label even though it didn't sign Buzzcocks, the Fall, Magazine, the Smiths or the Stones Roses. It had Joy Division and Happy Mondays but mostly it channelled and celebrated provocative northern imagination.*

*He was convinced I was the writer to chronicle the changes in the North he knew would happen. He wanted me to stay up north, where he could see me. I left. It took years for him to (almost) forgive me. I eventually accepted that his surreal seeming mission to remake Manchester wasn't complete madness. I have taken on the role he always saw for me. I think he always knew I would. We used to make fun of Wilson and the mantle of grandeur he often assumed – the telly side could be especially silly – but all along we knew really that in his idiosyncratic and subversive way he was a great and important figure. Things happened for the good because he was around.*

*This flamboyant, infuriating, pushy hybrid of light entertainer and anarchic Situationist was someone so in love with life, with Manchester, with music, with ideas and intellectual energy, that he infected you with his uncompromising, sometimes dangerous passion. In the end, no matter how far you moved from Manchester, if he had you in his thoughts, and his heart, you couldn't escape his plans for a better, brighter and definitely stranger North. He became the metaphysical militant Mayor of Manchester, and the kind of great campaigning iconoclastic northerner he always loved.*

### The Observer – 12 August 2007
b/

*Sometimes, Tony Wilson was just too much. Perhaps he was just too much all of the time. Sometimes I hated that he was too much, too sure of himself, too convinced that his ways were the right ways, rampant with self-assurance, self-belief, self-confidence, self-indulgence, a man crammed with busy, swashbuckling selves to the extent you were never quite sure what he was up to, and what he was. Could someone so forward, so garrulous, so indiscreet be trusted? Was he really the idealistic northern philanthropist determined to fight a lazy, complacent and derelict South, discovering and enabling all kinds of local talent to help in his battle for an absurdist form of Northwest independence? Or was he pompous, tricky TV buffoon exploiting musicians, fans, viewers, colleagues, Manchester while he talked up his own place in social and music history?*

*Sometimes I loved the fact that there was no one quite like him, that he could be at any given time Jerry Springer and/or Malcolm MacLaren and/or Marshall McLuhan and/or Theodor Adorno and/or David Frost and/or Melvyn Bragg and/or Andrew Loog Oldham, an unstoppable, fiercely smart hybrid of bullshitting hustler, flashy showman, aesthetic adventurer, mean factory boss, self-deprecating chancer, intellectual celebrity, loyal friend, insatiable publicity seeker. How could you not love this freewheeling, freethinking bundle of contradictions, even as he drove you up the wall with his non-stop need for adventure, quest and peril and his loathing for mental and moral inertia?*

*There was so much of him, and so many of him, from the slick, charming television host to the seditious impresario, from the surreal activist to the baroque loudmouth, all of this Wilson constantly needing to be at the churning centre of things. This was what people had trouble with: there was no precedent for such a combination of unlikely driven personalities to be so compressed into one mind and one body. Ultimately people tended to suspect it was all about his ego, and how he, and the rest of us, could best serve it. His ego, though, was part of his genius, and his genius consisted of the way he could flatten everything in front of him with sheer force of personality, and sweetly, sternly persuade the world to become what he wanted it to become. A place where talent, and imagination, and ideas could thrive, and make the world not just better, but more beautiful.*

From the very first moment I became aware as a teenager of this loud, ebullient and slightly unsettling man on the telly, it was obvious he was so full of life, and so full of himself. Initially that just seemed the natural energy of a born broadcaster. He charged out of the screen determined that you would notice him if not necessarily like him.

In the early and mid-1970s he became well known in the Northwest as a slightly naughty young Granada television newsreader with longish hair and flapping flares. He was one step below the great Granada god Bob Greaves – the suave Johnny Carson to Wilson's irrepressible Dave Letterman – a vaguely hip alternative to the BBC's more traditionally madcap Stuart Hall.

At the time it would have seemed more logical that the breezy, professionally friendly Wilson would have gone on to present It's a Knockout or The Krypton Factor rather than be inspired by the Pistols and avant-garde social theory. But then we didn't know at the time, even with that insubordinate, even sinister twinkle in his eyes, Wilson's background in anarchic politics, his knowledgeable passion for Shakespeare, and his proud appreciation of Manchester's radical, reforming, progressive history as the birthplace of the industrial revolution, the Guardian newspaper, the public library and Granada itself. He had decided it was his duty to ensure Manchester's intellectual tradition was not toppled by the emergence of popular culture but enriched by it. This kind of ambition was not what you expected from newsreaders.

He knew all about Friedrich Engels' time in Salford in the 1840s, and probably knew how Wittgenstein spent time experimenting with flight in the North during the early 1900's on his way to Cambridge, where he eventually lectured to Alan Turing, who would be based in Manchester when he began to imagine what became the computer. Tony perfected the ingratiating Wilson television personality almost to camouflage the strongly intellectual side of his being, so that he could smuggle through his weirder, wilder and often disruptive ideas.

Those of us who spotted the curious Wilson at those early Sex Pistols shows at the Lesser Free Trade Hall in June and July 1976 couldn't quite believe what we were seeing. A few of us there might have remembered the time he turned up at a Free Trade Hall Rory Gallagher concert a couple of years before and was cheerfully jeered by the entire audience. It seemed inappropriate that the clumsy, slight camp man from the telly should infiltrate the rock world, and then even more impertinently the new, anti-cliché punk world, and this was the source of the suspicion that there always was that somehow Tony was a dilettante, an outsider. Even at his most triumphant and obviously groundbreaking this always made him something of an underdog, a misfit, but he liked it this way, constantly identifying with the marginalised, the unloved and the isolated.

When he merged the two sides of his character, the brazen cultural theorist with the slick television presenter, and created the magnificently pretentious pop programme

*So It Goes, putting punk music on TV before anyone else, the clash was so far ahead of its time there still wouldn't be a place for it now. After the demise of* So It Goes, *he withdrew, wounded, and worked out how to keep his two lives together yet separate, maintaining his lighthearted Granada presence even as he was organising and inspiring the subversive Factory Records collective. Somehow he managed to be related to both Joy Division and* Coronation Street. *How Manchester was that?*

*He splendidly acted out being super villain and local hero, clown and philosopher, cynic and romantic, schemer and dreamer, charlatan and generous spirit, and seemed driven by the feeling that if he wasn't as dark as he was light, as profound as he was trivial, or as aggressive as he was gentle and patient, he couldn't complete his mission. His mission seemed to be nothing less than the modernisation of Manchester in a way that reflected his Situationist-inspired belief in a kind of urban utopia, the idea of a city as much made up by poetry, pleasure, philosophy and dreams as politics, business and architecture. He might have known this was his mission all along – he might have just articulated it that way after the events had happened.*

*As history settled into place, as it does, as the shrewd, analytical Wilson understood better than most, as he became associated with the influential, gorgeous and riotous Factory Records, and the Haçienda nightclub, and the life-changing Madchester scene of the late eighties and early nineties, it seemed as though all along he was destined to become known as Mr Manchester. He accepted the role with ridiculous gusto, happy as always to sacrifice dignity as long as he was the catalyst for change and excitement. He became the personality most identified with the changes the city had gone through since the Sex Pistols visited a few times during 1976. There was no one better – there was no one else at all – to play this role, and the vigour with which he did never particularly dampened the suspicion that he had manipulated history and exaggerated his own role in proceedings to ensure his own notoriety.*

*He relished the confusion people felt about his manner and motives, and was totally pragmatic about, even flattered by, the often extreme, occasionally violent vitriol directed his way by those who'd got him pinned down as a TV twit like John Stapleton and couldn't understand his other life as self-styled, self-regarding rock and roll revolutionary.*

*When Joy Division's Ian Curtis committed suicide in 1980, Wilson was already a monstrous master of mixing up fact and fiction in order to produce the truth of history. He approached the turmoil surrounding the death of Curtis as if it was raw material he could play around with, already planning how he could bend history to suit his purpose. It sometimes seemed callous, but he was ahead of everyone else in understanding how great a cultural impact the suicide would have.*

*He had marked me out as the man who would write the history of Joy Division. I initially resisted the role he had given me, annoyed that he was putting me in a place where he wanted me to be. His presumption that everyone would fall in with* his version of events could make him seem like a bully. Even as it was happening, he seemed to know that 25 years later there would be films, and documentaries, and books about this story, which was both his story, and not his story.

He realised more than I did that I would be writing about this period, from the Sex Pistols in Manchester via the launch of Factory Records as preposterous idea to the stunning death of Ian Curtis, for the rest of my life, hunting down the meaning of it all, following the clues that Wilson alone seemed to leave. If he didn't actually know then that this period of Manchester life as it revolved around his galvanising presence would become history, he was convinced he could make it happen, by making enough noise, by ultimately willing it to happen.

He willed it to happen because he believed that what happened directly and indirectly because of him as he tore through Manchester, as he rampaged through the seventies and the eighties, launching TV shows, clubs, labels, bands, bars, events, creating scandal sometimes for the sheer sake of it, was important, and that everyone should know about it – both as a major part of rock history, and as an important new part of the history of the North as a radical, progressive place that was still pioneering and still evolving.

After Factory and the Haçienda collapsed in glorious failure in the early nineties, Wilson sneered at while actively encouraging the films and books that were shaping the history he always had in mind. He was frustrated that he could not follow up Factory Records or the Haçienda with what always interested him the most – the new, the next, the unexpected – and anxious, yet flattered, that everyone was fixing him in time as the man who multiplied Marx with Warhol and the Sex Pistols to make Madchester. He hated to be fixed, to be pinned down, to be filed away in the past, even as he fought to make sure the history of his extraordinary times was being properly recorded. Death may quieten him down a bit, but it won't slow him down. Later in the year he appears as fiction in Anton Corbijn's film about the life and death of Ian Curtis, Control, and as, to some extent, himself in Grant Gee's Joy Division documentary and Chris Rodley's BBC4 film about Factory. The history he helped set up moves more and more into the mainstream.

In all of the years I've been involved in the music business, in journalism, in television and writing – and I would not have been as involved without his generous, constant, inspiring and occasionally annoying mentoring – I've never come across anyone so energetically brilliant. Without Wilson – and we now find ourselves to some extent without Wilson, which seems even more outrageous than being with Wilson – there may well have been in some form Joy Division, and Factory, and New Order, and the Haçienda, and Happy Mondays. There may well have been Peter Saville's dream designs, and Martin Hannett's timeless production, and a Manchester that managed to move on from its sad post-industrial decline. But none of it would have been so farfetched, so dramatic, and so fantastic. It took courage to be Tony Wilson, to then become, in the face of certain derision, Anthony H. Wilson. Only he knew how much.

*The Guardian* – 13 August 2007

*c/*

*If you lived in the Northwest at any time after 1973, it was impossible to ignore the indefatigable broadcaster, music mogul, social activist, proud northerner, football fan, writer and exhibitionist Tony Wilson, who has died aged 57 of a heart attack after being diagnosed with cancer earlier this year.*

*For years, he was known as plain Tony Wilson, both as an extremely opinionated, unashamedly populist Granada television presenter who could be seen on Northwest television screens almost non-stop for decades, and as an idiosyncratic, inspirational Manchester music impresario who dedicated his life to making the city internationally famous for its music, nightlife and distinctive pop culture spirit. From the moment he appeared on television, and especially after he combined his daily Granada duties with his extraordinary antics as self-appointed ringleader of the Manchester music business, he was someone you loved, or hated, or loved and hated at the same time.*

*In the 1990s, typically writing his own history as he went along, he made it clear he preferred to be known as Anthony H. Wilson. The pompous self-publicist part of him, enjoying the fact the bigger name sounded grander and would take up more space, announced that this was because he wanted 'to wind up all the people in Manchester who think I'm a flash cunt.' The more reflective Wilson, rarely seen in public as he set about promoting Manchester and himself with relentless vigour, admitted to me that 'I never liked Tony. I was always Anthony to my mum. I just wanted to be Anthony again.'*

*Anthony Howard Wilson was born in Salford, Lancashire. His German grandfather came to Salford in 1901 and his family ran three jeweller's shops in the city before moving when he was five to the leafier Marple, in the country near Stockport. His mother felt it would be a better place to bring him up, but he kept in contact with the grittier, more darkly romantic Salford. After passing his eleven-plus, the bright young Wilson won a place at the Catholic boys' school De La Salle Grammar in Salford, and travelled every day by bus and train between 1961 and 1968. Early interest in science was transformed into a lifelong love of literature and language after he saw a performance of* Hamlet *at Stratford-Upon-Avon.*

*He felt, as someone who very quickly understood the accelerating importance of popular culture, that he was always in the right place at the right time. Having been thirteen 'in the school playground when the Beatles happened', he started studying English at Jesus College, Cambridge when he was eighteen, 'when the revolution in drugs happened'. A flirtation with anarchic politics at Cambridge possibly contributed to his underperforming 2.2 degree, but certainly infected his unique, often haywire approach to life, work, art, music, family and business, the way he would take everything ridiculously seriously, and not seriously at all.*

*After Cambridge, he returned north and at 23 began his career in journalism as a news reporter for Granada television. Granada was at the time one of the great northern institutions, and he revelled in the atmosphere. He found a home at Granada, one that could, occasionally only just, indulge his tendency for a naughtiness that in the bland context of a teatime magazine show was almost dangerous. With grammar-school-boy long hair and a vaguely hippy/glam twist to his news reading suit, he exploited his sweet and charming side and became a local teeny bop hit and grandma's favourite. Many in the North never forgot when he was a cross between David Cassidy and David Frost, when he would be not so good-naturedly booed as he arrived at rock concerts, and this contributed to the lingering suspicion later when he pursued more serious, provocative activities.*

*Wilson, though, quick to adopt new personas, and adapt to new circumstances, adored the attention, and shrewdly exploited his role as local minor celebrity when it came to what he was really interested in — helping Manchester to develop as a major city with its radical, inventive and progressive traditions intact and positively enhanced by what he was unembarrassed to describe as a post-modern spirit.*

*As a now respected mainstream professional broadcaster, in 1975 he accepted a job offer from BBC's flagship* Nationwide *magazine show. Having resigned from Granada, he was driving down to London to a new life when he had misgivings. A few miles outside London he rang his boss at Granada and asked if his old job was still open. It was. He turned back. He would never entertain the idea of leaving the North again.*

*The first sign of Wilson's interest in the counterculture, in radical ideas, something you could only have noticed in the cosy teatime Wilson from the mischievous twinkle in his eye, was when Granada allowed him to present his own 'What's On' section of* Granada Reports. *This covered the local arts, entertainment and music scene, and in 1976 it turned into his very own pop music show,* So It Goes. *His suit replaced by a hopefully hip leather jacket, his hair still heart-throb long, the overeager Wilson looked out of place, as he did as one of the 40 or so people who turned up to see the Sex Pistols play at the Lesser Free Trade Hall in June 1976.*

*Everyone in the audience was inspired by this revolutionary performance to react in some creative way. Many formed bands —* Buzzcocks, Magazine, Fall, Smiths, Simply Red, Joy Division *members were all present. Others became designers, writers or took up various roles in the music business. The intrepid Wilson was galvanised by the event, by the combination of anarchy and music, philosophy and pop, danger and delight, image and protest, and it changed his life, as it did Manchester itself. He immediately invited the Sex Pistols onto the second and final series of* So It Goes, *which was never shown in more than three ITV regions. Taking pop culture seriously as a social and political force, it was ahead of its time. It still would be today.*

*By 1978, still a grinning Granada personality, Wilson formally entered the* music business by opening the Factory Club in Hulme to showcase new local music talent. Factory, named part for Manchester's industrial past, and part for Andy Warhol's arts warehouse in New York, became a record label. Wilson ran it with fellow northern Catholic grammar school boys, the designer Peter Saville, the producer Martin Hannett, actor and manager Alan Erasmus and Joy Division manager Rob Gretton. Inevitably the label was like no other; deeply northern, stubborn and disorganised, it released records with a reckless anarcho-capitalist verve and an indifference toward profit that verged on performance art. It became the great Manchester label despite not signing Buzzcocks, Magazine, the Smiths, the Fall or the Stones Roses. What it did have was Wilson, part glib newsreader, part cultural curator, part exuberant nuisance, part revolutionary warrior, inspiring, or needling, those around him. The design-conscious, discreetly subversive Factory Records became the link between Manchester's reforming radical past, the Sex Pistols' incendiary performance and the new modernised Manchester that Wilson had in mind.

Factory's best-known group Joy Division became New Order after the 1980 suicide of singer Ian Curtis. Wilson fed off even this dark energy, confirming the views of those doubting his motives. He blithely carried on with his great plan before anyone really understood he had one. With Joy Division/New Order money Factory 'gave back to the community' by opening the Haçienda Club in a textile showroom turned yacht salesroom. Beautifully and wittily designed by Ben Kelly, it looked like something you only found in New York, and anticipated a new, bold 21st century Manchester filled with canal-side apartments and boutique hotels. After a shaky few years, by the mid-eighties it found its function as a dance club importing experimental house music from Detroit and New York.

Factory's Happy Mondays bound together the exotic new dance rhythms with a groggy Lancastrian verse, and the movement known as Madchester was born – the commercialisation of the abstract, agitating spirit of Factory, and the spirited post-modern skittishness of Wilson. Wilson, as the self-appointed public face of the movement, became the tabloids' Mr Manchester, and enthusiastically presided as militant marketing mastermind over the transformation of the city into a global brand.

Factory farcically collapsed in 1991 with debts of £2 million. The Haçienda was eventually shut down in 1997 by order of the police after a frenetic decade of being the night-time home of hedonism and a magnet for thrill seekers and cool hunters. Wilson was still a now slightly more weather-beaten Granada pin-up. He claimed to be the man who brought loft living to the city. He became increasingly vocal in his only slightly ironic call for regional self-government in the Northwest, fancying himself as Chairman of the North to the horror of Liverpudlians. He was played by Steve Coogan in the 2002 film 24 Hour Party People, which represented his life as chaotic comedy and Wilson as daft Dada daredevil. He sportingly wrote the subsequent novelisation of the film.

*He attempted new versions of Factory, endlessly curious for the next new thing, the next pop culture revolution, the next dangerous movement, but he never managed to follow his great innovations, Factory, or the Haçienda, or So It Goes. The history he had written for himself as audacious post-punk saviour of Manchester was too powerful to improve upon.*

*He lived out his final months after having a cancerous kidney removed with typical restlessness, curiosity, anger, good humour and fearlessness. His enormous impact on his beloved Manchester over the last 35 years is undeniable. To some extent, even if he did say so himself, this compelling, unique hybrid of selfish visionary, TV hack, charming bully, generous tyrant, commissioning editor, playful philosopher, inconsistent genius and down-to-earth intellectual regenerated a declining city both economically and culturally.*

*He was married twice, to Lindsay, and Hilary, who was the mother of his two children, Oliver and Isabel. In 1991, with his surviving partner, Yvette Livesey, he set up the In The City Music Conference, another enterprising attempt to put Manchester on the world map. 'I am the boss,' joked Yvette. 'He's just the mouth.'*

*Anthony Howard Wilson: broadcaster, impresario, record label boss, writer, philosopher, urban planner, wit.*
*Born 20th February 1950. Died 10th August 2007.*

On the Saturday morning, the morning after a *Newsnight* where I talk about Tony with Peter Saville and the luminously self-confident, Wilson-esque broadcaster Richard Madeley – with Stephen Morris beaming down from a Manchester studio – I appear on BBC1's *Breakfast News*. On *Newsnight*, with his Factory friend Saville, his early 1980s Granada colleague Madeley, and one of his annoying darling musicians, Morris, there's a slight sense that this might yet be a particularly unsettling Wilson scam.

We've not quite yet settled into taking this recent death seriously, and discuss Wilson as if we might actually be on some kind of surreal *This Is Your Life*, and the man himself might yet come cascading around the corner any minute, a jumble of coat, bonhomie and wise-boy grin, and join in the party, happily recalling some of the fine, fraught events in his life.

On *Breakfast News*, following the item about Big Ben and just before the piece about snoring, it all becomes even more surreal, and certainly more serious. I have not quite yet got used to the fact I must talk about Tony in the past tense, but I begin to get the hint from the way the conversation goes that I must move, as quickly as possible, however absurd it seems, from, 'I've known Tony for 30 years' to, 'I knew Tony for 30 years.'

The female newsreader interviewing me mentions in the seconds before we go live on air that around 1990, when she went to university, everyone she knew wanted to go to Manchester to study. It was the place to go, because of the Haçienda and the energy of a city that had by then, without knowing how or why, caught onto Wilson's subversive exuberance – the whole city had become a Fac number. She sadly tells me that she didn't make it to Manchester; she ended up at Bristol. I wonder to myself what kind of life she would be living now if she had gone to Manchester – the same, or something less grimly embedded in the bright, fizzy early morning? – and then we are racing through Tony's life, in a matter of breezy morning moments. I find myself gently but firmly pressed into supplying lively soundbites, nudged into summing up Wilson as the man who first put punk on TV, the man who brought Madonna to Britain – her first appearance was on the *Tube* television show broadcast live from the Haçienda in 1984 – and as Mr Manchester, the rave man who made the city go pop. I am whisked off to make way for the snoring item before I can mention how, following Madonna's uncomfortable appearance at the Haçienda, miming intently with tired looking male dancers for *The Tube* in front of a sullen, suspicious crowd of locals wearing clothes that were more post-punk than baggy, Rob Gretton and Hooky had offered her 50 quid to perform for them in more intimate circumstances. She had, without being particularly polite, declined.

Back home, finishing off the *Observer* tribute, an email comes through from the *NME*, asking me if I could contribute to a Tony Wilson special they are producing. I'm not sure I have enough Wilson words in me – after the television, halfway through the *Observer* piece, with *The Guardian* to come and the short one already done – but decide there is something appropriate about writing about Tony for the *NME*. The paper was the location for the early Factory plugs Tony smoothed out of me, the scene of many of our fights, and for some of the inevitable make-up moments. I agree to write something. As soon as the *Observer* piece is finished, on the Saturday afternoon, I move onto the *NME*, accelerating back to the late seventies and early eighties where every week I would write thousands of words for the paper, some of them, up to about 1981, being for and about and because of Factory and associated palaver. I still have the *Guardian* obituary to write, but find that I could in fact write about Tony from many different perspectives, each one having a different tone, a different style, a different Wilson, and that this is the whole point of him – that to sum up the size of the character, to capture all of his skins and personalities, you would need to write about him not just for the *NME* and *The Guardian* but also for *Broadcast*, for the *New*

*Yorker,* for the *New Left Review,* for *The Big Issue,* for *Radio Times,* for *OK,* for *Playboy,* for *Interview,* for *iD,* for the *New Statesman,* for *Arena Homme,* for the *Manchester Evening News,* and for *Prospect.*

The piece I write for the *NME* is about one third of the length of the pieces I used to write, back when the twentieth century seemed to have no end, and Thatcher seemed immortal, and vinyl seemed safe, and there was just the *NME,* Peel and *Top of the Pops* – even if there was also *Melody Maker* and *The Old Grey Whistle Test* – in a world before *Smash Hits,* MTV, Live Aid, *Q,* Britpop, *X Factor* and downloads, and Madonna was a distant dream, or nightmare. There were also possibly about a hundred music critics in Britain. There are now, roughly speaking, a million.

The new *NME* – which is an *NME* that exists because, since I wrote for them, there has been *Smash Hits,* Oasis, the Strokes, independent radicalism becoming indie fashion, the end of *Top of the Pops,* and enough time since the death of vinyl for there to be a return to vinyl – is not built to accommodate my old-fashioned length. My piece is snipped into the right kind of brief, bright size for the new *NME,* and the full length version, which I would consider short but, in the commercial modern world of rock writing, is considered excessive and possibly heretical, is posted on the *NME* website, where, in its blog-like length and self-referring eagerness, it belongs.

### NME – week ending 18 August 2007.

d/

*My daughter Madeleine asks me on Thursday if I would ever again write anything for the* NME. *I haven't written for the* NME *for nearly a quarter of a century, although some people, who like the idea that the world never really changes, assume I still do. Some thoughts about Morrissey were printed a couple of years ago, but that was more by me as old acquaintance of Morrissey rather than me as old* NME *writer.*

*I reply that, no, I won't ever write again for the* NME. *Those days have passed, I've moved on, so has the* NME. *The world must change, or there will always be Wham and the Shamen. On Friday Tony Wilson dies: I consider his timing to be not just sad and appalling, but also laced with a typical final show-business flourish, as if he is drawing attention by so dramatically disappearing to the Joy Division films, books and re-releases that are about to happen. A uniquely inventive seeker of publicity to the amazing bitter end.*

*Where I've moved on to, a grownup world, or maybe a less grownup world, means I am asked to talk about Tony on BBC2's* Newsnight *and the BBC Breakfast News, and write about him in* The Guardian *and* The Observer. *The* NME *calls as I gather and share my memories of someone it's suddenly not too* unreasonable to call a legend, and it soon becomes clear that in fact there are circumstances where I will write again for the NME. How can I not write about Tony for the NME, the place where I started writing in 1976, encouraged and hassled and needled by the mighty, relentless, unpredictable Wilson?

The world changes, but in some ways the world stays as it was – and there is a world where Tony Wilson is always hopefully, defiantly launching Factory Records, and I am writing about it in the NME, and the debut Joy Division album is about to be released as FAC 10, and the future is always about to happen, made up of these moments that are submerged in the past, but so special and powerful they seem constantly alive and in the present.

I got a job on the NME because of a fanzine I made in my bedroom called Out There. Tony, then a minor local celebrity, an oddball Granada television personality, approached me at a gig and told me how much he liked the fanzine. I think he was the first famous person who ever spoke to me. I was flattered, if a little bewildered that the man from teatime telly was interested in a fanzine that wrote about Patti Smith, Sex Pistols and Buzzcocks. Someone later told me that it was his close friend and later Factory colleague Alan Erasmus that first found the fanzine, and told Tony how good it was. This would be typical Tony – never quite the first to notice a new movement, a new event, but the loudest and best at exploiting that newness, perhaps for his own ends, perhaps because his sense of community spirit, his love for the North, for innovation, was so strong.

After Out There, even before I started writing for the NME, Wilson took a personal interest in my progress. To some extent he always thought that Out There was the best thing I ever did, a great northern debut that I never quite repeated. He wasn't surprised that it led to a job at the NME. Often when writing something it was very much in my head that I must impress the demanding Tony, my strongest critic, and eventually my biggest fan – for him, the 2000 publication of my memoir Nothing, a book about the North, about suicide, and about the power of the imagination, was a kind of follow up to Out There, and I was more pleased than I ever let him know that he thought so much of it. His liking of the book was typically perverse of Wilson, as he didn't necessarily come out of it too well – your personal opinion of Wilson constantly changed as you tried to work out whether he was sincere or insincere or insincerely sincere or sincerely insincere. When I wrote the book, I was going through a doubting Wilson period. Funnily enough, when I was going through a phase of not quite trusting Wilson, if only because his appetite for experience could seem overwhelming and a little suspect, he would pop up in some way, with a phone call or an appearance on television that reminded you, once or twice in the nick of time, that he was a force for good, and definitely not bad. It was just that sometimes he could be truly (usually tactically) mischievous in how he pursued the goodness.

*I started writing from a Manchester where groups such as Buzzcocks, the Fall and Magazine were working out how to respond to the Sex Pistols' June and July 1976 shows at the Lesser Free Trade Hall. The NME needed a Manchester correspondent and Manchester needed an NME correspondent. It was my wonderful fate to be that correspondent. Everyone seemed to be assuming their roles handed out by specific northern destiny, as though this had been orchestrated because the Sex Pistols came to play, or just to shake the city into action – Pete Shelley as avid pop romantic, Howard Devoto as the pulsating, unsettling brain of Manchester, Mark E. Smith as ravaged bent poet, Ian Curtis as tormented myth-in-waiting, Morrissey as agitated unloved loner, Malcolm Garrett as Buzzcocks designer, Richard Boon as Buzzcocks manager, and then Rob Gretton as protective Joy Division manager, Peter Saville as visionary Factory designer, producer Martin Hannett collecting and sensationally storing the sound of Manchester, Alan Erasmus as famously silent Factory director. And, at the head of it all, right behind everyone, off in the distance, in the midst of everything, plunging into action, Wilson as Wilson, a law unto himself, ensuring that what everyone did had a focus, even if only he knew what that focus was. Eventually, that focus would be represented by the Factory Club in Hulme, by the sandpaper sleeve of the first Durutti Column album, by A Certain Ratio's drummerless debut single, by 'Love Will Tear Us Apart', by New Order's 'Blue Monday', by the Factory catalogue (a combination of poem and Dada filing system), by the Haçienda nightclub, by the high, jumpy Happy Mondays, and ultimately by Madchester – Manchester filtered through the striving, craving, colossal, endlessly stirring imagination of Wilson. Wilson, more and more Wilson, Wilson always playing Wilson, hiding behind Wilson, showing off Wilson, challenging everyone to achieve greatness for the sake of Manchester itself and, by implication, Wilson. Wilson bloody Wilson.*

*I had a few fights with Tony, especially when he considered I was not using my growing role at the NME in proper service of Manchester and Factory. He stopped talking to me for a while when I moved to London to take a full-time job at the paper, livid at my betrayal of Manchester, and the North, and its future soul. Gradually, he started to call me again, usually when he wanted a mention of a Factory release, or a Factory event. Eventually, I wrote so much about Factory music – right down to the dust, bone and drone of Section 25, Stockholm Monsters, Crispy Ambulance, the Wake – that the NME banned me from writing about anything to do with Factory Records. I switched my attention to what I called New Pop – ABC, Orange Juice, the Associates, Fire Engines, Josef K, and even Dollar and Haircut 100. Wilson was furious with me once more, assuming I was turning my back on him, on Factory, on his important, developing vision of the North. I was more in love with it all than ever, but I couldn't show it. He didn't believe this. I tried to demonstrate this love by helping to form a record label, Zang Tuum Tumb, that was*

*obviously influenced by the art, style and personality of Factory. We had a hit with*
*a northern group, Frankie Goes To Hollywood, but they were from Liverpool, and for*
*Tony the whole thing seemed too crude and commercial and blatant. I was surplus to*
*requirements, and Factory was doing just fine without my reviews and interviews.*

*He knew in the end that eventually I would start writing again about the*
*North, about Factory, and about the importance of Joy Division and New Order. He*
*knew that I would eventually write about a book about Joy Division, even as I*
*initially resisted the idea because he seemed to be forcing it on me. He knew, even*
*when I didn't, that my role would be to become an historian of the period, that what*
*happened between the Sex Pistols' coming and the opening of the Haçienda, in that*
*period between the Buzzcocks' first EP and the Smiths' first single, between the*
*opening of the Haçienda and the chaos of Happy Mondays, would supply so much*
*intrigue and mystery and creativity that a whole series of feature films, documentaries*
*and books could not completely record what happened, and how, and why. He knew*
*that he would be mocked and reviled for the way it always seemed to be about him,*
*even if in the end it was always about his love for Manchester, and controversy, and*
*ideas, and music, and innovation, and argument, about the need to make the future*
*happen based on the best thoughts you can possibly have about life, and art, and*
*love. In the end Wilson was prepared to sacrifice his own reputation, and be turned*
*into a crude caricature as Mr Manchester, as long as the North didn't passively sink*
*into its industrial past but extended its enterprising, radical traditions into a post-*
*modern, post-pop culture future.*

*He probably knew that eventually I would write again for the NME, and that*
*it would be about him, as stupidly dead as his fallen comrades Curtis, Hannett and*
*Gretton, and that he would be a little easier to understand and appreciate now that*
*he had, with as much shocking abruptness as the others, come to an unbelievable*
*standstill. He probably knew that I would write the piece, hoping that wherever he*
*was – did the 'H' he used to make his name better reflect the size of his ego stand*
*for heaven or hell? – he thought it was one of my better pieces. I always have that*
*sense that I must improve as a writer, get better all of the time, because of Tony*
*Wilson and the high standards he set as thinker, dreamer, broadcaster, provocateur,*
*critic and, to the very end, activist.*

And then, because Wilson wouldn't want anyone to shut up, at least for
a while, until a truth if not *the* truth had settled into position, a note for
*Arena Homme +*'s autumn 2007 issue:
*Walking through the Manchester city centre at 6am, as the city starts to wake up, I*
*take in all the changes that there have been there in the last 30 years, as the city*
*moved out of its dark, neglected industrial past, and an atmosphere of no future, and*

no wonder, into a bright, changing new world that might just mean boutique hotels, loft apartments, gliding trams, glass-fronted buildings and posh department stores, but which at least gives the city a thriving visual sense that it's directly connected to modern Europe, and doesn't have to scrape and bow to the soft South, and the churning, indifferent capital.

I wonder how many of those cosmetic, but also quite fundamental, changes have happened directly because of the agitating, persistent presence of Anthony H. Wilson, the great smiling anarcho-populist subversive, an unsettling combination of entertainment impresario and psychic urban planner, the only buoyant daytime television presenter who also ran − eventually into the ground − a unique and influential record label and helped launch a night-club that contributed significantly to a history of British hedonism.

How many of these changes happened because Wilson enabled the situation to happen where the designer Peter Saville could, in the late 1980s for a New Order album sleeve, vaguely, but very specifically, brief the experimental photographer Trevor Key to take a photograph of the kind of flower 'that would be in the IBM reception area in 2000'? Manchester is different to what it would have been because Wilson gave Saville and Key the abstract freedom to put sublime futurist flowers and beautifully rendered cosmic cherubs on the covers of pop records.

Wilson died probably a few decades before his friends, and enemies, and fans, and colleagues, and viewers, thought he would, three years before he was 60, the age he might have been when he'd become the official, as opposed to metaphysical, Mayor of Manchester, or the Chairman of the North, a part of the UK he considered an independent country. He would enjoy the idea that we're all wondering how, God help us, to best remember him − a statue? a road named after him? a music prize? everything he'd hate − and having, under the circumstances, to be a little more pleasant than we might otherwise be, if he was still around, acting like he owned whatever space he happened to find himself in, knowing that he knew best and one day everyone would agree with him.

The night before I'd interviewed the Joy Division/New Order bass guitarist Peter Hook in front of a sold-out audience at the Urbis exhibition centre, the kind of architecturally bold building celebrating adventurous aesthetic northern pursuits that is certainly a by-product of strategic, chaotic, post-punk, post-reasonable Wilsonian activity. It was the kind of occasion Tony would usually have been present at − either as charming host or dogmatic intellectual zealot, annoyed at the nostalgia, thrilled at the way ideas actively changed his city. He was missing, and it was bloody obvious. On the other hand, for better or worse, he's everywhere you look in Manchester, and I'll remember the tender tyrant just by walking around the city he was always so determined to make new, newer and newer still.

## LXII

**Meanwhile, since 1991, Alan Erasmus⋆ has sent enigmatic telegrams to acquaintances stating that he has not yet died.**

⋆He is known to have been for a brief time, in 1999, a physical education instructor at the athletic academy in Mexico City: he was preparing a lecture on Egyptian art. We lose all trace of him shortly afterward in the Gulf of Mexico, where he cast off one night in the lightest of small craft.

## LXIII

Because Hooky played a bass guitar solo that would last a thousand years and which was cut up into sections and used throughout the songs of Joy Division

because Bernard played his guitar round and round in brilliant fraught circles from inside, and outside, another hundred years

because Stephen could race through a hundred years in four minutes flat

because Martin Hannett had enough patience to wait out the hundred years and then work out how to make it all sound acceptable to those who didn't have a hundred years to hang around

because Ian sang as though he'd already written the words down, with a wonderful, ragged right-hand margin, keen to get it all out before the ruin, and something was giving him the heebie-jeebies

because his early life, and then the one that followed, was very strange, and then after that there wasn't much but death and posthumous fame

because he said, 'I ain't going to give you a fucking cigarette, there's a shop on the corner, you can go down there and buy a fucking pack of cigarettes, don't ask me for cigarettes.'

because it's necessary to force a coherence on the scene that it didn't necessarily have

because there was no philosophical core to it

because it wasn't all just goofiness

because cultural undergrounds develop in the void left by the abdication of an official culture

because eventually what with one thing and etc it, the it of the group, the forward-looking it of the sound and the sense, the meaning and the melancholy, the drum and the drama, the bass and seriousness, the guitar and half-lit faces, the size and scale, the voice and sensitivity, the drastic openness and miscellaneous pain, the hyped-up enthusiasm and caustic disaffection, would all lead and trend and voyage across the decades around the Cure, Depeche, Echo and U2, for better or worse to Low, Coldplay, Interpol, Franz Ferdinand, the Editors, Arcade Fire etc etc

because of rock music's sheer ubiquity

because the urge to transform one's appearance, to dance outdoors, to mock the powerful and embrace perfect strangers is not easy to suppress

because of the amount of dope and booze that got consumed

because of what happens if you try and make the most of each day in life

because life is a means of extracting fiction

because we know to an extent the beginning of the story and certainly the end but not quite the jumble in the middle

because mundane incidents can often be elevated to fable

because history is manmade

because each life makes its myths

because myths have a force that can never be entirely tamed by ironic aesthetic contemplation

because suicide takes some getting used to

because the dead have their own kind of knowledge

because if no-one tells the story there is no story

because memory is an internal rumour

because Ian in his terrace house had a deep connection to the existentialist tradition of God as an absence, a negative presence we live in terms of because he had a sense of a transcendent plane from which he was barred but wanted to work against

because, if it was there, Hannett found a sound, and if it wasn't he found another

because Ian kept trying to answer the question we must constantly be asking ourselves, who do we think we are and what do we think we are doing?

because the threat of violence is very close to us all

because Ian wrote songs to deal with the violence in himself

because his instinct was to turn disaster into art

because he once told me I use too many commas

because someone faces a challenge bravely and succeeds or fails

because Wilson aroused hostility in an extraordinary number of people, even when he stayed in the background

because Curtis died a death, followed by one or two others, and didn't get to watch as his life and death was turned into a kind of industry

because Wilson was a poseur and Gretton never read Proust

because Erasmus was interested in spies

because Ian was shaken by glimpses of another world

because he cast a cold eye on life and death

because he couldn't keep his pessimism and his life in separate compartments

because the Factory train ran out of coal and they tried to keep it going by breaking up the train itself and feeding into the fire for fuel, until the train was just a fire on wheels

because Hannett and Erasmus and Gretton and Saville and Wilson and

Hooky and Bernard and Stephen said let's not end it this way

because the procession had moved on and the shouting was over

because the phrase 'unknown pleasures' was strongly reminiscent of Yeats, not to mention Lovecraft

because his various delusions and manias caught up with him

because all you have to do is die

because when he killed himself there was a fly buzzing away on the windowpane

because, thanks to David Bowie, he never lost sight of an everyday audience

because we like to know a lot that we aren't told

because Wilson was Catholic, communist, northerner and celebrity

because they never used the word 'baby' in a song

because he was striving to keep a terrible temper under control

because, for a single instant, flaming horror lit up Ian's mind, opening before him a black abyss, and the black abyss swallowed him

because it came to pass

because he finally remembered a moment of suffocating ecstasy

because everyone involved was hungry for fame and praise

because Saville sensed the connection between things that weren't the same

because if life is not worth living, songs are not worth singing

because the group felt they were underpaid in a ridiculous and insulting manner because Wilson responded with, 'You can't be any more broke than I am.'

because Ian was preoccupied with his own shortcomings

because Gretton teased him about his lust for a Belgian and indulged in friendly misogyny

because Factory resembled a male-dominated sect and on the outside were the women, only let inside where their uses and virtues helped the sect jump into glory or excellence

because blankness and minimalism are balms poured upon our overused optical nerves and overcrowded brain cells

because we all feel the same grief when someone is in mourning

because the source of information was permanently deficient

because their music was indebted to the avant-garde of northern Europe whilst stealing openly from infernal American rock

because someone on the bus whispered in his ear that the world does not exist and he couldn't help but agree

because Wilson quickly took the measure of people and ideas

because the world carries weight and always weighs the same

because we need someone to explain to us what happened

because they met and parted in the centre of the city

because of the railway line that took you from Macclesfield to Manchester in less than half an hour

because Ian craved to be released from bothers, from daily demands and urgencies, from responsibilities and tempting distractions

because he was up against it

because death slipped into an arrested moment in a cold room of a hopeless house

because clouds came and went without thunder and lightning

because at the same time, he could kill himself or just sit down and listen to records

because our lives, stripped of their padding and numbness and habit, do appear horrific, flickering and absurd

because only the fear of life and death could beguile him to find the slightest meaning

because for him one day in May was the last day of the year

because he decided that he was no-one who had invented everything he saw

because his wife was young and had an encouraging smile

because she had a life too

because she depended on him

because she was in the shadows in her nightie

because she was struggling at home and his girlfriend was continental, sensual and poetic

because she was at home crying and he was on stage shaking the earth

because she was cleaning the dishes and he was inventing a fresh incarnation for himself

because she was alone with her baby and he was strenuously negotiating with immortality

because she thought when she guessed that he was in love with another it might have been Bernard because, you know, she'd always suspected, the shirts, the ties, the fastidious crease in the trousers, the combed hair, the love for Ziggy, the crust of campness that covered the boyish manliness, the closeness between two men you couldn't just put down to music and touring, surely his sexual nature was fluid?

because she dealt with the next-door neighbours and he longed to rush off and hide no matter where

because she was crushed and he was disgusted with himself

because she shopped for sugar in the local grocery store and he had an inkling of how singular in the vastness of our creation is the richness of our opportunity

because he wrote love letters to one woman and not to the other

because true love is the swiftest of all modes of thought

because we all live in dream worlds

because we remember when we were young

because the helpless dead tend to be visited by the sentimental, and not necessarily profitless, exertions of the living

because his wife was dismissed like a messenger in Shakespeare

because she dreamt of domestic bliss and he experienced Dostoyevskian fits

because she was lighting fires and he was raising eyebrows

because she listened to the breath of ambition in his sleep

because his body was lean and strong against her hand

because he tossed and turned amid the rumpled sheets and untied threads of the plot

because she paused at the door and felt in the pocket for the key because it was killing him

because he was writing songs the week before he killed himself

because the two incompatible realms of Ian's universe collided

because his imagination was out of place

because the house was quiet and the world was calm

because he borrowed courage from Iggy, and suave delirium from Morrison, and towards the end the caged rage of Sinatra

because he sang as deep-voiced as a cello, tipped with a flame

because he learnt as a performer that everything should be done coldly, with poise

because she found him turning icy blue on a dirty carpet

because one was the wife and wrote the book and kept the name and the other was the lover and faded into time and had nothing to say

because 27 years after his death he was still emerging with evidence of his greatness

because his abashed and constant sorrow keeps breaking through to touch the listener, aided and abetted by Hooky's endless, empathising bass, Bernard's tender, fitful guitar, Stephen's dogged, lyrical drumming, Martin's acute, clairvoyant sensibility

because a loved one leaves like air from the lungs

because frozen memories gleam amid the blackness of loss, there was, after a few years, yet another film.

Whereas *24 Hour Party People* filmed this particular unstable universe with Wilson at the centre, director Anton Corbijn put Curtis at the centre of his gentler, less stylistically abrasive film, *Control*. Corbijn found the mythical end of seventies North of England at the edge of his own imagination, located a tender young man finding danger because of love, and hate, moved through a story without resorting to flashbacks, without resorting to the kind of hectic, anxious visual style that only arrived in the years after Joy Division, and by making up history, putting together one selected moment with another using light and shadow, scenic beauty and searching songs.

He tells the story simply, and with a kind of rapturous care, deciding that no one has ever heard it before, and he is merely introducing for the very first time the idea of this young, nervy, relatively obscure musician from quiet, unchanging Cheshire who managed to change his life so extremely, he lost it. He's pictured as the kind of wiped-out English boy who achieved just enough O-levels to get a menial, mentally exhausting job, who wondered what it would be like to win over the world like Bowie with pure blasts of charisma, who crept to the edge of fame, of making it, and also at the same time found himself on the verge of losing everything because, once he was forced to think about it, he chose to view his life as something that was his to take.

In this story the route from the Sex Pistols, who come out of approximately nowhere with the suddenness of an assault, leads to a particularly messy, largely inexplicable suicide, and no further – in the fiercer Wilson world the suicide was somewhere in the jumbled middle, just one step on the way to Factory's maddening rise and its sloppy collapse. Curtis dies in the dingy front room of an oppressive terraced house in Macclesfield, surrounded by damp, chill fields, not completing his grand escape as planned in his bedroom listening to the Velvet Underground. Or, he dramatically completes his escape, smuggling himself out of the town inside his own dead body. There is, as Johnny Rotten had pointed out, no future.

Because Curtis is at the centre of *Control*, the most vivid presence in his own story, the film could not have worked without a completely believable performance of Ian Curtis – a representation of Curtis not just as mesmerising rock performer with some sensational stage tricks that involved moving the body and mind like no one ever has, but also as a loser, liar, loner, as chauvinist, as diseased soul, as naïve young dad, as embarrassed friend, as miserable fatalist, as urgent fantasist trapped inside persistent, grinding reality.

If the Ian Curtis in *Control* was just a plain combination of mime, wig and copied gesture, then quite naturally people would have wondered why there was another film set in this time and place, and it would have seemed simply an indulgent memorial, a biopic taking refuge in nostalgic reconstruction, not a serious, resoundingly uncynical and tactful attempt to grasp the strange things that happen in a small town, that happen behind the entertainment scenes.

## LXIV

**An article published in the *Observer Music Monthly*, September 2007.**

001

Stephen Morris cannot believe it.

When he talks about what he's lived through as a simple, dedicated drummer, first for Joy Division, then for New Order, one classified as the fifth greatest of all time in a recent online poll, he can start to sound like a post-punk Victor Meldrew, increasingly indignant at the chaos that unfolded all around him mainly because he found himself, through no real fault of his own, a Factory Records recording star. Don't get him started on the Haçienda, the Manchester nightclub his two groups helped finance early in the eighties for up to £10,000 a month, where he never got a free drink in eight years. He still hasn't really recovered from the time 27 years ago when Ian Curtis, his 23-year-old Macclesfield friend and the singer in his band, killed himself the day before Joy Division were due to start their first American tour. His producer Martin Hannett started to die in the eighties, was dead by 1991, his manager Rob Gretton died later in the nineties, and now, would you credit it, the immortal-seeming Tony Wilson, boss of his record company, the crusading mouth of Manchester, has joined his comrades in the great Factory in the sky.

Steve acts as if he has been singled out for the strangest kind of persecution. And the farcical pain doesn't stop. There was a frenzied, facetious film made about this obsessed-over period in recent Manchester history. *24 Hour Party People*, a conceptual comedy in at least 100 parts, was directed by Michael Winterbottom, and Morris, just a plain hardworking northern drummer with a stupid fondness for a quiet life, had to suffer the indignity of seeing himself played by an actor. And now, bugger, it's happened again. Anton Corbijn, the singular Dutch photographer and video maker, whose lush, severe work you will know if you own records by U2, Depeche Mode, Bruce Springsteen, Nick Cave, has made *Control*, a film observing this fussed-over Manchester era more through the young life and sickening death of Ian Curtis than the unique tactlessness and tactics of Wilson. Manchester as hallucinatory urban bedlam is transformed into Manchester as exotically, dangerously mundane North European outpost seething with domestic, and cosmic, secrets.

Steve will often tell you he's not a bitter man, but surely no one should have to see their life story turned into a film not just once but twice. 'It just shouldn't happen,' he grumbles, resigned to the fact no one is paying attention to him even as they keep turning his life into fact-based fiction.

002

The Leeds musician and actor Sam Riley found out that he got the role of Ian Curtis in Anton Corbijn's film *Control* on his 26th birthday. His acting career hadn't really taken off, just a couple of roles in minor TV shows, a small part as Mark E. Smith in *24 Hour Party People* that never made the finished cut, and his band, 10,000 Things, had just been dropped by their record label. As an actor he'd been worried that the level of work he was being offered, usually TV ads, would interfere with his chances of being taken seriously as a musician. Now he didn't even have a music career. 'I always thought that it would really help if perhaps I got the lead in a really cool black and white movie where I talked all the way through.'

He'd auditioned a few times for *Control*, preparing by watching rare early videos of Joy Division and listening to the coarser, punkier group they were before, Warsaw. Sometimes it seemed as if all anyone wanted to find out was his ability to do what he calls 'the thing' – Curtis' explosive, implosive dance, an unholy combination of stasis and momentum, extreme mental pressure released through extravagant physical display. 'Can I see you move?' Anton would murmur softly in a Dutch accent straight out of a bad porn movie.

At one audition in Manchester a nervous Riley had dropped his script on the railway lines at the station. As he quickly learned some lines from a borrowed script, he looked up and could see through the window of the audition room the red-faced, bug-eyed actor before him desperately attempting to recreate the dance. He raced downstairs to the toilets for some last-minute practice.

'Do I get music?' Sam asked. An iPod was strapped to his arm, and away he would go, around the room, Anton and company solemnly watching him flail away in silence. Anton, not quite satisfied, would get up and show him what to do with his feet. 'Lighter, lighter,' he'd implore, showing the way, two grown men – one of them, being Dutch, well over six foot tall – flapping around an empty room attempting to pin down Curtis' unconfined, seized-up dancing.

003

A naïve, resourceful 24-year-old Anton Corbijn came to England in 1979 in part because of Joy Division, one of his favourite groups. He'd been photographing Dutch musicians for a few years, but knew he needed to move into a bigger world. He left the small, timeless village in Holland where he was surrounded by a low-level, austere and dramatically abstract landscape that would feature constantly in his photographs and videos. He found ways to set the musicians he photographed inside his own mysterious, playful imagination as formed by his isolated and isolating upbringing.

The trees, grain and shadows in his work with U2, Beefheart and Depeche, found in deserts and locations far from his home, often resembled the view he would have from his home as a youngster. A friend once pointed out that in every single Anton Corbijn video there is a tree. Often, there is also water, and in his photographs an atmosphere that seems to change as you look at it.

He came across the channel in search of Joy Division, with no money, little English, and no contacts, and somehow this droll, intuitive and deep-thinking Dutchmen found them.

004

Peter Hook, Joy Division and then New Order bassist, is talking to me on the phone from his house after a weekend DJ session in Singapore. 'I played the original version of "Love Will Tear Us Apart" and also "Transmission" in a total dance club, and people were going absolutely crazy. What's that about?' Hooky is the sentimentalist among the surviving members of the group, the one most blatantly proud of Joy Division's achievements, and the enduring life of the music, the one still stricken by Ian Curtis' suicide. Bernard Sumner, his old sparring partner in Joy Division and New Order, who he is currently in dispute with regarding the future of New Order, is less likely to luxuriate in the past. 'When I saw the film in Cannes earlier this year, after Ian had died, "Atmosphere" is played, and it's bloody heartbreaking, it really is, it's like going through it all again to be honest. Especially with all the problems with New Order. I'm going through hell and people start to applaud! It's bizarre having your life flashback like that for other people to see. It's like when everyone laughed in *24 Hour Party People* when we lost money on every copy sold of "Blue Monday" because of the expensive sleeve. I thought, you bastards – that's my life, that is, that really happened!'

005

'I grew up as the son of a Protestant minister so ill, dying people and death was never far from our dinner table talk. So it doesn't faze me as a subject. I think the things that matter in life and death, the beginning and the end, the essential things, it is a lot in my work. I want my photographs to have a function. It's the Protestant thing, that everything you do has a reason, nothing throwaway. Even in my videos, even if they're funny, or bad, which happens, there are some fundamental things being told. I want that function to be showing someone in a way you have not seen them before. Make a photo that does not double up anything you have seen before. You create something that makes sense because it does not exist yet.'

006

Anton and I talk in his large, immaculate office in Shepherds Bush in the early summer of 2007. After being filmed during the summer of 2006, after two years of tough, challenging pre-production, Control has been completed. People have started to see it, and it is being liked, even loved. Anton is extremely relieved. At times it looked as if there was no chance of it ever being made, and becoming the graceful, inquisitive partner to the riotous, hellzapoppin 24 Hour Party People. At times, it seemed as though Anton was going to be defeated, being the first-time director wanting to film in black and white, using a first-time director of photography and an unknown actor as the main lead.

007

Sam is talking to me from Berlin days after winning an actor's award at the Edinburgh Film Festival for his spectacularly convincing performance. 'Almost a year to the day that we finished filming.' He now lives in Berlin with Alexandra Maria Lara, the actress who in Control plays the quietly exotic Belgian journalist Annik Honore. The sensitive, impressionable Ian Curtis fell in love with Annik whilst touring with Joy Division. His toiling young wife Debbie – played by Samantha Morton – looked after their new baby back in their tiny terrace in Macclesfield whilst this new secret love bloomed and Ian's group became exhilarating post-punk cult favourites.

It's this story of a life breaking into two, into bits, of an anguished conscience expressed at the time so achingly in Joy Division's solitary official hit, 'Love Will Tear Us Apart', that Control eloquently and patiently monitors. The film, in bright, illuminating black and white, is more gently paced kitchen-sink art movie than sensationalising cutup biopic – the conflict between the old working class life Curtis was manically escaping and a new, apparently liberating life as desired, damaged rock star, which rapidly led to mental and physical breakdown, and then suicide. 'It's like the Bible,' says Corbijn. 'You know the end. He dies. So how you tell the story along the way is more important than ever.'

As Riley lived out the role in an intense ten-week period in the old Central TV studios in Nottingham last year, he admits that the reality of playing the young singer, trapped between family and a poetic seeming new love, careering towards suicide, had an effect on his own life. 'I think Ian went after fame and glory and to an extent he did it because he wanted to look after his wife and baby. Then he started resenting them because they were spoiling his new life, and then he hated himself for resenting them. He loved them and hated them in equal quantity. And Annik seemed his future. I got wrapped inside his problems. I found it very gruelling filming his epileptic fits. I found it tough knowing where it all led. It did cause me some major heartaches and depressions and all sorts of behind-the-scenes problems . . . I don't want to talk about it too much, but I committed myself so much to this, not wanting to waste this chance, terrified that I wasn't going to be able to pull it off, that I would let everyone down, that I half-morphed into what was going on within the film, and there was a kind of crash, and I had to pick up the pieces. I suppose you could say I was rescued by a German movie star. I moved to Berlin within two months of finishing the film. It's looked upon in the film world as a cliché I know, even more so given the characters we were playing, but the movie reality broke into my reality. I guess it's the kind of thing that happens when you get close to this kind of story. It can change everything. It's complicated, but I couldn't be happier and Berlin is beautiful.'

008

'Can you believe that the film Ian went off with the film Annik?' marvels Hooky. 'How hilarious is that? Talk about fact being stranger than fiction.'

009

'Sam just went for it,' says Anton. 'He gave everything to the film. For a lot of known actors it is really scary to portray an icon because you can only disappoint. In his own life he had nothing to lose by giving his all and taking all kinds of risks.'

010

'Well,' says Hooky, '*Control* is a hell of a lot more factual than *24 Hour Party People*. You can see that Anton knew us, and he knew us well, and he took the original script, which was very English, like *Queer as Folk*, and which would not have travelled, and quite subtly he made it deeper and have a broader appeal, so that it would not just make sense to an English audience but to an international audience.'

011

'Within fourteen days of arriving in England,' Corbijn remembers, 'I had tracked down Joy Division's manager Rob, and I met them at Lancaster Gate tube station. They were staying at a hotel nearby. That's where we did the first photographs. Being a well-brought-up, good young Dutchman I wanted to shake their hands, but nobody would shake my hand. After we had done the photographs, then they shook my hand. We didn't say much. I couldn't say much. Not only was my English really poor but I had trouble with accents. I could just about make out good English. The Manchester accent didn't make it easy. Also I was in awe of them. It didn't make for much conversation.'

012

The photographs Corbijn took that day, crossing the boundaries of language, silence and shyness, helped create the enduring image of Joy Division as serious, intensely introverted post-punk rock group as much as the conspicuously inscrutable artwork of Peter Saville. The photographs weren't rock photographs but photographs of young northerners on some unspecified mission, and Saville's designs defiantly avoided all rock clichés in the unashamed pursuit of stark, stirring beauty. At the time, such solemnity and indifference to conventional rock ideas might have seemed precious and presumptuous; in the long run it consistently maintained an insulating layer of mystery that ensured the group never dated.

The group may well have been four ordinary, mischievous young punk fans from grey, dingy Salford and disconcertingly quaint Macclesfield – with Manchester, their cultural playground, in the middle – but the contribution of Saville, and then Corbijn, alongside the way Martin Hannett transformed their violent live sound into compressed disquiet, helped present them as cryptic adventurers on a journey into awe-inspiring metaphysical darkness. These collaborators helped the group themselves believe, without being able to explain it apart from through their music, that they were more than just another group following up the influences of the Stooges and the Pistols in the politically-charged, socially restless late 1970s.

013

As soon as Sam got the role, he asked if he could actually sing as Ian. Anton was initially adamant that you would hear no other singing voice than Ian's. Riley tried to coax his director into believing that he could pull it off. 'It seemed impossible,' he admits. But once the actors playing the band got together they all started to learn the songs and, encouraged by the fact the songs were powerful but never complex, quickly mastered instruments they'd rarely, if ever, played. James Pearson as Bernard Sumner, Harry Treadaway as Stephen Morris, Joe Anderson as Peter Hook, along with Riley, became a group, hanging out with each other, generating the unruly, insular 'us against the world' attitude that the once real Joy Division had. The fact that the acting Joy Division play those early songs with as much edgy, scared and relentless commitment as the once-upon-a-time real thing helps lift the film above being another sterile rock biopic mime show.

Having the actors replay the urgent original group demonstrates how there were always two Joy Divisions – Joy Division's Joy Division, the one that played live with an unfettered metal fury, and Martin Hannett's Joy Division, a strategically processed studio intensification, and fragmentation, of the live entity. In the film, the bruising wildness of the live music helps make sense of the damned, psyched-out Curtis dance much more than Hannett's hallucinatory concentration, which attempted to make sense of Curtis' incredibly private thoughts.

'Up to a week before the film,' says Corbijn, ' I thought they were going to play to playback. They ended up so good they played live as Joy Division and Sam sang as Ian. According to Bernard Sumner he had exactly the same timbre as Ian. I can't think of it any other way now. That was a great gift from the actors. They wanted so badly to be a band and they behaved like a band.'

In the end, the only Joy Division music you hear played by Joy Division are the songs 'Love Will Tear Us Apart' and 'Atmosphere'.

014

One Anton Joy Division photograph in particular froze the group in time, but a time that was not necessarily 1979, or any particular known era – it was their own time, in a space between one reality and another, an otherworldly place their music seemed to slip and slither into and out of. Three members of Joy Division had their backs to the camera, their hands in their pockets, and were staring down a tunnel, at a distant light, at an entrance or exit. Ian Curtis, in long dark overcoat, having just remembered something, or forgotten something, had turned away from them, and was about to move in another direction, away from the light, towards what could be perceived, let's face it, as the unknown. It was a photograph that led you to believe how Ian, without dressing up, without saying much outside of his songs, in his own withdrawn, thoughtful and fundamentally disobedient way, was an artist and a star. It is such images that have carried Curtis and his band out of where they were right into the middle of now, and beyond.

015

'I'm bound to say this as a musician and as one of the musicians involved, but I sometimes think,' reflects Hooky, 'that it's mainly because of the music that the story is still so much alive — that we did something so uniquely simple that's ended up so powerful and timeless. It reached into people's souls. It had such an impact on people's lives. Sure, there's the dead rock star thing, the myth, there's Factory, Tony Wilson, and the Haçienda, and Ian's death cemented it, but I don't think it would all still be so fascinating to people if it wasn't for the music.'

016

'It's one of the few conceptual photographs I took at that age. I had in mind the album title *Unknown Pleasures*, and I had this idea that if people walk away they walk towards unknown pleasures, and I just thought it would look good if one of them looked back. It wasn't planned beforehand. It's just the way it happened. It became very iconic in the end, with Ian committing suicide. It looked like premonition, but to be honest my English was so bad I didn't understand the gravity or severity of Ian's lyrics. I could feel it, but I didn't really understand. I suppose it created an image of the music using their bodies. Initially no-one wanted to publish the photograph because only one guy was looking at the camera. The group liked it and they used it on the cover of the special limited edition Sordide Sentimental "Atmosphere" single. Rob paid me £25 and a copy of the single.'

017

'I was terrified,' admits Riley, remembering the time the *Control* Joy Division turned up to recreate an early real-life Joy Division gig in front of 150 extras, most of whom were hardcore fans looking for a sign of weakness. 'I was terrified just of acting, especially with Samantha Morton as Debbie, just in case she wiped me out. But to actually have to be Ian on stage . . .'

Riley had already made the mistake of checking an online Joy Division chat-board for reactions to him playing the role. There was mostly consternation. After early reports of Jude Law and Cillian Murphy, this unknown failed musician from Leeds seemed a comedown. 'It was like, who the fuck is Sam Riley? Still is, to some extent.'

Some fans even lobbied for the return of *24 Hour Party People*'s Ian Curtis, Sean Harris – he went on to play Ian Brady in a televised drama about the Moors Murders, and perhaps him playing alongside Morton, who has played Myra Hindley, might have conjured up some of that poisonous, unsettling edge-of-the-moors atmosphere which seeped throughout Joy Division's music.

'I really felt the pressure then. 150 extras all checking me out – so what makes you think you can be Ian? It was written all over them – it'd better be fucking good then. I thought, they're seeing if I'm too small, too tall, wrong face, if the hair's wrong, the clothes. Actually, they were just waiting to see "the thing". They just wanted to see me dance.'

018

'It was important to keep the film in black and white,' says Anton, never totally convinced by colour as a way of explaining things. 'That's how I remember it. The North was so grey and Joy Division always seemed in black and white. Their record sleeves were in black and white and the way they dressed was not colourful. I can't even think of a group shot of Joy Division in colour. I have a theory that in those days before you had a hit you were only published in black and white magazines. Joy Division had never had a hit so they were never published in colour magazines! Your whole memory of Joy Division is through black and white photographs, so the film just had to be in black and white. It was amazing, the opposition to this. This just made me more determined.'

019

Another film that tells the Joy Division story, Grant Gee's big budget documentary, is being released almost simultaneously, and there is Chris Rodley's Factory documentary being shown on BBC4 – I ask Hooky whether people will get sick of the obsession with Joy Division and Factory and Ian Curtis' suicide. 'Well, I've lived with it every day for 30 years, and I'm not sick of it.' Is it just nostalgia, a sentimental retreading of a period that's over by those who cannot bear to see time slip away, a morbid cashing in? 'Bernard gets pissed off with me for being so sentimental, nostalgic and melancholy, but that's just the way I'm built. For Bernard, it's over, let's get on with something else. But I think there's nothing wrong with looking back and seeing what happened, where you've been, what difference that made to how things are now. If you leave everything behind, how can you tell whether anything special happened or not? If what you did is worthy of being history it can take being retold from different points of view.'

020

In the 1980s, now settled in London, the gangly, single-minded Corbijn provided classic, unnaturally glamorous covers for the *NME*. His photography, of Siouxsie, Bowie, Ferry, was of unusual people who happened to be rock stars, not of rock stars in traditional, hackneyed poses. By the mid-1980s, his photography was helping to create the images for U2 and Depeche Mode, elevating the disturbed, romantic idea of them above their everyday laddish appearance just as he had captured, through their presence and an unsettling accompanying absence, the elusive ambition and depths of Joy Division's music. Even while his fame as U2 photographer increased, he continually experimented with the subject, form and content of his photographs.

He has directed videos for David Sylvian, Nirvana, Metallica, Johnny Cash, Mercury Rev, the Killers, as well as for U2 and Depeche Mode. A melodramatic video for Joy Division's 'Atmosphere', where midget monks and hooded entities hauled a momentous iconic photograph of Ian Curtis across a typical Corbijn wasteland towards, or away from, the ends of the earth, was typical of the way his videos combined high-minded seriousness with the deliriously lightheaded.

He wanted to make a film, but wary of the classic rock biopic traps, the wigs and sweeping generalisations, not a music movie. Producer Orian Williams had optioned Curtis' wife Debbie's poignant memoir, *Touching from a Distance*, and was searching for a director. Established directors such as Danny Boyle were being considered, but ultimately all paths, for better or worse, led to Anton. At first he was adamant that he was not going to do it. 'It's always been a battle for me to be not known as a rock photographer but just a photographer. Making a music film meant I would always be known as a rock photographer. The reasons to make it in the end overcame even that.'

021

'Life in the late seventies wasn't so fast, and so stimulating, you had more time, and

I wanted to get that across, rather than interpret the time through what has happened since. I didn't want to make an action film or a commercial, I didn't want to shoot it like a hip modern film. I wanted something that is actually beautiful where you can just enjoy the actors and feel that this was something real that happened with real people. Think about that, not the flashness of approach. It is old fashioned in that way, and that seemed the brave thing to do – not to play up the mystery, not to make more myth, but to try and clear things up, so that you can clearly see Ian, the deeply troubled young man, and what happened to him.'

## 022

Hooky compares the two film Ian Curtises that there have now been. 'I don't think either of them got Ian 100 per cent, but that might just be my version of Ian. But they were both fantastic. Sam caught Ian as a person, the way he spoke, the way he moved, little inflections, and he's certainly Ian as a good looking young chap. Sometimes it sent shivers down my spine. That was more the Ian I remember being with, whereas Sean in *24 Hour Party People* was perhaps the better stage Ian.'

## 023

'I was worried that I would take away the mystery, but in the end I also wanted to tell a simple story, and take the story to a wider audience who would be interested in the story at the heart of it, if not the music. The cult audience knows this story. It seemed time to take it further, hopefully without ruining the secret. Making the film took the mystery away to an extent – when you are young, you look up to a band whose music you love and think are half-gods, and only later do you learn they were just normal lads who had a bit of chemistry. I didn't think of it as a music film. I just wanted to make a film that was natural to me, and I didn't want to make it look like a music video at all, because the story has nothing to do with music videos. I just made it a film that happens to have a lot of music in it.'

## 024

'When I saw it at Cannes,' says Hooky, 'I knew that it was a great film and that it would be very well received because, even though it's two hours long, only two people went to the toilet the whole time. In fact, one of them was Bernard. The other one was a 70-year-old woman.'

In 2004, Corbijn worked on an epic book of U2 photographs, which involved looking at contact sheets from the early eighties. 'It went beyond being a technical project, and I started to feel just like I did back then. Having no money, waiting for a bus, looking for somewhere to live, you're in a foreign country, unsettled, working as hard as you can to do good work, and many of those feelings were linked to Joy Division. I realised the film could be a personal project for me, the fact that my motivation to go to England was Joy Division. It was looking at a part of my own life as much as it was just telling the story of Joy Division. It meant so much to my life. It justified making the film for me.'

Within three days of agreeing to make the film, in 2005, he was sat, unprepared and a little bewildered, at a press conference in Manchester alongside co-producer Tony Wilson and another producer, Todd Eckart. On the way to the conference, Anton thought of the title. At the conference, it was, naturally, the extreme self-publicist Wilson who did most of the talking. What with one thing and another, Wilson never got to see the finished film, his death in early August drawing attention in the most emphatic way possible to how this film, as a delicate by-product of the agitating cultural commotion he helped orchestrate, is about the fierce strangeness of disappearance as much as the fearsome and astonishing miracle of appearance.

026

Wilson swoops onto set one day with his dog, one of those large, floppy William Wegman Weimaraner dogs from a New Order video. He has no intention of getting involved, of interfering with Anton's plans, and simply works the room, like a professionally interested royal visitor, joking about the clothes, checking on the odd detail, geeing everyone up, happy to see the story told through Ian. His dog runs amok, causing chaos, shitting all over the wires, bumping into scenery. Wilson keeps grinning at everyone as if the trouble the dog is causing is absolutely nothing to do with him.

027

'When I was at Tony's funeral in August,' Hooky recalls, 'I came out of the cathedral with Natalie, Ian's daughter, and they were playing "Atmosphere". Bloody hell, I said, sometimes I wished that I'd never written it – it's like

Robbie Williams' "Angels" is for weddings, and "Atmosphere" is for funerals.'

028

Corbijn was finally making his first movie, but it soon became clear that no-one really wanted it – or, no-one really wanted it the way that he wanted to do it, used to working mostly on his own, to just following his instincts. Potential financing quickly fell away, with those prepared to give money demanding things that would have made the film exactly the conventional, crude, American-style biopic Corbijn was determined to avoid. Players in the British film industry looked unfavourably on all of his ideas for the film, right down to the fact he, a video maker, was directing it. If it's a music film, then the only way the system says it can be done is to be more Cowell than Cassavettes, more Hornby than Jarmusch, or be loaded with Richard Curtis, *Four Overdoses and a Suicide*. The film looked doomed.

Corbijn stubbornly kept it alive. He took on the role of producer as well, determined now to make a movie not directly of Debbie Curtis' book, not as an offshoot of Wilson's defunct Factory empire, not necessarily playing along with the Joy Division death industry, but just as a distinctive northern story set in the 1970s, based around various memories of Ian's life in the few years between his late teens and his death. The soundtrack would just happen to include Bowie, the Stooges, the Velvet Underground and Joy Division.

He financed the film himself with a couple of friends and streamlined Matt Greenhalgh's light, functional script. As the filming start date was postponed from the winter of 2005/2006, to March, to May, to July, a battered, distracted Anton was sure that this was the only film he would ever make. He was dealing with budget problems, with a lack of distribution offers, with the egos and sensitivities of the living characters he was portraying, trying to keep both Ian's wife and his lover happy with their portrayals, dealing with the tricky, picky New Order as they wrote the soundtrack, running across all the grudges that still exist within the formal and informal families 27 year after the fact. 'When it is your first movie you are ignorant of the problems ahead, thank God. I quickly learnt about the amount of things that can go wrong with a movie and the way it can disappear in front of your eyes. I was prepared to lose my money. It is amazing that it didn't happen. If you want to take a photograph, you can just take it. Here, to make the movie I wanted to make, it looked as though I would have to sell my home. It didn't stop me. I went for it, stayed positive on set, and somehow it worked out.'

029

'The whole beauty of the story,' says Hooky, 'is that everyone remembers everything differently. Everyone has a different memory of what happened. Not that anyone is right or wrong, you just saw it from a different point of view, and there was so much to see, so much happening. What Anton has done is make the story from his memories of how he felt at the time, and you can tell that he's a fan. You could tell he's a fan from his "Atmosphere" video. The film is incredibly personal to him and I'm immensely proud of him, the way he was so single minded, and would not compromise his vision of the film.'

030

I visit Anton on set in Nottingham in late August 2006. It's a hot sunny day. 'I thought it would be very cloudy and grey and of course it's been the sunniest summer for years. We got one great cloud, above the crematorium when we filmed there.'

He's at his calmest and gentlest, despite the pressure and the fact there's still no-one prepared to distribute the film. I watch him carefully piece together the chaos of Curtis' last days, on the road, in the studio, at home, homeless, in love, out of love, lonely, surrounded by, and increasingly separate from, friends and family, sure of the way he wants to tell the story, relieved that there was no-one demanding more pace, more sensation, more madness.

In the studio, Bernard's little house where Curtis fled after being kicked out of home sat next to Wilson's front room just across from Hannett's recording studio. You can stroll in a few seconds from Macclesfield to Stockport to Salford.

A hushed, stunned Ian and Bernard discuss Ian's mounting personal problems and then, minutes later, sonic enthusiast Hannett organises the backing track for 'She's Lost Control'. A distant, disappearing Manchester, a fluid, contradictory set of memories, a brood of heroes and villains, a crushing together of time and emotion, a tragic story, a collapse of personality, Ian at the centre with, in this case, the other characters all supporting his story, symbolically fading behind his evaporating intensity, it was all being fed through Anton's decision to make the story be both as real as possible, without it sinking under too much camp period detail, and also dreamlike and subtly disorientating.

A film Manchester is made up, approximately resembling a lost Manchester, and it takes an outsider's eye – the reflective Dutchman refusing to give up, searching for clues to his own uncompromising need to make the world better and more beautiful – to tell this very British, very English, very northern and very lonely story. He was able to make it because, now an internationally renowned, considerably experienced and sophisticated photographer and video maker, he directed the film with an innocence echoing that with which he took that first photograph of Joy Division. It broke all the rules, but he didn't know those rules even existed, and even when he found out they did, he didn't believe them and refused to follow them. This attitude makes him an honorary member of the radically imaginative collective that formed Joy Division and Factory Records.

031

Anton calls me from Belgium at the end of August 2007, his slow-moving black and white film with unknown lead actor that he was told again and again wouldn't work about to be released. He's in one of his more sentimental moods. 'It was 35 years ago yesterday that I took my first photograph – a local Dutch group called Solution.' He's just done the Belgian equivalent of the Jonathan Ross show, gamely selling this fatal love story to as wide an audience as possible. He's looking at the poster for the film. 'It's like a combination of *Scarface* and Godard.' He's sold the film in America – to notorious indie monster Harvey Weinstein, which is deeply Wilsonian. 'Harvey called me, said, "I loved your film, don't change a thing, and don't believe what you read about me. Classic stuff." We'll see . . .'

I tell him Sam says he wants to work on whatever film he's going to do next. 'Sam and I were the virgins on this film and we depended on each other to get through it.' So there will now be another film? 'Oh yes. It will probably be a thriller. In colour. Something very different.'

032

The film is shown to a standing ovation at Cannes in May. After the showing Sam visits the toilet and finds himself standing next to Peter Hook. Joe, who played him, was making a film in Hollywood. 'I said, what do you think, Hooky? He said, "Well, if you'd played me, you'd be in Hollywood now." No slap on the back, but a basic Manc gag. That's good enough for me.'

033

'I went into the toilets after the Cannes showing,' remembers Hooky, 'and I find myself going to the toilet next to the young Bernard and the living Ian. I can't tell you how weird that is.'

## LXV

**Last lines collected between 1987 and 2007 for a Joy Division book that may or may not ever be written/to be entitled *Where Will It End?***

Life will dissolve into itself, rivers into the sea, and the known into the unknown.

Shadows embalm me.

I know that everyone thinks about the crowds and carrying on.

Of course, this vicious blurring is also a blotting out of a private reality that has become too harsh to bear, and it sustains, rather than dilutes, the emotional force of the song.

Each morning, over 16,000 hearts will break.

It all worked out just like he said it would.

Moments can be an instant or indeed an eternity.

Say goodbye.

But that's another story.

When will it end?

When we talk about the past we lie with every breath we take.

In 1980, there were about two hundred people living in the Manchester city centre. By 2007, there were over 20,000.

The last time Peter saw Ian they were together in the front of Peter's car and they were leaving for America in a couple of days and they were happy and excited, they couldn't believe their luck, and Ian was dropped off at his mum and dad's house.

We are dealing not with reality, after all, but that image of reality which reaches the surface through the cracked looking glass of the media.

Let us go back to the facts, to the false facts, distorted facts, concealed facts, empty facts, secretly rich facts, and unspecifiable speculations of our narrative. Or not.

Gretton grinned, and grinned, and eventually pulled them out of interviews, deciding their silence would seem more mysterious, and winning, than their stilted pause-packed conversation.

Now, we know less than before about what might be possibly going on.

Yet it is not.

Time is running out.

Of course, in the end, it was Bernard, a former graphic design student, who came up with the idea for the cover of *Unknown Pleasures*.

Our vicissitudes (but not our souls) stand revealed in the mirror, or given another day, and another mirror, there we are, feeling wretched, but looking splendid.

Let us spin on the vertigo of that thought.

Of course we also live in a world more dazzling with the montage of startling connections than a David Lynch film.

Proceed.

The end is all there is, the end is.

That's my professional opinion.

They want to be invisible.

More and more so, as days go by.

It so easily might have been otherwise.

I cannot consent to let Heaven and Earth, this world and next, be beaten together like the white and yolk of an egg.

I think my favourites would be Susanna and the Magical Orchestra's 'Love Will Tear Us Apart', Low's 'Transmission', Grace Jones' 'She's Lost Control' – and New Order's first single, 'Ceremony', which was a Joy Division song.

But then Iggy ended up with one leg shorter than the other.

I couldn't have put it better myself.

I've said it before and I'll say it again. Life moves pretty fast. If you don't stand around and look at it sometime you could miss it.

A cheerful conclusion, amidst bleak perspectives.

I tried never to mention what Tony had shown me in Macclesfield, in case people felt I was morbidly exploiting the situation, cashing in on something – guilt or embarrassment or just plain confusion – abusing the privacy of others, dwelling too much on an isolated incident, romanticising grief, but ultimately, the only reason he showed me what he showed me was so that the episode would become a chapter in a book, where it would belong, shimmering between fact and fiction, meaning just what he always meant it to mean.

Behind every stark fact we encounter layers of ambiguity.

Let's not end it this way.

And then, just as I thought it was all over, begun, middled and ended, at least for now, for a while, approximately tidied into shape, I received an email about a detailed, authoritative documentary that director Grant Gee and writer Jon Savage had made about the group. The film, non-fictional but made up, an emotional documentary, had found new gaps in the story, opened up new questions, filled some gaps, and answered various questions. It had completed one version of the history, and started yet another. It told you all you needed to know about the ways, means and historical movement of a real life and an imaginary Joy Division, up to the point of knowing there would always be more to know, and find out, and think through. The email said: 'We'd love you to chair the Joy Division masterclass at Sheffield this year, referring to the Joy Division documentary that is being released in early 2008. The class will concentrate on the production process of the film, so we'll have the director, writer, editor and producer on stage, and the idea is to tease anecdotes out of them on how they approached capturing the story and dealing with the legacy of such an influential band. The film itself is also about myth-making and Manchester. I imagine that you will have things to say about this yourself.'

Whichever way, however it happened, I am part of it.

Maybe it was a good thing for it to seem random.

'And the first question at this Q&A session in Greece,' said Hooky, 'was from someone who said . . . let me get this straight. For fifteen years as a group you never said anything of any consequence. You never really said anything. And then for the next fifteen years you never stopped talking.'

For us, life is a fact, no less, and above all, no more.

It seems you kill yourself in the same way that you dream.

Sometimes I regret not having bought that clown.

Shoot, create new situations.

He conned them, one and all.

Joy Division won an award at the ceremony, for being icons, for being great all these years, for being filmed, for not being forgotten, for letting the cat out of the bag, and the story had now reached the stage where the actors who had played Ian and Debbie Curtis in the movie gave the award to the real Debbie Curtis and Ian's daughter Natalie and someone who to an extent resembled the real Peter Hook.

The beautiful must be incongruous.

Knowing is always more or less pretending to know.

A point of view, alas, which he was one day to abandon.

I had fallen into an unwritten Wilson novel, and the author was about to appear on the scene.

I didn't feel so bad anymore, because I knew he was still with them in spirit.

When you look at a body, you realise how temporary it is, how it can all end in a matter of minutes.

Then he laid down his napkin and left the room.

'Meet me at the usual place,' said Rob, 'I'll have it with me.'

Upon the place beneath.

*Woyzeck* is a blackly comic satire based on a true story of a nineteenth-century barber. Johann Christian Woyzeck was the foundation for Georg Büchner's play *Woyzeck*. Woyzeck was beheaded in 1824 for the slaying of his mistress. Prior to his execution, Woyzeck was assessed by a doctor to determine whether he could be considered accountable for his actions. The doctor determined that Woyzeck was of sound mind and that any irregularity was due to his physical constitution and moral degeneration.

Saville visited the cemetery where Wilson was buried, looking, perhaps, to see if there might be some kind of monument he could design that would suit the place, and the stunning fact – and he couldn't get over this – that Wilson's body had actually been dropped into the ground, and covered with dirt, and left to rot. As he stared at the place where Wilson wasn't, but was, working out if anything could be done that wasn't silly or sentimental, he saw a shadowy figure in the distance approaching him. There was no one else around. Slowly the shadowy figure moved towards him. Saville was a little spooked. Surely not . . . He couldn't make out the features of the figure. It disappeared behind a tree, and then appeared right in front of him. It was Erasmus, holding a huge spliff. Saville breathed a sigh of relief. Erasmus said to Saville, 'Well, we're the last two now.' Saville laughed a little nervously, and held his breath.

For this, on various planes, is the tendency of dandies.

We were standing at the end of a decadent epoch.

In the end, 'Love Will Tear Us Apart' is 'about' its melody.

With the passage of time it will become more and more beautiful.

You couldn't miss it.

He jumped into himself all by himself and all the way up to himself.

Don't go down the road to ruin.

In the post-modern world, it seems that history no longer provides autonomy or identity, but is another commodity served up in television reruns, nostalgia, and endless repetition, so that instead of improving upon the work of a previous generation, each new generation merely repeats it with only a slight variation.

As if one needed to be told.

Although I am not in the habit of saluting the dead, retracing this existence here has both pleased and displeased me.

This doesn't change the fact that you can't have a dialogue with the dead.

And nowhere else.

This is the starting point.

Working on such a project is really more a working on oneself.

Perhaps it wasn't so that he would destroy himself, but so that he could put himself back together again.

And why did it have to happen on that particular day, and no other?

Some day, I shall write about all this in great detail.

Between them, they leave no nerve unshaken.

Later that morning Gretton caught the train back to Manchester, and I never saw him again.

Wilson just happened to be nearby.

The pale sun shone down on this Eucharist of the Madonna of the hoardings.

The music swells and merges with the shrieking wind.

Because it is impossible to be right, to tell the truth.

We were in good humour because otherwise we would go to pieces.

The little time that separates us from emptiness has the flimsiness of a dream.

They actually thought, the show must go on.

Now we are getting somewhere.

I never thought of asking him.

Be careful what you wish for.

If instead his death is fetishised and the story told again and again to the last gasp and beyond, then the body becomes a relic or a kind of cultural bookmark.

The more things change, the more the story stays the same.

No, no story, never again.

What are we but puppets, manipulated on wires by unknown powers? We are nothing, nothing in ourselves; we are the swords that spirits fight with – except no-one sees the hands – just as in fairy tales.

But it is his refusals which animate his legacy with an incandescent rage, a passionate and profound fury that did not cry out for death – but for just the opposite.

Quickly and slowly.

When the world is not the same as our minds believe, then we are in a nightmare.

And I realised there are no 'sicknesses of the soul'. There are only words.

Tomorrow, they would talk, and embrace, and recall the time everything was ruined, and no one died.

## PART THREE:

### Future/Life

### LXVI

After Ian Curtis' funeral, shaken manager Rob Gretton did his bit, in his own way, to make things seem better, to cheer up his devastated group. He tells the surviving band members that, well, at least this means that in an awful sort of way Joy Division's future is ensured. People will still be remembering you in ten years time, he said. Ten years seemed a long way off then. Who gives a fuck, thought Peter Hook, about the future? Who gives a fuck about Joy Division being remembered when you've just lost your best mate?

'The funny thing is,' he will eventually say, 'when it is ten years later – and then twenty years, 30 years, you do give a fuck that the group is remembered. You do care that people still care, even if it is because of the suicide. You hope that really it's because of the music.'

Within days – within minutes, perhaps – of Ian dying, the three remaining members decided to carry on.

'Yeah, we all decided that very quickly,' says Stephen Morris. 'We had no choice really, and I think it was just the way we were that there was no question of us carrying on. I think it actually says a lot about the strength of Joy Division that even when one of us killed themselves, we just decided we would still be a group. Not even that could break us up.'

Hook: 'It was like someone had snatched the prize away, after you'd worked so hard for it. So we decided we would go out to win it again.'

Sumner: 'We'd worked for four or five years to make the group succeed. We'd written a whole set of songs and suddenly it was all gone. Suddenly it was decimated. The beauty of it was that even after what had happened we stayed friends and we stayed together.'

The replacement for Ian was not really the replacement for Ian. No-one moved into the middle, no one was suddenly expected to stand in the shadow. Another young man didn't become part of the story. Instead, it was a young woman, gentle, a little bewildered, but part of the community already, aware of its intensity, but also its straightforwardness.

Steve's girlfriend, Gillian, an early fan of the group, present at the night of the Stiff/Chiswick challenge in March 1978, slipped onto the stage, almost floated into the group encouraged by the mischievous Rob Gretton in what turned out to be a clear-thinking masterstroke. She had already played with Joy Division on a night at the Eric's club in Liverpool, when Gretton had revealed another side of his perverse genius as manager by cutting open the hand of guitarist Bernard while they played with bottles backstage. As Bernard said, 'As you do.' Gillian played a little guitar that night, and was blooded into the scheme of things.

Gillian was not now part of the new group as a singer. It was immediately clear that the singer had to come from within. 'If we got another singer in,' recalled Stephen, 'it would just look like Joy Division Two, and whoever it was would be under a tremendous amount of pressure and instantly compared with Ian. That would be impossible. So we had to have the singer sweepstakes and Bernard drew the short straw.'

Bernard: 'I didn't see it as being difficult taking over from Ian. I saw it as an honour really.'

Without Ian, it was the same group, but completely different, and it needed a new name. A few were discussed, some straight, some silly, none right – the Witch Doctors of Zimbabwe, Black September, No Name, Bernard, Stephen and Peter, Barney and the JD's. Rob found New Order in an article on the Cambodian Khmer Rouge, and all of them were oblivious to the idea that talking of a 'new order' didn't exactly lay to rest the idea that here was a group of individuals dangerously obsessed with black-hearted fascist imagery. 'We just thought in the end,' said Bernard, with a dispassionate flatness that made cynics assume he was hiding the full, dubious truth, 'that whatever we chose it would just become our name after a few months.'

Being so neutral and blankly provocative, the new name, with that bold and confident 'new', helped the development of the post-suicide myth better than having a name like the Witch Doctors of Zimbabwe. New Order immediately sounded like a group that would emerge once a group called Joy Division had, somewhere between naturally and supernaturally, shed their skin.

For Gillian, bringing a lacerating simplicity to things, an innocence and an unexpected femininity that helped supply the bracing strength required to patch together a profoundly fractured system, the name basically meant that there was now a new order to the group.

## LXVII

In 1991/after the group had found enigmatic eighties fame by breaking with and yet somehow continuing the ideas and ideals of Joy Division/moving beyond Martin Hannett/becoming Factory pop stars/a 1990 number one/a football song/for England/ hiding/revealing themselves/behind a succession of formal subversive Saville screens/signing to London Records following the disintegration of Factory Records/beginning a cycle of comebacks, fall-outs, regroups, arguments, reunions and breakups/forming other groups/Bernard's Electronic/'New Order without my bass,' said Hooky/'I wish Hooky would stop playing fucking bass guitar solos all over my songs,' said Bernard/Hooky's rocky Revenge and Hooky's poppy Monaco/Stephen and Gillian's the Other Two/the stress of Joy Division finally catching up with them/finally they could argue amongst themselves without feeling that they were betraying the memory of their ex-singer/an introduction to the documentary *New    orderstory*/an introduction read by Jenny Seagrove/in a state of shock after it was explained to her about the eleven-year-old suicide/to reflect the feminine side of New Order/the unusual – within the Factory walls – feminine side.

*New Order have been together in one form or another for sixteen years. From a shadowy underground first as Warsaw, then as Joy Division, their distressed songs about depravity and deprivation seemed to shake and writhe out of deep, craven trouble. Their music was . . . fantastic.*

*Not many noticed, because after two volatile, fantastic albums, just as Joy Division were heading off into their own sensational rock adventure, maybe even destined to become perverse superstars, their singer Ian Curtis, snagged on the jagged edge between the pleasure of it all and the pain, killed himself.*

*This was some end.*

*Four years' hard work disintegrated.*

*This is the story of New Order and how they endured, how they rebuilt, how they began again, changed their mind and the whole body of what they were because of a death, a new girl member, a change of name, an adoring manager, because of obscure disco music and Manchester nightlife, because they cared, because they couldn't care less, because you have to laugh, because you have to cry.*

*This is the story of New Order, who turned a pop life into something perilous and maddening.*

*They longed for success and recognition yet needed to keep themselves to themselves, wanting resounding glamour and chaste anonymity all at once. They could have signed to any record label in the world and, on the sly, sold as many records as any group ever has.*

*In fear, or in defiance, of a normal fate, they obliquely, indulgently stayed with their wilfully uncommercial record label Factory Records. This was the only record label on earth romantic enough to let the group do as they pleased, how they pleased, when they pleased.*

*They were very pleased.*

*Even when the group signed to a major label they were allowed to be as dreamy as they wanted.*

*The group were spoiled and they audaciously sneaked out of the shadows of Joy Division to become the most elusive and drastically secretive of pop groups, on the very edge again of becoming almost lifelike anti-superstars.*

*They must have known exactly what they were doing.*

*This is the story of New Order, a story that begins with the story of another group. The story of Joy Division.*

## LXVIII

In the few minutes after there was no Joy Division, in the few minutes before there was another group, as more darkness led to more darkness, it was as though everything happened that was going to happen in the coming years. Everything stopped, everyone held their breath, and an amazing future stormed into that dead stillness.

The group that the ex-Joy Division boys became formed whilst in the middle of an abrupt realisation, a sudden rush of knowledge, that what was about to come was 30 years of a formation of truth, of legend, of myth that would incorporate a gathering force of memories, recollections, books, films, gossip, documentaries. In an instant, New Order knew that they were having not only to follow the death of Ian Curtis, but also somehow follow what lay ahead, follow where the suicide, directly and indirectly, would lead – the death of their manager, the death of their producer, the death of their record company boss, the invention of a new Manchester, the fulfillment, and death, of their dreams. It would all lead to overkill.

There wasn't just the pressure of continuing after the death of their friend and colleague, but knowing that ahead lay the lows and highs of the Haçienda, the rise and fall of Factory, and no matter how many hits New Order had, no matter how intriguing and developed their music became, how much it anticipated and kept up to date with changes in fashion and style, no matter how many great albums they made, there would always be the sense that they were not quite Joy Division, that they were a mere electric echo, the shock waves spreading out from an extraordinary blow to the heart.

The future flashed before their eyes, scenes arrested in their essence. It had already happened, as in scenes from a distant life long forgotten and now recollected only in their bare essentials. What was to come: the dead laughter of a friend, the hidden brilliance always tracking their thoughts, millions of memories overlapping theirs, the best selling twelve-inch of the 1980s, a private, melancholy song stuttering across its deliberate circling electro–rhythm, a song about war and death, about real life loss, a song that they insisted on playing live on *Top of the Pops*, that would eventually be used in a Mars Bar TV commercial, each copy costing more to make than the price it was sold for.

What was to come: the new group not being able to contemplate playing songs by the old group for over fifteen years, the cold and magnificent Joy Division songs, hanging on to haunt another generation or two, like wind whirring at a window, full of life, and naturally death, always moving through a midnight gloom, lost forever in their own eternity, classic ruins, slowly entering the canon, slowly becoming part of a soundtrack of cool orchestrated by those appropriating and exploiting avant-garde pop and outsider imagery for their own commercial ends.

What was to come: Gillian coming a long way from somewhere as if it was always going to be this way, hesitantly learning new rules, the world gently shifting under her feet; the gradual replacement of Hannett as producer, his sound ghosting the next sound; Hooky's rampant reinforced bass motioning from one space to another as if nothing had really changed, even though everything had; Stephen's drums, now increasingly combined with his computer feelings, becoming harder, swifter, sweeter, stranger, as if nothing had really changed, even though nothing was the same; Bernard's guitar still squinting and spurting and breaking the surface and making pop music seem irresistibly precious, as if nothing had changed, even though he was now the singer, never climbing as high or falling as far as Ian, singing songs about not being lost, but not being here, doing the best he could with his illusions, singing love songs with adequate eloquence, all the while knowing, whatever happened, that there was something missing, all the while knowing his voice would always sound like he'd been so close, so involved, with unrelievable loneliness.

A future that would mean it would take a quarter of a century for the participants to begin to make sense of what had happened between June 1976 and May 1980. The participants – those in the group and those nearby – would try and work it out by making music, producing music, listening to music, writing about music, releasing records, designing sleeves, taking photographs, dreaming up concepts, printing manifestos, developing inside jokes, following private pursuits, opening clubs, planning tours, talking, and not talking, confronting the issue, and avoiding the issue, re-entering the movie at different points, losing their place, finding it again, only half-believing what they were hearing. The story, and stories, would take shape, the pieces would come back together, and almost fit, and the truth would exist more strongly now that it was fiction.

Gradually, it might as well be pointed out now there's a provisional end in sight to at least this point of view, everyone involved, over time, after about 25 years, give or take, even though it was sort of sensed immediately, began to see how all the stray things add up and everybody adds up to the same thing and the damn thing's still growing and this movie – it's always a movie, now – is made up out of a lot of parts of other people's films all glued together and one life is a lot of people's lives hung together in space only it's all kept in the dark it's all kept coiled away except for one small frame at a time flashed upon the screen of the present.

374

Before they were even officially New Order, they knew that all this would happen, that ahead of them lay everything that was going to happen because they had been abandoned, even though it was absurd to read too much into it, even though it was no-one's business but their own. Before they could even begin, they knew what it meant to carry on, even though, when all is said and done, they were just a pop group, give or take one that emerged out of trauma.

They knew, somehow, that to carry on was not going to make things any easier, that the scene ahead was fraught with sticky interest, with cracked mirrors and shattered shadows, that every way out turns out to be just another way in, but they carried on anyway. Within a few days, with everything behind them, and everything ahead of them, they were playing shows as New Order, sounding as though they were just returning to, or just emerging out of, a dream. Sometimes it seemed as though the dream was emerging from holes in their head.

There wasn't as much sound and fury as there had been earlier in the year, and the holy heights they'd reached in the final weeks before the finale were a fading dream, but they had memories to mull over, an immense future to get used to, and new machines to operate. Bernard could barely open his mouth, Hooky couldn't lift his gaze from the floor, Stephen refused to be caught out and Gillian's eyes were averted, as if she was intent only on herself.

At the time it seemed more than a few months, it seemed a lot longer than a year, it felt as though they had disappeared from view for ages, but it was just twelve months after I reviewed Joy Division for the *NME* that I was reviewing New Order. There they were, making themselves up, playing into the hands of a future that could only be what it was, filling in the facts that no one yet knew.

They played on a Monday, which meant that I had to deliver the review to St Pancras station early Tuesday morning, into the hands of editors on the way to the printers in Kettering to put together that week's issue. This meant I had to write the review overnight. New Order didn't make it onto the stage until the early hours of the morning. By the time they had played and I had said my goodbyes, it was two in the morning. By the time I got home it was three in the morning. I was a little shaky, possibly because of Bernard's Pernods, possibly because of my latest deadly deadline, possibly because I had glimpsed the future that New Order knew only too well, as if it was all behind them, a future that was permanently pressing down on them.

I had a couple of hours to write the review. I wondered if I would have anything to say about the group that Joy Division had become. How on earth would I begin? Would I be able to make it to the end? An hour before I had to leave for the station where the *NME* editors were waiting, because they had a hole in the paper they needed to fill, I was still staring into space.

## LXIX

**Live review – New Order's first London show, at Heaven, 9 February 1981, *New Musical Express* (published 14 February).**

It was the most difficult thing in the world for them to continue. And yet it was so natural. And yet . . . they're still so young. And yet again. New Order: so far so silent and cunning, stumbling against the false legacy of expectation, their central language bare and taut.

It's hard to rationalise that the group exist in this rock space, in this abusive context with all its endless blathering, its farcical structure of feeling. It's hard to report that New Order were hesitant, flawed, unformed and that it could all stop tomorrow and the sound was abysmal and they were intensely nervous and yet . . .

The music was touching, it could be perceived as being utterly profound, and there was a rich acceptance that in dealing with its drama we should respect the nature of imagination and liberation rather than simply respond to any direct appeal.

New Order were erratic and dangerously informal and inevitably vulnerable, and yet they achieved enough clean power to prove that they can (once more) redefine a whole range of attitudes and justify their simple but vigorous rejection of standard rock conditions. New Order are a new group: and yet a group caught up in a conventionally made rock myth. They want to be accepted and enjoyed for their direct, self-revealing address rather than stiffly looked at and complexly criticised: but nothing's that easy.

New Order are a simple group. They treat what they do seriously but don't take themselves seriously. At times I feel they're unaware what three of them achieved in a different place and have little confidence in their own capabilities.

But for whatever reasons – conscious, accidental, engagingly cheerful, charitable, convenient – the group cut right across rock's feckless rush, the stupid evading and posturing. Perhaps they're just incredibly natural – a pure body that reflects greed, pretension, stupidity and dishonesty in anything that comes near it. Perhaps they're just incredibly naïve . . . or too knowing.

And yet their music – a form and a blurring of form – can cut deep into all our experience.

Well . . . on the quiet New Order are deeply determined. It's a determination that has never been obviously articulated, but which can't buckle under cynicism, criticism, negativity. It's a determination that shapes the savage honesty of their music.

Offstage New Order are so bloody normal – retiring or pissed or completely nervous or inarticulate or as restless and lost for direction as you or me. And onstage they can be pretty opaque or disorganised. But their music and the central passions suggest such a violent/isolating confrontation and concentration. Onstage they look out-of-it or bored or trapped or maybe wistfully confident: but you can't resist the energies released or deny their essential – and paradoxical – nobility.

New Order – like their acclaimed and shaded predecessor – are unreal.

This may sound like a dumb thing to say, but everything's so unconnected. Not only are New Order unrock 'n' roll: all that and its connotations should by now go without saying. They're also just so unconcerned and – this is a real ache for you people with blind spots – the most unpretentious people I know and so lacking in ego and conceit it's . . . unreal!

I'm on edge for having to use the dumb word *unreal*: but the tension and conflict and character and even the actual existence of New Order is unreal.

And New Order at Heaven – the atmosphere, anticipation, conversation, HAPPINESS, the widespread elemental desire immediately to find greatness in New Order, perhaps even a refusal to admit it could fail, and the communal reverence for a mighty past *and* because a lot of the gathering had never seen You Know Who – was unreal and only unreal.

Or maybe it would be less dumb to call it an 'event'. Those aren't too frequent these days.

There was a bit of excitement about. London was looking forward to this appearance – an important part of the show was how it drew together people and implied that there's greater contemporary action and spirit than people like to pretend. It was the most atmospheric do I've been to for a long time: for London it was a rare rave.

I got a little bit drunk – no, *very* drunk – and burst into tears when New Order appeared onstage. New Order manifestly proved that pop can still lift people out of their slumbers; can still create those important new loyalties and get our hearts working.

New Order at Heaven: it was meant to be secret, but the lovely Final Solution people slipped up a few weeks ago . . . Rumour has it 10,000 people went after tickets; 1,000 got in and isn't it great that things can still be special and important, and not be fashioned and fadded out of all proportion by gossip and idiots?

New Order at Heaven: true love. Great place, new group, lots of people: perhaps the eighties will get moving.

The New Order Interview:

Hey, Barney, you want a drink?

'Yeah, I'll have a triple Pernod with blackcurrant and a bit of water. Where are the toilets?'

Lethal drink Barney's got, Mr Hook.

'Dutch courage. I'll just have a pint of lager.'

New Order have been doing things in the right order. A London show of course comes way down on the list of things to do. Those who live in London can view it as punishment that it's taken months and months for New Order to visit the blackening hole whilst they get on with visiting Blackpool, Nottingham, Brighton . . .

Their first shows – unsure and as a cruelly cropped trio after initial thoughts that they just didn't want to continue – were in the clubs of New York, not through exotica but simple practicality. NY audiences were dimly aware of a far away commotion that could've been fashion: they were not forced by preconceptions to accept New Order any particular way. New Order were fumbling – in a way they still are – but the NY dates reaffirmed balance and perspective.

Morris, Albrecht and Hook were a brand new group that was fated to inherit demented pressure. Pressure of a reputation that had grown fearfully mystical, the absurd pressure of a hit single, the ominous pressure that they may well have touched that sort of mastery that results in a New Sound, and the ultimate pressure of ghosts.

They've dealt with those pressures in the only way: they've ignored them – as much as it is possible. They've rejected any temptation to exploit reputation or myth: for New Order it could never simply be that there's a gap onstage – that *would* be cheating. Their loyalties are focused, because it's easy and a challenge, on overturning the 'obvious' or the regular ways – on making their own space.

New Order have done no interviews because, as a brand new group finding their new way, they felt they didn't deserve exposure or weren't ready for it: implacable, ingenuous and ultimately very effective.

They've grown their own sweet way. They could never have succumbed to the particular comforts of those old songs (although soundcheck voyeurs could thrill and chill to brill instrumental snatches of 'Transmission', 'Control', 'Atmosphere', 'Dead Souls' . . . aaah, teenybop passion for those songs the New Order show treated as so distant and separate) because that's *too* easy and fairly boring.

New Order are rising to a deep and substantive challenge. They are starting again but transmuting certain energies: a new group who have a tradition all of their own to redirect. Unrealer and unrealer. They have slowly and without bother achieved a majestic balance between extending suggested possibilities from that disturbed past and embodying novel principles and fresh threatening passions. They're doing what you wouldn't have thought possible: rubbing out the dark shadow of that past without minimising its impact.

They've a long way to go before they're revolutionary: but they're so much better than could be sensibly expected. They will be great!

At Heaven I wanted so much for them to be crushing and awesome, but the sense of occasion got in the way. They were nervous and most of the audience were nervous as well.

Whilst no one was looking they've become a four-piece. Steve Morris' girlfriend Gillian – they've been together since the early days – of all the girlfriends and wives was the one who took most interest in the music. Whilst the trio played around she helped out with keyboard parts. She was grafted into the group – and contributes guitar and keyboards. This little yet gigantic operation is typical of the group's emancipating informality.

Without any fuss, just their simple discipline and manager Rob Gretton's mixture of mischievousness and methodical magic, they've moved so far outside of the creatively/emotionally/intellectually inhibiting rock routines it's massively . . . unreal. Perhaps they can destroy those routines. More realistically they'll educate enough people to produce substantial damage.

The set drifted away. I was both transfixed and inattentive. The music lilted and lifted, reminding me of those tough and regular instrumental patterns in songs like 'Dead Souls', of the dramatic richness and indefinable structural grace of works like 'Atmosphere', with soft edges and accelerating rhythms and snaking textures and floating tunes and fluid, heady dynamics: pure seduction, a force all below the surface . . . untitled songs that float from far away, elusive, beautifully orchestrated, with words that in the unreal Heaven were simply sounds . . . sense comes later, when the shadows rubbed out.

The one link with that group was the poignant and scary performance of a song that was played once. Another group/another place. New Order didn't look as clumsy as they have been: but clumsier than they should be. There was no encore: how could there be an encore? Too showbizzy: too real.

New Order are incomplete. The (mainly Albrecht) vocals are boyish, fragile, uncomfortably mannered, the music is so delicate it desperately needs perfect sound quality. There was no anticlimax – but equally no transcendence. New Order are still coming: there are moments of greatness, it's such a revealing fusion of desires, and it has to be acknowledged that New Order ARE NOW LETTING US DOWN. And that is a lot of something.

This is just the start of a different story. Seeing New Order, those faces, those gestures, that nervousness, Gillian's disconcerting gentleness, sensing peculiar inexperience . . . it was, honestly, unreal.

In a way, from everyone's point of view, it was a relief to get it over with.

## LXX

I knew that ultimately I would think of an ending because eventually I would think of a beginning.

I knew that ultimately I would think of a beginning because eventually I would think of an end.

Joy Division would help me work it all out.

They would help me remember what happened.

For Tony

And for

Ian

And for

Martin

&

Rob

And for

Bernard
Hooky
Stephen

And for

Alan

&

Peter

&

Gillian

**& thank you**

to Paul Woods at Plexus for asking the question at just the right time so that the book got started and then tirelessly making sure that everything, within reason, was in the correct order and that the book got finished. Also to Sandra Wake and Coco Wake-Porter at Plexus and to Dick Porter.

to Anton Corbijn for the cover photograph

to Paul Barnes and Peter Saville for type thoughts

to Rebecca Boulton in the Joy Division/New Order office

to Kevin Cummins for the snow photo

to Neil Spencer, Tony Stewart, Phil McNeill, Monty Smith, Lynn Hanna, Angus MacKinnon at the *New Musical Express* for commissioning the *NME* reviews

to Adrian Thrills for his contribution to the Ian Curtis obituary

to Ian Penman, Danny Baker and Chris Bohn in the *NME* offices

to Mark Johnson for commissioning the face/pieces for his book *An Ideal for Living*

to Jon Savage for commissioning the *Heart and Soul* essay

to Julian Loose, my editor at Faber and Faber, and also to Faber's Walter Donohue

to Emily King and Frieze for commissioning the Peter Saville essay

to Rik Blaxill at 6music for commissioning the 25th anniversary Ian Curtis piece

to Paul Lester and Allan Jones for the *Uncut* interview

to Nick Stewart at Warners Music for commissioning the *North by North West* compilation

to Roger Alton at *The Observer*, Robert White at *The Guardian*, Paul Stokes at the *NME* and Joann Furniss at *Arena Homme +* for commissioning the Anthony H. Wilson pieces

to Caspar Llewellyn Smith at the *Observer Music Monthly* for commissioning

the Northwest/Manchester/Liverpool and *Control* pieces, and to Luke
Bainbridge at the *Observer Music Monthly*, who also commissioned the Best
Manchester 'Front Man' piece as editor of *City Life*

to Kevin Hewitt for *neworderstory*

to Devoto, Shelley, Diggle, Maher, Boon, Linder, Reilly, E. Smith, Clarke,
the Postman, Solomar, Witts, ACR, OMD and Cabaret Voltaire

to Sophie Hoult and David Godwin at DGA

**& love and special thanks**

to Leslie and Dilys Morley/x

to Carol for the Chinese thinking/x

to Madeleine Morley for the dreams and the future/x

to Elizabeth Levy for advice, guidance and inspiration, on the page and
beyond/x